legend

Previously published by Peter Jeffs

Pompey's Gentleman Jim
Breedon Books (1988)

The Golden Age of Football
Breedon Books (1991)

Portsmouth FC: The official centenary pictorial history
Bishops Printers (1998) *with Colin Farmery and Richard Owen*

Previously published by Colin Farmery

Portsmouth FC: The official centenary pictorial history
Bishops Printers (1998) *with Peter Jeffs and Richard Owen*

Portsmouth: From Tindall to Ball
Desert Island Books (1999)

Portsmouth: Champions of England
Desert Island Books (2000)

legend

Alan Knight

with Peter Jeffs and Colin Farmery

Legendary Publishing

PUBLISHED BY LEGENDARY PUBLISHING
PO Box 402, FAREHAM, Hants PO14 4ZQ

The right of Alan Knight, Peter Jeffs and Colin Farmery to be identified as the authors of this work has been asserted under the Copyright Designs and Patents Act 1988

British Library Cataloguing-in-Publication Data
A catalogue record for this book is available from the British Library

ISBN 0-9526760-1-X

Printed in Great Britain by Biddles Ltd, Guildford

For my father and mother, Edward and Joyce, for all the sacrifices they made which enabled me to pursue my dream.

And for my daughters Jade Rachel and Rebekah Paige, for their constant love.

Contents

Acknowledgements

We are grateful to the following for their valuable assistance in different ways: Andy Awford, Alan Ball, Frank Burrows, Chris Gibbs, Ray Crawford, Elaine Giles, Amanda Hughes, Bob Jenkins, Dave King, Clive Leatherdale, Di Lloyd, Ross McInnes, Richard Owen, Brian Porter, Kevin Ryan, Lisa Samways, Mark Saunders, David Streten, Mike Walker, Steve Bone and Dave Bowers of *The News*, and Christian Vaughan, Nick Bain and Emily Moon of Intuition Design.

The majority of photographs in this book are courtesy of *The News*, Dave Jordan / *Portsmouth Football Club* and Mike Walker / *M&Y News Agency*. The remaining pictures have been taken from private collections of the authors or supporters. It has not been possible to trace the sources of these pictures, however any photographer involved is cordially invited to contact the publishers in writing providing proof of copyright.

Back cover photography: Mike Jones (top) Mike Walker / *M&Y News Agency* (bottom).

Foreword by Jim Smith

Alan Knight's career is virtually unique, not only in club terms but in the game as a whole. We can be sure that his appearance record, as a keeper for one club, will never be surpassed. Not only that, his record of goals conceded to games played surely stands alongside those of the very best keepers this country has ever produced. Alan found his niche at Portsmouth and, while some may say that he could have gone on to greater things, he can look back at a great career at a great club. There have been some legendary names associated with Pompey in its history going back more than 100 years, but his name is right up there with the very best who have served this famous old club.

Alan is one of the best keepers I have worked with, and that includes the likes of David Seaman, Russell Hoult and Mart Poom. He is up there with them all and the key to that was his consistency, week-in and week- out. Alan could have played at the highest level, I am sure of that, but he was just too loyal to Portsmouth and too important to them, for that matter. He will admit that he had a period in his career where he let his standards slip and lost his way. But to his great credit he realised that, knuckled down, and went on to have one of the finest careers, at club level, that any keeper could ever have. He always had great respect from all the players at the club for what he had achieved, mainly because of his ability and the number of games he had played.

In my time, his experience helped out the youngsters in defence, like Kit Symons and Andy Awford, and they are great buddies of his to this day. But it seemed to me that he always had a great rapport with whoever he worked with over the years. By the time I came to work with him as his manager, he was already very experienced and knew the game inside out. He had all the attributes of a top keeper and inevitably his experience came to the fore. He was brave, knew what to do in every situation and read the game well. Importantly, he was also looked upon by the other players as a leader. All of these attributes played their part in his memorable performance in the Highbury FA Cup semi-final.

I always felt that his great affinity with Pompey, and his pride in playing for the club, were his main driving forces and the reason he played so many games. I remember that I brought Mart Poom in to displace Alan in 1994, as I felt he was coming to the end of his career. Poom was a fine young keeper but, to his credit, Alan rose to the challenge magnificently, went on to play unbelievably well and never gave Poom a chance to claim his place. Alan had one of his best seasons for Pompey. That was the pride factor in him coming out, which is a fantastic ingredient to have in a player.

When I came back to assist Harry Redknapp at the club, it was great for me to find Alan still working at Fratton Park. It's good to see that he is still getting the rewards from what he achieved at the club, through being a very important member of our staff now. He brings a great deal of experience to his role, talks a lot of sense, and works our keepers in the right way. Not only that, he is still continuing to do a lot of work off the field, in and around the city, in the community representing the club. This has been a feature of his career and for many years he has been a great ambassador for the club. All in all, Knightsie, not a bad career, despite all those fags!

Jim Smith
July 2003

Introduction

"Keeping goal is a lot like real life" - Anon

Who wants to go in goal? Not me. Surely you only end up in goal if you're small, bad at football, bullied by your peers or plain injured. In football, they say you have to be crazy to be a goalkeeper. No wonder, when a goalkeeper's work is so quickly forgotten – but let him make a mistake and he's not allowed to forget it. Keeping goal is one sporting activity measured only by perfection – goalkeepers simply cannot afford to make the kind of mistakes that outfield players routinely make. For Alan Knight stopping goals has been a lifetime's work – an occupation perpetually and precariously balanced between likely failure and unlikely triumph. His contribution to Pompey's cause over 25 years is immeasurable, in terms of certain goals saved and of points gained. As Mike Neasom of *The News* once put it so succinctly: "One day someone will work out the debt Pompey owe Alan Knight."

Pompey's greatest-ever goalkeeper played across four decades for the club he loved. He was nicknamed 'The Legend' by his Pompey team-mates, after he shattered Peter Bonetti's record for most appearances by a goalkeeper for one club when he played his 601st league game against Grimsby at Fratton Park on January 13, 1996. He then went on to spend four more years extending the landmark, finally racking up an astonishing 801 appearances in all competitions, from his league debut at the age of 16, at Rotherham, in April 1978, through to his final appearance at the age of 38, at Norwich, in January 2000. A record which will surely never be beaten, given the modern football climate.

Of other Pompey goalkeepers, only John Milkins, with 389 appearances, comes anywhere near his achievement, but still over 400 short! Apart from the late, great Jimmy Dickinson, who signed Knight as an apprentice and gave him his debut, no-one has played more games for Pompey. Dickinson retired in April 1965 having made 834 appearances in all competitions. After making the number one jersey his own at the start of the 1981/82 season, he was a model of consistency, winning England Youth and England Under-21 international caps. On Pompey's return to the first division, Alan made another piece of history in the opening match of that 1987/88 season at Oxford when he became the first player to represent the club in all four divisions. Unfortunately, it was during that brief stay in the top flight that Alan sustained horrific facial injuries at Wimbledon but, typically, it was not long before he was putting that behind him and showing all his old bravery and courage in Pompey's cause again.

The 6' 1" Balham-born goalkeeper was regularly involved in promotion and relegation battles, whilst the club fought its own off-the-field survival battles. During the bad times it was often said that only Alan stood between Pompey and a heavy defeat and in the good times he kept an astonishing 21 clean sheets in the Division Three championship-winning season of 1982/83. He equalled that record, ten years later. In the 1986/87 promotion campaign he conceded just 28 goals in 42 league games, and kept 19 clean sheets in the process.

Originally signing schoolboy forms on his 14th birthday, Alan's subsequent performances in the youth team meant that Pompey had to fight off advances from, amongst others, Aston Villa and West Ham, before he signed on as an apprentice at Fratton Park. During his long reign between the posts Alan has fought off competition for his place from many pretenders, ranging from Andy Gosney, Brian Horne and Jimmy Glass, through to Andy Petterson. Like others, he has also had to adjust to several rule changes imposed on goalkeepers in recent years.

Alan is one of the most popular figures ever to wear a Pompey jersey and there was universal approval when he was made a Member of the

British Empire in the 2001 New Year's Honours List, not only in recognition of his service to Portsmouth Football Club and the game itself, but of his record of service to the community. Some years earlier the only medal he had won in his long career – the Division Three championship medal – was stolen from his home by thieves. A public appeal, organised by the Supporters Club, raised funds to enable a replica to be made and awarded to him in replacement. After three player-of-the-year awards in his Pompey career, his popularity was amply demonstrated at his long-overdue testimonial match against Southampton in May 1994, when 17,500 fans crammed into Fratton to pay their tribute to him. Known as one of the best shot-stoppers in the league, Alan's hallmarks were a safe pair of hands, sharp reflexes and a consistency of performance, coupled with bravery and courage. In league football today the one-club man is almost extinct, but his legion of fans are gratified that he has been able to continue in Pompey's service and, as goalkeeping coach, make a significant contribution to the team's extraordinary success in 2003.

Now Alan tells his own story. From childhood to his apprenticeship and upbringing at Fratton Park, to his first team debut at 16, through his subsequent extraordinary playing career and on to the pain of stopping playing and adjustment to a coaching role. He also tells the hitherto untold story of the personal off-field battles he has fought.

His own life has, in many ways, mirrored that of Portsmouth Football Club; they have always been inextricably intertwined. If you are reading this book looking for the real Alan Knight, you will find him. It is not warts and all, or even kiss 'n' tell, as some parts of his life remain resolutely private, including his family life. What you will discover is a man with great modesty, quiet humour, and a determined career focus, combined with an ever-present, underlying insecurity, who finds it difficult to open up and face the realities of his life. This book, however, leaves no room for doubt that Pompey and football have been at the centre of his life, and as a consequence have naturally brought with them some incredible highs, and difficult lows.

Alan Knight, aged two years, three months.

1 - A legend is born

So near and yet so far. Perhaps the phrase which sums up my playing career. As near as three minutes 42 seconds, just long enough to boil an egg, or even to take a break during the TV commercials. Or as far away as three or four inches, the length of the palm of my hand. You can measure it whichever way you choose, but that was as close as I was ever to get to Wembley or an FA Cup Final as it transpired. For me and the thousands of suffering Pompey fans at Highbury that Sunday lunchtime in April 1992, it might as well have been a lifetime or a million miles away.

I remember thinking, as I hit the ground from my dive, "I've saved it" after getting a finger tip to the ball, then seeing it hit the inside of the post. I instinctively looked back, helpless as I watched the ball rolling back across me, inches from the goal-line. In almost slow-motion mode, a Liverpool player reacted first and knocked the ball into the net. Like any life-changing moment, you always look back later and think about the 'what-ifs'. What if the post had been round rather than oval - perhaps the ball might have come out at a different angle? What if it had not come so late in the game – the lads might not have been so tired and one of our defenders might have followed the shot in, after the kick had been taken, in case of such a rebound? What if Ronnie Whelan had been sent off earlier in the game – would any other Liverpool player have been so ideally placed to score?

Whelan should not even have been on the pitch to score that equaliser which earned Liverpool that subsequent replay at Villa Park, which we finally lost after a penalty shoot-out. Early in the game Mark Chamberlain had been making regular inroads down our right and in that mood, he might well have caused Liverpool real problems. But he was quickly scythed down by Whelan, and carried off as a result. There's no doubt in my mind that Ronnie should have gone and nowadays it would have been a certain red card.

I even looked back to a childhood injury which had slightly reduced the length of one of the fingers on the decisive hand. At the tender age of three an accident almost put paid to any hopes I might have had of becoming a goalkeeper at any level. I caught my hand in a door slammed by my sister and the top of a finger, almost an inch, was severed to such an extent that it was hanging by the skin alone. But I had two pieces of fortune, which not only saved my finger, but also my future career. First, a neighbour had the presence of mind to wrap and pack the two pieces of finger together and, secondly, a skilled hospital surgeon managed to successfully sew the two back together. Now, all there is to show is a marked scar and a slightly bent finger. Perhaps if that finger had been fully extended it might have been able to deflect John Barnes' shot rather than merely touch it on to the post.

The game itself was a bit of a blur, but I didn't have a lot to do that day or, indeed, at Villa Park in the replay. That's a measure of how well we played and how well our defensive system worked. But I can't, to this day, bring myself to watch either of the two videos of the games. I did have one let-off at Highbury, when the ball was played through to Ian Rush. I came out to save at his feet, but my knee caught him and the ball bobbled away as a result. The referee promptly gave a foul against Rush but he didn't touch me and, in fact, I had brought him down.

At the end of the 90 minutes Jim Smith met us in the middle, in the break before extra time, and said: "You've done fantastically well, they haven't caused us any problems, just keep it going." Suddenly, out of the blue, thanks to a great through ball from Warren Neill, Darren Anderton scored and I started to think "it's coming – we have a chance here – we're nearly there". In that situation you can't take anything for granted and must try to stay concentrated. As the minutes ticked by we naturally tried to play time out; to slow the game down and to try to waste as much time as possible by getting the ball into the corners.

Then, Andy Awford brought down John Barnes just outside our penalty area and Liverpool got out of jail. As soon as we had kicked-off again I looked up at the clock and, under my breath, exclaimed: "Three fucking minutes from Wembley!" Instinctively, our next thought was that we didn't want to lose the game. Again, this time as we hung on for the replay, we looked for ways to play out time. Then, it was all over. We had worked so hard and everything had gone according to plan, but it was such a shame that they scored in the way they did.

Awfs has never, to this day, been allowed to forget giving away that free kick and we still laugh and joke about it today. Nobody blamed him. It was just one of those things. I give him stick about it, but then people still have a go at me, saying that I could have pushed the free kick away for a corner. Others say Alan McLoughlin should have scored, rather than hit the bar, in the replay. You can go round and round, replaying moments in those games, but it doesn't change anything. After the first semi-final we were not in any way despondent – that was soon to follow – and our fear of Liverpool had gone. We certainly felt a lot better about facing them the second time around and we knew now that this wasn't the Liverpool of old. We thought we had more than matched them and that if we stuck at it in the replay, as we had done at Highbury, we had a good chance. And that was the way it worked out at Villa Park – we made the better chances but unfortunately, this time, the goal just wouldn't come. Once it went down to penalties, however, I did feel we were going to blow it.

Out in the middle, in the break before the penalties, it was a question of hunting around to find people who wanted to take them. We had made no preparation for a penalty shoot-out – no firm decisions had been made beforehand as to who would take them. On the night, there were one or two who didn't want to take them, who you might have expected to come forward. One or two others didn't want to take them unless it was absolutely necessary. The key thing about penalty-taking is that if you're not confident about it then you shouldn't be taking one. In the end we found four volunteers – Martin Kuhl, Kit Symons, Warren Neill, and John Beresford. Of those, I would never have thought that Kit would have put himself forward and yet he was the only one to score and was the coolest customer of the bunch. I faced three penalties from Liverpool and they all scored but, for us, first Kuhlie shot wide, then Kit scored, but Warren's was saved and Bes also missed the target.

There was such an overwhelming sense of anti-climax in our dressing room afterwards. A number of the players were in tears – younger ones like Shaggy and Awfs, as you would expect, but also some of the senior players. I was just numb but no tears would come. I just turned to the young lads and said: "Boys, you will get another chance, but I never will." Knowing that we could have beaten Sunderland in the final added to our extreme sense of disappointment. However, we had gone out to Liverpool in the most honourable way possible. After the semi-final draw had been made we had worried that, in facing the great Liverpool, we might let everybody down and it might end in some ignominious way. In the end though, everybody gave it 110%; we had given a good account of ourselves and we just didn't have that bit of luck which might have got us through. But it was not the worst I have ever felt after a game. Worse was still to come in May 1993, as we missed out on promotion, first after we were beaten 4-1 at Sunderland and then after we had lost out to Leicester in the play-offs.

However, it would be churlish of me to suggest that I have been anything other than extremely fortunate in my career. To have been able to make over 800 appearances at a club like Pompey, in front of such magnificent supporters, to spend 25 years at the club I love and to be able to play a small part in bringing promotion to the Premiership and the first division title to Fratton Park is a dream come true. I have also been fortunate enough to be honoured with the award of the MBE. On the very day that I went to Buckingham Palace, though, amongst all the excitement and tension of the occasion, amidst all the messages of congratulations, one person's words came echoing back to me. From nearly thirty years before, the words of my form-teacher at Henry Cavendish Junior School in Balham, a Mrs Hills, rang in my ears: "You'll never make anything of your life!" she raged, as her frustration with the daydreamer before her boiled over. At the time few would have doubted that she was right, as I stared out of the window dreaming of becoming a goalkeeper.

It would have been a shame if my life had been wasted because a great deal of blood, sweat and tears was expended in bringing me into this world. My birth was described to me by my mother as 'difficult'. That seemed to put it mildly, given what I have learned subsequently of the events of July 3, 1961, in Balham in the two-bedroom ground floor maisonette at 11 Burnbury Road, London SW12. Mum and dad wanted a boy – they were apparently few and far between in our family – a brother for Elaine, aged nine and Glynis, aged three. It was due to be a relatively straightforward birth at home, with my mother Joyce having my aunt, Gladys Knight, and a midwife close at hand. As it happened, I nearly died in the process. I am told that I was found to be in the 'breech position' – refusing to come out and with my chin stuck – and eventually, after a long struggle, not only was my mother in some danger of expiring, but I was weakening considerably. A life-and-death situation was apparently avoided by the big strong midwife who, throwing caution to the wind and with no regard to the damage which might have been caused, climbed on to the bed and literally yanked me out.

I was born into a typical working-class area. Our home was in an urban sprawl of property, built after the first world war. It amuses me to go back there now and find that it has taken on an air of affluence; invaded by yuppy-types, with inflated property prices to match. In our rented accommodation, with only two bedrooms, it meant that I shared with my sister Glynis until I was about five and, thereafter, had to sleep in the front room. My father had been a 'Desert Rat' with the Eighth Army during World War Two. He was a munitions expert, with a penchant for 'dirty tricks' with explosives, not that he ever spoke much about it to anybody. When I eventually came into the world he was a plumber with Ashford and Mall in Smithfield. He was with them for most of his working life, making his way up to foreman and even ending up as a director. My mother spent most of her early married life at home bringing up the three of us, but later worked as a dinner lady and a machinist.

We were a very close family unit, and both sets of grandparents lived in the same road. I was particularly close to my father's parents and especially to grandad Knight, whose first name, Edward, is my middle name. He was a real influence; an East Ender who had worked as a driver and a policeman. Hard as nails, but a loving man for all that. As my father worked such long hours, I spent much of my time with grandad, often walking the dog on Tooting Bec Common. He taught me how to tie my shoelaces and how to tell the time, but more importantly he instilled a passion and pride in me. Very often he would bring our conversations back to how important it was to make up your mind what you wanted to do in life and then really go for it. He died suddenly, when I was about eight years of age, and it came as a massive shock to me, being my first experience of death. My father was hit hard too, and was very quiet for some time afterwards.

I had no aggressive side to me as a boy, but grandad was keen to get me to stick up for myself. I remember being with him once, after I had a regular haircut – a 'short back and sides' – and some passing school friends proceeded to give me some stick. For grandad there was only one suitable response and he immediately made it clear to me that I should go over and have a fight with them. So, over I went, and ended up attacking one of my friends, Stephen King, rolling around in the gutter with him. We were the best of mates the following day, but I suppose I earned the respect that my grandad thought was so important. As it happened, my father had been a boxer during his army days and I gather his brother, Frank, had been a goalkeeper at Crystal Palace at one time without really making the grade.

I had a very happy childhood with my mother as the cornerstone of the family, my father always seemingly at work. I would say it was a fairly strict upbringing, with the real threat of having a whack on the backside for any misdemeanours. Good manners and family values were instilled in us from an early age. I remember my mother taking me for my first day at Telferscott Infants School, just four streets away, in a huge cold and draughty, turn-of-the-century building. Right from the word go, however, both there, and subsequently at Henry Cavendish, I never showed any real interest in school work. Some of the teachers were frustrated by my indifference, particularly as they clearly felt that academically I could have achieved more. Mrs Hills summed it all up with her outburst. In my case, it was definitely a case of 'the lights are on, but there's no-one at home'.

My footballing life began about fifty yards or so from home, at the age of about ten, on Tooting Bec Common, which is a huge expanse of open fields rolling through to Streatham. Three or four of us would regularly go over there of an evening for a kick about, although the other lads were two or three years older than me. We would organise our own games, putting coats and jumpers down as goalposts or practise headers and volleys, with me usually being the one who had to save them. I had many a battle with my mother over those trips to the common, mainly because there was a main road to cross to get there. I got into trouble with my mother one day over football, when, for the very first time at junior school, without notice, I didn't go home to lunch. There was a big game on in the playground during the lunchtime, which I couldn't bear to miss but while I was playing, in marched my mother and dragged me off home, to my great embarrassment.

However, it wasn't until the very first games lesson, at junior school, that I first went between some posts. The school games were played on a cinder pitch and on that day we all had to line up as the two teams were picked. Eventually, I was left as the last one to be chosen and, being the tallest of all, the sports master, Mr Hutchings, ordered me to go in goal. I remember that a few shots hit me in the face and on the backside that day, as I struggled to meet the demands of the position. But the seed had been sown in my mind and from then on I would make a point of watching the goalkeepers on *Match of the Day* very closely, with Peter Shilton, Ray Clemence, Peter Bonetti and Gordon Banks as real influences. Their every move was imprinted on my brain and I would take every chance to ape them. I was fascinated in particular with the contrasting styles of Shilton and Clemence – 'Shilts' the more spectacular, with Clemence using his anticipation and positional sense.

The daydreamer at school, who wasn't really very good at anything, could not wait to get out to the big embankment wall, built to keep people off the railway line between Balham and Streatham. There I would spend long hours, usually on my own, kicking a ball against the wall and grabbing the rebound. The indentations in the wall meant that the ball came off at different angles and speeds. Many a passer-by would have seen this young lad diving around on the small strip of grass in front of the embankment.

The Knight family came from the East End of London originally and a tradition of supporting West Ham was passed down. The men of the family would go to Upton Park on Boxing Day and I went from about seven or eight years of age onwards, on the North Bank, often being passed down to the front for a better view. I did start to go to Upton Park with my friends from about age 13 – Mervyn Day or Phil Parkes were in goal for them then – but there was often a hooligan problem on the tube that was quite scary and it really put me off going. We turned to non-league Tooting and Mitcham, where we would position ourselves behind the goal. I remember an FA Cup game there against Swindon Town when Frank Burrows and Stan Harland who, ironically, were both to play such a big part in my early career, were probably playing. We were right little troublemakers that afternoon, positioned behind the goal at one end. We took a great delight in throwing teasels – small prickly plant heads which stick to garments – at the back of the Swindon keeper.

It was a major blow, in more ways than one, when my time came to move to a senior school. Due to the catchment area it had to be Wandsworth School – which involved a daily one-and-a-half hour journey each way. I can recall the journey to this day – a train from Balham Station to Clapham Junction, a number 49 bus to Southfields and then a bit of a walk to the school. Not only did I loathe the travel, but they didn't play football there at all and I had to take up rugby, basketball and fencing. For six months I pestered my parents to get me a move to the nearer school, Ernest Bevin in Tooting. It was a desperately unhappy period in my life and I regularly cried myself to sleep. Finally, after my parents had given in to my pleas, they made the necessary applications and I was able to move, but even there no football was played in the first year. Luckily both the cub scouts and Balham Colts teams gave me the football I craved during this period.

By now I was set on becoming a professional footballer and it was through a teacher at the nearby Henry Compton School, who was a scout for Queens Park Rangers, that I began training with them on a Thursday evening. Not long after I began to train with Fulham as well, this time on a Tuesday evening. From the word go, my mother and father would take me in the family car and be there throughout the sessions. Looking back it must have been a real chore for them, particularly with the heavy traffic we often had to endure across London. Their early backing and encouragement, at great cost in terms of time, energy and finance was to continue for many years. Looking back, it was crucial to my making a career in the game. Many of the boys at these training sessions became associated on schoolboy forms with the London clubs. Sadly, after a while, it became apparent to me that I would not be signed by either QPR or Fulham, with whom I was training. I did, however, manage to make some use of the Fulham connection by getting a ticket for Wembley for the Fulham-West Ham FA Cup Final in May 1975. I was a West Ham fan of course, and had to be very quiet standing at the Fulham end.

It was just before my 14th birthday – early summer 1975 - when a colourful, larger-than-life character called Reg Lock came into my life. He made the introduction that I had been longing for. Reg was a freelance scout with links to Ray Crawford, who was looking after the youth set-up at Portsmouth at that time. "Do you fancy a week's trial at Portsmouth?" Reg said and, to be honest, I had no idea where Portsmouth was, although I might possibly have heard of it through the football results. My father had been based on the Isle of Wight for a short time during his army training, so he had a pretty good idea of the location.

We were both keen to take the opportunity and I was booked in for a suitable half-term week. My parents took me down to the south coast on a Saturday and, on arrival, we watched the youth team before being taken to my digs for the week in St Ronans Road, Southsea. As a 13-year-old I had never been away from home on my own – obviously I had been away on holiday, but always with my parents. They drove back to London and I was left on my own on the Sunday and stuck with nothing to do. I walked the streets and found myself down at Canoe Lake near Southsea seafront. I sat down for some time in a shelter there and cried my eyes out. I suppose I have to admit I was a bit of a 'mummy's boy'.

On the Monday morning, armed with directions, I had to find my way to Fratton Park to join the other lads down for the week. I walked into the ground and the dressing rooms for the first time and found it all awe-inspiring. The whole atmosphere and aura of the place from the unique smells through to the blue-painted floors were intimidating, but in a strangely positive way. I knew nothing of the history or tradition of the club. Very quickly though I discovered the honours boards, the trophy cabinet and the pictures of latter-day heroes. I immediately gained a great respect for what had obviously gone before at the club. After changing, the whole staff moved to the Eastney Barracks grounds for training and I even found myself with the first-team squad for a couple of days. There were plenty of young lads in the squad at that time – the likes of Keith Viney, Billy Eames, Steve Foster, Chris Kamara, Peter Denyer, Leigh Barnard and Paul Bennett - and it was great to mix with senior professionals for the first time.

When the morning sessions were over, it was back to Fratton Park for me to join in with the apprentices as they got down to the various daily chores which were part of their lot. I loved every minute of it – whether it was cleaning the boots, washing floors, or sweeping the terraces. I even got to clean out the public conveniences around the ground, which included, if necessary, putting my hands down the toilet if it needed unblocking. The apprentices are not allowed to carry out much of that work nowadays and I think that is a real shame. It was a good grounding, character-building and taught a respect for people. In those days, it was very much a case of an apprentice not speaking to a professional unless he was spoken to. There were other signs of respect too, like having to knock before going into the senior dressing room.

When the week was all over I was left with an overwhelming desire for more of it – this was definitely what I wanted to do with my life. I felt I had a chance of making it and that I would get a fair crack of the whip at a club like Portsmouth. There was no sign of the prima-donnas and cliques that I had noted whilst training with Fulham and QPR, where the influence of the parents had been a key factor in determining whether a boy was taken on or not. Then, to cap it all, Ray Crawford came over and said that they would like to sign me on schoolboy forms on my 14th birthday in July 1975. Immediately my parents were adamant that we should notify Fulham and QPR, out of courtesy. Ron Howard at QPR, was a terrific, straightforward guy and, after we had explained our decision, he wished us all the best. It was a similar situation with Fulham. From then on it was back to completing my schooling for a year at Ernest Bevin and getting down to Portsmouth in the school holidays, for more coaching and training. With the club in such financial difficulty, Ian Chase, who owned a couple of hairdressing salons in the area and who was involved with the SOS Pompey Committee, volunteered to put me up free of charge at his Gosport home for the majority of the holiday periods.

As a rule, I was not called into the club's youth side in the South-East Counties League, so arrangements were made, through Reg Lock, for me to train in the weekday evenings with Kingstonian Under-16's and on another night, the Tooting and Mitcham first team. I also played for the former on a Sunday. That arrangement continued for a couple of years, even after I had broken into the Pompey youth team at 15 years of age. Whilst I was with Kingstonian, as a 15-year-old school-boy, based in London, out of the blue I had a call-up for the Pompey first team. The two senior goalkeepers, Graeme Lloyd and Phil Figgins were both injured for the FA Cup first round tie against Minehead, but in the event, to my great relief, the youth-team keeper Paul Bennett played. As for Ernest Bevin School the emphasis was on rugby, under physics teacher Mr Drake. I had the odd game and we all went to Twickenham for the varsity matches. I even turned out twice for the Old Boys at full back, after leaving school.

Football-wise, it soon became apparent that an offer of an apprenticeship at Fratton Park on my 16th birthday was there for the taking. But, before that, I suffered a kick in the head whilst goalkeeping, that could well have put my infant career in jeopardy. It occurred whilst I was playing for Inner London Schools against Lanarkshire at the Spurs training ground at Cheshunt. I got a knock on my head and was carried off in a groggy state. Everybody seemed quite happy for my father to take me home, but we were warned that if I felt sick subsequently, then I was to go to hospital.

Sure enough, I was ill in my father's car and by the time we reached the local Accident & Emergency I was slipping in and out of consciousness. I was kept in hospital for three days under observation, with severe concussion diagnosed. During that time, my parents were scared out of their wits by the news that a 'brain swelling' had been observed and that it might be necessary to operate. Holes would have had to have been drilled in my head as part of the procedure, to correct the problem. In the event I was simply discharged, with instructions that I shouldn't play football for three months, to avoid the risk of getting another knock in the same area. In my usual stubborn way, I still went up on the common and joined in the makeshift games, but it didn't do me too much good, as I recall, with a couple of dizzy and feverish spells as the outcome. I sometimes think that I may have suffered some form of brain damage, either then or at some time later in my career. Even now, I do occasionally suffer from a slurring of my speech, with a feeling of being 'punch-drunk'. I have often wished that I had insisted on having a brain scan, using the club's medical insurance, when the spells occurred.

In the months before I signed for Pompey, my school time drifted interminably to a close and there was no doubt that my school work suffered considerably. I turned up for CSE examinations in Maths, English, Physics and Geography. They were all made up of multiple-choice questions, so it was just a question of taking pot luck with where I placed my crosses. Looking back, I do remember being interested and I still am, in History and Archaeology, particularly the Greek and Roman Empires. I'm not sure why I never came to take an examination in History, given my interest. To be honest though, I only had time for a teacher if he showed an interest in football. I had to go through the 'careers advice' scenario of course, but after explaining that my football career was already laid out before me, the headmaster then proceeded to tell me that I would be better off going in the army. Tony Meo and Jimmy White are old boys of Ernest Bevin and I wonder what advice they were given when they announced in similar fashion that they wanted to become snooker professionals.

It was during the last months of my schooling that I sustained my first broken nose. In fact, it turned out to be the first of three in just six months! As far as I can remember, I only ever broke my nose once in the next 25 years or so – when I had my face rearranged during a collision at Plough Lane against Wimbledon. The first time was a strange one. I was walking away from school, making for home the same as I always did, with my friends, down the road to the Tooting Bec Tube Station. An adult male quickly jumped from a van that was waiting at traffic lights and punched me on the nose, breaking it in the process. He promptly jumped back into the van, just as the lights changed, and away it sped. My mother was really upset and reported it to the police, but no trace could be found of either the van or the individual concerned. It really put me off going to school and walking back down that road again. Weeks later the nose was broken again. This time, it was during a piggyback race in training at Portsmouth. We all fell over and in the resulting scramble I suffered a sharp blow to the face. No sooner had that second one healed up then, shortly after taking up my apprenticeship at Fratton Park, one of the apprentices accidentally caught me on the bridge of the nose with the handle of a mop, as we cleaned up the dressing rooms. This third one really got me into trouble at the club, mainly through the amount of blood which was spilled on my playing kit.

I had been with Pompey for about two years as an associate schoolboy, with an apprenticeship just weeks away from being taken up on my 16th birthday, when, in May 1977, fate almost intervened. In the weeks before I was due to leave home, my father had become increasingly unwell with his chest. At the time, the prospect of being away from home and not being close to him and my family, if things got worse, was not too appealing. West Ham became interested and got in touch with me. Whether it could have been considered as an illegal approach or not, I really don't know. Eddie Baily, the former England and Spurs inside forward, spoke to my father and I, and we were invited to Upton Park for a first-team game as the club's guests. We met manager Ron Greenwood and he offered me a one-year apprenticeship, followed by an initial one-year professional contract.

We were flattered obviously, but I had some good friends at Fratton Park and was really settled there. I had a great deal of respect for Ray Crawford and in no way did I want to disturb our good relationship. In the end it came down to whether or not Pompey were prepared to agree to my release – it was in their hands really. If they still wanted me, then I was prepared to stay. I understand Greenwood came down to Fratton Park to see Pompey manager Jimmy Dickinson, who had just taken over from Ian St John, in an attempt to secure my release. I've learned subsequently that a fee of £5,000 was offered by West Ham and a player exchange involving myself and Pompey's Clive Green for West Ham's Mick McGiven was discussed.

In fairness to Jimmy Dickinson the club were in dire financial straits at the time and were desperately trying to bring in some new faces to improve their lot. Jimmy phoned Ray Crawford, who was at home on a day's holiday and painting a ceiling as the call came. Under protest, and not knowing what it was all about, Ray arrived to find Greenwood in Jimmy's office. Ray immediately took Jimmy aside and he told me later that he protested in no uncertain terms saying it would be a mistake to let me go – that I would be worth tens of thousands of pounds within a few years. To his credit, Jimmy took Ray's advice and, probably to his surprise, Greenwood went back to London empty handed. So, in effect, the decision had been made for me.

*'I had a quiet word with Jimmy
(Dickinson) outside of the
meeting and told him that Alan
would have a good career and
be an enormous asset.'*

Ray Crawford

For a budding young goalkeeper growing up in the late 1960s and early 1970s, when it came to choosing a role model the young Alan Knight was spoilt for choice. It was the golden age of British keepers. In singling out Peter Shilton and Ray Clemence as his particular heroes, he picked two players who were – in their contrasting styles – the epitome of goalkeeping excellence at the time.

Shilton represented the appliance of science in matters custodial. The third keeper in Sir Alf Ramsey's Mexico 70 squad, Shilton had emerged as a promising young goalkeeper at Leicester City once Banks had left for Stoke in 1966. While naturally gifted and extrovert on the field, he went one step further on the training ground where he relentlessly honed his technique. By a quirk of fate, he followed in Gordon Banks' footsteps, becoming the most expensive keeper in Britain when he moved to the Victoria Ground in 1974 for £325,000. His adoption of roll-necked goalkeeping tops, in non-traditional white or blue, added to the feeling that, like all keepers, he was, just slightly, mad. Idiosyncratic, certainly. Usually playing second fiddle to Clemence for the England jersey during the 1970s, Shilton, initially at least, paid a high international price for a shot from Domarski which squirted under his body during a World Cup qualifier against Poland at Wembley in 1973, which knocked England out of the competition. It wasn't until another big-money move to Nottingham Forest in the late 1970s, as Brian Clough guided them to European Cup glory, that Shilton was finally acclaimed England's number one. He went on to represent England in three World Cups – his last, 1990, at the age of 40 – and continued his playing career well into the 1990s: a tribute to his preparation and fitness and a role model for any aspiring goalkeeper to follow. Clemence, on the other hand, was arguably the more 'natural' goalkeeper, with superb agility coupled with an unerring positional sense. Having started his career at Scunthorpe, he was signed by Bill Shankly in 1968 and starred in the first truly great Liverpool side, which dominated English football in the late 1970s. He also profited from Shilton's World Cup disaster and generally was first choice for England from 1974 onwards; surviving his own high-profile howler, when Kenny Dalglish 'nutmegged' him to secure Scotland's 2-1 win at Hampden Park in May 1976.

As with any youngster in the 1970s with goalkeeping aspirations, Knight couldn't fail to appreciate Gordon Banks either. 'Banks of England' – as he was known – was an unassuming Chesterfield-born player, whose starring role for Leicester City had established him as England's Number One by the time of the 1966 World Cup. He carved his name in immortality as a member of Alf Ramsey's 'wingless wonders' who lifted the Jules Rimet trophy on a damp, sticky afternoon at Wembley in July of that year. His unflappable temperament and powers of concentration were married to an astute positional sense, which contributed to his 'greatest-ever' save in June 1970, when he swooped to claw Pelé's downward header up and over the bar. At 34 he was still playing in the top flight for Stoke City, when a car accident in October 1972 cost him the sight in one eye and effectively ended his career.

By contrast, another of Knight's heroes, Peter Bonetti, would have inspired anyone who regarded goalkeeping as an art, rather than a science. His game was based on instinct and agility and his nickname, 'The Cat', was never more aptly used. With his exotic name – he was the son of a Swiss restaurateur – he was an equally exotic goalkeeper. Invariably brilliant, but always prone to the occasional blunder, he ended up being 'best' remembered for his role in England's downfall, when they gave up a 2-0 lead against West Germany in the quarter-finals of the 1970 World Cup, with Bonetti arguably at fault for two of the goals, after Banks had been forced to drop out of the side with a bout of food poisoning. He played a record 600 games for his only league club, Chelsea, and the young Knight could scarcely have thought, while watching him star on *Match of the Day* and the *Big Match* that one day it would be a milestone he would more than emulate. With such a wealth of talent to admire – it should not be forgotten this was also the era of the likes of Phil Parkes at QPR, Pat Jennings at Tottenham and a young Mervyn Day at Knight's favourite team West Ham – it was no wonder the prospect of donning the gloves in the school playground, with jumpers for goalposts, or afterwards on Tooting Bec Common, would have been an alluring one for any lad growing up in this decade.

Knight's sister Elaine recalls her brother was always keen on football: 'He was a quiet, well-behaved young lad, who was never in any trouble, but he was very sociable, however, and he had a lot of friends who he played with on the common. From a very young age he really loved the game, and he thought of almost nothing else through his schooldays. People remarked on his great reflexes and intuition – he appeared to always know where the ball was going. Our mother believed his talent as a goalkeeper was a gift and my parents gave him enormous support financially, despite not being well-off, and in terms of time and energy,' she explained. Elaine is now a university librarian living in London, while his other sister Glynis is a social worker in Yorkshire.

By the time Knight had come to the attention of Portsmouth Football Club in the mid-1970s, however, joining the Blues must have seemed a far from attractive proposition. At that time the club was a mess. The optimism of mid-1973, when new chairman John Deacon had liberally sprinkled chunks of his property-boom profits over Pompey, had long gone. High-profile signings such as the £100,000 paid for Arsenal starlet Peter Marinello and Paul Went, acquired from Fulham for a record £155,000, were now expensive millstones around a sinking club's neck. The promised return to Division One had turned into a catastrophic relegation to the third division in 1976 and although Pompey's gates remained good by lower-league standards, they would not pay players on first-division contracts. Knight had first come to the attention of Pompey when football-lover Reg Lock had recommended the then chief scout Tony Barton take a look at the young keeper.

The club had just taken on Ray Crawford, who had left Fratton in 1958 before embarking on a long career in the top-flight which bought him a championship medal at Burnley and England honours, to run the youth team. The new man was clearly impressed when he first saw Knight in action in the summer of 1975 as he now recalls: 'In that week that Alan came down as a 13-year-old, I could see that he had a lot of ability. He was agile, had plenty of confidence, a good pair of hands, and talked to his co-defenders. He was a tall lad, which was in his favour, and, like his father, he was well-built but lean. I reported back to Tony that I thought we had a good one in the making, and the club agreed that we should offer him schoolboy terms. We had several other goalkeepers who turned up that week, who had been recommended to us, but Alan was always better than any of them.'

Having signed as a schoolboy in July 1975, 15-year-old Knight spent the summer of 1976 at Fratton Park, lodging with five different people during his stay, including local hairdresser Ian Chase, who also went on to be the founder of the Portsmouth Young Supporters' Club. By the time Knight had returned home to London for his final year at Ernest Bevin School, his potential had been underlined by youth team coach Crawford when he gave the youngster his South East Counties League debut on September 4, 1976. It was no bad debut either. He even kept a clean sheet as Pompey travelled to Crystal Palace and won 2-0. But Pompey's financial problems had also finally come to a head early in that 1976/77 season and so it was against the backdrop of the SOS Pompey – Save our Soccer – campaign that Knight would have been introduced seriously to the club. The fading memories of two league titles 25 years previously hung heavily on a club that was all-but bankrupt.

Its spirit, and most importantly that of its supporters, remained intact, however, and through their efforts extinction was avoided. And from Knight's point of view it must have appeared to be a club where the emphasis was on 'youth'. For the first time in a generation – in fact since the then manager George Smith had proclaimed in the mid–1960s that 'there was nothing but fish in the sea' around Portsmouth – Pompey sought to develop their own players. Adversity had already meant young players such as Peter Denyer, David Pullar, Chris Kamara and Portsmouth-born Steve Foster, who would play for England in the 1982 World Cup finals, had been given their head by first team manager Ian St John (who had replaced John Mortimore in September 1974) while Crawford was busily nurturing the next batch of talent.

Although still only 15, Knight was the first-choice goalkeeper of a Pompey youth team which reached the fourth round of the FA Youth Cup, before unluckily bowing out to Tottenham 2–1 in a Fratton replay in March 1977, with a striker by the name of Mark Falco grabbing one of the Spurs goals. Knight had already made his Fratton debut four weeks previously when a South East Counties League game against QPR had been switched from Eastney Barracks to the Frogmore Road ground. However, Crawford maintains his best performance in that inaugural season came in a Southern Junior Floodlit Cup tie at Portman Road in November 1976: 'It was probably Alan's greatest display in the youth team, even though we lost 1–0 on the night. He was absolutely outstanding against a strong side, which included lads like Russell Osman, Terry Butcher, George Burley and Alan Brazil. The then Ipswich manager, Bobby Robson, was there to see it and it was such a pleasure to see one of our lads put on such a display.'

The end of the 1976/77 season was to prove a turbulent one, as manager St John paid the price for taking Pompey to the brink of relegation to the fourth division. Replacing him was Pompey legend Jimmy Dickinson MBE, a veteran of 764 league matches and two championship medals. In May 1977 he accepted a caretaker manager's role and with three points from the last three games guided Pompey to safety. In the euphoria which followed that escape he was persuaded to take the role permanently and one of his first jobs was to decide on Knight's immediate future as he fast approached his 16th birthday. It also meant a change of role for Crawford, who had been instrumental in bringing Knight to the club in the first place. He was promoted to first-team coach, but continued to monitor Knight's progress closely as it was clear a number of other clubs were interested in signing him when he reached 16, in July. Crawford met Knight's parents to insist the club were still keen to sign their son. It had been an open secret since early 1977 that Knight was assured an apprenticeship, but there was still a danger his head could have been turned by other offers.

However, the main threat to Knight's Pompey career getting off the ground at all was the club itself. Still strapped for cash, especially after a fund-raising end-of-season friendly against either Aston Villa or Liverpool to tide the club over the lean summer months fell through, Dickinson's head was being turned by overtures from West Ham United manager Ron Greenwood, who fancied his chances of prising Knight away with an offer of £5,000. It was no mean sum for a player who had yet to play a reserve-team game and potentially a lifeline to a club whose finances were as parlous as Pompey's. Crawford takes up the story: 'He was one of the best young keepers around and West Ham wanted to take him from us when he was 15 years of age. I was at home on holiday at the time, when Jimmy phoned me to say Greenwood was coming down to sign him that morning. My immediate reaction was: don't sell him, whatever you do. However, Jimmy begged me to come in for the meeting, which I did. Greenwood was prepared to pay £5,000 for him, which, at that time, was a lot of money for a player of that age. In fact he was so keen that I felt that if we had asked for £10,000 he would have agreed to pay. I had a quiet word with Jimmy outside of the meeting and told him that Alan would have a good career and be an enormous asset and that it would be a great shame to let him go now. In fairness to Jimmy he had seen enough of Alan to know I was right, and we agreed to hang on to him.

'Alan knew by then that he had the ability, and had probably got to hear of West Ham's interest. I suppose, with hindsight, in some way I probably held him back, by hanging on to him at Portsmouth. But I wanted the best for the club and it was our job to try and keep our best players. Alan had seen players like Steve Foster, Graham Roberts, Dave Pullar and Leigh Barnard come through so he knew he would get every chance at Pompey,' added Crawford. So shortly after his birthday Knight, accompanied by his parents, met up with Dickinson and Crawford at Fratton Park to officially become a Pompey apprentice. And no-one could have imagined how quickly his chance to play in the first team would come.

2 - Growing pains

When my 16th birthday arrived, I was relieved to finally put pen to paper and started my first season, 1977/78, as an apprentice. Ray Crawford had moved up to assist Jimmy Dickinson with the first team and a Scot, Billy Hunter, had taken over as youth-team manager. As it happened, I was chief scout, Tony Barton's last signing before he moved to Aston Villa to join up with his former Pompey team-mate Ron Saunders. In fact, Tony took me up to Villa Park to have a look around with a view to moving my apprenticeship to the Midlands instead. But I had already signed for Pompey and didn't want to go back on that commitment.

When I arrived I had to go through the customary 'blackballing' initiation ceremony for all new apprentices. That meant being stripped naked, painted all over with black polish and then being taken out and left in the centre circle in the freezing cold. The secret was to willingly allow it to be done – if you struggled then it got worse, with Algipan rub put on your vital parts. Some unfortunates even had their pubic hair shaved, or so legend had it. It wasn't long after that the practice died out, but unfortunately not before I had been initiated.

I went into digs close to Fratton Park, at Warren Avenue, with another apprentice, Graham Marriner. Other than for meals, we were hardly there, but I am not sure that the elderly lady who put us up was really too happy with the arrangement. Within a few weeks we gave her what she thought was some cause for complaint, when she accused us of damaging the house. We had returned one day to find the front door locked, which was most unusual. Our reaction was to force the door, because we imagined that there was some sort of emergency situation. On discovering the damage, the lady ignored our explanation and contacted the club to complain that we were 'breaking her house up'. It was not a good start to my Pompey career and we had to be moved, to stay with a really nice lady called Hazel Penny in St Ronans Avenue. It was a much better arrangement as we were based opposite a guest house in which the other apprentices were lodged. We lasted with Hazel for a few months until, with her husband being posted overseas, we had to move again, finally ending up in the Normanhurst Hotel, in Southsea, with a gentleman called Fred Sutch looking after us. Later on, when I started going out with Jennifer, my future wife, I took to lodging most of the time at her mother's house.

We had to be at the ground for 8.30 am to sort out the kit with Gordon Neave and to work at the chores around the dressing-rooms and the stadium. 'Gordie' was a hard taskmaster, but fair and, looking back now, it's the way apprentices should be treated. The discipline didn't do anybody any harm at all. In between all that work, we would train in the morning and the afternoon at Eastney Barracks. Probably the most talented of the bunch was Keith James, whose early Pompey career matched mine. He was a right full back and he signed professional at 17 and became an England Youth international. He was a bubbly, mischievous character – simply a lunatic who would do crazy things – but great fun to be with, for all that. We were so bored in the evenings, and we had little money to spend – something like £18 per week to start with – although our digs were paid for. I started smoking at 16, out of boredom as much as anything else, and have been doing so ever since! We would go to the nearby pub The Leopold, in Albert Road, to play pinball and darts, as well as buying a pint of orange and water for ten pence, rather than orange and lemonade which would set us back 50 pence. Thursday was payday and on that night we would treat ourselves to pints of lager. I swear it was Keith's idea originally. On a Saturday night, we would go to the notorious Joanna's Club in Southsea and stand around watching the fights, which would often involve women. It was all a real eye-opener for me.

Billy Hunter was a good coach, who had originally been brought to Fratton Park by Ian St John, as his assistant. It was obviously difficult for him when St John left. He had a year left on his contract, the club couldn't afford to give him a settlement and he had little option but to accept a job with the youth team. Billy was hard but fair and he gave me a good initial grounding. Things did not go so well for the new first-team management partnership of Jimmy Dickinson and Ray Crawford. Jimmy wasn't really a tracksuit manager at all and left the coaching to Ray. They found it hard to get a response, or even respect, from the players, many of whom were well past their sell-by date in my opinion. As the club slid towards relegation many of us youngsters felt that we couldn't do any worse than them.

I didn't have a lot to do with Jimmy that season, but he was obviously a nice man, in fact, too nice to be a manager. Jimmy loved the club dearly and he took the manager's job out of an overwhelming desire to help out at that desperate time, but I sensed that he never really wanted it. What was sad was that the players had little respect for him as a manager. They obviously respected his amazing record as a player, but they felt that he was out of touch with the modern game. I heard the little comments they made about him, saying things like: "He's up in his office puffing away on his pipe, pretending to do the *Daily Telegraph* crossword, but he's probably got *The Beano* hidden behind it."

There was also a story going around that Jimmy turned up at a training session at Eastney Barracks in the rain and stayed in his car to watch what he thought was a Pompey practice match between the first team and the reserves. Afterwards, he is supposed to have said that our number seven wasn't bad, but what he was actually watching was a naval match between two ships' sides. Similarly, it was said that he turned up at Cold Blow Lane to watch Millwall reserves for a 7 pm kick-off, when in fact the match had already been played at 2 pm. That has happened to me since and I know people tell the same type of stories about a great manager like Bobby Robson. It was unfair on Jimmy, who I had a great respect for, after all he had stepped in to help the club he loved at the time of its greatest need. Nevertheless, it's true to say that he didn't understand the modern game, which had changed considerably over the years since he had played. I felt he would have been happy to have remained as secretary, as a figurehead based on his legendary status at the club. I don't suppose the job was directly responsible for his subsequent death, but it certainly didn't help.

Believe it or not, the first team's poor performances even led Billy to complain about us youth players having to watch the games on a Saturday at Fratton Park – he thought they were a disgrace. Like St John, Billy was a great believer in giving youth a chance and he would push Jimmy and Ray hard to get myself and others games in the reserves, who played in the Midweek League. For my part, there were two goalkeepers in front of me – Steve Middleton, who had just joined from Saints and Phil Figgins. Whichever one of them was not playing in the first team had to get match practice in the reserves.

The appalling state of the club's finances, even after the SOS Pompey campaign had been so successful, meant that the club were only able to offer professional terms to a select few of us. Graham Roberts was a powerful centre forward, but he was released and went to non-league Dorchester. He was, of course, later picked up by Spurs and converted to a central defender, who went on to play for England.

Neil Hider was our youth-team captain and he was not offered a contract at age 18 either; he was not considered to be tall enough for a centre half. I thought he was desperately unlucky. There was an outcry locally and a number of Pompey supporters were even prepared to pay his wages to enable him to stay on. Neil was a local lad and a staunch Pompey supporter, who found the decision hard to take. It hurt him a great deal and he was very bitter towards the club for a while. He has played out most of his football career at Bognor, after not attracting any other league club attention, which surprised me. He's now looking to move into management in non-league.

I remember playing at Highbury against Arsenal in the Southern Junior Floodlit Cup. I picked the ball out of the net six times, which was a harsh lesson. I was impressed by the marble staircase and the stadium though, but it has become one of my least-favourite grounds and that was the first of my bad experiences there. We beat Ipswich, who were the best youth side in the country, at Portman Road in the South East Counties League Cup and were indebted to a great supporter, Harry Garcia, who paid for us to have an overnight hotel stay. After beating Chelsea in the semi-final – one of my best games of the season – we went down to Norwich in a two-legged final.

Frank Burrows, who was to be such a big influence in my career, came into my life, and Pompey's, in February 1978. He arrived to assist Jimmy Dickinson and he immediately got the youth team training with the first team. He also got the first team training in both the morning and the afternoon, and instilled an unheard-of discipline at the club. He ruled through fear and I have to admit that initially I was scared of him. He was big, loud, with a strong Scottish accent and really intimidating. But he was always very straight; you knew exactly where you stood with him. Hunter, a fellow Scot, got on well with Frank and I was aware that he was pushing my case for inclusion in the reserves on a more regular basis, if not the the first team. So, in many ways, it was mainly through Billy that I was given a chance in the last league game of the season at Rotherham, after we had already been relegated. I don't think Jimmy would have picked me so soon. It was rumoured during the week before the game that I might be picked and then Frank came over and told me on the Friday. I had a range of emotions – obviously I was very excited and proud – but also very nervous. We travelled up to Yorkshire the day before for an overnight stay. I was offered a sleeping pill if I couldn't sleep, but I refused the offer and, in fact, slept pretty well. With just one reserve game behind me, I had not previously spent any time to speak of with the first-team squad and hardly knew them. I had been an apprentice to one or two of them over the previous months, however. Steve Foster, Billy Wilson and Peter Denyer were good as gold towards me. Billy, in particular, was very funny that day and helped me relax. Over the years I've seen many youngsters in our dressing room before their debut, some of the other players will say just the usual "all the best, just go out and enjoy it", while others, like me, with a more wicked sense of humour perhaps, can't resist winding them up with something like "bet you're nervous, I would be".

It was a dour and dreary game, played in front of a handful of our supporters, and not too many of theirs. The Millmoor ground hasn't changed from that day to this. Even the dressing rooms are the same, as far as I can make out. We were already relegated, but Rotherham were poor on the day, despite apparently still needing the points to be mathematically safe. I had this awful feeling that the first thing I was going to be doing was picking the ball out of the net. Who knows what that would have done for my confidence? As it was, early on, one of their players headed towards goal and shot. It looked like beating me, but Billy Wilson cleared the ball off the line. For me, the game just whizzed by and was a bit of a blur. Peter Denyer scored a smart goal and then it was a question of hanging on to that. I had absolutely nothing to do and I can't even remember making a save. Whether our lads in defence worked extra hard to protect me, or whether they were playing for contracts, or perhaps just looking to impress Frank Burrows, I'll never know. I was extremely anxious during the last five minutes and desperately wanted to get through with a clean sheet. At the end, when I came off, I was absolutely exhausted mentally and had a splitting headache from the concentration.

My parents came up for the game and afterwards my mother was clearly very proud, although my father wouldn't say it to my face. The lads were elated with the win but Burrows got me to shift the skips containing the kit back to the coach from the dressing rooms. I was still an apprentice of course, so it was my job, but I felt that it was Frank's way of bringing me down to earth immediately. As an apprentice, my bonus for the win amounted to £4, not that the money came into it at all, but on the coach on the way back Phil Roberts and Billy Wilson organised a whip-round so that I could in some way match their bonuses. There was a mention of the players contributing £5 each but I never saw any more money and am still waiting for the pay-out from the collection.

At the end of that season, the youth-team squad travelled to Amsterdam for an international tournament. It was memorable for me as it was the first time I had ever been abroad. There had been a great deal of fund-raising around the city to support the trip, which was by mini-bus, via the cross-channel ferry. We lost in the final, but my abiding memory of the trip is the stomach-ache which I suffered, the like of which I have never experienced before or since, with all the consequent embarrassment. We were placed with Dutch families and whether it was the diet of non-stop cheeses which contributed to my discomfort, I don't know. I do know that on the first of my regular visits to the toilet, at the family home, I couldn't find the flush. Embarrassed and anxious not to leave the toilet in such a state for my hosts, I looked for almost an hour, with my absence going unnoticed. It ended happily with my finding some sort of pole which had to be pulled. Some of the lads went up to the famous red-light district of the city, but I was too ill, with my head in a bucket for most of the time.

On our return and throughout the summer break, after my first season as an apprentice and having had a taste of the big-time through my first-team outing, all I could think of was that I wanted more of it. Lots more of it. It's just as well that I didn't realise then that it would be almost another two years before I got a real chance. My impatience was to be a recurring theme throughout my second season, but looking back it is obvious that Frank knew how and when to play me and how to get the best out of me, without hindering my development. I appreciate now that he made me wait because he knew I wasn't ready. Eventually though, when he reckoned I was big enough and old enough, he did give me my chance.

Before the club started its first season in the fourth division, Phil Figgins had been released and gone to Australia and a new goalkeeper, in the large shape of Peter Mellor, had been signed. On the coaching side, Crawford had left to join Fareham Town, Hunter had gone back to Scotland to work at Queen of the South and Stan Harland took over as youth-team coach. When Mellor first came to the club he seemed larger than life – a real extrovert, unlike anyone I had ever known before. Peter was a showman and also a well-built muscleman. He was possibly a bit too bulky and I felt that it restricted his agility somewhat. There is a place for weight training in the game, but I have never been too keen on putting on any bulk for that reason. Both of Peter's little fingers were bent from previous dislocations and that didn't help his handling. With his size, he covered his goal well, got his angles right and was a good talker. He was a bit unfortunate, a few years earlier with Fulham, to concede a goal, through his legs, against West Ham in the FA Cup final. At the time, stood up there at Wembley as a Hammers fan though, I enjoyed his discomfort enormously!

I had a moan to Frank about his coming, but Peter did help me a lot during his stay at the club. For my part, I think I helped him by keeping him on his toes, knowing I was after his place. I knew I could never be like him – throwing sweets into the crowd, wearing funny masks, taking on forwards down by the touchline and so on. That sort of showmanship was not my style at all – I found I always needed complete concentration and that if I played around it affected my game. Frank told me: "I want you to learn the good things from him and ignore the bad things." When I asked how I would recognise the bad things, Frank smiled and added: "You'll be able to tell the difference..." Peter and I were never bosom buddies but we had great respect for each other. I only got closer to him, and socialised with him, much later after I had taken over from him as first choice. At the time, when I finally displaced him, he knew he was coming to the end of his career but was naturally upset about it, just as I would be many years later, when my turn finally came to be replaced. To be fair, Peter never showed it and, like the good professional he was, he never stabbed me in the back.

For me, the only highlight of that 1978/79 season was my involvement with the England Youth team. For most of the season, with Steve Middleton, as Mellor's understudy, needing match practice, I was not even able to get in the Pompey reserve team and I had to watch as other lads from the youth team, like Marriner, Grant, Tindal and Gillespie, got a chance. Keith James and I got our chance for England in January 1979, through our performances for the youth team against Crystal Palace, whose manager John Cartwright was also the international team manager. Frank was as proud as we were that we had been recognised and we were touched when he went out and bought us, with his own money, new boots and training shoes to take with us. With the club in dire financial straits, Pompey players had to buy their own boots and ours were looking the worse for wear. We were suitably equipped therefore when we made our debuts at the Heysel Stadium against Belgium and the Leeds goalkeeper, John Lukic, who was already a regular member of the squad, and I played a half each on a frozen pitch.

Cartwright was a very good coach, who was heavily influenced, through his involvement with Palace, by Terry Venables' methods. He got some stick for leaning towards southern players, but obviously he could only pick what he knew. After Pompey, getting involved with England was a big culture change for me. It was not only the mixing with first division players, but the FA resources, with money seemingly no object, meant there was a marked difference for me in the nature of the accommodation and training facilities. In February 1979, Keith and I travelled to Rome for the first leg of a qualifier against Italy, for the Little World Cup Finals to be held in Austria in the summer. The game was originally scheduled for a venue in southern Italy but was switched to the Olympic Stadium in Rome – where no England team had ever previously won. Steve Cherry, of Derby, was in the squad and fancied his chances of playing in goal, but I played for the whole game. There was hardly what you would call a crowd in the huge stadium but we were shocked when we came up the tunnel to see guards with guns around the running track. We won 1-0, but one incident during the game stands out for me, involving both of us Pompey lads. I came for a corner, caught the ball, but as I landed an Italian spat in my face. I could feel the spit running down my face as I held on to the ball and then kicked it upfield. Keith James then came up, hit the offender full in the face with a little jabbed punch and, with a cheeky grin, ran away. The incident was missed by just about everybody else, including the ref and certainly would have brought a vital penalty to the Italians.

I had been doubtful for the game after getting a 'dead leg' in training in Italy beforehand. With the help of some compression bandages and anti-inflammatory tablets I got through the game but unfortunately, on my return to Fratton, I got another blow on the leg in training. That caused me to miss the second leg of the qualifier at Villa Park a few weeks later. I had some ultrasound treatment from Gordon Neave, who was doubling up as physiotherapist and kitman, but the calcified haematoma, as it was diagnosed, continued to grow rather than reduce in size. Subsequent x-rays showed an enormous growth, with my thigh double its normal size and I was struggling to walk by this stage. I was referred to Haslar naval hospital in Gosport and they had only ever seen such a growth on American footballers, who had to have them surgically removed. However, it was possible for such an enormous calcification to be cleared by continuous friction from the thumbs of a physio, but it was a very painful business which often reduced the patient to tears. I had to suffer that for a week but I was fit enough to travel to Austria for the finals.

We stayed just outside Salzburg for a couple of weeks, with the

Germans also in our camp and I was understudy to John Lukic. Keith James played in all the games, and there were lads like Clive Allen, Paul Allen, Steve Mackenzie and Mark Falco, who would go on and make the grade in the first division. One memory of that trip surrounds Clive, after he had missed a vital penalty during the finals. I was very disappointed and surprised at his post-match reaction to the miss and remember him laughing and joking in the coach afterwards. I couldn't help but remember that when later he was transferred for £1 million.

Ironically, a 6-0 thrashing by Forest on a wet night at the City Ground, in the FA Youth Cup, was one of my best games of that season. I really felt that if I had not been on top of my game it could have been something like 15-0 that night. The youth team had a mixed season. We won 4-2 at Ipswich but, disappointingly, went down 3-0 at Fratton to Chelsea in the Southern Junior Floodlit Cup. There were some new youngsters like David Leworthy, Kevin Bartlett and Trevor Roberts showing up well and the former two would go on and have successful league careers.

Stan Harland was a strange guy, who I found hard to get along with. I suppose he did have to take the brunt of my frustration at not being able to play in the reserves. In similar fashion to the boss, Stan ruled by fear but, nevertheless, got the same respect. I did feel, however, that he went over the top with the discipline aspect at times. Stan also put us through an awful lot of training – literally morning, noon and night. It was a great culture shock at the time and I felt that there was too much weight-training, with the main emphasis on getting us all to become bigger and stronger. Goalkeeper Steve Middleton was put on the transfer list during the season, as I understood it, to try and clear the way for me to have a chance. Steve had a bad time and being an ex-Saint also didn't help his relationship with the Pompey fans. He got very depressed and disenchanted with the game, such that he gave up football altogether by the end of the season.

After Jimmy Dickinson's heart attack at Barnsley, at the tail end of that season, Frank took charge for the second season – 1979/80 – in the fourth division. With Peter Mellor still in my way and being over-age for the youth team, I faced up to a diet of regular reserve-team football. However, in November, I had the call at last, after Peter had let in four at Newport the previous week. I had certainly made enough fuss about getting another chance and now, here it was. Strangely, I was more nervous at Fellows Park, Walsall, than I had been on my debut at Rotherham, 18 months earlier. The game ended in a 1-1 draw and I was gutted at letting in the goal, although it wasn't really down to me. I had to feel sorry for young Rob Green, my opposite number, who, minutes from the end, let a 'daisy-cutter' from Colin Garwood go through his hands and legs for our equaliser. All Frank would say afterwards to me was: "There is no number-one keeper, if you are playing well enough then you will keep the jersey." I did keep it, and made my home debut the following Saturday against Lincoln in a 4-0 win. This was the real big one for me, playing in front of the home crowd as more or less a local boy by now. I was conscious that people often form impressions on a first sighting, and that many of our fans had never seen me play before.

It was a great relief to get that home debut under my belt and that the side played so well was a bonus. After that clean sheet, my confidence was high for the following Saturday at Fratton, this time for my first FA Cup tie, against Newport County. I was happy with my performance again in our 1-0 win, but it was a bout of gastro-enteritis which caused me to miss the next game and let Peter back in. I had taken a fancy to a girl who worked at the bank where I had my account and asked her out for something to eat. As it happened, we went to the pub first for a drink. In there I came over really queasy, was sick and had to make my apologies and beat a hasty retreat. I never saw her again. The last thing I wanted was not to be playing, but I had to cry off on the Friday before our home game against Halifax. Happily, after recovering, I regained my place at

Peterborough the following Saturday and had a really good game. It wasn't long before I was left out again, but this time it was largely my own fault. We had beaten Northampton 6-1 at home on the Saturday after Christmas 1979 and played Aldershot at home three days later on New Year's Day in front of a big holiday crowd. We were sitting nicely, second in the table and clearly in with a big shout for promotion.

We had trained on New Year's Eve and I went back to my digs for the evening, with a complete curfew on all the first-team squad. Obviously the players not in the squad for the match the next day were free to go out and see the New Year in. I was left in the house on my own, with all the other young lads having gone to a Southsea nightclub for the evening. I went to bed early, as required, but couldn't get to sleep. At 11.30 pm I got up and decided to walk down to the nightspot just to wish them 'Happy New Year'. When I arrived at the club, I became aware that some people had spotted me going in. Portsmouth is like a goldfish bowl and I might have known that I would be seen. However, no sooner had I turned up than the lads told me to get home and not to be so be stupid. I left immediately, without having a drink, and didn't even see the New Year in with them.

The following afternoon I had a torrid time in goal. I was done by three carbon-copy near-post corners, which gave Aldershot a 3-1 win. Frank was very upset afterwards in the dressing room but, no sooner had he started his rant, then there was a knock on the door and he was passed a piece of paper. After reading it, Frank turned to Joe Laidlaw and confronted him with the report that he had held a New Year's Eve party in his flat at Waterlooville. Then, turning to me, he said: "And you're in trouble. I'm told that you were seen stumbling out of a night club in the early hours of the morning, drunk, unable to stand up." Then, he took Joe straight into his office, so I didn't get a chance to reply and decided not to hang around to face the consequences there and then. Joe was fined two weeks' wages for his misdemeanour. That was a black weekend for me and I had to wait until the Monday to get to see Frank to give my version of events, which he accepted. But, unfortunately for me, he said: "As you've broken club rules, you've given me no option but to give Peter Mellor his place back. You've been a mug and you've got to learn from it. I'm not going to fine you, because it will cost you money not being in the team, through losing appearance money and bonuses."

In any event, I deserved to be dropped for the way I had played. It was a hard lesson for me and I knew that, through my stupidity, I had let Peter back in again. Frank explained my omission to the local press by saying that he had decided it was time to give me a breather because I was getting a bit tense – adding that he didn't want me to become "the youngest grey-haired man in Portsmouth". Over the years there always seemed to be someone else there, waiting to take my place in goal, even if it did make for healthy professional rivalry. It's easier to keep the jersey than to get it back. I had worked hard and waited long, to get that jersey from Peter and I hadn't wanted to give it up that easily. Despite all my time in the game, deep down I have always had a great deal of self-doubt and been very self-critical, but tried not to show it. I suppose it could be argued that this underlying lack of confidence has kept me on my toes over the years. It wasn't until mid-March before I got back into the side, after Peter had been carried off at Stockport in the previous match with an injured ankle, which meant Joe Laidlaw had to go in goal. It gave me my chance but, looking back on my performances over the next two games, it might have been better if Joe had stayed in goal, with my confidence being so low.

It was getting very tense at the top of the table, with us in third place and we went up to Darlington desperate for a win against a side in the bottom three. Alan Rogers scored to put us ahead, but 20 minutes from the end I gave away a penalty which brought the Darlington equaliser. A long ball had been played over the top of our defence and their lad was on to it and through on goal. I came out, brought him down and he got up and scored from the penalty. Frank was in a rage in the dressing room afterwards about the goal and before he got round to me, Archie Styles gave me a word of warning: "Whatever you do, don't answer him back." But when Frank 'enquired' what I was doing by coming out and bringing their lad down, I still tried to interrupt his rant and explain, but it only served to increase his wrath. Out of the corner of my eye I could see Archie shaking his head at me. Frank then turned on Steve Davey, blaming him for being out of position and his rant continued while we were in the bath. Eventually, Steve couldn't take any more, and jumped out of the tub and went for him. I think he tried to throttle Frank, but not before someone had been able to get there first and hold him back. But it was all forgotten minutes afterwards.

Against top-of-the-table Walsall at home the following week, I gave away another penalty which cost us a point. I was promptly left out, with Peter returning for the remaining eight games of the season. The win at Northampton in the last match, which brought our promotion, has gone down in Pompey folklore, but I didn't go and stayed at home. In those days, there was only one substitute, which was never a goalkeeper, and only the 12 players involved travelled. Nevertheless, given what a crucial game it was, I was upset at not being asked. Keith James and I were in Portsmouth in our digs that afternoon trying, successfully as it happened, to stay away from the radio. We waited until the result came up on the TV teleprinter and then literally jumped around the living room with joy. It didn't take us long to get down to the Craneswater Snooker Hall nearby and start celebrating with a few pints of lager. We went over to the ground later and met up with the lads as the coach arrived back and then spent the rest of the evening with them in the Pompey pub. It was my first real taste of success and, even though I hadn't been too involved, I was absolutely overwhelmed.

It seemed as though the whole of the city came out to greet us during the open-top bus tour and at the Guildhall for the civic reception. The celebrations amongst the players and the fans went on for the whole week and were a very special experience for me. After all, we had only scraped into the promotion frame in fourth spot and it really came home to me just how much the city had been craving any sort of success for their football team. I have since experienced other promotions with Pompey, but nothing has lived up to that one. The memory always sends a tingle down my spine.

I have such great memories of the players involved. One or two of them found it difficult to maintain that level of performance in the next season in the third division. Joe Laidlaw, the skipper, was a typical Geordie, a real terrier and a 'miniature Gazza' for us. He had great vision and passing ability and also scored some vital goals. Frank had gone for experienced players to get us up and, despite being in the twilight of his career, Joe was one of his best buys. Colin Garwood was also a great character. He came back for pre-season training once with a 'full-set beard' and looking like a beer barrel, as if he was about four stone overweight. Frank was not too impressed, and Colin had to have sweat bags fitted to enable him to lose that weight. It was a hard slog for him and he lost some stamina as a result. It was really the beginning of the end for Colin and he was sold in mid-season to Aldershot. At centre half was Steve Aizlewood, a very brave guy, who would go through a brick wall for Pompey and gave 110%. He was the ugliest man in the world, but a big softie really. Baz, as he was known, always seemed to be in the wars, with plenty of blood to show for it, mainly from cuts around the eyes which were down to his unusually soft tissue in that area. Steve Davey alongside him was a very funny man, a great character and the life and soul of the dressing room. Not the tallest centre back in the world, but a very good pro who read the game well and had a tremendous leap. Keith Viney, at full back, was my future brother in law – a very fit, athletic guy, who could run all day and get forward well. Possibly not the best defender, but he still won the player of the year award the following season. On the other flank John McLaughlin was a decent right back and a very good defender. Terry Brisley picked up a lot of goals from coming in at the far post, hence his nickname 'far-post Bris', to connect with crosses from Alan Rogers, who was himself a great winger who could deliver a great ball. Jeff Hemmerman was a good goalscorer and a really nice guy and very family-orientated. He perhaps didn't mix socially as much as most of the others. Rogers, too, was very much the family-man, with a dry sense of humour. He was not really one for the club scene, was not a big drinker and preferred to go out for a meal with his wife and friends.

For pre-season training in July 1980, we went to HMS Mercury, a shore establishment out in the Hampshire countryside, and underwent a two-week programme with the naval physical training instructors. It was really hard – getting up at 7 am for a four-mile cross-country run, and, if you got back in time then, and only then, there was some breakfast available. Other than a lunchtime break, the day was made up of fitness work around the PTI's circuits. Although we were billeted at Mercury, we were allowed home on Wednesday evenings provided we got back by 10 pm. Otherwise, we were taken in to Portsmouth to the cinema or to a bingo hall. At one such bingo trip some drinks got to be served and Joe Laidlaw, being Joe, over-indulged and missed the bus back. All the talk amongst the squad was about his disappearing act. It transpired that he had called at one or two other establishments on his way back to Mercury and was much the worse for wear by the time he arrived back in the early hours of the morning. Unable to find his own room, he then proceeded to move around, banging on everybody's door. When he reached Stan Harland's door, he fell into Stan's arms as he opened his door to him. Joe had been skipper through the previous season's promotion and was voted player of the year, so Frank had a lot of time for him, although he recognised that he had a few problems. Despite suspending and fining him for this breach of club discipline, Frank was still happy to re-appoint Joe as skipper.

Peter Mellor started in goal, kept his place and I had just one first-team game that season. That wasn't until February either, against

Exeter, after Peter had injured his shoulder. Mick Tait scored a hat-trick in a 5-0 win, our best of the season. I had nothing to do in the match and would really have liked to have had a chance to shine. It was a very frustrating time for me and I desperately wanted to play in the first team. It affected me badly, such that I usually ended up down the pub drinking too much and wallowing in self-pity. I was close to going off the rails that season and, looking back, it's clear to me that I thought I was better than I really was.

In the reserve team with me were a number of disgruntled senior pros and, as a young lad, there's no doubt that their influence rubbed off on me. On those Fridays, for instance, when the first team squad were travelling to the next day's away game, I was left with them and we would work on our ball skills in the morning. Then, I would be dragged down the pub or snooker hall with them for a lengthy liquid lunch, before returning to weight circuits in our small gym at the ground. Obviously, I wanted to be one of the lads and that's when the drinking culture really started for me. It had probably gone on for a long time before that - just as it had done at most clubs through that era. People at all levels in the game saw it as a team bonding thing and the proper thing to do, having trained hard and played hard.

I was away from home and didn't have a family life to fall back on. It wasn't until I began to spend a lot more time living with Jennifer's parents and became part of their family, that I started to settle down. Also, I spent a lot of time with Keith James, who was in a similar position, having played for England Youth but who was now unable to break into the first team. We wound each other up about it, went out to pubs and clubs and got drunk together. It's probably true to say that we were not good for each other. Keith was a stronger character than me and often got the blame for leading me astray. Unfortunately, it all came to an end for Keith halfway through the season when his contract was terminated and paid-up. Initially, along with some other players, he was made available for transfer and he was unhappy that the first he heard of it was when he read about it in the local evening paper. Nothing happened, although he did have a trial at Norwich. Keith went back to the London area and played non-league for Walthamstow and Hayes, but is now working in a bar in Spain.

Throughout that season I was pestering Frank for a chance and then, when I was really down, for a transfer. I would go to see him in his office at least every two weeks on average and often hand him a written transfer request. He would routinely tear up the letter, place it in the waste paper basket and the meeting would be over in 30 seconds. It all became a bit of a joke between us. I saw other players doing well and I felt that my career was drifting away. I saw myself as 'the forgotten man'. To hear that John Lukic, who two years earlier I had kept out of the England youth team, was the first choice keeper at Leeds and training with the England senior squad, didn't help my mood.

By now Graham Roberts, another Pompey youth contemporary of mine, had made it to the Spurs first team, even if it had been via non-league Dorchester. It didn't help that Keith Viney, my girl friend Jennifer's brother, was in the Pompey side for most of the season. Frank's argument was that I wasn't yet experienced enough, but I argued back that I wasn't going to get the experience all the time he wasn't playing me. Frank told the press that he didn't feel that I was prepared to accept the responsibility for organising the defence in front of me and running the penalty area. He felt that I wasn't prepared to shout at some of the senior professionals. For my part I felt that you had to build up a relationship with the senior players and earn their respect, before you could get them to accept your orders. I argued that I needed a long enough run in the side to enable me to achieve that.

What also really upset me in October that season was not being invited to travel up to Anfield for the now legendary League Cup tie against Liverpool. I went out with Jennifer that night in a beat-up Ford Escort I had bought from Steve Bryant and drove up and down Southsea seafront listening to the radio commentary. With all the atmosphere and the noise coming from our supporters over the radio, that was one match in which I wished I had played. Another upsetting situation for me that season was my training ground collision, in a five-a-side, with Graham Marriner, who was in digs with me. Graham was up front, when a ball was played forward to him and I came out to intercept. I spread myself to block the ball, but he stopped and my momentum took me into the back of his legs. The weight of my   stomach, as we fell together, broke his ankle. I was gutted for Graham and he was out of action for a very long time. He was never the same player after that and it effectively ruined his career.

My first taste of specialist coaching came that season through an FA seminar for keepers, to which Peter Mellor and I went. Up to then, the training for keepers amounted to no more than people hitting shots and crosses at you when full training had finished. For the first time I was able to come across one or two ideas which might improve my game. After that dreadful season for me personally came the realisation, through the summer, that it was now or never for my career. I was 20 years old and I had been at Fratton Park for four years. It was time for me to be positive and make things happen.

*'Quite honestly he is potentially
the best young keeper I have
ever worked with, but the key
word at the moment is
'"potential".'*

Peter Mellor

Having finally signed his apprenticeship forms, Knight reported for pre-season training in July at a club optimistic it could finally start bouncing back from the trauma of just avoiding relegation to the fourth division. On the goalkeeping front, Pompey had released Graeme Lloyd, formerly of Liverpool reserves and Motherwell, and youngster Paul Bennett, whose sole first-team appearance had been in a 2–1 victory over Minehead in the FA Cup. The season started with Steve Middleton, signed on a free transfer from Southampton as first choice, with home-grown Phil Figgins his understudy, now he had recovered from a serious wrist injury earlier in the year which had threatened his career. Although now first-team coach and manager of the reserves, Crawford still kept a watching brief on the young players at the club and he showed admirable prescience; writing in the programme for the Leicester City League Cup tie in August 1977: 'Alan Knight in goal is a potentially excellent keeper. I say "potentially" because he is still only 16 and it would be a pity if too much was expected of him too early, but in his own age group he will be in a class of his own.'

Pompey couldn't quite take the cue from Knight, however, and it was soon clear that the first team remained well short of even third-division class. A 2–0 win over first division Leicester in that cup match was the only bright spot of a calamitous run in the autumn of 1977 which saw Pompey pitched into the thick of the relegation battle once more, entering 1978 bottom of the table. By this time Billy Hunter –

first-team coach under Ian St John – had been redeployed as the manager of the youth team and he too was of the opinion Knight would go far: 'Alan has something extra as far as boy goalkeepers go. He has truly high-class talent, likes to work hard and he's got the right character – that's always a good start,' he told the *Sports Mail*. Knight played his part in an unbeaten start to the season for the youth team, including an impressive 3-0 replay win over Ipswich in the South-East Counties League Cup. Knight also experienced the bitter taste of a derby defeat, although by all accounts, not least Hunter's, he put up a fine show as the team lost 4-2 at Southampton in the FA Youth Cup in November. According to *The News* Knight displayed the 'coolness of a veteran' in the game. The Saints side included Steve Moran in their team, whose path would cross Knight's again in a slightly more important derby just over six years later. The same month Knight was also recognised for his contribution to sports at his old school, Ernest Bevin, where he was presented with the 'Sportsman of the Year' trophy by Lord Pitt, to record the fact he had been selected for the Inner London Schools' team as well as taking part in England trials for volleyball and being 'very active' in the lacrosse, swimming and water polo teams. Knight's potential had also been spotted by the England selectors and he played in a match for a Youth XI in front of what the *Sports Mail* described as a 'select audience' including Sir Stanley Rous, president of FIFA, and a clutch of top managers, including Bobby Campbell, the ex-Pompey midfielder, who was destined to become his boss at Fratton.

Despite some indifferent form in the league, after such a promising start, the youth team were making significant progress on one front and in March 1978 they were able to relieve, to a certain extent, the gathering gloom of the impending relegation of the first team, with a 2-1 victory over Chelsea in the semi-final of the South Eastern Counties League Cup, in which Knight and Neil Hider had played a crucial part, to set up a two-legged final with Norwich. Despite the fact fourth-division football was a virtual certainty for Pompey for the first time in their history, off the pitch a coaching appointment had been made in February which was very quickly to have a highly significant impact on Knight's infant professional career. Crawford had left the club in January in slightly cloudy circumstances after an alleged 'breach of contract', although he had been offered the alternative role of chief scout at the club, which he predictably declined. His replacement was former Swindon Town centre half Frank Burrows. Realising the playing staff was rotten virtually from top to bottom, with Dickinson's willing support, the pair began clearing out the dead wood ahead of the drop. Burrows was also an advocate of giving youth its chance, when the circumstances were right, and it was clear Knight's star was a rising one at Fratton. In April 1978 his picture featured on the cover of the official programme for the third–division clash with Carlisle and he also reinforced his credentials with a penalty save in the second leg of the final against Norwich – who had John Fashanu in their line up – which Pompey lost 2–0 and 3–1 on aggregate.

And when the squad sheet for the final match of the season at Rotherham was pinned up on Friday April 28 with the name of 'A Knight' on it, to many it seemed no less than the young keeper deserved for his season's efforts: a trip away on the first-team bus to carry the kit and sit on the bench. But Dickinson, prompted by Burrows, had other ideas and at 16 years 299 days and with just one reserve appearance to his name Knight became Pompey's youngest-ever first-team goalkeeper. The elevation of Knight was in part down to the regime Burrows had introduced since his arrival. Where Dickinson – ever the traditionalist – had the youth team and senior players training apart, Burrows had insisted they train together, giving the young goalkeeper ample opportunity to shine. Knight's debut was actually signposted in the previous Saturday's *Sports Mail*, where Dickinson had said: 'The boy will play next week and at the moment he is more likely to get his chance at Rotherham than Chester on Wednesday.' A baptism of fire it was not, however, as Mike Neasom noted in his match verdict in the Mail after the match: 'Young Alan Knight's big day was quieter than many he could have known in the youth team. For after being rescued by Billy Wilson after being rounded by Dave Gwyther the young keeper knew scarcely a moment's difficulty.'

So Knight went down as being surely the first Pompey goalkeeper to come from the ranks to make his first-team debut with just one appearance for the reserves to his name and, with hindsight, he should be forever grateful Dickinson decided to pitch him into the fray against struggling Rotherham rather than promotion-chasing Chester, who cruised to a 2–0 win against rock-bottom Pompey three days before. Picking Knight was a cannily-judged move by Burrows and Dickinson, but it was also clear the young Knight was nowhere near the finished article, clean sheet or not. In the summer of 1978 Pompey shuffled their goalkeeping resources once more, with Figgins being released and signing for a club in Australia. Portsmouth-born Middleton's Pompey days were also numbered, although he was there for pre-season training as the Navy put the players through their paces at HMS Mercury. His Fratton career was blighted by an inability to live down his Southampton past, not to mention a series of blunders, culminating in a classic cock-up where he missed Paul Cahill's throw back to him in a home game with Plymouth and Fred Binney scored to set Argyle on their way to a 5–1 win, which all but relegated Pompey in March 1978.

The new goalkeeper at Fratton Park was in the larger-than-life frame of Peter Mellor, who had been an England Under-23 international at Burnley in the early 1970s, but whose career had nose-dived after a couple of howlers of his own, while playing for Fulham, handed West Ham the 'cockney' 1975 FA Cup final. Blond and brash, a free transfer move from Hereford had re-ignited his career and his impressive form. As Pompey challenged for promotion from the fourth division, he snuffed out any dreams Knight might have had of making any more first-team appearances, in the short term at least. For Knight the start of the 1978/79 season saw him continue to impress in the youth team – now under the guidance of Burrows' former Swindon team-mate Stan Harland, after Hunter had been appointed manager of Queen of the South – but the continued presence of Middleton was frustrating his ambitions of breaking into the reserves, who competed in the Midweek Football League. Dickinson acknowledged the problem for Knight and the club: 'Alan is a very fine prospect but at the moment I don't think he is ready to go into the first team for the extended run. It is something we are trying to sort out and we know how important it is,' he told the *Sports Mail* in September 1978. The situation resolved itself the following month, when Middleton was released from his contract, deciding he'd had enough of professional football.

On the field things were looking up. Mellor's arrival had galvanised Pompey's previously leaky defence – and even claimed a club-record six-match run without conceding a goal – while Burrows' know-how in the transfer market had moulded a side capable of challenging for promotion. Knight was now number two to Mellor, and even as Pompey's promotion charge faltered, as a bitterly cold winter took its toll in early 1979, the club were keen to sign Knight as a professional – three months before the end of his apprenticeship – to prevent other clubs trying to muscle in on his burgeoning talent. Knight signed his first professional contract at Fratton on February 23, 1979, on a weekly wage of £60. His growing reputation was underlined in the same month by his call up – along with youth team-mate Keith James – for the England youth set up as they prepared to meet Italy in Rome, in the Stadio Olimpico, for a 'little' World Cup qualifying match. Knight had been given his debut in January, replacing Leeds' John Lukic at half time in the 4–0 win against Belgium, and for the pair to be chosen to start in such an important representative fixture was a coup for the fourth division club. It might even have been a hat-trick of players involved for the club as centre half Trevor Roberts was also put on stand-by for the game.

England emerged 1-0 winners, but the comedown for Knight was immediate. Three days later he was keeping goal for the youth team in a rearranged fourth round FA Youth Cup tie and was forced to pick the ball out of the net six times as Pompey tamely submitted to Nottingham Forest without reply. In effect, that match was the end of Knight's youth career at Fratton. His challenge now was to make Mellor work hard for his shirt and, ultimately, step into his shoes, although the fact Mellor was voted the supporters' player of the season underlined the scale of that task. He also had England honours to chase, earning another call up for the second leg of the clash with Italy at Villa Park. However, the leg injury he picked up in training cost him his place in the return – which England won 2-0 to book their place – and almost scuppered his chances of making the finals of the tournament in Austria. He made it, however, but only played one game – a 3-0 win over Malta in the group stages, as England earned third place in the tournament with Lukic established as the first choice. James was luckier, being an ever-present.

Knight reported back for pre-season training in July 1979 with Pompey a transformed squad. Burrows had replaced Dickinson as manager after the original Fratton legend had suffered a heart-attack at Barnsley in March and with the money raised by the sale of centre half Steve Foster to Brighton he set about building a squad capable of getting Pompey out of the basement. In came midfielders Joe Laidlaw, Terry Brisley, defenders Steve Aizlewood, John McLaughlin and Archie Styles plus winger Alan Rogers. That Burrows didn't feel the need to add a goalkeeper to his shopping list confirmed that 18-year-old Knight was now the pretender to Mellor's throne, although he had an injury scare in pre-season when he was knocked out during a friendly at Ventnor on the Isle of Wight, and had to leave the field suffering from double vision. His chances of breaking into the first team seemed remote as the team set about the fourth division with a vengeance, racking up 12 wins and 40 goals in the opening 14 matches. Knight would no doubt also be casting envious glances as his rival the previous season for the England youth jersey, Lukic, was clocking up the appearances in the first division for Leeds. However, Knight's chance finally came as Pompey wobbled. Three defeats in four, culminating in a 4-3 loss at Newport in which Mellor and his defence were held culpable, as the hosts' goals all came from headers, opened the door. Knight's second first-team appearance came as Pompey prepared to face Walsall at Fellows Park on November 10 and the first to telegram wishing him good luck before the game came from the usurped Mellor. Knight told the *Sports Mail* at the time: 'Peter was tremendous. He was the first to congratulate me and say that he hoped things went well. Although he knew I was after his place he has helped my game tremendously. I was still very nervous before the match but the save I made early on helped settle me down quite a lot.' Knight went on after the 1-1 draw: 'Now I've got the taste of it I intend to stay there – it will be tough on Peter if I do, but knowing he's there waiting will make me try all the harder.'

And stay there Knight did. Even when he picked up an injury before the home clash against Halifax on December 1, which enabled Mellor to get back in the team, Knight was reinstalled the following week against Peterborough – and he kept a clean sheet, this third consecutive shut-out. He made it four in a row as Pompey held third division Wimbledon to a 0-0 draw at Plough Lane in the second round of the FA Cup. After that game Mellor commented: 'Quite honestly Alan is potentially the best young keeper I have ever worked with – but the key word at the moment is "potential". Technically he's already a very, very good keeper but obviously with his experience so limited he's got a lot to learn. Most of all he's got to come out of his shell a bit and really demand of the players around him, but that is something that will come with games. I'll certainly help all I can but as I do so he'll know I'm thirsting to push him out of the team again. At the moment I think I am the better keeper, because I've got the experience.'

It was that 'lack of experience', in more senses than one, which cost Knight his place. He might have got away with his ill-timed Southsea seafront sojourn on New Year's Eve 1979, had it not coincided with a poor performance the following day as he patently failed to dominate his area and Aldershot helped themselves to three goals, sending Pompey spiralling to a shock defeat in front of more than 23,000. Diplomatically perhaps, more than 20 years on, Burrows cannot recall giving his young keeper a dressing down in the privacy of his office after receiving those letters from supporters who had spotted Knight 'out on the town' and he was equally sensitive to Knight's feelings at the time: 'Alan had reached the point where he'd gone a bit tense and it was time to give him a little breather. But he will come again. He's still a very good keeper and a better one than he was two months ago before this run in the team,' he said on the eve of Pompey's trip to Wimbledon for a cup second replay. With Mellor back between the sticks, Pompey won 1-0 and set up the glory of a clash at Fratton with first division Middlesbrough. But for Knight it was back to the grind of mid-table Midweek League action as Mellor kept his place even as Pompey's promotion charge faltered. Knight was recalled for a couple of games in March, after Mellor injured his leg at Stockport and skipper Laidlaw saw out the final minutes in a 1-1 draw and earned himself forever the soubriquet the 'flying pig'. These were still the days of just one substitute, after all. Although Knight didn't disgrace himself, the two penalties he conceded in the matches against Darlington and Walsall respectively, cost Pompey a couple of points they could ill afford. It was Mellor who returned for the decisive run-in as Pompey clinched promotion amid tense and emotional scenes at Northampton on May 3.

Pompey began their preparations for a return to third division football with Mellor still clearly the first-choice goalkeeper, as he took a leading role in the pre-season friendlies and it was no surprise when he was named in the team which began the season with a 1-0 win at Plymouth in the League Cup on August 9, 1980. However, it was clear Mellor was beginning to prepare for a life after professional football – he was almost 33 by now after all – setting up a series of highly-popular goalkeeping schools in the city. And by that time Knight's future competition for the number one jersey had already arrived, in the 6' 4" frame of Andy Gosney, a Southampton-born 16-year-old who had signed apprentice forms that summer. Youth team coach Jack Smith had already marked Gosney down as one for the future recommending him for England Youth trials. Whatever thoughts Mellor may have been having about his retirement, however, were clearly at the back of his mind as he started the season in inspired form. In one performance he almost single-handedly kept second division Oldham at bay in a League Cup second-round tie.

Now also coaching Knight and Gosney, the magnanimous Mellor had words of comfort for his understudy, but still clearly aimed to keep his place, as he told the *Sports Mail*: 'We spend a lot of time training the three of us. I think I've helped Alan a fair amount and this little group is good for us all. The boss knows goalkeepers need slightly different work and he is prepared to let us get on with it. But apart from that I hope I've helped Alan off the field as well, with his attitude. I know it's frustrating for him playing in the reserves and it's difficult to be patient, but if he is his chance will come... over my dead body though!' Whatever his feelings, Knight could have no complaints about being kept out of the team as Mellor continued to star as Pompey's push for a second consecutive promotion gathered pace. He was also in goal as Pompey lost 4-1 at Liverpool in the third round of the League Cup, with poor Alan having to make do with listening to the 11,000 or so chiming Pompey fans on the radio back in Portsmouth, having been left behind by Burrows. What would have happened had Mellor been taken ill, or injured himself in the warm-up, before the game, must remain anyone's guess. At least Laidlaw was in the squad...

Knight's impatience would not have been helped as Mellor, having just signed a new two-year playing contract, revealed to Neasom just before Christmas that he almost considered becoming a full-time goalkeeping coach after Burrows had dropped him 12 months previously, allowing Knight his first run in the team. 'When I was left out after we lost at Newport I had a long chat with the boss about it. I thought it was time to move over, but decided against it when I got back in the team. Now I'm delighted I did. I think I've probably been as consistent this season as at any time in my career. Now all I'm aiming to do is keep my place – and keep playing for as long as possible.' The accidental collision with Graham Marriner on the training ground, which left the young defender with a broken ankle would hardly have helped Knight's morale, but Mellor finally proved he was fallible, when he picked up a shoulder injury in the 2-0 home win over Walsall in February and Knight was in for a re-arranged home game with Exeter City. It was an eventful evening as Knight made two fine early saves and ended up concussed after a goalmouth collision. As the Grecians clearly had one eye on their impending fifth-round FA Cup tie at Newcastle, Mick Tait finally stole the headlines, helping himself to a five-minute second-half hat-trick as Pompey cruised home 5-0. Not surprisingly, Mellor was back the following week for the game at Brentford and followed that up with a nostalgic return to his old stamping ground at Fulham's Craven Cottage. Not even five goals conceded in those two games could persuade Burrows to shift Mellor and Knight was left to contemplate the rest of the season in the stiffs.

The news in late March 1981 that his contemporary Lukic – who despite some question marks over both his form and confidence of late – had been called up to train with the England senior squad, as they prepared for a friendly international with Spain, was an ironic counterpoint for Knight, who was making do with outings against Southend reserves on a Tuesday night watched by the proverbial one man and his dog. He tried to maintain a philosophical view as he told the *Sports Mail* in April: 'I was a bit choked when I read of John's call up. That brought home to me how things can change in this game and I've also got the memory of what happened to Keith James to keep me going. He was in the England team with me and now he's with Walthamstow. But it's also made me more determined to take the next chance I get. I still hope I might get a game or two this season – but if I don't then I'll be out to win my place at the start of next season and keep it.'

Alan Knight collection

Alan Knight (front right), aged ten, picks up his first football award. His father Ted is directly behind him.

Alan Knight collection

Knight training at Bransbury Park in 1977, shortly before signing as an apprentice.

INNER LONDON EDUCATION AUTHORITY

HENRY CAVENDISH SCHOOL

Hydethorpe Road, S.W.12.

REPORT FOR SCHOOL YEAR ENDING JULY 1971

Name: Alan Knight   Form: 3H

SUBJECT		ASSESSMENT	REMARKS
ENGLISH	Reading	Fair	Alan has made some progress with his reading but he must still try to practise it as often as possible in order to bring it up to the level of his age. His written expression has also shown some improvement. Alan must also make a big effort to learn all his multiplication tables.
	Composition	Fair	
	Comprehension		
	Spelling	Weak	
MATHEMATICS		Fair	
	Tables		
HISTORY		Good	
GEOGRAPHY			
SCIENCE			
ART		Fairly good	
HANDWORK			
NEEDLEWORK			
WRITING		Fair	
MUSIC		Good	Alan has learnt many new songs this year. AB
	Choir		
	Orchestra		
PHYSICAL EDUCATION		Excellent	Alan shows outstanding ability in all aspects.
	Swimming	Excellent	

GENERAL REPORT   Attendance Satisfactory.

Alan tries hard in all his work but he has difficulty with most subjects. He is always pleasant & helpful & is popular in class.

_____ Hills.   Form Master / L. R. Saunders _____ Head Master
                      Form Mistress

P. 929

Alan's junior school report in July 1971, aged ten. His PE teacher remarked: 'Alan shows outstanding ability in all aspects'.

Knight (second right), shakes hands with Pompey manager Jimmy Dickinson watched by his father, right, and Ray Crawford.

Fratton for me says Knight

Speculation over the future of 15-year-old goalkeeper Alan Knight, from ston-on-Thames, has ended with the announcement that he will be joining pey as an apprentice professional on his birthday next month.

Knight paid his own far... for Po...

The News reports Knight's arrival in June 1977 (left).

Alan Knight collection

Knight on trial at Portsmouth during the summer of 1976.

Portsmouth FC

Alan Knight, Pompey apprentice. July 1977.

Knight (back row, far left) lines up with Roy Race, David Kemp (with ball) and some
fellow apprentices for Roy of the Rovers comic in September 1977.

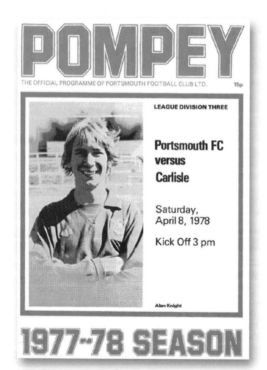

Knight's progress is marked with
his first-ever cover appearance on
the programme for the home
game with Carlisle in April 1978.
Pompey are already relegated to
Division Four.

NAME ... KNIGHT   A...

WEEK NO. ...4... DATE 28..4..79

GROSS WAGES
BONUS   60 £ -

DEDUCTIONS   £ 60 -

Grad. Pension
Income Tax   7-10
Nat. Ins.   2·88
Superannuation
Dr. Barnado's

TOTAL DEDUCTIONS   9 . 98

NET WAGES   50 -02
TAX REFUND

                    £ 50 . 02

An early professional wage slip. In 1979 £60 per week came out as somewhat less, after deductions...

Alan Knight collection

Knight (far right) with the England Under-18 squad in Rome, February 1979. Keith James is fourth from the left.

The News

Keith James (left) and Knight celebrate their England Under-18 call up.

Mike Walker / M&Y News Agency

Knight is presented with a plaque by former Pompey favourite Steve Foster to commemorate promotion to Division Three in May 1980.

3 - On the up

I reported for pre-season training in July 1981 in my best-ever
state of fitness. As part of my positive approach I had trained
very hard throughout the summer on my own. Every night would
see me out running around the streets of the city and I played lots of
squash, but stayed away from football altogether. I had felt Peter Mellor
was no longer the automatic first choice towards the end of the
previous season and, on our return to training, was given the strong
impression that I would get a real chance. That impression was
reinforced when I played in both pre-season friendlies against West
Ham and Arsenal, then confirmed when I was included for the
opening league match against Lincoln. We then went to Southend, in
midweek, in the League Cup, where I had my best performance for
the club to date in a goalless draw. I remember saving everything that
night, and it gave me enormous confidence. After a second-leg
victory, we were through to the next round where we were due to
play Queens Park Rangers, with the first leg at Loftus Road, on their
controversial artificial surface.

It proved to be a strange and ultimately disastrous experience, which
went a long way to shaping the team's and the manager's fortunes that
season. For some reason, Frank seemed especially wound up for the
game. QPR were in the first division then and had a tremendous side
who had adapted well to the surface. For our part, we had practised
on the pitch on the morning of the game and had got hold of some
special boots. It was a miserable wet night and the ball was skidding

and flying around. It didn't stop Chris Kamara and Mick Tait getting in some sliding tackles but they both suffered horrendous burns to their legs as a consequence. We went in just one goal down at half time and that was down to the pitch. I was moving to get behind a shot when the ball was deflected off our defender Peter Ellis. On the surface, I just could not change my position and with my feet rooted to the spot, the ball flew into the other corner.

With the home leg at Fratton Park to come, we went into the dressing room at half time thinking we had done well to hold them to the one goal. But Frank came in and shocked me and many of the other players with his reaction. He went mad: "That performance was simply not good enough," he raged, with no justification that I could see, accusing us of showing a lack of commitment and letting down our travelling fans. We were all astounded and, in a very strange move, he ordered us into all-out attack: "You've got to give it a go," he said. The strategy simply left us wide open at the back, Rangers took full advantage and tore us to shreds. We lost 5-0 and were very lucky to get away with that score line. Frank was normally tactically sound, but that was one occasion when I just couldn't work him out. The QPR forwards, Simon Stainrod in particular, took the mickey out of us in the second half as we poured forward and lost all shape. We drew the meaningless second leg, but our chances had long since gone thanks to Frank's curious second-half tactics.

That beating at Loftus Road affected our performances for some weeks afterwards. We lost three on the bounce and only won once in eleven games subsequently. I was the fans' player of the month and no wonder, because we were being battered and I had plenty of chances to show what I was capable of. During that spell I had one of the best games of my career, in a goalless draw at Plymouth's Home Park, on a wet and windy afternoon. It was a performance that I ranked with that at Southend in the League Cup earlier in the season. It really was one of those days when I was saving everything. Plymouth could have gone on and played all night and they would still not have scored. It was one of those rare occasions when I even got letters from the opposition supporters congratulating me on my performance: "The best goalkeeping performance I've ever seen at Home Park," said one, which was touching.

Then, in November 1981, we were drawn against Millwall in the first round of the FA Cup. That brought one of the worst penalty decisions I have ever had given against me and subsequently one of the scariest experiences of my career. We were one-up at Fratton Park when, in the second half, I dived to push away a long shot. Whilst I was getting up, one of their lads tried to jump over me but landed on my back and went over. The referee gave a penalty, which I was pretty upset about and, when Millwall scored for the equaliser, it meant we had to go to Cold Blow Lane for a replay. It was a wet, horrible night and, aside from the fact that we lost in extra time, I came in for some vile treatment that night, for no other reason than that I was the opposition goalkeeper. Some idiot was selling toffee apples and these were being bought to throw at me. With their crystallised sugar surrounds they were hard and jagged too. Add to that the fact I was spat on every time I went to take a goal-kick meant that I was also becoming covered in spittle. When they weren't spitting at me they were directing their phlegm at my glove-bag in the back of the net which also became well covered. These creatures were not youngsters, but middle-aged men and women.

My parents came to all our games, and I had real concern for their safety that night, which didn't help my concentration on the game. It was not unusual for missiles to be thrown in those days. One of my earliest memories, during my time as an apprentice, was being told by the other lads that, after we had played Millwall at Fratton once, they had to clear knives, darts and marbles from the away terrace, the moat below and the pitch. It's a disquieting thought for me now to think that I could have had a dart hit me at some time. The only occasion when I was hit on the head by a missile was at Grimsby many years later. I felt a sharp pain on the back of my neck, and went down as if I had been shot. It turned out to be a fruit pastille.

A trip to Doncaster a few weeks later in that season brought another new experience for me; having to play for a whole second half with concussion. Tempers were already close to boiling point in the game when Doncaster's veteran striker Alan Warboys caught me on the head, following through, after I had snatched the ball away from him. Warboys was a typically big, old-fashioned centre forward, the type who was invariably called 'bustling', who gave no quarter in his challenges. All he got was a finger-wagging from the referee. I had double vision with pins and needles down the side of my face. I couldn't see out of one eye, and even with my remaining eye, I couldn't focus properly, with everything appearing in squares. I did finish the game, after treatment from Gordon Neave, but only with him staying on behind my goal. I even kept a clean sheet. All that happened after the game was that I was put on the coach and sent home. After that experience I could always tell if I had been concussed in any collision – the first sign would be a numb feeling spreading down into my hands.

It was proving to be a very disappointing season and Frank's position became more and more tenuous. I felt the writing was on the wall for him when his assistant Stan Harland was sacked in the New Year – I know the players felt that it was a ploy to push Frank to resign. When Bobby Campbell was appointed as coach that further undermined Frank's position. Sadly, those are the sort of moves which most clubs adopt to force the manager's eventual departure. There was no revolt amongst the players against Frank – but the players simply didn't perform to help his situation. It's now a well-used cliché, but generally it is the players who get the manager the sack. In any event Frank was becoming a bit stale in the job, however, and I thought the club needed a change.

I have great respect for Frank Burrows, who was the hardest manager and greatest disciplinarian I have known. With Frank there was always a fear factor, but along the way he gained a lot of respect from the players. Some of the players couldn't handle his fierce ways, but it was just what was needed at the time. Frank deserves a lot of credit for what he achieved at Pompey and the club owe him a great deal. He kick-started the club and turned it around when it was at its lowest ebb. Without him, who knows what would have happened. Frank instilled professionalism into the club at the very time when it needed it most. He made everybody much fitter and built a decent side. Even though we had scrambled out of the fourth division, he provided the launch pad for Pompey to move towards some sort of respectability. Frank was also good to me, even though I very often didn't realise it at the time.

When Bobby Campbell arrived I was playing well and it was nice to hear that he rated me: "He's got to be the best young keeper in the country," was what he was reported to have said at the time. When I also heard, before he left, that Frank had recommended me to Ron Greenwood for England Under-21 consideration, then, at least for me, if not for the other Pompey players, it had turned out to be a very good season indeed. I missed just one game that season, ironically, out of pure coincidence and not through any design of mine, at Millwall, when I had a thigh injury. Andy Gosney, who, like me, had come through the youth set-up and played for England, came in for his debut, after signing professional earlier in the season.

When Bobby arrived I could imagine him thinking that he had inherited a team, full of older players, which had probably run its course. I was the lucky one – I was still young and learning fast. With hindsight it was a transitional season, with us stuck in mid-table, which marked the end of Frank's era. Bobby came in with his own agenda and nobody could really have foreseen how he would transform things. What did become clear straight away was that Bobby was a very good coach and, looking back now, we played some very good football under him. It's surprised me that after leaving Pompey he only flitted in and out of the game. He was a fiery guy, with a real temper and plenty of self-belief – even to the point where some would say he was arrogant. I did have a real row with him early on, one which was soon forgotten, but it gave me an early insight into his nature. It all arose from my award as the fans' player of the year, which was a great honour and recognition for me in my first full season. It was the custom for the winner to be given a sponsored car by a local Toyota main dealer, but I was upset when I heard from Bobby that the garage concerned had decided to cancel the sponsorship. Their decision came after the previous year's winner, Joe Laidlaw, had returned the sponsored car in what they considered to be an unfit state. I was still not on very good wages at Pompey and was driving around in a six or seven-year old car at the time, so it was quite a big disappointment for me to miss out on the chance of a new car.

Putting aside the player of the season sponsorship deal, Les Allen, the club's commercial manager, stepped in and was confident of persuading the dealership to sponsor me anyway with a car, so the two of us went down to the garage showroom for a meeting to try to clinch a deal. By coincidence, Bobby Campbell was there at the same time to collect his club car and the three of us met up face to face in the showroom. There and then, in full view of other customers and staff in the showroom, Bobby lost his temper with me: "What the hell are you doing here? I've told you you're not getting a car and you're not having one. How dare you go behind my back like this. You're acting like some sort of big-time Charlie." Les and I were stunned at this onslaught; we simply didn't know what to say. I tried without success to explain that it had nothing to do with the player of the year sponsorship, but Bobby wasn't listening. After it was all over, and we had all got back to Fratton Park, I went to see Bobby and told him he was out of order with that outburst. To his credit he promptly apologised and the matter quickly blew over. I never did get the sponsored car anyway. This was to become a sore point for me, particularly when, in the following season, all the new signings got club cars as part of their deals, including Neil Webb, who was younger than me.

Bobby had plenty of new ideas, but there was one routine of his that I just couldn't take seriously. It was called 'shadow play' and involved two teams of 11-a-side playing without a ball. It wasn't a match as such because each team took it in turns to play against no-body, for 10-15 minutes. It was the funniest thing I have ever seen, as players pretended to have shots and make passes. I would always claim to have made fifteen world-class saves, whereas the strikers would always claim to have scored each time. To this day I don't know what purpose it served. I was reminded of those games again recently when I saw the film *Mike Bassett, England Manager*, and there was a sequence in that when the squad had forgotten to bring any footballs to training and had to play a practice game without them.

At the end of the season, Bobby released Keith Viney, amongst others, and it was a big blow for him and difficult for me. There was I, player of the year, having just signed a new three-year contract and living with me in the same house was Keith, who was, in effect, out of work. Jennifer and I were married that summer and happily, as it worked out, Keith went to the West Country with Exeter City and carved out a decent career down there.

When we all met up again for the 1982/83 pre-season and I saw the new players that Bobby had signed, I began to think that perhaps he and the chairman were really going to have a go at getting promotion from the third division. Certainly John Deacon had backed Bobby to the hilt that summer. In defence Ernie Howe came in to partner Steve Aizlewood, which meant two big guys at the back. We had been looking for someone in there to win the ball and Ernie was very solid and a good professional, even if he was not the best in the world on the floor. Young Neil Webb was a bit quiet at first, but teamed up with Alan Biley who took him under his wing and was a good influence on him. Clearly Webbie was a big talent, and I felt that he took a bit of a gamble coming to Pompey when some bigger clubs were interested in him. As it turned out, it proved to be a good springboard for his career. Dave Thomas came with a reputation earned with England and QPR, but it was Biley who made the biggest impression when he arrived, particularly with that Rod Stewart-like haircut. Biles was a larger-than-life character, but a genuine guy who we quickly realised was an excellent goalscorer. He formed a great partnership with Billy Rafferty up front and Raffs was a good target man who worked really hard. They complemented each other well and both would admit that they owed a lot to the service they got from Alan Rogers, wide on the left. I always felt that Raffs never got the recognition he deserved at Pompey and was a bit of an unsung hero of our championship success.

Bobby Campbell was a very astute tactician and we were a very well balanced side, who stuck to our 4-4-2 system throughout. There was no way we were going to change the way we played – it was down to other sides worrying about us. The players came to have great respect for Bobby, and you always knew that he was the boss. He was a very single-minded guy, a typical Scouser, who did not suffer fools gladly. There were plenty of disagreements, but Bobby was never one to publicly attack any player. As time went on I gained a lot of confidence from him. He had faith in me and it was good to have him say positive things about me in the press.

Mick Tait was a key figure that season, mainly because of his versatility. He played inside forward, switched to right midfield and then filled in at centre half during the vital end of season run-in. Campbell described him as 'PA' – as in 'Play Anywhere' – Tait. Those sorts of players are not around anymore. Now, you have to adjust the formation to fit the players you have available. Mick was a rough, tough Northerner who always gave 100%, but was a great lad off the pitch and close mates with Bobby Doyle. I have never known anybody who could drink like Mick. He would drink lager for fun, mostly at Cowplain Social Club, with Bobby as company. Oddly, the two lads were complete opposites. No disrespect to Mick, but Bobby was more the Trevor Brooking-type and always seemed very intelligent to me.

There was a lot of socialising that season amongst the players, as most lived in and around Waterlooville and Cowplain. We didn't break any club rules and wouldn't drink two nights before a game. It never affected our performances either in training or in games and everyone knew when to stop. In those days such drinking was not a big deal, and was a culture prevalent at most clubs. It wasn't just Pompey where it went on, as people have tried subsequently to portray. It's completely different today and the culture has changed entirely. Then, if you didn't socialise, you became a bit of an outcast. I lived in Portsmouth, but I would travel to have nights out with the lads who were a tremendous bunch. I was very close to all of them. There was a very sad period early on that season when we heard that Jimmy Dickinson had passed away. I had known him better than most, in that he had originally signed me for the club. Seeing long-standing people at the club, like Jenny Powling his secretary and Paul Weld, the club secretary, so upset at the Memorial Service, really brought the loss home to me.

What was remarkable that season was the number of penalties we missed during this period and it became a running joke at one time. It was just one of those things which seemed to affect us and it became a confidence thing in the end. I think we missed eight out of 14. At one time Bobby Doyle missed three on the bounce and everybody was having a go. Even I was taking penalties in training in a bid to be considered. What added to the lads' embarrassment was that even I was saving their attempts in training. The problem was only really solved when Kevin Dillon joined us on transfer-deadline day from Birmingham. For that promotion season and for thereafter, Kevin was, in my opinion, Bobby Campbell's biggest and most important signing. I rated him very highly indeed, for his all-round ability, great vision and passing. More recently Pompey fans have enjoyed seeing the likes of Prosinecki and Merson, but I would put Kevin up alongside those two great players. He was part of a group of players at Birmingham who were regularly in trouble – 'The Crazy Gang' comprising Tony Coton, Noel Blake, and Mark Dennis – and manager Ron Saunders was looking to split them up. Dillon was a feisty and somewhat strange character, who was not a problem for

Bobby Campbell initially. He dropped down a division and he no doubt thought he was a cut above us, which was probably true. Typical of his perverse nature, he chose to live on Hayling Island, well away from most of the lads in the Waterlooville/Cowplain area. He was very single-minded, making up his own mind about most things and later this led to some interesting confrontations with Alan Ball, Bobby's successor.

Out of the blue, as the climax to the season approached, I had a late call-up for the England Under-21 squad as an overage player. The match against Greece was due to be played at Fratton Park on the Tuesday, but the first-choice goalkeeper, Manchester United's Gary Bailey, had been injured on the Saturday. By the time I was contacted however, I was in London with a big group of Pompey players for the PFA Awards dinner on the Sunday night. We had a drink at a club in the afternoon and then went on to the Hilton Hotel, where I eventually went up to my room for a nap before getting into my dinner jacket and bow tie. There, I took a phone call from Jennifer to say that I had been called up for the squad and had to join up with them immediately. To be honest, I took some convincing that it wasn't a wind-up, because I had not the foggiest idea that I was in the minds of the selectors. In fact, I had not played well that season, not by my own standards at least, and had been disappointed in my form. I spoke to the England physio in their hotel on Hayling Island and he was insistent manager Howard Wilkinson wanted me there straight away. So, I had to leave London there and then, get on a train, go home to collect my gear and drive over to Hayling that night.

I did not expect to play and many people saw my call-up as a token gesture to arouse some local interest in the game. The England players and staff didn't seem to know who I was and when Howard Wilkinson proceeded to call me 'Paul' for the best part of the first day, it didn't give me too much encouragement. We went into Portsmouth to train at HMS Temeraire, a naval shore establishment, as all the local pitches were unfit. We arrived to find the Pompey squad there and about to finish, so I had to endure some mickey-taking. I remember that one of the England squad, Mark Hateley, of Coventry City, was very interested in cars and on that day he was impressed with the Pompey club cars. At the time, I doubt whether he noticed the modest yellow Fiesta that I had hired after my old banger had blown up. Mark also seemed to take a great interest in everything about Pompey and in particular the wage structure. There was not much I could tell him, because at that time, unlike today where players' wages are right out in the public domain, no-one had any idea what anybody else was earning. Little did I know that Mark would move to Fratton a few months later and I often wonder whether the seeds had already been sown in his mind during those few days on the south coast.

On the morning of the game I was shocked and proud to be picked to play. Oldham's Andy Goram, who was a lovely guy, was very upset at being left out. In retrospect, perhaps I did him a favour, as had he played in that competitive game then perhaps he wouldn't have been eligible to be selected by Scotland, by virtue of his father's nationality, who he went on to represent with distinction in the World Cup finals later in his career. As for the game, standing for the national anthem is a strong memory, but I had virtually nothing to do for over an hour, other than field a few backpasses. We were one-up when one of the Greek lads unleashed a thunderbolt of a shot from 25 yards which just flew past me. It was their one and only shot in the game, so it was certainly a great relief for me when we scored the winner. I did have a problem in that game with the different rules, which I was unaware of beforehand, which were being applied to goalkeepers in Europe and Britain. I knew something was amiss when I was twice penalised early on when, after I had made a save, I had then rolled the ball a few yards and picked it up again to kick it out. I was penalised for picking the ball up a second time, but happily we defended both free kicks in the penalty area successfully. Still unaware of what was going on, I resorted to taking the safe way out and kicking clear from wherever I had first handled the ball.

Afterwards I was reconciled to the fact that it would be my one and only game. About a month later I was called up again to play against Hungary at St James' Park, Newcastle and I was really chuffed. To be honest, it meant more to me than my original call-up. This time my name was there when the squad was announced. What really struck me as strange was Howard Wilkinson's motivational ploy leading up to the game. He pulled me over on the bus, as he did with all the other players, and asked me if my grandfather had fought in the first world war. When I said he had, he went on to tell me that the Hungarians had made the bayonets with which the Germans were armed and that they might have been used on my grandfather. It really was the strangest form of motivation I have ever come across. It certainly did nothing for me and was not something that I took into the game at all. Again, I had very little to do in our win and was rarely brought into the action. I found that the pace of the game at international level is different to the domestic arena. From my experience, it seemed to me that it was rare for an international goalkeeper to be busy, that there was a greater need for concentration and consequently more scope for error.

Once Gary Bailey regained his fitness and I was never called up again. But Bobby Campbell was not only unhappy that I wasn't considered again but also that I was not notified of my omission, despite being in two winning England sides. Bobby was insistent that the then full England manager Bobby Robson should apologise to me. He proceeded to get Robson on the phone, in my presence, so that he could make his apology to me. For my part, I was quite happy to get those couple of games. I felt that I had done myself justice, had been steady rather than spectacular and didn't ask for anything more. When you move into an international set-up people automatically think that your head is going to be turned by mixing with the stars and hearing about other players' earnings and trappings. After I had come back from playing against Hungary, Bobby Doyle had a go at me about my attitude: "You think you've made it now, don't you," he said. It did make me have a good look at myself, but there's no doubt the other lads would not have allowed me to get any ideas beyond my station.

Other than three successive goalless draws in March, when for some reason the goals dried up, we cruised to promotion after looking strong all season. It was a great relief when we beat Southend to go up, with a couple of games left. We wanted to be champions and tied that up three days later with the home win over Walsall. You had to give John Deacon a great deal of credit for what he had achieved. He had backed the club and the manager to the hilt throughout and it was a very harmonious period, with no real upsets or scandal to rock the boat. We were lucky with injuries, with defender Ernie Howe being the only long-term injury we suffered. I was ever-present that season and that meant that Andy Gosney found himself in the same position as I was in four years earlier – waiting patiently for a chance that never seemed to come. He accepted that position a bit better than I did. Some people even accused him of being content to be Number Two, but that really wasn't true. It was probably truer, however, that later on, Andy did get a bit too comfortable with the situation.

The last game of that season at Plymouth was a bit of an anti-climax, although thousands of our fans travelled down and we rewarded them with another win. It had been a long hard season and after that game we just wanted to get home to our families, but the chairman took a reluctant squad out to a celebration dinner at a Torquay hotel that night. There had already been two celebrations – after both the Southend and Walsall home games – with champagne all round, and now came the customary bus tour of the city followed by the civic reception. Again, it was terrific to see the happy faces of our supporters and there were some unbelievable scenes in the Guildhall Square. An absolutely unforgettable experience for me was opening the doors at the top of the Guildhall steps and seeing the whole square below us. The square was jam packed with our supporters, covered in blue and white, hanging off the rafters and even from Queen Victoria's statue. I was still a relative youngster, had never experienced anything like that before and it has stuck in my memory to this day. At the end of the season Mr Deacon treated the players and their wives to a ten-day holiday in Marbella. One or two of the players were not too impressed at having to take their wives, given that it was not the normal practice for such trips. We found ourselves in the Andalusia Plaza, a high-class hotel at the very expensive end of the resort. The older players quickly made themselves at home in this swankier, expensive part of the resort, but a few of the younger players, including myself and Andy Gosney, were happier to make our way to the less salubrious end.

The 1983/84 season, with new signings Mark Hateley and Richard Money in the side, got off to a bad start for me and the team. I was lying concussed in the goalmouth, after a collision, when Middlesbrough scored the winner at Fratton in the opening game, as the team made their return to the second division. I really thought I had broken my neck in that incident – I was paralysed, but fortunately, only with fear. What really frightened me was that I had a sharp pain in my neck and another pain running down the back of my arm. I laid there for about two minutes feeling physically sick and didn't want anybody to touch me, least of all to move me. Eventually I was persuaded that everything was OK and stayed on for the second half – but it was only adrenaline that got me through. The next morning I couldn't move at all and shoulder ligament damage was diagnosed, meaning I had to wear a brace for a few days. That Middlesbrough defeat was our first introduction to the big names in a tough league – there were others to come, like Manchester City, Newcastle, Leeds and Chelsea. We found it difficult and it soon became clear that our squad wasn't good enough to make any sort of impression. There was still a great togetherness, with no real cliques or problems and the lads gave their all that season, but we did find the step up a bit too much.

One game that season stood out above all others – the fourth round FA Cup tie against Southampton at Fratton in late January, 1984. There was inevitably a massive build-up beforehand and it was the biggest pressure game that I had played in up to that stage in my career. I thought I knew the strength of feeling between the two sets of fans but, until you have played in such a game, you can't understand the depth of the rivalry. The importance of the game to our fans was not lost on the players, and it's true to say that it meant just as much to us. So we were just as shattered by the defeat. We gave a good account of ourselves and to lose in stoppage time made it even harder to swallow. We played ever so well, even had chances to win it, and at least deserved a replay. To his credit Steve Moran took his chance clinically for the winner. I was totally gutted – up to that time it was the worst that I had ever felt after a defeat. We saw fans crying afterwards which brought their distress home to us even more vividly. The result had severe repercussions for several weeks afterwards and it was probably instrumental in Bobby Campbell losing his job eventually.

That cup defeat by Saints knocked the stuffing out of us and affected our confidence. To cap it all we then had three of our hardest games of the season to follow. We had to play Newcastle in the next game a week later at Fratton and Kevin Keegan, Peter Beardsley, and Chris Waddle tore us apart. We were lucky to lose only 4-1. A week later came another stern test at Maine Road, Manchester. We lost 2-1, after being one up at half time through Paul Wood's first league goal. City's two goals came in the 80th and 90th minutes, the winner being a penalty. Worse was to follow, with Leeds United next up at home. It looked like we might get our first win in eight when we went in 2-1 up at half time, but we gave away two in the second half and lost 3-2. Confidence was now at an all-time low. Our luck changed at Cambridge, where they had gone 20 games without a win, and a brace of goals from Mark Hateley gave us a welcome 3-1 away win and, sort of, got us back on track.

What we didn't know, as the season dragged to a close, with us in mid-table, was that the chairman was frustrated with the results and gates we were getting. Campbell still had the respect of the players but, looking back, his relationship with Mr Deacon had clearly broken down. It was still a surprise when Bobby got the sack with just one game to play. We all thought that if he was in any danger, then at least he would make it to the end of the season. I can only think that something between them forced the break at that time, although I wasn't aware of what it was. On Bobby's side he would probably say that he didn't get the backing he needed to strengthen the side. We were unlucky with injuries and the defence, in particular, suffered a lot of disruption as a result. In the end, basically, we seriously underperformed for much of the time and the squad was not good enough to make any impression on the league.

Mark Hateley was one player, of course, who did make an impression that season, to the extent he was picked to play for England and secured a lucrative move to Italy. Mark was a real family man, despite being only in his early twenties, and heavily into cars. He was a very dedicated professional who consistently played well in our struggling side. I really rated him. Obviously he was very strong in the air, but he was better on the floor than people gave him credit for. Once he had scored for England against Brazil, it became obvious that we would not be able to hold on to him for very much longer.

Alan Ball was the youth-team coach and he was genuinely upset for Bobby, who had originally given him his first chance in coaching. Ballie, himself, really enjoyed working with the youngsters and he was a natural with them. To be honest, I had not had a lot to do with him up to then. The chairman obviously rated Ballie and, when he was asked to take over as caretaker, I think he felt awkward at being put in that position. My only previous encounter with Ballie had given me a taste of his sense of mischief. I had been called in by Campbell to be hauled over the coals for being late for training and Ballie had happened to be in the office at the time sitting on the floor. I came up with a convoluted story that my car wouldn't start and that one of my tyres was flat, which gradually became more and more unconvincing. This load of bullshit clearly didn't impress Bobby, but it did, unbeknown to him, amuse Ballie immensely. He was sat on the floor against a wall, with his cap pulled down over his face, but with his shoulders shaking with his laughter.

We still had to play Swansea in a meaningless last match of the season at home. Ballie picked the same side which had lost in Campbell's last game, a 2-0 defeat at Derby, and his pre-match team-talk was to the point: "You have got Bobby the sack, now give a performance which will show to me, the supporters and yourselves, what you are capable of," he said. We won 5-0 and Biles got a hat-trick. Ballie was set on rebuilding the squad of players he had inherited, however and we were headed for a three-year rollercoaster ride that was to bring great camaraderie and the long-awaited elevation to the top flight. But not before a fair measure of pain and disappointment along the way.

*'If Alan Knight was picked to
play for England he would not
let them down.'*
                    Bobby Campbell

The buzz went round Weymouth's antiquated, but charming, Recreation Ground like wildfire: Alan Knight was starting the game. For the four hundred or so fans who had travelled to see Pompey's first pre-season friendly against Alliance Premier League opposition – that's the Nationwide Conference in modern money – in August 1981, it represented the first clue that Peter Mellor's undisputed reign as the club's number one was coming to an end. Knight only played the first 45 minutes – Mellor was there for the second half – as Pompey eased to a 2-1 win; but more crucially manager Burrows, from day one, had established the goalkeeping pecking order. Knight was also in goal for the two 'glamour' pre-season friendlies against West Ham United and Arsenal – this time playing a full 90 minutes in each – while Mellor had the ignominy of keeping goal as a Pompey XI crashed to defeat against an Isle of Wight select XI. So it was no surprise when Knight was named in the starting line up for the opening game of the season against Lincoln City at Fratton Park. And it didn't take the 20-year-old long to start setting the division alight, even if the team struggled. Pompey owed their 0-0 draw at Southend in the first leg of a League Cup first-round tie to Knight, which prompted Melvyn Cawston, the Southend goalkeeper that night, to write to his counterpart congratulating him on his display and enclosing a copy of the *Southend Evening Echo* report on the game. 'That was the best display of goalkeeping I've seen,' commented Cawston in the story. He followed that up with another classy display in a 1-0 defeat at Preston.

Meanwhile, Peter Mellor was pledging to fight for his place in the team, but betraying a sneaking pride in his prodigy's achievements, as he explained in September: 'It's the first time I've started a season in the reserves since I began at Burnley and I don't intend sitting around feeling sorry for myself. I don't mind admitting I was a bit disappointed when Alan got the nod. I thought I had a pretty good season last time, 24 clean sheets, and I thought I'd get first crack again. But Alan has waited for a long time and had to have a chance. Now he's got it, he's the one under pressure and it is up to him to prove he can stand it. I like to think I've helped Alan become better. I've spent hours talking and working with him and I'd like to think in the future I'll derive quite a lot of pleasure from that. If he goes on to play for England, and I think he could, then I will know that I did a bit towards getting him there. In the meantime I want to see Pompey win every match this season. Something like 10–9 will do!'

Winning every game was far from Pompey's agenda though, as they took until late September to record their first-ever three points for a win, after a 2–0 win over Bristol City at Fratton Park, marked by a stunning goal from another youngster, Steve Berry. Throughout the autumn Pompey would hover around the fringes of the relegation zone, with plummeting gates putting manager Frank Burrows under severe pressure. The wheels fell off Pompey's wagon spectacularly in early October at second division Queens Park Rangers, when they were thumped 5–0 on the London club's recently-installed artificial pitch, in the second round of the League Cup. Although Knight was not at fault for any of the goals he did confess at the time it was difficult to adapt: 'Some keepers wear knee and elbow pads, but I've tried them before up at Alexandra Park and never feel comfortable in them; they make me feel bulky and clumsy. I found it a funny sensation diving on it. I didn't get the usual amount of lift and, of course, the pace was difficult. The only good thing as far as I was concerned was that at least you could trust the bounce. It was true, which was something,' he said after the match.

As Pompey struggled to get their season moving, Mellor's appetite for the fight was clearly draining away, with his latest off-field venture seeing him move into the luxury hire-car business, to add to his coaching schools. The news that Andy Gosney was set to sign his first professional contract when he turned 18 in November was also a clear indication Mellor's days at Fratton were numbered and early in that month he was offered a free transfer. It came as no surprise, coming as it did in the week Knight produced, perhaps, his best performance yet. With the October player-of-the-month award under his belt, Knight produced what Mike Neasom described as a 'staggering' performance to keep a clean sheet and earn Pompey a point: 'The best save came in the second half when he somehow managed to throw himself backwards to scoop out a shot by Jeff Cook, which had clearly beaten him,' he wrote in his post-match verdict. Mellor, understandably perhaps, turned down a move to bottom-of-the-league Northampton, but Burrows could hardly make himself plainer: 'Peter's been good for us – but at the same time I think he would admit Pompey's been good for him – and this was a way of saying thank- you. At the same time it would have speeded Gosney's development,' he said at the time.

The under-fire boss was also working hard to keep the emerging Knight's feet firmly on the ground in the wake of rave reviews after the Argyle game: 'He made two or three good saves, but the rest was normal goalkeeping work as far as I was concerned. The boy has it in him to have a very good career for himself, but he has a lot to learn. Most of all he has to prove that he has learned to organise his defence and really boss those around him,' he told the *Sports Mail*, and he twisted the knife with a pointed comment about his commitment after the manager had given the players a couple of afternoons off: 'Really I was expecting them to come in for voluntary training. I wanted to see who was keen to work on the skill side of the game and their weaknesses, without being told. I expected Alan to be there and some of the other younger players, but he wasn't and neither were they. I just hope Alan isn't beginning to believe the things he's reading about himself. If he is, then he'll get an awful shock.'

Harsh perhaps, but by his own admission, even as a young pro, Knight was prone to make the most of the social side of his profession and clearly Burrows was more alive to the potential ways he could yet ruin his career, prompting him to go public with his criticism. One thing was for sure though; the boss couldn't fault his goalkeeper's courage, as he plunged in where the boots were flying and took a kick on the head from Doncaster striker Alan Warboys during the first half of a game at Belle Vue in December. An anxious Gordon Neave, the Pompey trainer, spent the rest of the game behind the goal, fearing Knight was suffering from concussion, but it made no difference to his performance as he produced a point-saving stop to deny Glynn Snodin late on. Knight's heroics on the field were not matched by his team-mates' however, and in January matters came to a head when Pompey gifted Chester – adrift in 24th place – their first home win of the season when they tossed away a 2-1 lead in the final 15 minutes. It left Pompey just one place clear of the relegation zone and chairman John Deacon reacted by firing Burrows' assistant Stan Harland and installing his own man, Bobby Campbell, as first-team coach. Campbell's arrival sort of galvanised a team which had been heading nowhere fast and by the end of March a potentially ruinous relegation had been all but averted. It was enough for Deacon and Burrows was sacked on March 31 with Campbell installed manager, to the universal surprise of just about no-one. Burrows had one parting gift for Knight, as he had written to the England manager Ron Greenwood just before his dismissal pressing his claims to be called up for the England Under-21 set up. Although Blackpool's Iain Hesford and QPR's Peter Hucker had both apparently pushed ahead of him in the pecking order to challenge Lukic, Greenwood replied that Knight's progress had not gone unnoticed. A relieved Knight revealed: 'That's nice to know. Obviously I want to play for England – who wouldn't?' Campbell too had also become a fast convert to Knight's abilities, adding: 'He's got to be the best young keeper in the country and if he can maintain his approach and his attitude to the game he can play for England. I am sure of that.'

In April, Mellor too, finally fled the Fratton nest, opting to extend his career in Canada, signing for Edmonton Drillers with the ultimate plan of moving to Tampa Bay in Florida, where he would start a business fitting stone fireplaces, as well as coaching goalkeepers. So Pompey would finish the season with just the youthful promise of Gosney as back-up and he was pressed into service sooner than anticipated, after Knight was forced to limp out of a midweek game at Exeter, having sustained a dead-leg. His brother-in-law to be, Keith Viney, took over between the sticks for the second half, as Pompey earned a creditable (in the circumstances) 3-3 draw, while the injury spoiled Knight's hopes of a 'full set' of appearances and gave Gosney the chance to make his debut on May 8, at Millwall. Consolation wasn't far away though, as Knight was voted *The News/Sports Mail* player of the season by fans and he received the trophy before the final match of the season. It was no more than Knight deserved, having shored up a pretty leaky defence time and again during the course of the season, but it was clear, that if his potential was to be realised, Pompey needed to start moving forward quickly, or else the club would find it hard to keep hold of him. In Campbell, they found the perfect man for the job.

When Knight reported back for training in July 1982, Campbell – aided by chairman Deacon's cheque book – had radically re-worked the squad in anticipation of a genuine promotion push. Arriving were Fulham defender Ernie Howe, Reading's highly-rated 18-year-old midfielder Neil Webb and former England winger Dave Thomas. Then, on the eve of the season, he produced a coup de theatre, announcing the signing of Rod Stewart look-a-like striker Alan Biley, whom Campbell had persuaded to drop two divisions from Everton for a £100,000 fee. Not surprisingly the bookies installed Pompey as favourites for the Division Three title and their early season form suggested a canter, but with Knight himself admitting he was struggling to match the standards set the season before, Pompey began to falter badly in the autumn.

The rot really set in with a 4-0 defeat on a Friday night at Southend – a little more than 12 months after Knight's heroics at the same venue – and after the game the keeper commented that ironically it was perhaps his best game of the season so far: 'I'm playing badly and I haven't really done myself justice this season. It seems the harder I try the worse it gets. I thought I probably had my best match of the season so far last week at Southend and look what happens – four goals. It's simple really, I'm not getting enough to do. That may sound daft and you would think a goalkeeper would love playing behind a defence where the ball never came through to him, but that's far from the truth. In fact, the busier you are, the better.' Knight was also coming to terms with a FIFA refereeing directive brought in that summer which meant goalkeepers who handled outside the area or professionally fouled a forward would be automatically sent off. 'It doesn't help when you go to clear a ball knowing that if you handle you are going to be sent off. People might not like the idea. I don't think I did really, but it's a fact of life. Now goalkeepers are really under pressure. What do you do? If you bring him down you're off, if you don't your side's a goal down and you're in trouble – difficult,' he said at the time. Knight's up-and-down season continued – his mood not helped by the theft of £100-worth of gloves from his goal at Huddersfield in October – and another heavy defeat, this time 5-1, at Bristol Rovers, the following month, left Pompey on the fringes, rather than at the heart of the promotion race. The club was also rocked, just before the Eastville debacle, by the sudden death of Jimmy Dickinson; the man who signed Knight as an apprentice back in 1977. But the team finally began to respond to the loss in the best way possible by picking up points and re-establishing their promotion credentials.

Knight was also showing some welcome signs of a return to his best form, producing a couple of superb saves at Bradford to build a platform for Biley to claim two late goals and an unexpected point. Four wins over Christmas and New Year propelled Pompey into the top three for the first time since September and the news in January that Fratton Park would host the England Under-21 European Championship qualifier against Greece in March meant hope sprung eternal that Knight might yet earn a cap as an over-age player, although Knight himself was quick to play down his chances. 'I'd love to think I might play but I can't see it happening. If it had been a friendly, it might have been possible, but for a championship match I can't see them picking an over-age player for his debut. And to be honest I know my form doesn't warrant me to be picked. I don't think I've had too many disasters, but I know I'm not playing well. I know I have a lot of work to do on my goalkeeping and that's why I've been coming in for extra training. The only person who can put it right is me and until I do I think I can forget about caps and things like that,' he told the *Sports Mail*. Knight's lack of luck continued in consecutive defeats at Sheffield United and Orient, where twice he got fingertips to penalties, but failed to prevent goals. Those defeats proved a turning point, however, as Pompey embarked on a seven-match winning run which would become the foundations of a title-winning season. Knight was definitely back to his best in the third match of that run, a 2-0 win at Millwall, although his 'best' save, a tip over of Dave Martin's dipping drive, he put down to his returning luck. 'Really I was badly at fault. I was caught in two minds and for a goalkeeper that is usually fatal. I intended to catch it and it went through my fingers and I thought I'd thrown it in. Instead I was lucky enough to deflect it up enough to get away with it.' For Gosney though, it was time to experience the frustration Knight had known under Mellor, although he admitted he had benefited from Knight's experiences. 'Alan is number one and a very good keeper and I know I've got to wait my chance. It wasn't easy for Alan, but he got his reward and I've learned from that,' he said.

Knight's return to form was also finally acknowledged by England, as he made his Under-21 debut in the Greece clash, although it was only an injury to Manchester United's Gary Bailey which saw him called into the squad. He was largely a spectator as England laboured to a 2–1 win. He could do little about the spectacular long–range effort which beat him and manager Campbell was convinced he'd done his cause no harm at all: 'He might not have had a lot to do, but what he did he did very well indeed. He showed a lot of class and composure in everything he did. He won't be forgotten.' And so it proved. Any thoughts that Knight's selection was simply down to a last–minute Football Association bid to boost the gate by playing a 'homer' were dispelled as he kept his place for the next game, against Hungary, at Newcastle the following month, allowing manager Howard Wilkinson to display his own brand of psychological preparation. Knight kept a clean sheet too as England earned a 1–0 win. By now Pompey had all but secured promotion, with the crucial points being earned in a 2–0 home win over Southend on May 7. Three days later – in Knight's 100th league match – he was in inspired form as he kept Walsall at bay during a second–half assault on the Pompey goal. Clinging to Steve Aizlewood's seventh–minute goal, Knight pulled off three sharp saves before climaxing his display with two minutes to go as David Preece put Kevin Summerfield through, only for the goalkeeper to come off his line in a flash and smother what looked like a certain leveller. The 1–0 win meant Pompey were champions, barring an arithmetical miracle, and Knight would be able to start testing his reflexes in a league which promised to have some big-hitters. Newcastle United, Leeds United and Manchester City – relegated from Division One by Luton on the last day of the season – would provide a more suitable stage for Knight to display his talents.

Campbell largely kept faith with the squad which eventually cruised to promotion, the recruitment of Birmingham midfielder Kevin Dillon and West Ham striker Nicky Morgan on transfer-deadline day had already given it a 'first division' air, but there was, of course, an ace up his sleeve. When Campbell somehow snaffled Coventry's England Under–21 striker Mark Hateley from under the noses of a host of first division clubs, eyebrows were raised. When a transfer tribunal ruled Pompey need only pay £190,000 for the out-of-contract son of former Liverpool centre forward Tony, the astonishment turned to envy and, in the Sky Blues' case, outright anger. Hopes were high at Fratton Park that Pompey could make it two successive promotions and return to the top flight they left in 1959. The opening game of the season suggested otherwise, however, although Knight was at the centre of the action as modest Middlesbrough battled their way to a 1-0 win at Fratton Park. The winning goal came midway through the first half when Hans Otto knocked the ball into an unguarded net, but that only told half the story as Knight was pole-axed on the six-yard line at the time, fearing he'd broken his neck, after an accidental collision with Boro striker David Currie. The decision of referee Eric Crickmore to allow the goal sparked a furious melée, led by Pompey defender Richard Money – another summer recruit from Luton – but the upshot was Pompey's punctured self-belief. Although he was able to finish the match after treatment, Knight missed the next game against Hereford, in the League Cup, as he nursed only a damaged shoulder. Afterwards, Knight said: 'I suppose it was panic really, but I really thought it was broken and I was scared to move. The lad didn't mean to get me. We both went for the ball and that was that. I'm not sure whether I got my hands to the ball, but as for Malcolm Allison [the Boro manager] saying I might have fouled his lad, well that's a joke!'

Knight was back for Pompey's first win of the season, and an appearance on BBC TV's *Match of the Day*, the following Saturday at Fulham, but the inconsistent start set the tone for a season which promised much, but eventually faded tamely away. Not that Knight could complain about a lack of action. Pompey's patently Division Three defence was no match for the second division's big-guns as a 4-2 defeat at Newcastle in October proved, but at least the goal-power of Biley and of Hateley, who was clearly playing a class beneath himself, did enough to keep promotion hopes lingering until a New Year slump. On a personal level, Knight was continuing to make headlines for the right reasons, but his chances of further England honours faded as new national team boss Bobby Robson overlooked him for the England Under-21 internationals in the autumn. Manager Campbell was adamant his man was still a contender: 'Football is all about opinions and it is Robson's which counts when it comes to the selection of the England team. My opinion is that Knight is one of the best keepers in the country, but I might be biased as I'm working with him day in, day out and I've seen him perform,' he told the *Sports Mail*. Interestingly, in October Knight came 'head-to-head' with one of his rivals for the England jersey, Aston Villa's Nigel Spink, who had been called up to deputise for Ray Clemence as England faced Hungary in Budapest in the European Championships. Although first division Villa shaded Pompey 5-4 on aggregate, Campbell said: 'I think Spink is a very good keeper and in the Milk Cup game he made three world-class saves, otherwise we would have won comfortably. Whether he is better than Knight is a matter of opinion. What I would say is that if Alan Knight was picked to play for England he would not let them down.'

As Pompey's season stuttered, Knight continued to impress, making his first-ever penalty saves in December 1983, first denying Kerry Dixon against promotion-chasing Chelsea, at Stamford Bridge, then four days later, on New Year's Eve, he stopped Cliff Carr's effort for Fulham at Fratton Park. The latter save was scant consolation as Carr had already tucked away a spot-kick as the Cottagers cruised to a 4-1 win, which left any pretensions of promotion in tatters. The FA Cup remained, however, and after Nicky Morgan's last-minute goal had seen off Grimsby in the third round, Monday's draw pulled out the game every Pompey fan wanted: Southampton at home. In their wilderness years in the lower leagues, Pompey fans had to endure the double pain of seeing Lawrie McMenemy establish his Saints side as one of the most attractive in England, featuring high-profile signings such as Frank Worthington, David Armstrong and Peter Shilton. However, it was a couple of home-grown talents, in Steve Williams and

Fareham-born Steve Moran, who were potentially the biggest threat to Pompey's hopes. The game was a 36,000 sell out and the atmosphere inside Fratton Park could have been cut with a knife. In retrospect, the game wasn't much of a spectacle, with the stakes too high for either side to risk a potentially fatal error. Knight did what he had to do, most notably turning aside a Mick Mills effort in the first half and claimed the man-of-the-match award. However, Pompey perhaps shaded the few half-chances there were until injury time – ironically added on by referee Lester Shapter after Saints' full back Mark Dennis had been felled by something hurled from the north terrace – when Worthington found the breaking Armstrong, whose right-wing cross was met by Moran rushing in at the far post. In what seemed like slow motion, the wrong-footed Knight's dive to save the mis-hit shot was a fraction too late and the ball squeezed in at the near post. The match was won... and lost.

With that defeat, Pompey's season disintegrated and although enough had already been done to mean relegation was never in the equation, it was Campbell who paid the price after an insipid 2-0 defeat in the penultimate game of the season at already-relegated Derby. Deacon, impatient for the promotion to the first division he had so spectacularly promised to Pompey fans back in 1973, but was yet to achieve, sacked him. Despite his growing army of admirers, for Knight it was evident his career was at a crossroads. Left behind by his contemporaries and no nearer the England jersey many – including Campbell – still thought he could wear with honour, it was evident Knight needed to prove himself in the top division before any such honours would come his way. Alan Ball, no stranger to wearing the three lions proudly on his chest himself, was appointed caretaker manager for the last game of the season against Swansea at Fratton Park. Could he be the man to deliver Pompey to the Promised Land and to ensure Knight's potential was finally realised?

4 - Into the big time

By his own admission, Ballie was putting together a team of
what he called 'rascals', and that was borne out by his signings
of Billy Gilbert and Mick Kennedy in the summer of 1984.
He always told us that he had no problem with what we got up to, as
long as we all gave 100% to the club. Ballie seemed to relish
controlling such players – even had some sort of affinity with them –
and certainly he saw them as a challenge. He liked their fiery
temperaments, which actually matched his, and for the most part it
was reciprocated by the players in question. Billy came from Crystal
Palace with a reputation after some 'skirmishes' there, but he really
was the 'salt of the earth'. Off the field, Ballie and the lads had no
problems with him whatsoever. On the field, of course, he regularly
had his problems. Mick Kennedy's reputation was such that he was
disliked by just about everybody he played against. There's no doubt
that he upset a lot of people with his approach to the game. Mick was
conscious of this, and it got to the stage where he wouldn't make an
appearance at any PFA functions, because he felt that everybody hated
him. Mick Baxter from Middlesbrough appeared to be a great signing
in defence, but none of us could understand why he really struggled
in pre-season. Even I was beating him in the cross-country runs and it
soon became apparent he was seriously ill. Tragically for him he was
diagnosed with Hodgkins' Disease. With Mick's illness, Ballie went in
for Noel Blake, who, with Kevin Dillon, was one of the 'Crazy Gang'
at Birmingham. He saw Blakie as another 'rascal' to add to the

increasing bunch. It certainly seemed to stimulate Kevin, having like-minded characters like Mick and Blakie coming to the club.

There was an extraordinary camaraderie amongst this group of players and a great team spirit, both on and off the pitch. For that reason alone it made them the best squad of players that I have ever played with at Fratton Park. All the lads were very close; not only in location – the Waterlooville/Horndean area – but in the way we spent so much of our time together socially. We were always out on Sunday and Wednesday nights at either the Bird in Hand at Lovedean or the Cowplain Social Club, and then after training we could be found at the Sportsman's Rest in Copnor Road on Monday, Tuesday and Wednesday afternoons. Mick Kennedy chose it – he liked a 'real local', and, not only that, Bob the landlord served great rolls. Looking back, it was fortunate that there was a 3 pm closing time in operation at that time. Ladbrokes the bookmakers were across the road, which gave the gamblers a chance to pop over and place their bets for the day. People talk about the Wimbledon 'Crazy Gang', but socially the Pompey squad at that time bore comparison. I would have to say that Ballie positively encouraged our 'social activities', and I think he thought that it was beneficial, from a 'bonding' viewpoint.

When Blakie and Billy came together at the back they were a great partnership, and complemented each other so well. Billy was a fantastic footballer – the best central defender I ever played with at Pompey. Billy could read the game so well, was so comfortable on the ball, and could pass it out from the back as well as anybody in the game. Billy's reputation preceded him - he was a bit fiery and it brought him disciplinary problems. I suppose his temperament let him down really and stopped him going further in the game, after he had been part of the Venables 'dream team of the 80s' at Crystal Palace. It was part of his make-up though, and made him the player he was; but I felt it held him back as far as playing for a top club or England were concerned. Blakie found it difficult to settle at first and it didn't help when he complained about the stick he was getting from the Fratton Park crowd. He maintained that some of it was of a racial nature and, obviously, that was totally out of order. We were shocked when he made those allegations and, at the time, I certainly don't recall ever hearing any racial abuse towards Blakie from our supporters, although it often came from opposition fans. As always, it was blown up out of all proportion by the media and Blakie got a great deal of sympathy, which he was, unwittingly, able to use to his advantage. Once he had won over the crowd, he responded well to that and it was reflected in his subsequent performances.

Another player who had a problem with the Pompey fans initially was Scott McGarvey, who had the difficult task of replacing Mark Hateley. With his permed and bleached hair, the fans took him to be a bit of a poser and playboy. But he was nothing of the kind and not a big-time Charlie at all. Scott was a terrific lad and a good pro. Once fans take a dislike to a player it can be very hard to turn things around, and, to make life even more difficult for Scott, the goals didn't come. Unlike Blakie, however, Scott never managed to win the fans over and it was a shame he never made the grade at Pompey.

Much was made that season of what Mike Neasom, chief sports writer at the Portsmouth local paper *The News*, called: "A string of expensive misunderstandings between goalkeeper Alan Knight and Blake". I admit it was one of those seasons when a few own goals went in, but there were no real misunderstandings, other than at Wimbledon, between myself, Blakie and Billy Gilbert. In fact, I thought we had a great understanding at the back. The own goals were largely unfortunate – a couple were unlucky deflections, and one occurred after a shot had cannoned into Blakie's chest and flown into our net.

However Blakie's own goal at Wimbledon in October, which is talked about by Pompey fans to this day, was something else. It was less than a minute from half time, and goalless in a tight game, when I managed to block a Wimbledon free kick, only for Alan Cork to knock the rebound past me for the first goal. In the process Cork's boot had caught me on the knee, and I was left hobbling around in the goalmouth, in some pain holding my knee. In the light of subsequent events, I should have gone down injured and called for treatment. From our kick off, with just seconds left to half time, the ball was played back to Blakie, and it was his intention that he should pass it back to me, so that I could take my time in clearing and use up the remaining seconds to the interval. So that's exactly what he did, without looking, expecting me to be ready to receive the ball. But, by this time, I was bent over and rubbing my injured knee, oblivious to the fact that the ball was rolling towards me. By the time I had reacted it was too late, and the ball had gone past me into the net. In the space of about thirty seconds we had conceded two goals. There wasn't time to kick off again, but I was in no hurry to reach the dressing room. It was a long and slow walk back for me and finally I was met with Ballie screaming and shouting: "What the hell was going on there!" but, in fact, he didn't dwell on it for too long because he still thought we had a chance in the game. If Kevin Dillon had not missed a penalty in the second half we would have got a point, and it wouldn't prove to have been so costly.

There were two other games over Christmas and New Year that season that everyone seems to remember, both at home. The first, against Oxford, was a few days before Christmas, and there seemed to be no way back for us as the game went into time added on for a pitch invasion by a fully-dressed Santa Claus. We were one-down, but Alan Biley went into Pompey folklore that day with his two injury time goals and the 20,000-plus crowd went home to have a very good Christmas. A few days later, on New Year's Day, came another extraordinary game at Fratton, this time against Fulham. We were surprised that the game went ahead, given the gale-force wind that was blowing straight down the ground. The wind was unbelievable that day – the worst I have ever known during a game. The team playing against it just could not get the ball out of their own half. We had the benefit of the wind first half and went in 4-0 up, but knowing that even that might not be enough. In the end, we were relieved to finish at 4-4, after we had conceded a penalty for their equaliser in the last minute. Both sides found it quite impossible to cope with the conditions, although, in our case, panic set in during the closing minutes. If the match had gone on for another five minutes I have no doubt we would have lost. That season also brought the start of a TV hoodoo which seemed to haunt us for many seasons thereafter. The belief that we never seem to win in front of the cameras in live games took root after the two vital games we lost at Fratton Park against Birmingham and Manchester City that season. Both teams were physically and mentally stronger than us and, looking back, proved that we were not yet ready for promotion.

It was about this time that I encountered the first in what turned out to be a catalogue of rows over the years between the club and *The News*, when Neasom was banned by the chairman from speaking to the players for a while. I had a lot of respect for Mike, even if I didn't always agree with his viewpoint. Since his retirement, the paper's style has changed, with a tendency to more sensational stories and headlines, and a need to fill even more pages. This led to some strained relations during the Pulis and Rix regimes in particular, as the club struggled, and even the current chairman Milan Mandaric has had his share of negative reporting. I know that reporters have a difficult job and I've had no problem with the paper at all. I have always felt that both the club and the newspaper need each other and are important for each other. The majority of the time they are a great support to the club and a vital source of news and information for the fans. However, I have felt at times that there have been stories that didn't need to be reported by the newspaper, and have not helped their or Pompey's cause. It's been a regular occurrence, over the years, for new players at the club to comment on the lines of: "I've never known a paper to be so critical and scathing as this one is", and make the point that, at other clubs, the local papers are more supportive, even through the bad times.

During that season two wingers, Vince Hilaire from Palace, and Kevin O'Callaghan from Ipswich, moved to Fratton Park. Vince came to us as a very quiet lad, who didn't drink, didn't go out, and sat and watched TV all day. In fact Billy Gilbert told us that when Palace went to the United States on tour Vince sat in his hotel room all day, in seventh heaven, watching cable TV. It didn't take us too long to convert Vince over to our ways. In a few weeks we had effectively destroyed his relationship with his then girl friend and introduced him to whisky and Coca-Cola. Now, to this day, he spends many an evening telling people of our exploits in that period. Cally was one of the funniest guys I've ever met – a great mickey-taker and one of life's biggest moaners – even worse than me. Put Cally and Kevin Dillon together, and it was a murderous combination – they would moan, groan and slate each other mercilessly. Cally seemed to be a 'big-time Charlie' when he arrived, and I suppose anyone might take an instant dislike to him, until such time as you got to know him really well.

It was in January 1985 that I came as close as I have ever been to moving to a 'big' club. It all started one morning, when I had a phone call from a friend to say that a newspaper was reporting that Arsenal had made a £250,000 bid for me. Later, as I walked into Fratton Park to report for training, Ballie caught my attention, from his office, by banging on his window and then, in what I took to be a reference to that report, shaking his head at me with a grin on his face. In the dressing room I took a lot of stick from the lads about the report and then we moved to Rugby Camp at Hilsea as usual for our morning's training. I was just about to go on our normal warm-up jog when Ballie took me aside and said: "There has been an enquiry from Arsenal. After training, go straight home and you can expect a call in the afternoon," adding, "Arsenal are a fantastic club. It'll be a great opportunity for you and, if you need any help whatsoever, I'll be there for you." By now my head was spinning. I was thinking of a million things and I was not really listening. The lads were all chuffed for me and very supportive. Typically, they insisted I must go down the pub with them as usual, if only for an hour. In those days, of course, there were no mobile phones. Once I got home I settled myself down by the phone. Every time it rang I dived to answer, and once had to tell my mum to quickly get off the line. But no call came.

The next morning I picked up the newspapers to find that Ballie was complaining about unfounded transfer stories being written about me, and saying that as a result I had come to him the previous day all starry-eyed asking if I was leaving for Arsenal. After reading that, I was in no mood to confront Ballie when I got in for training. To this day the truth of what when on that day has never been explained to me. All I know is that, shortly after, Arsenal bought John Lukic from Leeds. From what I could make out subsequently, the deal faltered because the chairman had been asking too much money for me. For me the worst part was the embarrassment of it all with my family and team-mates. The fans were none the wiser, thankfully, but the disappointment did linger with me for a while thereafter.

One guy who did move that season was Alan Biley. He was sold, controversially, to Brighton in the spring of 1985, despite being a big favourite with the fans. I have to say that it was a mystery to me why, from day one, he and Ballie didn't see eye to eye. You just have to say that he was simply not the type of player that Ballie wanted in his team – it was nothing more sinister than that. There were a lot of fanciful rumours around about the circumstances of their fall-out, but I can't give any of them any credence.

We went into the last game of that season needing to win at Huddersfield, and for Manchester City to fail to beat Charlton at home. Ballie told us: "Whatever you hear about what's going on at Maine Road, just go out and win the game." It was my first experience of such a situation, where, inevitably, you have one eye on what's going on elsewhere. Soon, I realised that you get a series of different results relayed to you and you have to make sure you just don't listen to any of them, and don't pass anything on to your team-mates. The realisation that you get misinformation coming over to you during the game was something that would stand me in good stead later on in my career in similar situations. That day, for instance, Ballie was even getting wrong scorelines being passed to him on the bench by Huddersfield officials. At half time he was absolutely insistent that we didn't listen to anything from Maine Road, although it was clear to me, from the reports being passed on by the fans, that City were well on the way to a convincing win.

We played well that afternoon and Cally scored an amazing goal. It was a great disappointment to miss out on promotion on goal difference, but the news that began to filter down to the dressing rooms from Valley Parade, Bradford, just a few miles down the road, soon put everything into perspective. We got garbled messages that families were dying in a fire in the ground and, as we moved into the players' lounge, we saw the scale of the disaster for ourselves on TV. It was a strange and eerie end to an afternoon when we had all been so focused on promotion, and, in an uncanny way, it temporarily took our minds off our own acute disappointment.

Ballie was devastated by missing out – his response immediately afterwards was to say: "I couldn't have asked any more of you – it's been a great season." It was his first season as a manager, and he took it really personally. He just wanted to get away, to have a break and dust himself down. But I think he knew that he had a team that could be there or thereabouts again, with some fine tuning. Ballie was a great motivator, but I always felt that he was a better coach than a man-manager. His training sessions were certainly more imaginative than those of Burrows and Campbell. He was keen to play free-flowing, attacking football, rather than the 'route-one' style which was around at that time, epitomised by Wimbledon. As far as man-management is concerned, different players need handling in different ways – some respond to a verbal lashing, for others the softly-softly approach, with an arm around the shoulder, works better. As I said earlier, Ballie liked players around him who were difficult to handle, and he certainly proved that he could work with them. He could clearly relate to them, perhaps he saw them as kindred spirits, and he felt that he could be more aggressive and abrasive in their company. That just didn't work with the more timid type of character, however, and he found it difficult to adjust his approach accordingly. Kevin Russell was a prime example. Early on in his career I remember Ballie giving him a verbal lashing in training – "You'll never make a player," he ranted. It was an approach that might have got a better result with a different player, but it certainly didn't suit Kevin. It was good to see him go on and do well for himself later in the lower divisions.

As a group, it had been our first year together and we were bound to reflect on that missing extra point which would have taken us up. I realised then that you can tear yourself apart wondering about this or that result in the season which would have made all the difference. In the final reckoning Manchester City, Birmingham and Oxford probably spent more money and had greater experience than us. I was out of contract at the end of that season and looking forward to signing a new one, which, with bonuses, effectively doubled my pay. That was exactly what had been promised to me verbally early in the New Year. I knew that the several players who had joined the club in the past couple of seasons were earning three or four times more than I was. I was then, and, as it transpired, was destined to always be, the worst-paid first-team player at the club. Several players have said to me, before and since, that to get a significant wage rise you need to get a transfer. But clearly that takes no account of loyalty to one club.

So, when the time came for me to visit club secretary Paul Weld to sign the new contract at the terms promised, on being shown the papers I was shocked to find myself, without any warning or explanation, looking at a derisory offer with an increase of between £20 and £30 per week. When I eventually got to see the chairman for an explanation, Mr Deacon said: "Are you sure that's what we agreed, because I really don't think that's the deal we discussed at all." In reality, it all came down to the fact that we hadn't been promoted:

"Our not going up has seriously affected our financial position," he said, and I was left with the clear impression that the chairman had been stringing me out to the end of the season over my contract, waiting to see whether we were promoted or not. It was certainly convenient for the club that it was not due for renewal until the season had ended. I should not have taken the original offer verbally; I now know I should have got the chairman to put it in writing. Ballie had said that if we were promoted then: "I will be the first one knocking on the chairman's door to get you what you deserve," but he was still reeling from missing out on promotion, and didn't feel that he was in any position to take up my case. "There's nothing I can do for you," he told me.

I felt very let down by the club reneging on its offer, and refused to sign the new contract. In the way that contracts worked in those days, I duly went on a week-to-week contract, and on to the transfer list, with a £150,000 price-tag. I didn't want to move at all, and it was simply a matter of principle. Ballie understood my situation and he went some way to sympathising with me when he said: "I don't want to see you go, but you've got to do what you've got to do." I was never money-orientated in my career, unlike many players – all I ever wanted to do was play, that was when I was at my happiest. Obviously, if the chance had come to move up a level for more money, then, like any player, I would have taken it, but it didn't bother me in the least when there were no offers for me that summer. When the start of pre-season 1985/86 arrived, it was made clear that if I didn't sign then I simply wouldn't be able to play. The psychological war began when Andy Gosney started in goal in the first-team friendlies. On the eve of the season, I swallowed my pride, took what they were offering, and signed for another year, largely because I couldn't face not playing and not being involved.

The big question was how we would react after last season's disappointment and whether there would be any sort of hangover.

The answer was immediate. The lads came back in really good heart and, after beating Sunderland in our first home game, we went on a great run, victory after victory, and it snowballed from there. We won our first seven games at home and were seven points ahead at the top after 13 games. Winning became a habit for us. Nicky Morgan, in particular, got off to a flyer, with six goals in as many games, and it was a good season for him. He was a quiet, unassuming lad off the pitch, who never said much, but a big, strong, bustling centre forward nevertheless. Neil Webb had moved to Forest. It was inevitable, given that his contract was about to expire, that he was destined for greater things and the club had to cash in while they could. Full back Kenny Swain came from Forest and he was clearly a disciple of Brian Clough, as most former Forest players were at that time. He idolised Cloughie, was heavily influenced by him, would talk about him a lot, and most of what he said seemed to come straight from the great man's mouth. Swainie was very experienced in the game by this time and he was a very cool customer, with an air of aloofness, who led by example. I don't remember him ever being overly loud or aggressive as a skipper, never flustered and he was very articulate in the way he talked about the game. He was very family-orientated and on the social front, one who would show up, have one or two drinks, and then go home.

Ballie's recruitment of Mick Channon from Norwich was a gamble, given his big Saints background, but his experience and know-how helped the other players. Despite his England caps, Mick didn't come in with all the 'big time' baggage, and he was great for the dressing room with his dry sense of humour. His banter was up there with the best of them, and some of his cutting remarks, for instance his "morning, reserves" greeting, in that Wiltshire burr of his, to those players not in the first-team squad, were in a different class and had us in fits. Mick Quinn, who moved to Fratton later in the season, loved Channon. They were both gamblers with a great interest in horses, like Ballie, with whom they had a great affinity, and were both strikers – "sniffers" – in the same mould. You couldn't expect a great deal from them outside the box, but inside they would really do the business. Mick helped Quinny's game enormously. Quinn was a chirpy Scouser who fitted in well immediately. Right from the off he was scoring goals and we could see that he was a decent player.

I remember vividly the three Milk Cup ties that season against Spurs; the first two were goalless, but fantastic games nevertheless. We finally won in the second replay, at Fratton Park, with a header from Noel Blake. There's no doubt that those games distracted us in the league and in that period we lost games that we should have won. We were very pumped up for those Spurs games, and were really frustrated when we failed to get the win we deserved in the first two encounters. After the second Spurs match, we had to travel to Bradford for a midweek league game and play in front of 4,000 at their temporary home at the Odsal rugby league stadium, in the pouring rain and freezing cold. With a handful of fans dotted around the huge bowl, it was just about the bleakest ground I have ever come across. They say that great players are able to turn it on week in and week out, whatever the circumstances, but, psychologically, we just weren't up for it and lost 2-1.

On the Sunday evening, before the second Spurs replay at Fratton on the Tuesday, I was injured after a road accident, on the Eastern Road, when I collided with another car and the occupants were injured. The problem was that I was way, way above the legal alcohol limit and was later charged accordingly. I had been with the some of the lads in the afternoon when we attended a charity event at a local cinema, and then I had gone on afterwards and met up with some friends in Cosham. After the impact I ended up in a ditch with cuts, bruises and a whiplash injury. I failed the roadside breathalyser test before being taken to a police station for the toximeter test. The readings were so high that I was advised to have a blood test before going home. I was distraught with worry and really concerned about the injured parties in hospital after the accident. The story of my accident was, of course, all over the media and I was ashamed of myself. I went to see Ballie the next morning and he was anxious to see whether I would be fit to play the following evening. Andy Gosney was one of the first to come and see me – hoping that it would give him the chance to play in goal – and the lads tried, unsuccessfully, to lighten things up for me with some banter. I wanted to play against Spurs and, after I had satisfied Ballie that I was physically fit, he agreed. I think my decision to play was justified by my performance that night.

A month or so before the case went to court I was told there was a possibility of a jail sentence but, after a lot of worry beforehand, I received a two-and-a-half year ban with a £300 fine. I was told later that it was a heavy sentence in the circumstances and that, with my 'local celebrity' status, I had been used as an example to others. From then on it was down to the other lads, mainly Kevin Dillon, to give me lifts everywhere, or me getting on my bike, although we did move back to Portsmouth to make things easier. After two years I successfully appealed against the ban and the final six months were dropped. Of course it was all down to my level of drinking at that time. I went through a form of repentance but, if anything, not having a car probably resulted in me drinking even more.

Drinking amongst the players was what I had grown up with, and what had been introduced to me as the norm from day one; it was what you did in those days, it was what was expected. I don't want to make any excuses, but I simply didn't know any different. The managers expected it – there was never any word of caution from them or anybody else. I now wish I hadn't drunk so much over the years. I think I would have been a better player if I hadn't. I drank far too much. It was excessive, I realise that now. How many pints I could down in a session – 10 or 15 in a typical night – had become a part of Portsmouth folklore. People would expect to see me in and around the city's bars and clubs.

I don't know what an alcoholic is – but I know I did have a drink problem all the way through my career. I always thought I could handle it whilst I was young and fit, and I really don't believe it ever affected my game. I never played when I was in any way affected by drink. As players we religiously kept to the club rules – no drinking in the 48 hours before a game. Beyond that we drank during every other available moment – as soon as a game ended we would be down to the players' bar to get smashed. Years later my problems would begin in earnest when I stopped playing and was no longer subject to the players' curfews. Nowadays such drinking by the players is frowned upon in a big way and I think that's right. Players just won't drink to that extent now, and certainly I wouldn't have done if I had been earning the equivalent of £5,000-£10,000 per week. There are good reasons why it's healthy for players to socialise and have a drink together, but not to the extent we were in those days.

We came up against Aston Villa in the third round of the FA Cup that season, early in the New Year, and that added to my problems. We drew at home, but not before Billy Gilbert had been sent off for retaliation against Villa's Simon Stainrod, who was a real pain in the arse. He had wound Billy up all through the game until, finally, he lost his cool. Stainrod was also involved in the incident, in the replay at Villa Park, when I broke my hand in extra time, in an attempt to prevent their winning goal. In trying to punch the ball away, I connected with his forehead instead. I knew I had broken it from the moment it happened, but played on for the remaining ten minutes or so, during which time I luckily never really touched the ball, as we poured forward, vainly, to get an equaliser. They say that things go in threes, and after my road accident, on the same day that I broke my hand and so ended my 129-appearance run, I learned that Jenny had miscarried. It was a hard time for us. My hand was put in plaster, and I had to wait six weeks or so for it to heal. Andy had his chance, during which period we lost to Oxford in the next round of the Milk Cup, which was very disappointing after our great struggle to get past Spurs. I didn't want Gos to do badly, but I always felt that Ballie wanted me back in as soon as possible for the promotion run-in.

We seemed to cross swords with Wimbledon on a regular basis during this period and Ballie hated playing against them. When we beat them 3-1 at Plough Lane that season – New Year's Day 1986 – he came into our dressing room with just four words: "Here endeth the lesson". There was a lot going on in the return at Fratton, in March, with players even winding each other up in the tunnel as both teams waited to go out, then keeping it up throughout the game. In our previous home game, four days earlier, we had beaten Millwall 2-1 and their centre forward John Fashanu had flattened Cally off the ball. Ironically, 'Fash' moved to Wimbledon from Millwall immediately after that game. So, in our next game, there he was again, coming on as a substitute and proceeding to repeat his antics. This time he caught Kevin Dillon with his elbow, off the ball, smashing his cheekbone, effectively rearranging his face. I saw the whole thing vividly. That incident was seen by a lot of people in the ground, but not the referee or his linesmen, unfortunately. In those days you had to accept that sort of thing – it was all down to the officials and there wasn't the exposure that such behaviour attracts nowadays as a result of games being filmed and highlights being replayed on TV. Little did I know that day that, a year later, it would be my turn to fall foul of another Wimbledon 'trick'.

With three games left we were sitting in second place, but had Charlton and Wimbledon sitting behind us with games in hand. The pressure was intense. Any slips and they would be there to overtake us. We went to Stoke, in midweek in April, and lost 2-0, and that meant we had to win our last two games and rely on the other two slipping up. The first of these was at Bramall Lane, against Sheffield United, which has been a notoriously unlucky ground for Pompey over the years. Ballie described it in the press beforehand as: "The club's most important match for 27 years". We had been banging in goals at will all season, but we just couldn't score that afternoon. Maybe the pressure really got to us, but the goalless draw was no good, and things were out of our hands after that result. For the second year running we had missed the boat, but the players gave their all and backed Ballie 100%, just as he had complete faith in us.

Unfortunately, for the second year running, I had to bear the brunt of much of the fall-out, particularly as it affected the chairman's thinking about my contract. With my deal due to run out at the end of the season, I had, once again, been in discussions with Mr Deacon in the spring over terms. I made it clear, given that I was playing week in and week out, that I was looking for equality, if not with the top wage earners at the club, then at least with the other regular players. He also, once again, verbally offered to double my wages to bring me in line with the other members of the first-team squad. Again, like a mug, I failed to get him to put it in writing. Aside from missing out on promotion, on a personal basis, it had been an awful year for me off the pitch, what with my accident, driving ban, Jennifer's miscarriage and my broken hand. So I was looking forward to the security of a decent contract at last, and a testimonial which would go some way to making up some of the money I had missed out on over the last few seasons. But once again, when it came to it, the original offer was withdrawn and replaced by the same old derisory increase of £20-£30 per week. Again it was put to me that the club could not afford any more. With the team being in the top two for the bulk of the season, I realised that, as a consequence, Mr Deacon had had to pay a considerable amount each week in the way of bonuses. But for me to be the one to have to suffer was hard to take, not to mention the fact that I had now allowed it to happen to me twice.

Some people felt that promotion was simply not meant to be. There was also the same old rumour, which comes around at such times, that the players didn't want to be promoted on the basis that they wouldn't survive at the higher level. That was nonsense, of course; no player works on that basis. But Mr Deacon may well have been influenced by that sort of thinking. So I turned down the offer, and was really despondent and disenchanted about the club going back on its promises again. Among the fans, the tired old line was trotted out : "It's the end of the season, and Alan Knight is on the transfer list again..." I heard that Norwich were interested in me, but in the end they went for Bryan Gunn, from north of the border, instead. Ballie's future was unclear, and none of us were sure if he would stay on. Certainly I knew he was considering resigning after we had failed to go up again. We knew that if he came back, then it would be for one last bash at promotion.

I did work extra hard in pre-season and, when we came back, I was, once again, on a week-to-week contract. Ballie was still there and, early on, the whole squad sat down with him and resolved to give it another go. It was a case of re-grouping, and we felt that, after being at the top for almost the whole of the previous season, we still had a great chance of making it this time around. However it was obvious that there was a lot of apathy and cynicism around the city, and that was only to be expected. Nobody could blame our supporters for being less than enthusiastic about our prospects, after we had promised so much in the previous two seasons and failed to deliver. But we didn't allow those feelings to affect us in any way. From our point of view we went into the season feeling that we had a lot to prove to our supporters and ourselves. As the season approached, I knew I wasn't going to get any more money, and I desperately wanted to play. So, I put to pen to paper and signed on for another three years at the terms offered, although I was unhappy at the way I'd been treated. From the word go that season, it was clear that Ballie was under a lot of pressure, and there was talk that his job was on the line. It was beginning to show as well; he was much more animated and would lose his temper more quickly than previously. There were to be one or two explosions from him as the season unfolded.

Mick Kennedy had been proud of the captaincy, and naturally he was upset when he lost it to Kenny Swain. Mick didn't hold a grudge over it, and, like us all by now, he had a great respect for Kenny, who had become something of a father figure to many in the squad. Mick was still finding it hard to curb his explosive temperament and was sent off in pre-season. As usual he started the season with the best of intentions in that respect, but it was always obvious that if you took that aggression out of his game then he lost a lot of his effectiveness. We were still a hot-headed bunch of individuals, and regularly one or other of us would spit out the dummy and throw the toys out of the pram, on or off the field. Blakie asked for a transfer early on and it was difficult to pinpoint one real reason for that. We knew that his family was struggling to settle, that his mother wasn't well in the Midlands, and that he still had strong ties up there. Blakie was a complex character anyway, who would have personality swings – one minute he would be out with the lads on the town, and the next he would be in ultra-professional mode and talking of staying in to study for his coaching badges. He was often quiet but would then explode and surprise everybody. As was to be expected, the whole question of his leaving soon blew over.

We had made a good start and were well placed in the league by the time we went to fourth division Wrexham, in late September, for the first leg of a League Cup tie. We were expected to hammer them and when we went two-up, early in the second half, the tie looked all over. But they came back at us strongly, and it was real 'backs to the wall' stuff. They had one kicked off the line before, finally, pulling one back from the penalty spot in injury time. We thought we had done reasonably well and afterwards went back to our hotel in Chester, where we were staying overnight. On arrival, Ballie called us together and went berserk, in a way I had never ever seen him react to a performance before. At the time it occurred to me that it was a symptom of the pressure he was under. He went through the whole gamut of manager's insults: "You are all a total disgrace to yourselves, to your families, to the club and you have let our supporters down in a big way tonight. None of you are fit to wear the shirt, you've shown no pride or respect and none of you deserve to ever play for this club again." Some of the players tried to argue with him, to little effect.

After all that was over, one or two of us went out to a club for a few drinks, and on our return to the hotel came across Ballie in the bar with director Jim Sloan. He was still very aggrieved about our performance and we sat up with him until about 4 am while he gave further vent to his feelings. And that was not the end of it. The next morning we were on our way home and soon our physiotherapist John Dickens was coming to the back of the coach, where some of us were enjoying a few beers and a game of cards, to say that Ballie was "going potty" up front. He was calling a meeting of the players at Fratton Park immediately on arrival and we were not to be allowed home first. The result was that players had to collect their cars from various car parks along the M27, then make their way to the ground for mid-afternoon. On our arrival it became clear that Ballie was due to face a board meeting and at our meeting beforehand he informed us that he intended to resign. Not before he had made some strong personal attacks on several players, however – Kennedy and Gilbert in particular – calling them "alcoholics and pissheads" among other things. Typically, Cally had a real go back at him, for what it was worth. Then Ballie left us in the dressing room, still totally bemused, and not understanding why it was happening at a time when we were second or third in the league. His final words as he left for the board meeting were: "I've had enough of you lot. I can't do any more with you and I am resigning." The next morning we went in for training as usual. Nothing had changed and it was all forgotten. It was as though it had never happened.

In many ways that incident proved that such strong opinions and feelings between players and manager could be expressed and aired in the open, and that afterwards they could all be forgotten, without the group and its spirit being damaged in any way. That entire group were very strong characters in their way, and any weaker characters in their midst would have buckled under the pressure and intensity. Players like young Kevin Ball were on the periphery, but he grew up through the early years of his career with that group of players. Kevin thrived in that atmosphere, and I believe that it formed his character and made him the strong-minded player he eventually became.

By mid-October we were top, but had a real kick up the backside with a 3-1 defeat at Leeds. The Elland Road crowd are always very intimidating and vocal and, that afternoon, they certainly made it clear that they didn't approve of the two black lads in our side – Blakie and Vince. What was ironic was that they both ended up moving there a couple of years later. Soon after that we played Millwall in the Full Members Cup at Fratton, a Mickey Mouse cup if ever there was one, although it was notable for the hat-trick of penalties scored by Kevin Dillon. Like all top penalty-takers, Kevin had great confidence in his ability to score. He always wanted to take them, no matter what, and that innate arrogance was the secret of his success. But, funnily enough, he couldn't often beat me from the spot in training.

Close to Christmas came our infamous meeting with Sheffield United at Bramall Lane, in which we had three players sent off. I have seen plenty of poor refereeing over the years, before and since, but have never seen a referee lose control as completely as Kelvin Morton did that afternoon, and be so swayed by a home crowd. To send a player off after just seven minutes – Billy Gilbert for something he said – was a complete joke. Then, close to half time, there was no real need for both Mick Tait and United's Peter Beagrie to go after an off-the-ball incident. Kevin Dillon had already been booked for sitting on the ball and refusing to play on after Tait had been sent off. So a minute or so after Tait and Beagrie had gone, Kevin was on his way for a second bookable offence after a trip.

We came out for the second half with just eight men, with the game still goalless. Paul Mariner moved to centre half and the boys worked so hard that we really deserved something from the game. To lose by only one eventually really showed what spirit there was in the side. Paul did really well, out of position, but the game was settled by his 70th minute own goal. A cross came in, and in trying to clear it, he only succeeded in blasting it past me – a great finish, but unfortunately at the wrong end. At the final whistle there were a few scuffles in the tunnel with their lads, not to mention Ballie having to be severely restrained as he tried to get at the referee. Our anger was carried into the dressing room with mirrors being smashed, and several doors kicked open in the heat of the moment. Our reputation as a team who would battle and scrap for every ball went before us and, at times, the referees were simply not strong enough to handle some of the situations which inevitably arose.

It was around that time that young Mark Kelly was coming to the fore, being capped by Ireland before he had even played in our first team. He was a very talented winger who Ballie, in his typically passionate way, described as "the next George Best". He had a knack of being extravagant with his praise for young players – he had done the same with Paul Wood – and there's no doubt that it did put some early unnecessary pressure on them. I felt desperately sorry for Mark, who was forced out of the game eventually, with a knee ligament injury. He worked so hard for so long on his rehabilitation, but had to give up the fight. It's sad to think that the sort of surgery that was developed three or four years later for that sort of injury would have saved his career.

Our hard-fought away win at Plymouth on Boxing Day that season stands out for me, mainly because I had been up all the night before in the hotel with a stomach upset that also affected Swainie and Blakie. Perhaps I should have tried that pre-match routine more often because I had one of my best games that afternoon. The next twist in that extraordinary season came with Mick Quinn's court appearance, and subsequent three-week jail sentence for driving whilst disqualified. We were all absolutely dumbfounded at the news and no-one had the slightest idea that he was banned from driving. In his typical Scouse scallywag way he never informed anyone of the situation and there he was driving around in a club car. Apparently, he was stopped by the police whilst going to the chemist to pick up some medicine for his girl friend and admitted he hadn't got a licence. Quinny was made an example of and sent to prison. At the time, I didn't see what purpose that served and I still don't. We all felt desperately sorry for him, as he was in no shape or form a criminal. I felt that it would have been a more positive response to send him out on community service; coaching in schools, for example.

We had, as usual, another eventful encounter with Wimbledon that season, in the FA Cup at Plough Lane. For some reason our whole approach to that game was poor. We got off on the wrong foot when we were caught up in traffic on the way to the ground, and our physio, poor old Gordon Neave, had to get off the coach and run for some distance down the road to hand in the team sheet. The pitch was icy and hard, and our attitude could be summed up easily: we don't want to be playing this lot on this pitch. And you simply couldn't go to Wimbledon in those days and be anything less than 110% up for it. We didn't get our footwear right either and, despite several changes during the game, were uncomfortable throughout. I was like 'Bambi On Ice' that afternoon, in front of thousands of our fans and the *Match of the Day* TV cameras, and most definitely "unusually hesitant" as the local press described me. Add to that an own goal from Blakie and we were lucky to escape with only a 4-0 thrashing. Again two completely contrasting styles were on show – we wanted to play a bit, against their direct route-one stuff, and that day there was only going to be one winner. As you would expect, after a let-down like that, Ballie was very animated to say the least. Besides our abject surrender, he also, above all, hated losing to Wimbledon. They were also becoming a real bogey side for me.

In the league we were enjoying our football, and in with a real chance of promotion at last, with a string of wins through the spring period. We didn't feel any real pressure this time around, simply because everybody, including many of our own fans, had written us off. We could hear everybody, in effect, saying: "There's Pompey up there again, but they will blow it." As a group we knew that people didn't really fancy us, and that nobody liked us. Even at a local level there were a lot of negative vibes around. The gates were well down and the stadium was a shambles with the Fratton End partially closed. Financially, there were severe problems and Ballie was not allowed to buy anybody. To add to that, it was becoming blatantly obvious to me that the chairman was thinking about selling the club.

I was overjoyed when our first child, Jade Rachel, was born on a Thursday afternoon, April 23, the day before we were due to travel to Grimsby. The lads got to hear of it through Mick Kennedy, who also told everybody that I had named her 'Stella' after my favourite beer. The result was that I had several cards and congratulations from people referring to 'Stella's' birth. To top my weekend, we got a vital win at Grimsby and we stopped our ex-team-mate Scott McGarvey from scoring against us. It's surprising how many former Pompey players have scored against me over the years.

When we met Millwall in early May, with just two games left, we could have been promoted with a win, but that was dependent on Oldham's result. So, again, we had another of those afternoons full of false rumours and scorelines, whilst trying to stay focused on the job in hand. We didn't know, until after we came off with a 2-0 win under our belts, that in fact we still needed another point to be sure. We might have known that it wouldn't be that easy. We went to Palace a couple of days later, on the Bank Holiday Monday, but with three minutes left and the game looking for all the world like a goalless draw, Ian Wright popped in their winner. It would have been nice to have clinched it there in front of thousands of our fans who had made the journey, but somehow we knew that things never worked out that way for us. I was gutted afterwards, with a real emptiness, but we still didn't really feel we would miss out. We felt that Oldham were getting a bit wobbly, and that the pressure was getting to them. We were now pinning our hopes then on something happening the following night at Shrewsbury, where they were due to play their holiday fixture and that's exactly how it came about. Jenny and I took the baby out in the back of the car that night, and just drove around the city for a while.

We didn't want to listen to the radio and soon went back home. I looked on TV's Teletext occasionally and saw Shrewsbury were winning. The first I knew that Oldham had lost and we were up was when Jenny's mother phoned her with the news. We all agreed that we would go over to Swainie's for a party. The chairman and Ballie phoned us all there with their congratulations and then, inevitably, we all got drunk. There was no sleep for anyone that night. The next morning we all met up at the ground for training, but, when it became obvious that the intense media attention would make it impossible to train, we all got drunk again in the Pompey pub. The celebrations were confined to that Wednesday and, by the evening, we had all gone home to our wives and girl friends. We were back training normally on the Thursday, and other than one or two of us having a lunchtime drink, it's untrue to say, as some have claimed since, that the celebrations went on all week and up to the game on the Saturday.

For the players, more than anything else, there was a huge sense of relief that we had finally achieved what we had been striving for over three long years. There was a pride that we had done what we had originally set out to do – that we had done our jobs. But it had taken its toll and, psychologically, we were exhausted. The squad had a siege mentality about it – it was us against the world, but it had worked. We had stuck together, through all those setbacks, and seen it through to its successful conclusion. Our relief and celebrations were, however, tinged with a great regret: we hadn't won promotion on the pitch in front of our supporters. We had missed out on that experience, and we knew that our supporters would have preferred it that way. It certainly took something away from the whole thing.

Much of our below-par performance in that final game at Fratton Park against Sheffield United was down to that nervous exhaustion, although I have to admit that one or two of the team were still the worse for wear from the celebrations earlier in the week. Ballie wanted the championship and was upset with the result but, as a team, we weren't as focused as we had been in previous games. United came to spoil the party, and were certainly up for it more on the day. I know that in football, when you are in the opposition, in such situations where a team is in celebration-mode, you really want to spoil the party and turn them over. They had plenty of experienced players who were capable of exploiting the situation, and so it proved. The Fratton Park crowd just wanted to get on and have a celebration there and then, and we just wanted to get the game over with. All I could think about was that I had achieved my lifetime's dream of playing at the top level against the likes of Liverpool and Manchester United. As a climax to the whole thing we had the open-top bus ride to the Guildhall and a civic reception. It was a simply fantastic day, particularly for the families. The colour and sound which greeted us was awe-inspiring, with the square filled to capacity and overflowing with our supporters, young and old. We all had a turn at the microphone. Typically Mick Kennedy sang an Irish song that nobody understood and Kevin Dillon persisted in wearing his Ronald Reagan mask.

When the dust had cleared we knew there would be question marks over all our heads for the next season. When you have done the job, then you like to think you will get the chance to start and show what you can do at the higher level. Money didn't come into it for me; I just desperately wanted to play in the top division. However, there is always a clear need, and even more so today in the Premiership, to bring in better quality players and have greater strength in depth, to enable you to compete at that level. But we knew equally that, given the club's dire financial position, Ballie was never going to be allowed to do that, in any event. Goodness knows what would have happened to the club if we had missed out on promotion again. The chairman would almost certainly have sold up a lot quicker and there's little doubt that Ballie would have gone.

*'He's a super keeper – not
flashy, but confident.'*

Mick Mills

Alan Ball had clearly galvanised Portsmouth Football Club as the 1984/85 season got underway. The sale of Mark Hateley to AC Milan for £1 million had given the new boss some money to play with and he had recruited wisely, with steely characters such as Gilbert and Kennedy providing the perfect antidote to the cavalier approach of his predecessor, Bobby Campbell. By the end of September Pompey were undefeated and in fifth place in Division One, having secured back-to-back 1–0 away wins, at Leeds and Birmingham, in the process, which typified the new approach. The latter victory had thrust 23-year-old Knight into the limelight once more and Ball became the latest to espouse his credentials. Responding to a journalist's post-match question about the strength of Pompey's back four – by now reinforced by former Blue Noel Blake – Ball retorted: 'Back four? You mean back five don't you. Don't forget the goalkeeper's doing great.' At the same time, Knight acknowledged that he had been out of form for the best part of a year: 'I didn't do myself justice last season and I don't need anyone else to tell me; I had an awful time,' he said. 'But so far this season it's gone really well. Playing behind Blake and Gilbert is something. They help me a lot all the time. So far it's been easy. I haven't had much to do and I just hope it goes on that way. But if we get a match when things don't go so well I just hope I'll be able to pull them out,' he added, before playing down the inevitable question about reviving his England chances.

Certainly, Pompey's defence had a mean look about it: just seven goals conceded in ten unbeaten games, from the start of the season, which had taken them to the top of the table. However, just as, for the first time in 20 years, Pompey were being taken seriously as top-flight material, a bizarre sequence of own goals and gaffes was just around the corner and about to threaten to derail the undoubtedly solid foundations Ball had created. The unbeaten run ended at Wimbledon, a game forever remembered for that own goal as Blake's back pass from the kick-off, following the Dons' opening goal, trundled past the injured and oblivious – until it was too late – Knight. 'Blunder boys' read the caption under the respective protagonists' pictures in the *Sports Mail* and it was difficult to disagree.

Blake was reluctant to shoulder responsibility though: 'I would play that back pass ten times out of ten,' he defiantly asserted post-match. 'There's no way I blame myself for it. A few people stabbed me in the back for it, but people like that do not bother me. I felt absolutely sick for Alan. I went over to him to see if he was OK and he said to me he was in a lot of pain. He should have gone down though and hopefully it is something he won't do again for a very, very long time…' However, Blake was clearly unsettled and proclaimed his unhappiness two weeks later in the local press, citing his move away from his Birmingham roots. Knight shrugged off the disappointment to return to form at Oldham on November 3, where he produced another virtuoso performance in horrendous conditions, to help secure a vital 2-0 win. Mike Neasom found no less than seven saves to remark on: '[Knight] three-times thwarted Mark Ward, three times 'burly' Mick Quinn and once Tony Henry.'

Four weeks later and Pompey were still in the thick of the promotion race when the gremlins struck again as top-of-the-table Blackburn arrived at Fratton Park. In front of 16,000 – the biggest gate of the season to date – Blake's chest got in the way of a rebound off the post to put Rovers one up, then Mick Tait managed to almost slice the ball out of Knight's arms to double the visitors' lead. Two goals in a minute, early in the second half, by Kevin Dillon and new signing Vince Hilaire, earned a point. However, the fragile nature of Pompey's morale was underlined in mid-December as Blake's increasing discontent came to a head when he went public with claims that sections of the Fratton Park crowd had racially abused him in the game with Huddersfield, after his mistake gifted them the opening goal. The fact he scored the winning goal with 11 minutes to go was, in retrospect, something of a watershed for his relationship with the fans. In pledging to forgive, if not forget, what those fans had said, and help Pompey win promotion, it also gave him the chance, once and for all, to lay the blame at Knight's door for that goal. 'The one at Wimbledon was Knightsie's fault and he has accepted that,' he told the *Sports Mail*, no doubt in a tone which brooked absolutely no argument.

1984 ended with Pompey being thumped 4-1 at Sheffield United, with, this time, Gary Stanley getting his goalkeeper into trouble with a poor pass across the face of his own goal, to set up the opener just after half time. 1985 opened with the never-to-be forgotten, wind-assisted 4-4 draw with Fulham. From Knight's point of view the key event of the moment was his supposed move to Arsenal, which hit the back pages of the tabloids the day after the Fulham debacle. At the time Ball denied Arsenal, who had just shelled out £500,000 for Southampton's midfield star Steve Williams, had made any contact with Pompey over the transfer. However, he did put a price on his young keeper's head: 'We want Alan Knight here, but I suppose if someone were interested we might be prepared to listen to them although it would take £200,000 or so to tempt us.' It seems there was more than just smoke to this story though, as Ball now subsequently acknowledges: 'It wouldn't have been a good move for Alan, as he would only have ended up playing in Arsenal's reserves,' he said.

Ball was clearly prepared to wheel and deal in the transfer market as he looked to freshen up the squad for a promotion push, which was in danger of evaporating on the back of a six-week winless run. The run of poor form ended emphatically with a 5-1 thumping of Oldham at Fratton in mid-February, including two goals by fans' favourite, Alan Biley. It was to prove his swansong, and within the month he had left for south-coast neighbours Brighton. Not that it affected Pompey's point-garnering ability, and Knight played his part with vital saves and clean sheets to earn points at Wolves and Shrewsbury in March. Easter Saturday saw a six-pointer at Fratton with Brighton and the importance of the game, and Biley's return, had persuaded the BBC TV *Match of the Day* cameras to the ground. Knight had to endure a dissection by commentator Barry Davies and pundit Jimmy Hill, in front of the watching millions, over his part in Brighton's equaliser. His failure to cut out Danny Wilson's cross led to poor old Blakie shinning another one into his own net. More upsetting still, the VT editor had also left a stunning save from Mick Ferguson to preserve a point on the cutting room floor. 'I was very disappointed when I sat down to watch the video recording on Sunday morning. I accept I should have gone for the cross, but I was looking forward to seeing the save again. Instead, I suddenly realised they had gone by it without showing it. I was choked,' he said the following week. 'I was pleased with the save because I was going backwards at the time and didn't think I'd be able to knock it over the bar – I'd have liked to have seen it again.'

A 3-1 win at Fulham on Easter Monday – with promotion rivals Birmingham and Manchester City still due at Fratton – had, seemingly, put one of Pompey's feet in the first division. Defeats in both those games however, sandwiched between a 2-1 loss at a rainy Selhurst Park, against Crystal Palace, left their hopes of going up in tatters. Three straight wins to finish the season, coupled with City's stumbling form, edged the door ajar again, but City's emphatic 5-1 win on the last day of the season, against Charlton, who fielded rookie keeper Lee Harmsworth, finally slammed it shut.

Despite the heartache of missing out on promotion, Pompey had made enormous progress on the field, although it was harder to say the same about Knight, whose career was approaching a crossroads. The collapse of the Arsenal transfer almost certainly was playing on his mind when he put in a transfer request, after the promise of a significantly-improved contract disappeared, as the financial reality of another season of the second division sunk in. The truth is his availability – well publicised though it was – failed to solicit a single serious inquiry. And had the move to North London gone ahead, one has to wonder whether it would have made any difference. With Pat Jennings reaching the end of his long and illustrious career, his replacement was already being groomed. John Lukic, Knight's contemporary and seemingly eternal rival, had been signed from Leeds for £70,000 in early 1984 and he made his Gunners' debut soon after Knight's move foundered.

It was a familiar refrain from Knight as he started the new season with a string of clean sheets at home, having seen off Andy Gosney's strong pre-season challenge by swallowing his pride and coming off the transfer list, 24 hours before the season started with a 2-2 draw at Hull. 'I didn't have a good season last year. I know that and don't need people to remind me about it, but I worked hard in pre-season, have lost a little weight and I'm determined to do myself justice this time,' he told Mike Neasom. 'Going on the list and then not attracting an offer doesn't do a lot for anyone's confidence and it certainly hurt my pride more than a little.' Knight signed a one-year contract and it was clear Gosney's presence was also making him sweat, just a little. 'The fact that Gos did so well in pre-season matches also adds a little bit of pressure. He's a very good keeper and if he once gets in the side, I might have a bit of trouble shifting him...' With Pompey's season picking up pace like an express train, though, Gosney must have been preparing himself for a long wait to make league appearance number two for the club. Knight preserved Pompey's impregnable home reputation until November and also made a rare penalty save, blocking Nicky Chatterton's effort at Millwall, setting up the platform for a 4-0 win. Stoke's player-manager Mick Mills joined the Knight fan club after a string of saves helped earn Pompey a 2-0 win over his side in the third round of the League Cup: 'He's a super keeper – not flashy, but confident.' Four successive defeats in November and early December were offset by a marvellous fourth-round win over Tottenham – Glenn Hoddle and Chris Waddle included – at the third time of asking, although Knight had to be grateful to his crossbar in the second replay at Fratton when a speculative Waddle effort sailed over his head. Ball was also working hard to rebuild Knight's confidence: 'He felt he wanted to get away at the end of last season. While people had come and gone he'd been part of the fixtures and fittings here since he was a kid. We talked it over and I'm delighted he decided to stay. He has worked hard on his game ever since. He's a pleasure to work with,' he explained.

Gosney finally got his chance as Knight's trio of misfortunes over New Year 1986 ended with him breaking his hand on Simon Stainrod's head as he attempted to keep out Aston Villa's decisive goal in extra time during an FA Cup third-round replay. Despite being well placed in the league, the jitters were already setting in at Fratton as a disappointing 1-1 home draw with Fulham saw Ball vent his fury at the attitude of his players and the fans. Gosney's first game was in a crucial six-pointer with title rivals Norwich, at Carrow Road, and he could do nothing about the two late goals which meant the Canaries pulled five points clear at the top of the table. That was followed by a 3-1 defeat at Oxford in the quarter-finals of the Milk Cup – again Gos was beyond reproach – but the feeling that Pompey might just blow it again was gaining momentum. Gosney was making the most of his chance, but aware it may not last long: 'I have always been one of those people who takes things one day at a time. Whether Knightsie will come straight back in again when he's fit, I don't know. I will find out when that day comes. If I'm playing well enough, hopefully, I will stay in the side,' he told the *Sports Mail*. In the end he did his cause no favours by being at fault for both Oldham's goals, as the mid-table side snatched a 2-1 win on a frozen Fratton pitch, at the end of February. Knight was back for the following week's trip to Blackburn, although even his return couldn't prevent a 1-0 defeat. Ball acted, finding £150,000 to sign Oldham's 'Mighty Quinn', before proclaiming: 'We'll not lose again this season'. A 3-2 win at Brighton on Easter Monday once again had Pompey with one foot in the first division while Knight was offered a new three-year contract, including a testimonial. Pompey's move was partly down to their desire to persuade Knight not to test the water again in the summer, when his contract expired. 'There are a couple of things to sort out, but it's a fair offer. It's nice to think the club think enough of me to make the offer in the first place,' he said at the time. Ball chimed in: 'The chairman has offered him a very good contract with a testimonial year and I hope he accepts it – he's done a great job and still has one to do,' he said.

The problem was the rest of the team failed to do theirs and it was *déjà vu*, as three consecutive defeats in April scuppered Pompey's chances again and left them three points short of promotion. Charlton claimed the runners-up spot that had looked Pompey's by right and Ball's *bête noire* Wimbledon came through on the blind side to steal third place. On a personal level, Knight had to contend with the double blow of seeing his aspirations of proving himself in the top flight snatched away again as well as seeing that tantalising contract offer whipped away as chairman Deacon set about tightening belts. Pompey's promotion challenge had failed to draw in the crowds and the average gate was down on the previous season. It was a very unhappy Knight who reported back for pre-season training at HMS Mercury in July 1986. To be fair he was between a rock and the proverbial hard place. Pompey had done the dirty on him over his new contract, yet there were precious few takers for an out-of-contract player, in effect free to sign for whom he pleased. Loyalty in football should work both ways and Knight was having his tested. The fact he opted to stay – on only marginally-improved terms – was perhaps the defining moment of Knight's career. His fate from then on was inextricably linked with the club's.

The pressure to mount a third – and this time successful – promotion campaign was intense and two points gleaned from the opening two league games did little to raise spirits. Gosney caused a flutter of anxiety early on, too, getting himself suspended for being sent off in a reserve game, leaving youthful third-string goalkeeper Tony Oliver as the only cover. The crisis passed, only for Gosney to go out and seriously injure his knee, but Ball decided to rely on a loan signing – 'I know exactly who I'll go for if I need him' – to cover for Knight. On the field, Pompey finally clicked, with Quinn earning the nickname 'Noah' as his regular two–goal hauls, backed by the meanest defence in the league, ensured regular three–point returns.

Knight was finally rediscovering his best form and was determined to exorcise his latest nickname at the club, thanks to Ball's appliance of his former Saints team–mate, Peter Shilton's training routines for the club's goalkeepers: 'It's hard work indeed, but two or three times a week it's all we do and I'm certainly feeling better for it. I'm trying to be more positive and get out to crosses better – perhaps it's got something to do with the other lads calling me "Flapper",' he said at the time. A point ground out at Stoke, after Paul Hardyman endured the ignominy of being sent off and carried off at the same time, was in part down to Knight stopping Keith Bertschin's penalty. The fragile nature of the confidence built up by the good start was underlined though when Ball flipped his lid after a sloppy last half hour at Wrexham. 'We had a long session and I did some very straight talking,' the manager told the *Sports Mail* at the time. 'Some of the things we did were amateurish and I wouldn't tolerate them from a team of kids – these were hardened pros. It made me wonder whether some of them had learned the lessons of the last two years. I didn't like what I saw and I don't want to see it again.'

Pompey's chastened players responded and were top of the table at Christmas, shrugging off the problems posed by the suspensions the eight–man fiasco at Sheffield United, in December, created. Knight's efforts were also recognised by the fans as he won the December player–of–the–month award, in part for a match–winning performance at Plymouth on Boxing Day – the scene of his heroics five years previously – as Pompey clung to a 3–2 lead. Promotion beckoned, but Pompey, being Pompey, endured a miserable January as leading scorer Quinn was detained at Her Majesty's pleasure for motoring offences, and further bad publicity winged the club's way as an administrative oversight led to Lottery and Gaming Board officials dramatically raiding the club's offices. On top of that

Pompey 'surrendered' 4-0 at Wimbledon in the FA Cup fourth round, prompting Ball to commit the white 'third' kit the team wore that day to the history books. And then it all came right again. Quinn – having kept his nose clean in Winchester Prison – was out on parole to play his part in a 1-0 win at promotion rivals Ipswich, thanks to Mick Tait's goal. Knight's path also, in a roundabout way, crossed his old rival Lukic's, as the pair vied for the title of the 'meanest' goalkeeper in the Football League, each having conceding just 16 goals in their respective club's first 27 games of the season. His form inevitably re-posed the eternal England question: 'I know how much I have to do,' he told Neasom. 'There are a lot of good young keepers around these days. Hopefully though, if we can get into the first division, there will be more chance of me being seen by someone who can drop my name in Bobby Robson's [the then England manager] direction.'

And get into the first division they did, although characteristic blips in form ensured the title went to a Derby side orchestrated by veteran midfielder John Gregory, who would, in time, have his own forthright view on why the Rams secured the title when he found himself in the Fratton hot-seat. After promotion was clinched, Knight – the sole survivor in Pompey's side from the fourth division days – was suitably emotional, and tired no doubt, as he told *The News*: 'I couldn't bear to listen to the radio to hear how Oldham were getting on, I felt it might be tempting fate. When my wife told me the score I didn't know whether to laugh or cry as I would have preferred it if we could have done it ourselves. This is a bit of an anti-climax, but I don't think that feeling will last for long.' Knight finished the season an ever-present with 20 clean sheets and just 28 goals conceded in 42 league matches – a club record. He was also voted the players' player of the season. The challenge of the first division awaited, but to paraphrase Knight, there certainly were a lot of good young goalkeepers around. And while Knight was certainly 'good', whether, at 26, he could be considered, in footballing terms at least, 'young' was now open to debate.

Knight makes his point at Southend in September 1981, assisted by Steve Aizlewood (obscured) and Billy Rafferty (left)

Page 18   EVENING ECHO Thursday, September 3, 1981

KNIGHTMARE FOR BLUES

Floodlight robbery

as Alan slams door

"THAT'S the best goalkeeping display
e seen," was the verdict of one
southend United player on the miracle
performance of Portsmouth's young
keeper Alan Knight last night . . . and
he should know!

Blues' record-breaking goalie Mervyn
wston was till marvelling at the perfor-
ce of the man at the other end of the
h hours after last night's pulsating
alless League Cup tie at Roots Hall.

"You couldn't fault
r strikers," said
wston, "They put
ens of shots and
ders on target, but
ight just had an
ired match."
     broke
          g at
          by

By HOWARD SOUTHWOOD

banged his head against a brick
wall all night.

"Some of Knight's saves
were incredible," said the
Irishman who topped Blues'
goalscoring charts last season.

"Against any other 'keeper
we would   finished three
                it is

he stopped some of our efforts
I'll never know. Portsmouth
have got him to thank for still
being in with a hope of getting
into the second round.

And unhappily Blues'
chances must be remote for
the second leg
although h

fans are in for a treat. Both
sides contributed towards an
enthralling 90 minutes — the
only pity was there wasn't a
goal or two to show for all the
sweat at the end."

Knight's list of glorious saves
must read like a horror story
for Blues but here goes:

● Mercer header brilliantly
saved at full stretch.

● Mercer's awkward, d
ot palmed out.

overworked defence down
both flanks.

● Spence touched on a hard
right-wing cross which was
clawed out.

● Ron Pountney's header was
pushed clear at the foot of a
post.

● Phil Dudley's cracking 25-
yard thunderbolt was deflected
by an almost classic arm as it
wards the top corner.

The headline from the Southend Evening Echo sums it up as Knight breaks Southend
hearts in a League Cup tie in September 1981.

Portsmouth FC

Knight lines up for the club's pre-season
photo shoot in August 1982 (above) and
August 1984 (right).

Portsmouth FC

Pre-season training in July 1982 with Jon Roles (left).

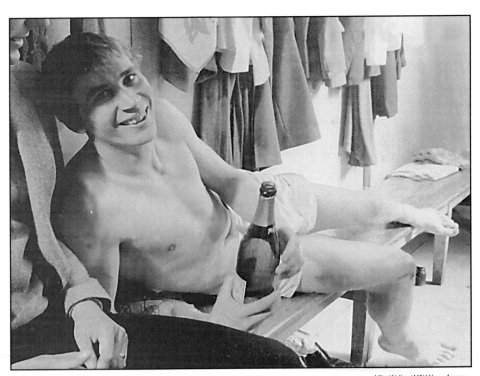

Knight celebrates with a bottle of champagne after promotion to the second division is assured with a 2-0 win over Southend in May 1983.

NIGHT TO REMEMBER

Late England winner pleases 'keeper Alan

ENGLAND UNDER-21 2, GREECE 1

Pompey goalkeeper Alan Knight's proudest moment looked in danger of turning sour until his South Coast neighbour, Saints' dynamic winger Danny Wallace, popped up to help snatch a last-gasp victory for England against Greece in last night's European Championship clash at rain-lashed Fratton Park.

Knight was virtually a spectator all evening — his hardest tasks had been collecting a timid lob in the first half and then claiming a high arching cross just inside his six-yard box after the break.

But, with five minutes left, a blistering 25-yarder from the left foot of Theodoros Vouzitilas beat on all ends up and he admitted afterwards to feeling "sick" at that moment.

BY STEPHEN BREACH

VITAL

But Wallace, who had earlier given England a third-minute lead with a typical deadly final back ...

by Coventry's Mark Hateley and Sunderland's Nick Pickering before the tiny Wallace applied the vital touches — must have been delighted to have seen Wallace's last-gap effort fly into the net at a packed Fratton end, and said: "I enjoyed the game although I did not have that much to do, but when the goal went in I felt sick.

"The goal came at a bad ...

the burly blond goalkeeper added: "It was a lovely togetherness and I was delighted with the reception I got from the crowd.

"It was just great to be involved with England and it was a bonus that we got the right result in the end.

Yet Knight has probably never experienced such a quiet evening in his short career. The first ...

...mpey goalkeeper Alan Knight ... to the crowd as the ... line up for the

The News reports on Knight's performance after his shock call up for the England Under-21 international against Greece at Fratton Park.

Private collection

Look back in anger. Knight can only watch as Grimsby's Paul Wilkinson scores in March 1985

A muddy Knight shapes to clear during the 1986/87 season.

Kevin O'Callaghan (left), Mick Quinn and Knightsie, with lager can, get into the party spirit.

Run for your life! The final whistle after Pompey's last home match of the 1986/87 game against Sheffield United.

5 - Itchy feet

In pre-season we had the usual HMS Mercury preparation and then went off to Sweden for a 14-day tour, which, somewhat reluctantly, the club had been asked to accommodate. It turned out to be an absolute nightmare. We were there for far too long, had far too much free time, and one or two of us were almost suicidal after a few days, mainly out of sheer boredom. It even got to Ballie before very long, and it was down to him to keep up our spirits. In someways, the luckiest man alive during our internment was Nicky Morgan, who was able to fly home, although the death in his family was hardly a recommended means of engineering an escape. We were based in the middle of nowhere and had to travel for three to four hours for each of the fixtures. Who organised that, I don't know. The games themselves were no better. We played a series of poor teams, and winning each time by five or six was of no real value. We sat in our rooms for hour after hour watching TV and videos, with Vince, our TV freak, as the video-master. What was extraordinary was the Swedish censorship – thrillers like Miami Vice would have the violent sequences removed, whereas sex films would have the hard porn sequences left in. Kenny Swain and Paul Mariner went on the trip determined to enjoy themselves. As Paul put it: "It could be my last club trip and I want to make the most of it," but it wasn't very long before we were struggling to make anything of it at all.

However, that trip could hardly be blamed for our dodgy start in the first division. When Blakie was injured, just before the big kick off, it immediately showed up our lack of resources, as Mariner had to play at centre half in the opening game. Going to Oxford's little Manor Ground was hardly the most glamorous of introductions to the top level, but they tanned us 4-2. Chelsea gave us another lesson in our first home game a few days later, putting another three past us, and suddenly, early on in the season, after those two bad results, we were already under a lot of pressure. Then almost immediately came the big one, with Saints the visitors to Fratton Park. The 2-2 draw was a fair result in the end with Colin Clarke scoring twice against us, something he would constantly remind me about when he moved to Fratton Park three years later.

With Blakie out long-term, Ballie was allowed to spend £70,000 on defender Malcolm Shotton from Oxford. On his debut, we were humiliated at Highbury against Arsenal, and their six goals illustrated the blatant gulf between the two sides. But their opener was so embarrassing for me, and Graham Rix, who played a big part in it, would often pull my leg about it during his time as manager at Fratton. Rixie had crossed the ball from the by-line but, in doing so, through his momentum, had run off the pitch temporarily. I had fielded the cross and then proceeded to roll the ball out prior to clearing it. Rixie had come back on and gone along the goal-line behind me. I heard him coming from behind me, but he was able to get round me, get a toe to the ball and knock it into the path of fellow Arsenal striker Alan Smith who put it into the net. As it happened Smith was struggling goal-wise at Highbury, at the time, and that first of the season set him up for an eventual hat-trick that afternoon. Whenever Rixie brings it up I always say that he should have been red-carded – a yellow for being off the pitch without permission, and another one for nicking the ball off me. But on that afternoon the goal was allowed to stand. It was 4-0 at half time and we went in at the break a bit shell-shocked, to say the least. It was really a question of damage limitation in the second half, although they had reached six with 25 minutes still to play, so it could easily have been a lot more. However, by the time we met West Ham two days later, on the August Bank Holiday Monday, Ballie had made a great signing in midfielder Barry Horne from Wrexham. With him in the side we got our first win but the injuries were mounting up.

Striker Ian Baird joined us in the summer, from Leeds, and from day one nothing would go right for him at Pompey. He had a really bad time; he wasn't scoring goals, and the crowd were soon on his back. The harder he tried; the worse it got. I really felt sorry for him. Bairdie hated every minute he was at Fratton Park. He heartily disliked the club and everything about it – I remember seeing him once in the dressing room, shaking his head, and repeating to himself: "What a shithole, what a shithole". Many of the disciplinary problems he had on the field were born out of his frustration. Happily for him, he got a move back to Leeds early in the New Year.

By Christmas we were struggling. There were no real indications that the club were in any financial trouble; after all we were in the top division with all the benefits that was supposed to bring. Then came our short trip to The Dell to play Saints, early in January, with a Sunday morning kick off. I was in the back of the coach on the way to the ground, having a fag, as usual, with Mick Kennedy. Out of the blue, Mick said to me: "This could be my last game for Pompey." My response was: "Shut up, you must be joking," but Mick replied: "Bradford and Manchester City have come in for me. The club have accepted their offers and it's up to me to decide what I want to do." He was really upset about the whole affair. It seemed crazy to me at the time to be selling one of our best players, and my feeling was that perhaps this was the first sign that the chairman was about to bail out. As for the game at The Dell, it was probably the most enjoyable game I have ever played in, although I didn't have a lot to do. We were up for it, big time, but nevertheless Saints had a few internationals in their side, and had a very professional approach to things. It was a hard-fought derby and there wasn't too much between the sides. We rode our luck at times, but they didn't take their chances on the day. For Saints, Clarkie missed a lot that morning, as I often reminded him a few years later. It was the only real bright spot of that season. I had always wanted to play and beat Saints, particularly after the cruel way we had lost to them in the cup a few years earlier. Above all, it was something to give back to our supporters for the pain of that defeat and for what they suffered at the time.

We had a decent little FA Cup run too, kicked-off by a great win at Blackburn on the Saturday after our win at The Dell. Kevin Dillon scored the winner with an amazing volley from about 40 yards, in the second half, but not before he and Ballie had been involved in one of their regular 'disagreements' in the dressing room at half time. Sure enough, as soon as he had scored Dill headed for the bench to make his point to Ballie. This was just one of the occasional feuds which sprang up between Ballie and Dill, which was not surprising given the nature of their respective characters. I remember once Dill being substituted at half time, getting changed straight into his suit without even taking a shower, and slamming the door shut as he left the dressing room. Whereupon Ballie interrupted his team talk to slate Dill: "There he goes, look at him, what a fucking waste of time; he's a disgrace, just when we need everybody to pull together…" Ballie was interrupted in mid-sentence by Dill coming back in through the door, having been just outside, saying: "If you have got anything to say, say it to my face and not behind my back." A potential fracas was only avoided by some of the players shepherding Dill out of the dressing room and the bell sounding for the second half.

In that FA Cup run we got to the quarter-final and played at Luton, on their artificial pitch, at Kenilworth Road. We went away for the week before to train in Spain, but our preparations were to no avail. We were well below par that afternoon and all uncomfortable on that surface. I know I was never happy with my footholds that afternoon. I felt the teams that played on those surfaces in those days really had an unfair advantage. Luton had got their footwear worked out; they were familiar with the way the ball played and had evolved a system to use on it. To add to our problems, Quinny was sent off early in the second half for elbowing Steve Foster. It was a neat bit of play-acting by Fossie, who made a real meal of it. Quinny did have a go at him, but Fossie's over-reaction didn't help the situation.

We were in a fair amount of trouble at the bottom with half a dozen games left when my season came to an abrupt halt at Wimbledon. Ballie had really wound us up for it: "You can beat them. We're the better footballing side and that will count in the end. They will try and bully you for the first 20 minutes, but you must stand up and be strong." Well, we were just six minutes into those 20 minutes, when I really copped it. Wimbledon had a free kick in the centre circle, and, as you would expect, goalkeeper Dave Beasant came forward to launch the ball into our penalty area, somewhere roughly on the penalty spot. Their plan was to have the two big men, Eric Young and John Fashanu, ready to make runs across the area to attack the ball. I came out to catch the ball close to the penalty spot, but both of their lads came in with their elbows raised to protect their heads. It was not done deliberately – it was just the way they played – but they knew full well that it might injure somebody. Young arrived first, and my momentum carried me into his flailing elbow, with the result that my face was seriously damaged. The referee carried on playing with me down concussed, but when I was finally helped off I could feel the whole of my face swelling by the second. After getting to the dressing room, I was put in an ambulance and taken to the Accident and Emergency department at St James' Hospital which, ironically, was the nearest hospital when I was a schoolboy, and which was in the process of closing down.

My mother, along with my father and two sisters, was at the game, but she didn't really like watching me play through her fear of me getting hurt. So it was fortunate that, as it happened, she was so busy chatting beforehand that she was late into her seat for the game and missed the incident altogether. By the time she had noticed that I wasn't in goal, I was already in the ambulance – that avoided one potentially embarrassing situation in that she would probably have wanted to get in with me. My family did come down to the hospital, but the swelling was too great for anything to be done there and then. The x-rays confirmed that the bone under the eye-socket had been shattered and my nose broken. Apparently, I was fortunate that the eye-socket itself had not been broken. I overheard one doctor saying: "If it had been an inch higher, then it would have been his eye, with the orb shattered and the sight affected." I should have been admitted to hospital that night, but there were no beds available. So, when the Pompey coach turned up at the hospital, I was laid out on the back seat and taken to the Queen Alexandra Hospital in Portsmouth. I'll never forget the looks on the other players' faces when they saw me with my face double its normal size.

The lads were in high spirits after they had dug out a decent result drawing 2-2. Lee Sandford was very chirpy after going in goal and doing really well. He couldn't wait to tell me what an easy job it was. I was under observation for a couple of days, but nothing could be done until the swelling went down. Funnily enough, I never had any real pain from it, at least, not until just after the operation to put it all right. The procedure involved cutting in both under my eye and up under my lip so that the bone could be pushed up into position again. Then some wire had to be inserted, with gauze being packed in around the sinuses, to enable the bone to be held and kept in place. When eventually the wire and gauze were removed, under local anaesthetic, it transpired that the whole area was infected. The smell from the considerable amount of pus which emerged was just too much for me and I fainted in the hospital.

There was very little fuss about the incident, which had ended my season. I never heard from Wimbledon or Young and I never expected to. Some might have considered suing for the damage which had been inflicted on me. Certainly, if such an incident had occurred today and been seen and dissected on TV, then I feel Eric could have been in big trouble with the FA. As it was, the chairman took the matter up with a view to having Young charged with bringing the game into disrepute, but they wouldn't look at it. Given that the referee didn't caution Young, or even give a foul for the challenge, there was little chance of getting any sympathy. There were a lot of naughty challenges around in those days which went unpunished and I was probably not the only player to have cause for complaint during that time.

My testimonial year was well underway, with plenty of events being organised by my committee. But, whilst in hospital, I had to miss my dinner at Bognor and a snooker evening, starring Steve Davis, at the Portsmouth Guildhall. My ex-managers were invited to the dinner, and it was typical of Frank Burrows that he drove down from Cardiff to Bognor for the evening, and back the same night. I was due to have a testimonial match that season, and my committee had preliminary discussions with Celtic and Rangers, but it never got off the ground, simply because the chairman wouldn't sanction it. I would have to wait another six years for it, all told!

Gosney took over in goal and, with plenty of spirit in the side, we still felt we had a chance of staying up, particularly after that draw at Wimbledon. There were plenty of rumours around at that time that the club was to be put up for sale and that was unsettling for the players, although I was more worried about my own situation at the time. In the end we couldn't wriggle out of it and were relegated. We were only three wins short of staying up, as it turned out. The feeling between the players was that, after all the blood, sweat and tears it had taken over three years to get up, we had been massively betrayed. I certainly felt cheated that, other than one or two cut-price buys, there had been a lack of investment in the club. We knew that things weren't as they should have been between manager and chairman but felt that, if Ballie had been backed and given a fair crack of the whip, then he could have achieved something. But then, I suppose if Mr Deacon was not in a position to provide any substantial investment, then you can't really blame him.

So it was back to the second division for 1988/89, with a new owner in Jim Gregory, and he had brought in John Gregory as Ballie's assistant. Although I never saw any real problems between them, you could just tell that Ballie didn't really want Gregory around, but he had to make a go of working with him. Ballie toughed it out for as long as he could, but it was clear that he was swimming against the tide that season, and that it was only a matter of time before Gregory took over.

Physically my face had healed and was back to its normal ugly shape but, psychologically, I had to prove to the manager that it hadn't affected me. In pre-season there were plenty of extra crosses for me to deal with and lots of diving around at people's feet. I didn't have any worries that my confidence would be affected and I was lucky enough to remain in Ballie's plans. Ballie appointed Kevin Ball as skipper and, although he was inexperienced, it was a good choice. Kevin got on well with Ballie and had thrived under him. He led by example, was not scared to say what he thought, and having bigger names and more experienced players around didn't bother him. Unfortunately, he missed most of the season through injury, which was an inevitable consequence of the way he played. He was a bit raw at that time and never held back from making challenges in which he was liable to get hurt.

As the season unfolded my form was patchy and Ballie was clearly less than impressed with some of my performances. It all came to a head in October, at Scarborough, when a 3-1 defeat dumped us out of the League Cup on aggregate. We had a real row at half time about their first goal. I had come out of the penalty area to try to claim a long ball, didn't get there before their guy, who went round me and scored. At the break I was greeted by Ballie saying: "What the fuck were you doing there?", to which I replied: "OK, I made the wrong decision." That was the signal for me to go into a sulk and retreat to the toilets, where I spent the rest of the half-time interval whilst Ballie gave his team talk. In there I decided that I wouldn't come out for any more balls in the second half. The result was that Scarborough's other two goals were solely down to me and we had been hammered. The row soon blew over, illustrating once again that you could have an argument with Ballie, but it was soon forgotten. We had some good players that season, and none better than Warren Neill, who was probably the best right back I ever played with at Pompey. But we were an ill-disciplined outfit, full of fiery characters, some of whom, like Warren Aspinall, a record summer signing from Aston Villa, and Dill, had very short fuses, which did nothing to improve our disciplinary record. I don't know how Aspers got away with half the things he got up to on the field. As a player, to fight for the cause, he was someone you would always want on your side. He had his disciplinary problems, but the main trouble came off the field when he went out for a drink. After a few he was really 'in your face', with a knack of rubbing people up the wrong way.

Our disciplinary record took a turn for the worse when Ballie signed Gavin Maguire, who was a good player but an extremely complex character – always liable to do something stupid on or off the field. We simply couldn't predict what he was going to do next. He was skilful enough at the back to be able to beat a player before clearing the ball, but the problem was that he could not resist trying to repeat the trick, which would often get him into trouble. Although I wasn't there, evidence of his volatile nature came at the team's Christmas party, when Gavin arrived late during the meal. One of the young players, Mickey Ross, made some comment or other, to which Gavin responded by picking up a plate and throwing it directly at his face. Mickey was cut and bruised, but could have sustained a nasty eye injury. The incident didn't get back to the team management, however.

Four defeats in a row in January put paid to Ballie, who would probably have resigned anyway, but for the fact that there was money at stake from the balance of his contract. There was a feeling that Ballie had 'lost' the players' support, but it was more a case of him having 'lost' the chairman. It was yet another situation where a chairman had brought somebody in earlier, who, by his presence, would put pressure on the manager and hopefully lead to his eventual resignation.

Gregory immediately turned into an aloof, stern character and when he brought in Steve Wicks as coach, with a nice-guy approach, it was the classic 'good cop, bad cop' scenario. Wicks was a chirpy cockney-type but didn't impress any of us with his coaching. Gregory soon alienated the players by, amongst other things, introducing a ridiculous dress code for training every day. We had to appear clean shaven, but more importantly in a shirt and tie. Gregory announced the rule by saying: "If it's good enough for Glasgow Rangers then it's good enough for you." We just could not see what difference that made to the way we played. Soon we were having a laugh, by appearing in loud Mickey Mouse ties and I remember Mick Fillery once turning up in a smoking jacket with a cravat.

Gregory labelled us as a 'pub team' when he reflected on his time at Pompey in his own autobiography. That was probably down to our habit, encouraged by Ballie, but thoroughly disapproved of by Gregory, of loading crates of beer on to the coach for away games, for consumption on the way home. As far as we were all aware, it was common practice at that time, as a friendly gesture, for the home club to put a couple of crates on the away coach before they left for the return journey. Gregory, apparently, first became aware of our practice, asking Kevin Ball what he was doing, when he spotted him loading the crates, bought from the proceeds of a 'whip-round' amongst the players, on to the coach before our trip to Shrewsbury for the first game of the season. When the bottles came out on the coach on the way home, after our win, Gregory could be seen in his seat shaking his head and muttering: "But we've got a game on Monday afternoon against Leicester!" The fact that 48 hours later we won 3-0 probably didn't affect his view of the situation.

In fairness we were a team of individuals, almost kamikaze-like in our approach to games, who were in need of some discipline, but Gregory had a real problem earning the respect of the players. From day one he was looking for any opportunity to stamp his authority on things – dishing out fines galore for 'offences' such as being two minutes late for training. His inconsistency and contradictions didn't help his cause and he always had a problem with the three players – Warren Neill, Mike Fillery and Gavin Maguire – who had played with him at QPR. He would scold us for some habit or another, only for one of those lads to invariably come back with the retort: "He's a fine one to talk, he was always doing that himself at Rangers." Ballie had originally nicked Fillery from QPR on the back of a contractual error there, but Gregory certainly couldn't handle him. He was a very talented player, possibly overweight at times, who took some motivating. Just when Gregory had got him training harder than ever, the manager chose to slate him in the press – describing him as "a 60-minute man" – which, not surprisingly, totally destroyed the relationship.

Often, new managers are wary of players who have been at the club for what they consider to be 'too long', and associate that with some lack of ambition on a player's part. Gregory was of that breed, and when he challenged me on that score I would come back and say that at least it shows that I have got some loyalty to the club. Unusually, Gregory thought that it would help the team to bond if we all attended a church service at Portsmouth Cathedral. In a reference to this in his autobiography, as an example of our supposed resentment to the proposal, he reports me as having asked, when it was announced, whether it was compulsory to attend. I have to say I have no recollection whatsoever of having asked him that question. In late February 1989, I picked up a hip injury at Bournemouth in a collision with Graeme Hogg, missed the next game through the knock but couldn't regain my place from Gos until he too was injured some 14 games later. Whilst I was out of the side my mother, who had been seriously ill, passed away, which hit me hard. Not just her death, but the feelings that it subsequently invoked in me, meant that my mind was not completely focused on football during that awful time for myself and the family.

I was extremely homesick when I first came to Pompey and found it hard being away from home, even though I was regularly going back at the weekends. My mother was a very loving woman and I really missed her. After I had signed professional I made a conscious decision to try to detach myself from home life and to make a life for myself in Portsmouth in a bid to rid myself of the homesickness. I realised much later that my mother found that separation difficult. With hindsight, I had been selfish throughout my career in ignoring my parents and being so insular, by making football the be-all and end-all of my life. That was never more apparent than in the days before my mother died when, as a result of my pushing her out of my life, I was unaware of how ill she had been.

She had always suffered from asthma and, after having breathing difficulties, she was diagnosed as suffering from lung cancer. Even after she had collapsed at home and been admitted to hospital I was lax in visiting her. I eventually got up to the Brompton Hospital when I was told she was in a poor condition. On the night of my visit, there were plans to let her go home to die, with suitable provisions to make her comfortable. The extent of my selfishness over the years in pursuing my career, and in particular not being there for her over the previous couple of weeks, hit me hard. My mother clearly had that in mind when, in what transpired to be her last words to me, she said: "You can love someone, but it doesn't mean you have to like someone." I stayed up there that night, but 24 hours after I had got back I had a phone call from my sister to say that my mother had passed away. Her last words still upset me, but I try not to think about them, that way they don't hurt me. As it happened, my guilt was compounded by the fact that I had advised my father to go home and rest, so he wasn't with her when she died.

My father is now aged 83, but suffers from emphysema as a result of asbestosis, brought about by years working in old hospitals ripping off the lagging from the pipes. Ted is partially disabled, with breathing difficulties himself, and finds it difficult to get around. Through regularly coming down to watch me play he got to like the Portsmouth area and has now moved to Gosport from London to get the benefit of the better air on the coast. He's been coming to Fratton Park for years, but unfortunately his increasing disability meant that he didn't get to any matches at all last season.

I struggled through the grief of my mother's death by focusing once again on my football and what was left of the season. It was about this time that Barry Horne was transferred to Southampton, although he was not overly keen on the move. There are very few really thick footballers, who fit the public's stereotype of the profession. However, Barry was a little bit out of the ordinary, being a very intelligent, articulate guy, with a university degree. It was no surprise when he put his talents to good use through his involvement with the PFA. I had to admit though that John Beresford was an astute purchase by Gregory. Bes turned out to be a good attacking left back – when he was flying he could be every bit as devastating as Matthew Taylor. However, he had a lot of injury problems, pulling muscles in particular. Some players are like that and it's possibly down to their physique and particular muscle structure. We lost our last six games that season and I was back in the side for the last two after Gos got injured at West Brom. My contract was up for renewal that summer and I signed it just for the sake of it, bearing in mind that I had not played well that season and I was hardly likely to attract any bids.

Much to my surprise, Frank Burrows returned to the club as Gregory's assistant, replacing Wicks for the 1989/90 season. It was a strange marriage between the two, and I am not too sure how it came about. But I was happy to see Frank back for a continuation of our love/hate relationship and it meant that I could again have the advantage of the extra goalkeeping coaching which he provided. On his return Frank was still the same old disciplinarian, if somewhat mellowed, but he immediately struggled to handle the players at the club, many of whom were bigger names than he had been used to dealing with. Players like Mike Fillery, Warren Neill and Gavin Maguire, for instance, through their London big-club upbringings, just didn't respond to his aggressive style of management. By now a real rift between the players and the manager had developed. Gregory was way out of his depth. Even the players he had signed, like Kenny Black and John Beresford, had turned against him. We were not working together, there was little bonding between the squad members. There was no real friction, as such, between the players, but that spirit, which had been the secret of our success in previous years, had been effectively destroyed.

We had our worst start to a season for many years and things reached rock bottom with a 5-0 defeat at Wolves at the end of September. We were goalless at the interval, but they murdered us in the second half. That may have had something to do with what Kevin Ball said to the Wolves star striker Steve Bull as were going out again on to the field after half time. He said something on the lines of: "Go on, show us what you're made of then…" After that, they were coming at us from all directions with two goals late on from Bullie. One shot he struck past me was the hardest strike I have ever come across in a game. That rift with the manager had grown to such proportions that, after that hammering from Wolves, on the way home, led by Gavin Maguire, several of the players joined in an impromptu hokey-cokey down the coach in 'celebration', for the purposes of upsetting Gregory. It was a clear sign that he had totally lost our respect.

Guy Whittingham had broken into the side after leaving the army and it was obvious, right from the time of his two trials with the reserves, that he had something about him – you could just see that he had the goal-scoring knack. It seemed strange that nobody had picked him up previously, in his earlier non-league days. Guy was a very fit lad, with blistering pace, and a good pro who worked very hard at his game. His army background meant he was very disciplined in his approach, although he did find it something of a culture shock moving from the services to professional football. He was a terrific guy – no pun intended – and perhaps a bit too nice in some ways.

After a home defeat against Leicester, on New Year's Day 1990, Gregory was gone and Frank took over as caretaker until the end of the season. Immediately, the atmosphere changed; the players lightened up and everyone felt much more at ease. In his first game in charge we won at Stoke who, ironically, were being managed by Ballie, with a couple of new faces in the form of Mickey Hazard and Gary Stevens. Mickey was a very strange lad who, from day one, never seemed happy about being at Fratton Park. He certainly found it a big culture shock coming from Spurs, and always gave the impression that he felt he was a bit better than the level of ability he found at Pompey. As for Gary, he was getting over a serious knee injury he suffered at Spurs and was just happy to be playing again, but it wasn't long before the problem recurred.

Despite an indifferent season, when it was all over the chairman paid for us all to go to Fuengirola in southern Spain for a break, with youth team coach Malcolm Beard in charge, in Frank's absence. We were all generally well-behaved, but I remember doing an impression of Spiderman one night by leaping from one balcony to another, despite being on the hotel's sixth floor. It was all for the purpose of getting Guy's training shoes and throwing them down into the pool below. It wasn't until the next morning that Guy woke up to see what I had done to his shoes. Another funny incident surrounded Mark Chamberlain, who had been out all night and returned to the hotel around 5 am. Chambo had gone into the kitchen looking for an early breakfast, hoping to find some rolls. Unfortunately, the kitchen staff took him for one of the beach-sellers, who come from North Africa to pester the tourists with their wares and thought he was trying to steal from the kitchen. The result was that he was chased out of the hotel.

Frank was appointed manager for the 1990/91 season, but both the team and I had a poor start. After five games, I had conceded 11 goals and then, after we had lost 2-1 at Notts County to a last-minute goal, I found myself dropped for the first time in nearly ten years. Ironically, it was Frank again who was involved, just as he had been when, after that New Year's Day 1980 incident, he had brought Peter Mellor back into the side. This time I was really upset and felt Frank was taking the easy option in using me as a scapegoat for the team's overall performance at Meadow Lane. Having worked with me before, I felt that I was a soft target for Frank. In that match I felt I had been let down big-time by Gavin Maguire, who had a nightmare game, but Frank didn't have the courage to drop him. In his earlier days Frank wouldn't have had any qualms in dropping anyone. A hastily-written transfer request from me to Frank was just as quickly 'binned' by him. I had to grin and bear it for 16 games in all but, no sooner had I got back in the side, I was injured at Hillsborough. I broke a bone in my hand making a save, although I had gloves on. Neil Sillett, our physio, knew it was a broken bone as soon as I complained of the hand being numb. I carried on, but Wednesday scored their winner during that period. I got a hand to the shot but had no strength there with which to stop it and it was clear that I had to come off, although Frank was against it. As I was passing him in the dug-out he made his feelings known by calling me "a soft poof". I went to hospital with Sills and, in fairness, Frank did apologise to me later for that remark, when he realised the extent of the injury.

I was out for 15 games in all, including our mini FA Cup run, during which time Frank resigned and Tony Barton took over as caretaker. It was a bit of a surprise when we heard the news, on our way back from a day's racing at Cheltenham. Possibly Frank needed more time to get it right, but obviously you know when things are looking difficult for the manager. Mike Neasom rang me with the news and asked me who I thought should be the new boss. We were on the coach, having had a few drinks and I said, jokingly, that I was "happy for my hat to be put in the ring". Sure enough I got home to find that it was the headline in the newspaper that night and I had to wriggle out of it the next day and issue some denials. The lads responded well to Tony, who was a very nice, placid guy. He was a players' man, with no side to him at all, and I felt, with his success at Aston Villa in the European Cup behind him, he might get the manager's job if he did well to the end of that season. But, with only five wins out of 12, it was not enough and I know that Tony was bitterly disappointed not to get the job. It hit him hard and he left the club soon afterwards. His departure heralded the arrival of the 'Bald Eagle', Jim Smith and an era which was to bring some fantastic times for everybody but, ultimately, some huge disappointments.

*'The trouble is that if you're at
a club too long people take you
for granted.'*
                    Kevin Dillon

Suspicion that Pompey were not going to find the first division
all that it was cracked up to be probably came on the
publication of the fixture list in June 1987, which presented
the club with a first-day trip to mighty... Oxford; long-time
lower-division rivals. Even if, to be fair, chairman John Deacon
had invested quite significantly in the team following
promotion – £285,000 for Leeds' Ian Baird and £200,000 for
Brighton's Terry Connor being the most significant signings –
it was clear Pompey were short of top-flight class, or depth, at
least, from day one. The fact that Noel Blake had picked up a
knee injury in training and was out for at least six weeks meant
that Knight had to rely on makeshift centre half Paul Mariner
to help protect him at the Manor Ground and none of the four
goals that flew past him could be laid at the keeper's door. It
was a similar story when Chelsea wrecked Pompey's home
return to the first division with a 3-0 victory that was more
comfortable than the scoreline suggested. Baird too was
unable to help the cause to begin with, having still to serve a
two-match suspension held over from the previous season. It
was an unpromising start for Pompey, as well as for the new
striker, who also had his 'former Saint' tag to live down.
However, his subsequent less-than-complimentary
description of the set-up at the time had a ring of truth. Fratton
Park's newest stand, and the traditional roost of the club's
most fervent fans, the Fratton End, had been half-shut since
1986 and not even the increased revenues first division
football would bring could get plans to renovate it off the

ground. The beautifully proportioned Archibald Leitch masterpiece, the South Stand, was largely unchanged – save for essential fire–safety work post-Bradford, which ruined its character – since it was opened in 1925. The North Stand hadn't been seriously altered since seats were installed in the early 1950s. Let's call the place decrepit instead.

The news got worse, as Blake's injury turned out to be more serious than first thought and Christmas was now the earliest he could be expected to return. Malcolm Shotton's stop-gap signing from Oxford was the first sign that Deacon's fortune was drying up and even a reasonable spell of form in September and October, which saw the team attain the heady heights of 11th, was offset by the fact that Baird was struggling to adapt to life at Fratton. The club were prepared to sell him back to Leeds for a cut-price fee, but the problem was compounded as the crocked Connor had yet to start a game. In addition, Pompey had been dumped out of the League Cup – in its Littlewoods guise – by second-division Swindon.

Promotion had failed to spark public interest – in part due to police insistence on the majority of games being all-ticket – and gates were only marginally up on the previous season. In November, Deacon announced the wage-bill had to be cut by a third. Mick Quinn's refusal to sign for Millwall, in a £300,000 deal brokered during the summer, was cited as a key reason for the growing financial crisis. On the pitch, Knight was increasingly exposed as injuries continued to bite. Shotton succumbed to a long-term knock and Billy Gilbert and Lee Sandford were added to the sick list. Nottingham Forest whacked five without reply past Knight in November, although there was a brief respite, as clean sheets against Norwich and Coventry garnered four points, which kept Pompey's head just above the automatic relegation places.

As the calendar turned from 1987 to 1988 the bubbling crisis at the club finally spilled over. The players were banned from talking to the press – and The News in particular – after a spate of sensational headlines highlighting the parlous state of the club's finances and a post-match bust-up between Ball and an unnamed player, following the 1-1 draw with Watford on December 28. As he was dropped, it seemed that Kenny Swain had paid the price for revealing the dressing room argument, as Pompey picked up a point against Arsenal – it would have been three but for a late penalty miss by Kevin Dillon – and then cruised to victory in the south-coast derby. Mick Kennedy's transfer to Bradford took the gloss off that result and the dressing room unrest came to the fore again as Dillon's granite look, after having secured a 2-1 FA Cup win at Blackburn with his wonder volley, only hinted at his crossed swords with Ball at half time. Amid the chaos, Knight finally shone, producing a series of acrobatic saves to secure a 0-0 draw at Chelsea. Through no fault of his own, however, Pompey's whipping-boy reputation was doing his hopes of impressing the England set-up no good at all, but at least the eye of the storm seemed to have passed. A win over Derby in early February lifted Pompey five points clear of the drop-zone and Kennedy's return to Fratton in the fifth round of the FA Cup saw Pompey cruise into the quarter finals for the first time since 1952. Knight too was getting down to business in his testimonial year, with the inevitable round of raffles, race nights and sportsmen's dinners, and his benefit match, it seemed, might yet be organised against the backdrop of a successful campaign against relegation.

Of course, it couldn't last. News of a £750,000 unpaid tax bill, and a consequent winding up order by the Inland Revenue, shattered the fragile optimism a ten-match unbeaten run had generated, far more comprehensively than the way unbeaten, runaway league leaders Liverpool ended the on-field run at Fratton in late February. Baird's 'Fratton hell' was finally ended with a £185,000 move back to Leeds, but not surprisingly, there was no replacement. Pompey were running on empty and not even another sterling performance by Knight at Sheffield Wednesday – which prevented a defeat of 'disastrous proportions' according to Neasom – could avert a 1-0 loss. The pick of the saves was a one-handed effort to deny a deliberately-placed Lee Chapman header in the first half. Knight also joined an exclusive club in April, as he made his 300th league appearance at Everton, but by the time Knight's season was ended by Eric Young's forearm at Plough Lane, ten days later, Pompey were all but doomed. Andy Gosney was in goal as a dodgy penalty at Coventry ensured defeat and put even the possibility of finishing in the newly-instituted relegation play-off place for the fourth-bottom side virtually beyond them. Deacon was also off. The Southampton-based property magnate had finally run out of the money and energy needed to sustain the club and he sold his interest to Jim Gregory, the former QPR chairman.

Suddenly it was all go at Fratton as the new broom arrived in June. The redundant upper-tier of the Fratton End was demolished – and a replacement promised – while both the north and south stands were given a major overhaul. Ball was, ominously for him, re-designated chief coach, with John Gregory appointed as his assistant. Ball was given a transfer budget, however, spending £150,000 on Manchester United defender Graeme Hogg, £200,000 to land former England winger Mark Chamberlain and a club-record £325,000 on the eve of the season to sign Aston Villa's stormy petrel Warren Aspinall. Early on it seemed to click. A 4-0 home win over Leeds, featuring ex-favourites Noel Blake and Vince Hilaire, not to mention a red-carded Ian Baird, put Pompey top of the table. A 3-1 defeat at home to Hull took some of the gloss off the start and Knight was back in the wars at Stoke, where another Pompey old-boy, Nicky Morgan, accidentally caught his now-recovered face. From the incident, Simon Stainrod scored the equalising goal. 'I was too groggy to think about Wimbledon, but I suppose it looked pretty bad from the stands. It was fortunate really. Nicky caught me just behind the ear, but it gave me a heck of a headache,' commented a rueful Knight.

Ball's tenure was undeniably compromised by the aggregate Littlewoods Cup defeat against league new-boys Scarborough in October, in which's Knight's first-half misjudgement and subsequent sulk, contributed to all three goals conceded in the decisive return leg. However, in the league the team continued to pick up points and returned to the top of the table in mid-November, after a 3-0 demolition of Barnsley, at Fratton Park. Meanwhile, Knight was approaching a significant personal milestone as Pompey's longest-serving goalkeeper – no doubt something assistant coach Gregory would have noted with suspicion – although the grapevine had Ball searching elsewhere for a goalkeeper. Hull's Welsh international Tony Norman had impressed in the Tigers' 3-1 win earlier in the season, but Ball was adamant there was nothing in it: 'I haven't inquired about Norman and that's all I can say. Alan Knight is the number one here and has been playing well. Gos has also been outstanding for the reserves and I believe he may have turned a personal corner. Goalkeepers tend to mature later than outfield players and I think he's perhaps lacked a little ambition, but I sense a new attitude from him this time and he's beginning to really push for a chance,' he said at the time. The manager even gave Gosney a rare run out in the Simod Cup tie with Hull but, new attitude or not, his luck was out as he ended up dislocating a finger, which ruled him out for four weeks and gave latest prodigy Alan Gough the chance to sample reserve football. Gosney had a novel way of keeping match-fit: he turned out as a striker for the second string.

Knight also had the misfortune of seeing a shot by Blackburn striker Howard Gayle slip from his grasp and over the line to give promotion rivals Blackburn a decisive edge, in a clash at Ewood Park. The eventual 3-1 defeat knocked Pompey off the top of the table and the season was soon drifting into freefall. Four consecutive league defeats, and an FA Cup exit at the hands of Swindon, over the holiday period gave Jim Gregory the chance to pull the plug on Ball's reign as manager and namesake John stepped up to take charge for the home game with Shrewsbury. Pompey had slumped to twelfth place and badly needed a victory to rekindle their promotion hopes. The automatic places were looking a long shot, but the still-fresh concept of the play-offs was a more than realistic target. Gregory got his win – 2-0 – and chairman Jim was in the press three days later to reveal plans for a £10 million stadium redevelopment on the Fratton railway goods-yard site. For the supporters, well accustomed to false dawns, both of these were to prove no different to the rest.

No points and a solitary goal in February meant Pompey's promotion hopes were dead and Gregory's 'get tough' policy with the players continued apace, with Lee Sandford picking up a fine of a weeks wages for getting sent off for the reserves. Knight was also suffering, as a collision with his own centre half Hogg, at Bournemouth, meant he missed the following matches against Ipswich and Plymouth with a damaged groin. That disappointment was nothing compared to his surprise when Gosney – albeit impressive in both games – kept his place in goal after he had recovered. It left Knight stranded four matches short of that all-time Pompey goalkeeping appearance record of 334 league games, held by John Milkins. 'I suppose I've got to trot out the old cliché that I'm going to fight to get my place back, but it's a fact,' he told the *Sports Mail*. 'But I'm not the sort to make trouble, I'm going to have a chat with the manager next week to see how the land lies,' he added. Boss Gregory, however, insisted Knight would be offered a new contract, when his existing agreement came to an end in June.

Gosney was certainly given ample opportunity to show what he could do as the team became more adept at collecting red cards than wins. Gregory's 'clean up' campaign had come to the attention of the players' union chief Gordon Taylor, who was busily warning the manager off any more fines, but his desire to instil more discipline into Ball's 'pub team' at least enabled him to off-load Billy Gilbert and Kevin Dillon, as their contracts came to an end. Knight also regained his place, as Gosney badly injured his knee ligaments at West Brom, and he was able to get within a game of Milkins' record, as champions Chelsea – managed by none other than Bobby Campbell – brought the curtain down on a bitterly disappointing season, by recording Pompey's sixth straight league defeat.

Gosney's injury meant that Knight, having put pen to paper

for another three years at Fratton Park, would start the season as first choice; it would be late September before Gos returned to the reserves. That left Knight with just the problem of what to call Gregory's new assistant, Frank Burrows, to worry about: 'I wasn't sure what to call him. When he was here before it was simple. He was "boss",' he explained at the time. In the end 'coach' sufficed, but only for the time being as it turned out. Gregory's reign was fast falling into chaos, as Pompey clocked up just two victories before November. The 'replacement' for fans' favourite striker Mick Quinn, who had exercised his freedom of contract and signed for Newcastle in the summer, was an underwhelming Jimmy Gilligan from Cardiff, although Guy Whittingham was establishing himself, having arrived the previous May for the £250 it took to buy him out of the army. He grabbed the goal which secured that second win at Bournemouth, but the victory was largely down to Knight's saves, as his manager acknowledged: 'This season he's been having a very, very good time. There have been the odd mistakes, but everyone has those. Some of his saves have been absolutely fantastic. He certainly did his bit to get us that win at Bournemouth and that's been the case several times this season. As a shot-stopper I don't think there are many better anywhere,' Gregory told the *Sports Mail*. Knight was closing in on his 350th league appearance and had targeted Jimmy Dickinson's all-time record of 764. Gregory added: 'Whether he makes it is really up to Alan himself. If he looks after himself there is no reason why he shouldn't have another ten years at the top. He's only 28 and when you look at people like Shilton, Parkes and Burridge, it's easy to see Knight has a great deal in front of him.'

Knight's form was also accredited to the return of Burrows, who recalls now how he was initially surprised how Knight had let himself go: 'When I left the club, Alan was a bushy-tailed, bright, talented young man, with the world at his feet. I lost contact with him but when I came back as coach and manager again, a few years later, I was disappointed to find he had clearly let his standards drop a bit. I pulled him in and told him that the player I was looking at was not the player I had left; that, as a senior player, I expected him to show more responsibility for his fitness and discipline and that he should not put his job at risk. To Alan's credit, he responded well, worked very hard and soon looked fitter and sharper. He was one of my successes in my second spell at the club. I don't interfere with players' personal lives but you've got to have discipline in sport. I treat players like men, but if Alan had let me down then he would have soon known about it,' he said.

Any initial uncertainty Knight may have had over Burrows' title was removed in early January, when Gregory's evident loss of control of the Fratton dressing room – five transfer requests in November, including that of Gosney, told its own story – saw him lose his job after less than 12 months and Burrows took temporary charge. A couple of encouraging results saw him given the job until the end of the season, and a second request by Gosney was given as short a shrift by Burrows as his predecessor.

But Knight was the man with the shirt and he continued to draw praise for his performances, notably a point-saving one at home to promotion-chasing Newcastle, who were managed by Jim Smith, spearheaded by Quinn and orchestrated by Dillon. After the game, which ended 1–1, the old pals' act delivered suitable praise: 'Knightsie's always done well when I've played against him,' said Quinn. 'I don't think people down there realise what a good shot-stopper he is. There aren't many better anywhere.' However, perhaps Dillon's comments were the more telling. 'I think he's been with Pompey too long. He should have moved on. The trouble is that, if you're at a club too long, people take you for granted and that's the case with Alan.' It was difficult to argue with Dillon's assessment, but Knight was back for pre-season training, with Burrows now installed permanently, after a nine-match unbeaten run at the end of the season staved off relegation comfortably. In fact, it was Gosney who had become the more restless, understandable given his lack of opportunities, but he too was still around come August 1990 and he soon got his chance.

Pompey started the season slowly, largely because the team was shipping goals at an alarming rate. Knight had been especially culpable during a 4-2 home defeat by Port Vale and the axe fell after the next game, a last-minute 2-1 defeat at Notts County. Gosney was in for the south-coast derby with Brighton, but was unable to prevent another defeat. However, Knight's undisputed reign was over. His feeling of being made a scapegoat for Pompey's start was reflected in his feelings at the time: 'I suppose Frank had to do something. We had conceded 11 goals in five games after all, but I don't think they were all down to me by a long chalk,' he moaned to the *Sports Mail*. A week later, his transfer request was slapped on Burrows' desk and shredded in front of him, but the keeper had softened from his initial stance, when he was prepared to bombard the club with requests until they let him go. 'There's no point. I understand Frank's decision and accept it. In any case I'm not the sort of person who can stay in a huff for too long,' he said. Whispers that Newcastle may be interested in signing him proved to be no more than that, so it was back to a diet of reserve-team football. David Pleat, then manager at Leicester, reportedly watched him in a number of Football Combination matches and Wimbledon, how ironic would that have been, also sniffed around, without taking matters further. By the end of November though, Knight was back, after two defeats and six goals conceded by Gosney had plunged the team back into the relegation zone. It was to prove a short stay as a broken hand at Sheffield Wednesday, on December 29, put Gosney back in the spotlight. Interestingly, on the same day Burrows attempted to prick Knight's conscience when his New Year resolutions for his squad were published in the *Sports Mail*. His wish for Knight? 'To give up the lager and the fags... some hope!'

By the time Knight was fit again, Burrows was part of Pompey's history once more, as he resigned in mid-March with the team hovering above the relegation zone. Knight had also missed a mini FA Cup run, ended by Paul Gascoigne's brace of goals for Spurs, at Fratton, in the fifth round. Taking temporary charge was chief scout Tony Barton, a former Pompey winger in the 1960s, and one of his first jobs was to bring back Knight, after Gosney endured a miserable evening at Barnsley, letting in a couple of soft goals in a 4-0 defeat. With Pompey in the thick of the relegation battle, however, Barton wouldn't want to have dwelt on the fact Knight had yet to appear in a winning team during the season. A 1-0 home defeat to Newcastle on his return kept that unwanted run going, but a 4-1 victory over Bristol City on Easter Saturday eased the pressure and, in the end, Pompey cruised to safety, although a 3-1 surrender at Wolves on the final day of the season almost certainly put paid to Barton's hopes of getting the job on a permanent basis. Knight was by now part of the fixtures and fittings at Fratton Park. Potential had finally given way to pragmatism as palindromic as the sound of the Pompey Chimes. Pompey could depend on Knight, a handful of games away from a 400th league appearance, and Knight could depend on Pompey.

6 - So near, so far

I was intrigued by Jim Smith's appointment, and you had to respect his record in the game. With no disrespect to the likes of Frank and Ballie, here was a manager who had worked at big clubs and achieved things in football. He had a real presence, was a tremendous motivator, and there was a fear factor among the players, borne out of respect for the man. As always when a new manager arrives, everybody was out to impress. Every player raised their game, were very much sharper in training, and the tackles were flying in as individuals looked to make their mark. Jim obviously looked hard at what he had inherited and it must have been immediately apparent to him that he had a good bunch of kids coming through. He set out to encourage them and clearly felt that it was the right time for them to come in. It took some courage to put them in and he was certainly brave to go with them for the opening game at Blackburn in August 1991. He got rid of the 'dead wood' and in came the likes of Andy Awford, Kit Symons, Darren Anderton and Darryl Powell, with Stuart Doling added for the first home game.

It worked out well for me because I had played with many of the youngsters during my longish spell in the reserves the previous season and I was well aware what an effective partnership Awfs and Kit had formed. As for Shaggy (Anderton), initially he was a quiet, somewhat withdrawn lad, but a real athlete and very fit. He had played in the youth and reserve teams without making any real impact, but then suddenly he really began to blossom and struck some amazing form. I had taken notice of him for the first time during a reserve game against Brighton – he was on fire that afternoon – and I began to feel that he had a real chance of making it. Physically, he was still a bit on the fragile side when he broke into our first team and even then was prone to injury, as some players can be. He worked hard in training, pushed his body to the absolute limit and it told eventually. Without the injury problems he has experienced in his career, which first attracted that unfortunate 'sicknote' label at Pompey, I feel sure he could have been an even better player at the top level and an established international.

Midfielder Chris Burns had been signed from non-league Cheltenham during the summer, where he had been working as a bricklayer while playing football part-time. Jim gave him his chance at the start of the 1991/92 season and, knowing his background, our fans took to Chris straight away. He was a down-to-earth guy who gave an honest 100%. He was not the most gifted player in the world but he worked hard and played out of his skin for a while. However, he simply couldn't sustain that level of performance. In reality, he wasn't good enough at our level and it caught up with him in the end.

It was early on in that season , during a goalless draw against Brighton at home, that I put on what I consider to be my best performance for Pompey. Brighton murdered us that afternoon but I managed to get something on everything they threw at me. I was the first person to get ten out of ten in the player ratings in the local paper, but I was sorry that, for once, Mike Neasom was not there to report on the game and rate my performance. He was away at the cricket with Hampshire for the Nat West final at Lord's and, with his reputation for being less than generous with his ratings, I would have loved to have seen what he would have given me.

Our FA Cup run started modestly at Exeter, where Ballie was now manager, and it was obviously a potential banana skin for us. It looked like going to a replay at Fratton, before Aspers popped up at the death with a far-post header, to win it. None of us had any expectations at all of doing well in the cup – we had been far too accustomed to getting knocked out early on. It was just nice to have the experience of being in the draw for the next round. Leyton Orient at home was the Shaggy show, with two fabulous strikes highlighted on TV's *Match of the Day*. Terry Venables fell in love with him that weekend and Shaggy was well on the way to becoming a household name. We were very disappointed to draw Middlesbrough in the fifth round. Other than the home advantage, there was nothing glamorous about it and they were a very difficult side to beat. We got our noses in front, but they squeezed an equaliser two minutes from the end and we had to go back to Ayresome Park for a replay. I didn't fancy our chances; it was a horrible place to go and from my experience we never had any luck whatsoever up there. I wasn't alone in my pessimism; no-one seemed to give us any chance and that may have extended to Middlesbrough, who seemed to take us too lightly on the night.

To prove how wrong you can be, it turned out to be one of the best nights of my career and possibly the best performance from a Pompey side in my time. There were two great strikes from Clarkie, who was a far better player than people gave him credit for, and another show from Shaggy, which included a freakish goal from a corner. It was simply one of those nights when everything goes right for you. Afterwards we all went out in a northern town and several of us got drunk. I was late getting up in the morning and it was only through Sills dragging me out of bed that I made it for the flight back.

By now, having reached the quarter-finals, we were starting to think that anything could happen. We were reasonably pleased with our draw, at home to first division Nottingham Forest but, with Brian Clough in charge, we knew it would be tough and that they would be expected to beat us. There was a lot of razzmatazz in the build-up to the game and Fratton Park was packed. We scored in the first couple of minutes through Alan McLoughlin (Macca) and then had to hang on for the rest of the game. We defended so well, but the Fratton End clock has never moved as slowly as it did that afternoon. I know, I kept a close eye on it from the other end. Everybody remembers the reaction save I made from a glancing header from Stuart Pearce in the second half, when I was able to get across and palm away his shot with my left hand. It might not have been the very best save of my career, but it was probably the most important. Afterwards, we were physically and mentally drained, but everyone was so chuffed with what we had achieved and overcome with the thought that we were potentially just one game from Wembley. Our success through the rounds had bred a great team spirit and, with a decent manager and a good blend of youth and experience, we began to believe that anything was possible. No-one was worried who we drew in the semi-final that night, but, when the draw came round, Liverpool were the one team we most wanted to avoid and there's no doubt we would have been more than happy to have taken on Sunderland or Norwich instead.

With everything in and around the club and the city focused on the semi-final, it was very difficult to concentrate on the league, although in the six matches in between, results were pretty good, mainly because everyone wanted to do well in order to get a place in the side at Highbury. We had a press day at the Meon Valley Country Club during the week before the game and then retreated to a hotel in St Albans to get away from the frenzy. At the time, our second child, Rebekah, had just been born but, unfortunately, was quite poorly. Jennifer was unwell too, with complications following the birth. It was a worrying time for us and more than an unfortunate distraction for me. The press got hold of the story and even went so far as to suggest that, such was my state of mind, I might not play. As it was, Jennifer couldn't join the other wives for the weekend away.

Jim had decided to play a deep defensive system, in effect defending from the edge of our penalty area, so that Liverpool wouldn't be able to penetrate us. He toyed with the idea of playing Gavin Maguire at Highbury, but that soon became a non-starter when we put the system into effect on the training ground. Gavin just couldn't get his head around how we were going to play, got frustrated and then got the hump. As for the system itself, it was a great success in both games and Liverpool couldn't break us down. In each, they had eventually run out of ideas and at the final count we had made the better chances.

We were held up in traffic getting to the game for the noon Highbury kick off and that, coupled with the thousands of our fans walking in the roads around the stadium, meant that we arrived later than planned. I was just so desperate to get out there and, above all, to get my first touch of the ball. I suppose I was a little bit more nervous than usual. You're not human if you are not affected by an occasion like that. But if you allow the nerves to get too much of a hold, then there is a danger that you will freeze. But I don't think any one of the side were affected by nerves in either game, at least until the penalties in the replay that is. Forty-eight hours after Highbury we were right back down to earth, looking for league points at Prenton Park, playing Tranmere in front of 6,000. Not surprisingly, we lost 2-0 and their vital second came when I miscued a drop-kick clearance and Tony Thomas volleyed the ball back over my head from what was reported to be 45 yards. I believe the goal features on one of those football gaffes' videos, but it was just one of those things. Credit to the player, but nine times out of ten I'd have got away with it.

After the Villa Park replay we had to play seven league games in just over three weeks and we were unable to keep our play-off dreams alive. As the season closed, we went to St James' Park to face a Newcastle side fighting for their lives against relegation. Kevin Keegan – their Messiah – had just arrived as manager and there was a great atmosphere, with a full house singing his praises. In that set-up, I really wanted to spoil the party, to send them down. We fought hard, but went down 1-0, to a good goal from David Kelly, five minutes from time. My attitude that day had nothing to do with Newcastle or Keegan, it was just the way I always approached such occasions. It's the way I believe every player should approach such games – some players have that sort of psyche and some don't. I remember, a couple of years later, playing West Brom at Fratton Park in the last game of the season, with thousands of their fans in the ground. They needed to win to stay up and we had nothing to play for. West Brom won 1-0, and survived but, quite honestly, some of our players were thinking about their holidays that afternoon. I suppose, in turn, Pompey have been the beneficiaries of that sort of attitude from other teams on occasions, but it doesn't sit easily with me.

Before the start of the 1992/93 season – Smith's second – Andy Gosney left for Birmingham after eleven seasons trying to take my place in goal. That season goalkeepers were also confronted with their biggest challenge yet. For some time the powers-that-be had been considering what to do about the backpass, which they felt enabled teams to waste time unduly. Now it had been decided to outlaw picking up the ball altogether. Early on that put most keepers in a state of panic. Many, including myself, started to think: "Oh God, I can't kick a ball straight", which left us, for safety's sake, fly-hacking it into Row Z and drawing an ironic cheer from the fans. It was a mental thing with many goalkeepers and it took some time for a lot of us to get confident and comfortable with our kicking. Some may argue I never achieved this! It certainly changed the game radically for keepers and also made the game a lot quicker. It's funny now, looking back to the old days when defenders could pass the ball back and we could pick it up, to see all the time-wasting which went on. I have to say it shows, in the end, that its introduction was a good thing for the game.

Everybody goes into a new season aiming to make a bid for promotion, to be there or thereabouts, after getting to the magic 50 points, of course. I suppose we were more hopeful than usual, after our previous season's exploits. Jim was looking for the younger players to improve and build on the experience gained in what was their first season. To their credit, people like Kit and Awfs did come on in leaps and bounds and a further major piece of the jigsaw was added when Paul Walsh came from Spurs. When Walshie arrived, people trotted out the usual patter about a 30-year-old player coming towards the end of his career who looking for one last pay-day. His appearance, with the long, blond, flowing hair, gave him the aura of a 'poser' type, but that was way off the mark, for there was no more committed player at the club. Walshie was a dedicated professional with a single-minded approach to his career, which he has carried into his business life after injury forced him to retire. I had met him previously in England parties and knew him as a likeable guy, who was a very funny 'cheeky chappie'.

I can honestly say that Walshie was the best player I ever played with and, even to this day, I rate him above players I have worked with subsequently and that includes Robert Prosinecki and Paul Merson. Walshie's skill and speed were second to none for me. He was certainly the most skilful with the ball at his feet I have ever seen – on his day he could beat teams on his own. His superb close control in taking players on enabled him to turn them inside out. For pace, I would compare him to Arsenal's Thierry Henry in today's game and you can add to that his astonishing work-rate, which was a tribute to his fitness. In the air, he had a good spring, which meant that he won more than his fair share of headers and could score goals with his head. Walshie was the perfect partner for Whittingham at the time and Guy would willingly admit that without him he wouldn't have scored as many goals as he did that season. Guy was quick too, so with Walshie's vision and ability it was a formidable partnership. However, with that all-round ability, I felt Walshie should have scored more goals in his career. His goals-per-game ratio didn't match his ability and that may have prevented him earning more England caps.

When Guy grabbed a hat-trick in our opening game at Bristol City, in which I had a shocker for some reason, it was obvious that he was going to get his fair share of goals, to put it mildly. Guy and Walshie developed a telepathy as the season went on, such that they seemed to be able to read each other's games. You need a top goalscorer if you are going to achieve anything and we certainly had one in Guy that season. His amazing record of 49 goals in total speaks for itself. His pace was extraordinary and much of that was down to the sprint training he obtained from a local athletics coach. That pace was a big part of his game, but once that left him towards the end of his career he was struggling as a striker. Typically, Guy was professional and disciplined enough to adapt his game accordingly and go on to play in midfield in the Premiership with Sheffield Wednesday. People ask me who was the best Pompey striker I ever played with. It's close, a toss of a coin almost, but, with no disrespect to two great players, I would just go for Mick Quinn. He was more of a natural goalscorer than Guy, a real 'sniffer' of chances anywhere around the box.

By now, my promised testimonial was well overdue and I kept going in and asking when it could be played. Finally, I got to see the chairman Jim Gregory, for what turned out to be a strange meeting. I just couldn't get a straight answer. He told me: "I don't believe in testimonials and I'd rather give you the cash," but he clearly wasn't going to do anything of the sort. He was intransigent, to say the least, despite my pushing the fact that it had been promised to me some years previously. I did get a lecture from him about all the difficult 'big-name' players, like Rodney Marsh, who had not been able to get the better of him. What that was supposed to convey to me, I'm still not sure. It was frustrating but, in fairness, it was a situation which Jim Gregory and Jim Smith had inherited. When I reported back to the boss, he said he would keep battling away at the chairman to get it sorted but, as it transpired, he had little more success than I did.

We were involved in the Anglo-Italian Cup that season which produced some 'interesting' games, to say the least, both here and in Italy. For me, it was fascinating to experience the different styles and play against foreign players who were often more technically gifted. For all that, most of the games were horrible and full of bad feeling. The Italians simply didn't like our tackling, particularly when studs were showing. They made it difficult for the referees by making a meal of every challenge and, if the challenge was above knee-high, then all hell would be let loose. There was also a lot of spitting in your face, which was not too well received here, as you can imagine. We didn't get too many foreign trips so we enjoyed some nice little breaks in Italy which, each time, gave us a few days away from the pressures of the league, even if the football wasn't too great. The most memorable, if only for the setting, was in Bari, where we played in a quite magnificent stadium built for the 1990 World Cup. It had a 60,000 capacity, but on the night we played it had just under 1,000 fans inside. More than 300 of them were ours, dotted around the upper tiers of one stand. It wasn't exactly the most prestigious competition in the world and clubs didn't usually put out their strongest eleven. Players were often anxious to avoid injury and this game, in particular, was more like a pre-season friendly.

Before the season was more than a few weeks old, Martin Kuhl was suddenly sold to Derby and it upset the fans, who saw it as a sign of the club's lack of ambition. It was a good move for him, as his contract was due to run out at the end of the season. The game was changing as far as contracts were concerned and players were beginning to have to move to improve their lot. There was nothing sinister about the transfer at all. The club had a good offer and, although Kuhlie was captain, we were well-covered in his midfield position. I was very pally with him, and he reminded me of Mick Kennedy in that he used to get very fired up and was very passionate in the way he played. Kuhlie was a good, honest player, a driving force for us in midfield, who had problems with his weight and had to work hard to keep fit. We called him 'Spit the Dog', for his habit of continually spitting, not at people I hasten to add, but on the ground, during a game.

The club were having problems with Stuart Doling at this time, which was a shame as Stuart was a fantastic young player with great ability. He was in and out of the first team, but had two troublesome injuries at inopportune times which brought him considerable frustration and caused him to really go off the rails. Neil Sillett publicly called him 'a problem child' and he and I took Stuart under our wings. At one time he was something of a surrogate son to me, staying with us on a regular basis. It's my experience that talented players often have complex personalities and Stuart had a real self-destructive streak. He had personal problems from a very young age, shortly after his father died. He didn't like living away from home, even though home was only a few miles away at Lyndhurst, in the New Forest. He was drinking far too much when he was injured and then, to cap it all, went AWOL at Christmas for a couple of weeks. Inevitably, he was released by the club eventually and ended up in non-league, close to home. There was still a drinking culture, of sorts, within this group of players, but with nothing like the sort of intake we managed in the 80s, when we were out every lunchtime. Now our outings were restricted to one night – Wednesday – per week when seven or eight of us would meet up at somewhere like Martines in Guildhall Walk, near the centre of the city. Our exploits brought plenty of public feedback to the club and every now and again Jim would give us his 'obligatory chat', to remind us of the rules regarding acceptable behaviour.

There has been some controversy in recent times about gambling amongst players. With the amounts being earned in the game, the consequent losses tend to take on dramatic proportions. I am not one little bit interested in gambling or horse-racing, although I enjoy the 'social' side of it, if we have a day out at Cheltenham, for instance. You will always find a group of players, at any club, who like a punt and, in fact, many of the managers too. Over the years I recall people like Joe Laidlaw, Micky Quinn, Mick Channon, Gary Stanley and, more recently, Durns, Awfs and Sills being particularly into it. Of course, Steve Claridge's exploits have been well-documented. I remember Steve winning £40,000 at Cheltenham during one of our trips, but you only got to hear of the large winnings. You rarely heard of the times when players lost a week's wages for instance. When I first started in the first team there were big card schools on the coach to away games which really got out of hand. People were losing a week's wages and more and, the longer the trip, the worse it got. It was the worst preparation possible for a game for a player to go out to play with a big loss hanging over him and Frank Burrows stopped it altogether.

We were live on TV one Sunday afternoon, early on in that season, against West Ham and I had the distinction of being named man of the match by summariser Jimmy Greaves, despite my mistake being responsible for the only goal of the game, which was the Hammers' winner. It was a horrible goal – a ball was played forward to the edge of our area and I came for it, whilst calling to Awfs to "leave it". He ducked, but the ball hit him on his oversized backside and squirted away from me. Clive Allen was able to latch on to it and score a good goal from an acute angle. We had a battering in the second half which enabled me to make a string of saves and recover some dignity.

Soon after that came that notorious game at Oxford which ended 5-5 and prompted Jim to say afterwards: "We will rue this result." The Manor Ground was not one of my favourite grounds and I remember Jim and Graham Paddon devising a special routine for our corner kicks, to ensure we were not caught on the break because Oxford left so many players upfield for corners. We started off unbelievably, going 3-0 up at one stage during the first half. Oxford were clearly embarrassed and gave it a good go in the second half, but we were still coasting the game at 5-2. Oxford did pull one back to make it 5-3 with just over ten minutes left, however. We were into the final minute at that score, when Warren Neill went down with an injury to waste time, and came off. Jim put on Stuart Doling at right back and immediately, with his first tackle, Stuart lunged in and gave away a penalty. They scored from it and it was 5-4 and we were into injury time. Gavin Maguire asked the ref how long was left and he told him: "Once you've kicked off there'll only be seconds left before the game's over. If you put the ball into a corner that'll give me the chance to blow." So the ball was played back to Gavin from our kick off, but unfortunately he mishit the clearance and it sailed straight through to their goalkeeper. He launched it down field again to the edge of our box, with everybody expecting the whistle to go any second. The ball bounced around the edge of our box, all the Oxford players having come forward for it, and there was an almighty scramble with several blocks. I got to block one shot but the ball flew out to one of their guys who poked it in. We kicked off yet again and then it was the end of the game – the most freakish I have ever played in.

Jim went absolutely ballistic in the dressing room afterwards, telling us, in no uncertain fashion, amongst a stream of expletives, that we had done well, got ourselves in a great position in the game, but had then been thoroughly unprofessional and thrown it away. He forecast there and then, as I've said, that it would come back to haunt us and plenty of people subsequently have pointed to the two points dropped that night as the reason why we didn't go up automatically that season. I don't think you can do that quite so simply as there were far too many things which went on in games before and after which cost us goals or points. I, for one, made mistakes which cost us points. It was just one of those crazy things which, unfortunately, in a season-long campaign, come along sometimes. It was early on in the season, and anyway, with the amount of goals we scored and points we gained subsequently, any other team would have gone up, and have done since, with that sort of record. Jim has since, for instance, often pointed to a penalty which Guy Whittingham missed against Peterborough that season. Guy was not our regular penalty-taker, but Warren Aspinall handed the task over to him to enable him to get the goal he needed to break the club's goalscoring record. We still won 4-0, with Guy scoring three, but Jim maintains that the loss of that goal was costly and that he should never have been allowed to take it. Guy scored nearly 50 goals that season so, for me, that missed penalty was just another of those many 'ifs and buts'.

I had a patchy start to the season and from then on there always seemed to be talk around in the press about some keeper or another coming in to challenge me. Andy Dibble was supposed to be coming from Manchester City for £300,000 and I know that Dave Beasant was close to signing from Chelsea, but it all fell through. I began to wonder whether it was all part of the Smith psychology, to keep me on my toes. But soon we were reeling off the victories over the Christmas and New Year periods and winning was becoming a habit. Along with the rest of the team, my confidence was flowing again and six straight wins in March really put us in the frame for promotion.

The Guy Butters/Symons/Awford threesome, at the heart of the defence, complemented each other well and they were absolutely tremendous as we hit the home straight that season. Butts was very popular, with a dry sense of humour and a great attitude to the game and life itself. He was a big, strong lad, good in the air, who could read the game well. His record through this period speaks for itself, but later on he seemed to get left out regularly and possibly Jim was worried about his lack of pace, particularly with balls played over the top. I felt that was probably the reason why he didn't make the grade at Spurs, his previous club, but Butts was still a reliable, solid centre half who always gave 100%. Looking back at the best central defensive backlines in front of me over the years – whether as a three or a four, Kit and Awfs would be at the forefront. As a three, Billy Gilbert with Kit and Awfs would be just perfect. In a four I would add Noel Blake to the line.

By the time of the run-in, Colin Clarke had been sidelined for the rest of the season through injury and we were short of a forward. Despite being linked with several strikers as a replacement, it soon became clear that Jim wouldn't get the financial backing he needed to bring someone in. In the end he turned to George Lawrence from non-league Weymouth and 'Chicken George' became his lucky charm. He was a great lad who did well when he played. Every time he was there as substitute, we didn't lose. With just three games left, things were getting pretty tense. We went to Notts County, who were close to the relegation zone and needed the points almost as desperately. We won 1-0 with a goal from Walshie twenty minutes from the end, but it was a horrible atmosphere that afternoon, with a lot of stick coming from both the County players and supporters. One or two of their players really dished out the verbals, causing some of us, particularly Butts, to get really wound up. Soon there were plenty of childish jibes being exchanged on the field – like, for instance, "you're not going up", with the response "and you're going down". It's not unusual for that sort of thing to go on, but I don't like to hear it and, normally, I don't get involved at all.

After beating Wolves at home we had won eleven out of twelve, with two to play and, like many others, I thought that promotion was within our grasp. Then, we went to Sunderland, who were in a real relegation battle and were really wound up, not only to try to secure their own survival, but also to beat the team at the top of the league. Kevin Ball was in their squad and, although he didn't play, we knew he would have been in there winding them up for it. We had a huge following and there was a great atmosphere. Their first goal came late in the first half and, to cap it all, we also went down to ten men. I remember the ball being played in to the box and coming out, choosing to punch, rather than catch it. I didn't make the best of connections and my clearance just reached the arc of the penalty area, from where it was looped back in over my head. Butts, who was covering behind me, dived backwards and chose to palm it over the bar to safety. Butts was sent off and Don Goodman scored from the resultant penalty. Butts and I have discussed it since and clearly he would have been better off letting the ball go in – we would still have been 1-0 down but with a full set of players. In the second half, Walshie was also sent off, for an elbow off the ball, after completely losing his rag in frustration at some of the refereeing decisions that afternoon, not to mention the fact that we were 3-0 down by this stage. He couldn't have been angrier with himself immediately afterwards, smashing a mirror and kicking stuff around the dressing room. We still had chances, even with nine men, but by then had totally lost our discipline. Suddenly, promotion was out of our hands.

Like everybody else, I was gutted after that match. It was the worst I had ever felt after a game up to then. But we tried hard to put it into perspective – we had been on a fantastic 12-match unbeaten run which had to come to an end sometime. It was just a shame that it had to come on that day, in circumstances which made it even harder to bear. It was frustrating, but not half as frustrating as what happened the next day, on the Sunday, when West Ham United, our closest rivals, played at Swindon, who were already assured of a play-off place. The timing of the game, in that West Ham were conscious of our defeat at Sunderland the previous day, was unfair to say the least and, on top of that, Swindon's performance was hard to take. We knew that, having the play-off games to come, Swindon probably wouldn't break sweat, but they didn't even put out a full-strength side and those who played clearly didn't want to get injured or make any effort on our behalf. It was live on TV but I didn't watch it and took my two girls down to Dorset, to Monkey World, for the afternoon.

So, it was down to the last game at home to Grimsby, where we had to match West Ham's result at home to Cambridge and score two more goals than them in doing so. There was almost a disaster for me in the first minute when, from a back pass, I smacked the ball into the back of one of their players and had to scramble back to our goal-line to desperately retrieve the ball. As for the game, it was another case of false information – this time on West Ham's score line – being relayed to the pitch. Early on there were loud cheers from our crowd for an apparent Cambridge opening 'goal', but we didn't realise that it had subsequently been disallowed. I tried to spread the message to all our players not to take any notice of information from the crowd. In the end, it came down to our failure to take enough of the many chances we made in the game. There was no blame on anybody – we could not have tried harder. We heard that West Ham had won 2-0 as we were coming off the pitch, having won 2-1 ourselves, and had the result confirmed in the dressing room. Funnily enough, that Cambridge 'goal', which was disallowed and might have changed the course of that game, was 'scored' by Steve Claridge. I gather that in recent years both Steve and Harry Redknapp (then a coach at West Ham) have looked back on it and agreed that it was a perfectly good goal. Certainly the TV replay of it showed it was a close-run thing.

Naturally, we felt very sorry for ourselves afterwards and we went away for a few days, to the Royal Bath Hotel in Bournemouth, before the first leg of the play-off semi-final against Leicester. To give Jim his due, by the time the game at the City Ground, Nottingham (played there because Leicester's Filbert Street was being redeveloped) came round, he had got us all refocused and well up for it. We went into the game confident and feeling we had a good chance over two legs. But, after Julian Joachim had nutmegged me for their goal four minutes from time, it began to look more of an uphill task. It was an edgy, scrappy game and 0-0 would have suited us fine. Looking back on it now, even the 1-0 score line was not the end of the world, with the second leg at home to come.

In that second leg we were the victims of one of those refereeing decisions which change games and leave you utterly baffled. We scored first, but Ian Ormondroyd's equaliser for Leicester was blatantly offside and it was immediately apparent to us out there. It wasn't one of those where you come off, see a TV replay, and then realise that you have been the victim of a bad decision. We knew there and then, with me stranded on the penalty spot and Ormondroyd behind me, that there simply were not two players between him and the goal-line. Apparently the referee Roger Milford has since admitted that it was offside and, when Jim Smith raised it with him a few years later, the only response he could get was: "Well, Jim, it's only a game, after all." That for me reflects the mentality of some referees as far as the importance of such decisions is concerned. For us, it was far more than a game and a dodgy decision. It cost us a possible Wembley appearance, potentially promotion and the subsequent glory, not to mention earnings. We staggered round the pitch applauding the crowd, who were just fantastic to us, but we could see a lot of tears being shed amongst the fans. Unlike the FA Cup semi-final at Villa Park, there were no tears in the dressing room. Everyone was just stunned, numb, silent, not knowing what to say. We were all just left in our own worlds, with our own thoughts. All Jim could say was: "You've all done brilliantly, there's no more I can say." It was the worst-ever feeling – total desolation. Like everybody, I was totally gutted. Your whole life is focused on promotion – everything revolves around it. It's a very draining experience, day-in, day-out, which takes a lot out of you mentally and physically and, when it ends like that, you are left totally devastated. All you want to do is to leave the ground and get home, to be left alone with your own thoughts of what might have been or, in this case perhaps, of what should have been. But the overriding feeling is a need to get away from everything, to get a holiday booked, to recharge your batteries and absorb yourself in your family. I thought then, and still do now, that the whole play-off idea is a joke and events that season confirmed it for me. We finished three places and 12 points better off than Leicester over a 46-game season, but were then forced to play them over two legs for the right to go to Wembley for a play-off final, where, as it happened, we would have met Swindon, who also finished 12 points below us.

Our fans were obviously shattered and distraught, but the level of their support and sheer positive thinking, on the night and subsequently, was absolutely brilliant and helped us get through it. They clearly appreciated that we had given our all and those little comments we got when we met them in the street through the summer, like "you did us proud", "you'll do it next year" and "you were robbed" meant such a lot. But then the fixtures for next season come out, you start training in pre-season, one or two new players arrive and suddenly it's all forgotten. You start to re-focus. During your career, as I was to come to realise, you tend to forget how quickly the seasons pass and how, before you realise it, your career is over.

For some weeks into the following season, I felt there was a hangover from the acute disappointment of missing out on promotion and our performances were clearly affected. I even pulled a muscle in training, a first for me, which caused me to miss three games and gave a chance to Brian Horne, who had been signed in the previous season from Millwall as my understudy. Brian was a decent keeper and a good shot-stopper, who had to work hard throughout his career to keep his weight down. Unfortunately, after patiently waiting almost a year for his chance, Brian then proceeded to let in nine goals in his three games.

After scoring all those goals the previous season Guy was obviously looking to capitalise on it and move into the Premiership. He had spent some years in the Army before coming into the game and, at 28, he wasn't a young man in football terms. There was, by now, some big money to be earned at the top level and I imagine he was tapped up by Premiership clubs during the summer. No-one could blame him for accepting Aston Villa's offer and I would certainly have done the same in his position. His replacement, Lee Chapman, arrived from Leeds, but from the off didn't seem to fit in or to want to be with us. He was a strange guy who gave the impression that, having come from Leeds United and won some medals, he was far too good for us. He played a couple of games and then Jim got him in and said: "If you don't want to be here, then you had better go," and a deal with West Ham was quickly struck. It always seemed to me that Lee wanted to be in London anyway, opening restaurants in his spare time.

The highlights of that season centred on the cup competitions, in January especially. First we went to Premiership Blackburn in the FA Cup third round and belied our league form by getting a 3-3 draw, thanks to a fantastic hat-trick from Alan McLoughlin. We went to Ewood Park and honestly didn't think we had a cat in hell's chance, but Macca got us the replay with his fantastic opportunism that afternoon. Funnily enough, during the coach journey up the previous day, Jim had put on the video of the FA Cup semi-final replay at Villa Park, and we had kept on replaying Macca's miss when he hit the bar from close-in whilst giving him some real, but good-natured stick. Macca was a good, honest professional, who didn't get anything like the credit he deserved for his dogged, hard-working performances for Pompey. Despite scoring the goal for the Republic of Ireland, which took them to the World Cup Finals, he was an unassuming guy and a real family man. But he was passionate about the game and someone who was a bit fiery at times, who could easily be wound up.

Four days after our draw at Blackburn, we went to Old Trafford in the League Cup and that was a fantastic night. They were all there that night for United – Cantona, Schmeichel, Bruce and Giggs to name a few – in a full-strength side. Despite Walshie's two memorable goals, my most vivid recollection is of the penalty we were denied when Macca was brought down. We stayed up in Manchester overnight after the game and a few of us went out to a drinking club and met up with Steve Bruce and Peter Schmeichel. Benny Kristensen, our Danish midfielder, introduced me to Peter and we sat up all night drinking and smoking. Given that, during his time at United, Peter had changed people's attitudes to goalkeeping, and the way it was played, it made for a long and interesting chat. Not that I learned anything really new, more that it was great to exchange views and ideas with one of the true greats in my position. We lost both replays at Fratton Park. Against United, we didn't hit anything like the same standards as we did at Old Trafford, and Brian McClair scored with a simple close-range header to decide that one. In the Blackburn game we were still in it, despite being 2-1 down, when Jason Wilcox punched in Rovers' third. The referee and linesman professed not to see it, unlike everybody else in the ground, and it was downhill in that game from that point. Gerry Creaney made his debut in the Man United replay and he was a strange guy, big and brash, who was, to use my favourite phrase, a true 'big-time Charlie'. Having come from a big club like Celtic, he clearly thought he was a cut above us, which was in stark contrast to another Scot, Mark Burchill, who also came from Celtic Park, and is a lovely guy.

Gerry used to think he was clever by running alongside goalkeepers, as they rolled the ball out prior to their clearance, and toe-poking it away from them just as they were about to kick it. He was invariably penalised and wouldn't accept that you couldn't raise your foot to a keeper, arguing with the referees that the ball was still in play. Towards the end of the following season, Gerry was beaten up outside a Southsea night-club and, in truth, there were not too many Pompey players showing much concern afterwards. He would get stick when he was out on the town, but didn't help the situation with the sort of comments he made. You don't, for instance, endear yourself to people when you tell them: "My shirt is worth more than you earn in a week," as he did on one night out. Mark Chamberlain was with Gerry on that fateful night, but had left Pompey by then to go to Brighton. At his peak, Chambo was a great player, who appeared laid-back, but that was just the way he came over. He had been fantastic for us in the cup semi-final season and the next, but had then begun to pick up a lot of ankle injuries, which affected his form. Despite the impression he gave, he was devoted to the game, and still works with youngsters in the Saints Academy. We lost the last four games of that season, without scoring a goal and, I suppose, the writing was beginning to appear on the wall for Jim. Looking back, the same could be said for me. At 33 years of age in the summer of 1994, it was probably the start of the beginning of the end for my career. That feeling increased when Jim paid a lot of money for a goalkeeper from Estonia, of all places.

But that was all put aside, temporarily, after the season had ended when I was finally able to stage my testimonial match in May, after a six-year wait. I had got really frustrated by the delay in arranging the match and had rejected some fairly unattractive pre-season friendlies against foreign opposition, like Real Sociedad. To their credit, my testimonial committee had worked hard in my initial year and I was grateful for the financial returns from their efforts. But the match was obviously crucial and it often looked as though I would never get it. Ballie taking over at Southampton was the key element and he got Lawrie McMenemy to agree, but with Lawrie insisting that both clubs sent out full-strength sides. Unfortunately, Pompey were committed to play in a tournament in Greece at the same time, but Jim agreed to let some of our first-teamers stay behind to play for me and then fly out the next day. With the addition of some star ex-Pompey players like Mark Hateley, Darren Anderton, Paul Walsh and Barry Horne, Lawrie was happy with our squad on the night.

Our fans had suffered a mediocre season and the omens were not good for the turnout. My testimonial committee members were showing great concern at the numbers in the ground up to half an hour before kick-off, no more than 4,000 apparently, but, before we knew it, the ground was bursting at the seams. There was a fantastic crowd of over 17,000 – a much bigger crowd than anybody expected – and my return of close to £120,000 was just fantastic. Pompey players, past and present, came from far and wide – every single player who said they would get there did so. Putting the financial aspect aside however, it was the most moving and touching experience of my life – topping everything from the promotions, through to my MBE award. It's a cliché I know, but you can't put that sort of experience into words. My personal reception and ovation were so memorable and leading the sides out at the start, with my two girls, was something really special. Some of the Saints lads were playing for contracts and we lost by five, although it was pretty irrelevant. Matt Le Tissier put on some of his tricks, and we even had the sight of Ballie coming on for them late in the game. We won a dodgy penalty, which gave me the chance to score from the spot at the Fratton End – the only goal of my career.

Afterwards, all my guests went to the hotel where many of the players were staying and had a party. The following morning I was greeted by local media reports of post-match running battles between Pompey and Saints fans. It later emerged that it amounted to nothing more than a wall being knocked over close to the ground and the cost of rebuilding it came out of my fund. It was a shame that the media blew the incident up to such an extent and cast a cloud over the night. But I was left with the thought that I could never thank the Pompey fans and my tireless committee enough for their support. All that waiting and wrangling over the years was finally worthwhile.

*'He deserves to be up there with
Jimmy Dickinson.'*
                    Frank Burrows

The team sheet new manager Jim Smith handed in on the first day of the 1991/92 season underlined Knight's 'senior' status at the club. At 30, he was the oldest player in a side freshened up by the emergence of a clutch of young players, such as Kit Symons, Andy Awford and Darren Anderton, who had been a central part of the Pompey youth team which reached the semi-finals of the FA Youth Cup in 1990. Smith's reputation as a man who got teams promoted went before him, but no one at Fratton could imagine the route he would attempt to take. Other senior professionals – costing big fees and on salaries to match – were unceremoniously dumped into the reserves. Warren Aspinall, Steve Wigley and Gavin Maguire were quick to bitch in the press about their lot, while Graeme Hogg was packed off to Heart of Midlothian; but Smith was vindicated by a promising start to the season which saw Pompey on the fringes of the play-off chase as summer gave way to autumn. Knight also had a new, albeit temporary, understudy in 20-year-old Alan Gough, who stepped up after poor old Andy Gosney – who had had an operation in the summer to correct his squint – suffered a serious ankle ligament injury in pre-season. Gough was a Republic of Ireland Under-21 international, despite having yet to make a first-team appearance.

Knight was relishing the chance to help nurture the raw talent of Kit Symons and Andy Awford – although his advice may well have been of the 'do as I say' variety – and he was also proving the old adage that keepers get better with age. It was The News' sports journalist Danny Griffiths who gave Knight those full marks out of ten as he single-handedly kept Brighton at bay at Fratton, singling out a double save early on from first Gary Chivers' diving header, then the follow up shot by Gary O'Reilly, as the pick. Team-mate Awford recalls that game vividly: 'Brighton should have won by three or four. I remember the one double save he made as being out of this world. All I could say afterwards to him was you must have stayed in the night before!'

The following week, Knight was targeting playing on for another decade: 'I can't see any reason why I shouldn't play on for another ten years at least, provided I can find someone to give me a contract. It would be quite something to play on into the next century and I think I can,' he said. If he was hoping Gosney would continue to keep him on his toes, he hadn't figured on his long-time rival's bad luck. No sooner was he back to form for the reserves, than he sliced open his thumb on, of all things, a tin of corned beef. Once it was healed, he finally got his first-team chance, but at York City, as Smith loaned him out. Gosney was philosophical and mentally preparing himself to leave the club: 'It'll give me a boost and I hope it will lead to a chance to go somewhere else permanently,' he said. Within three weeks he was recalled, as Knight's tweaked hamstring opened the door briefly, but his appearance in the 3-2 win at Swindon on November 16 would be his last for the club, as a knee injury in January would end his season. Gough, too, saw the writing on the wall and demanded to go on the transfer list, a request which was accepted.

Pompey's season truly clicked into gear with a 4-0 thrashing of promotion-chasing Middlesbrough, in the final home game of 1991. Among the goals was Guy Whittingham, who had been struggling to recapture the form of his first two seasons with the club, but at last he began to provide the cutting edge which had prevented the side from seriously making a promotion bid. However, it was the FA Cup which really cheered. Another Whittingham goal helped see off third division Exeter, managed by Alan Ball, in the third round, then Darren Anderton's televised double-blast accounted for Leyton   Orient in round four. Whittingham's solitary strike took Pompey to the brink of the quarter-finals at home to Middlesbrough, only for Knight to be haunted by Alan Kernaghan's late strike which went through his legs. 'That was really gutting. Anywhere else and I think I might have got some part of my body to it and stopped it,' he commented post-match. However, it merely set up one of the most memorable of Pompey nights, as they travelled to Ayresome Park for the replay and came away with a 4-2 win, thanks to Colin Clarke and Darren Anderton's respective braces. In the sixth round, new signing Alan McLoughlin netted the goal which would carry Pompey into their first semi-final since 1949, but Knight played his part, notably with a fine one-handed save to deny Stuart Pearce, who had stolen in to meet a Nigel Clough cross with his head. Knight told Neasom ('eight out of ten, Alan...') afterwards: 'It wasn't a bad save. To be honest I'd started to come for the cross but it was bending away from me and then I noticed Pearcie making a late run and started to go back. Fortunately I was able to take off and knock it away.'

In the semi-final Pompey drew Liverpool. At the time, the Reds were still a renowned force, although their truly great days of the 1980s were behind them. The first match at Highbury was probably the greatest Pompey occasion of the past 50 years. More than 19,000 fans were lucky enough to get tickets for the game and, although most travelled in hope rather than anticipation, on the day it soon became apparent their favourite team were more than up for the match. Liverpool were contained rather more easily than anyone might have imagined and, when Anderton's shot found the back of the net with six minutes of extra time to go, like Knight, fans' thoughts turned to a first Wembley appearance since 1942. Three minutes and 42 seconds remaining were showing on the clock when Ronnie Whelan followed up the John Barnes' free-kick. Knight's fingers just couldn't quite stretch enough to push it round, rather than on to, the post and the bitterest of sweet sensations, for all concerned, was assured. The replay defeat, by penalty shoot-out, after Alan McLoughlin had rattled the bar late in normal time, had an air of inevitability about it.

The date with Liverpool had overshadowed just about everything, but Smith's Pompey 'babes' were also progressing well on the play-off front, until the fixture backlog caught up with them. Two days after the match at Highbury, Knight was brought down to earth with a bump as Pompey's promotion hopes took a nose-dive, ironically on Merseyside, as they lost 2-0 to Tranmere. The second goal put Knight centre stage for all the wrong reasons. His scuffed attempted clearance fell to Tony Thomas, 45 yards out and his first-time volley sailed over an embarrassed Knight's head and into the net: 'The boss wasn't too amused, but I've just got to live with it. Give the lad credit for having the bottle to attempt it. He was lucky I suppose and he'd probably try it another hundred times without getting it on target. It was down to me. I scuffed the ball and it went straight to him, but the shot never gave me a chance. They reckon in this game there is always something new. That was the first time something like that's happened to me and I hope it's the last.' Knight was less philosophical about Tranmere striker John Aldridge that night. The former Liverpool striker had developed a penalty taking technique which involved a 'shuffle' in the middle of his run up. Although the Rovers' player-manager put his effort wide against Knight, the keeper was less than impressed: 'It's a total con and completely illegal. It was only justice he missed. Guy Butters didn't handle in the first place. I'd thought a lot about what I would do if they got a penalty. I tried to keep my eye on the ball and ignore Aldridge completely. In the end he took so long to sort himself out, I went the wrong way anyway, but I don't think it should be allowed.' Pompey endured their own penalty nightmare in the replay against Liverpool and the play-offs slipped away, but optimism was high that the following season could well be one to remember.

Inevitably, clubs in the newly-founded Premier League had woken up to the young talent on display at Fratton and it was no surprise when left back John Beresford invoked his right, at the end of his contract, to move on, although it was slightly disappointing, when a move to Liverpool broke down, he opted to join first-division rivals Newcastle. The sale of Darren Anderton was a different matter, as Pompey opted to cash in on him, but the deal Smith brokered with Tottenham ended up being a canny one. The supposed 'make-weight' in the £1.7 million deal was Paul Walsh. He was a patently talented striker, who, at the wrong side of 30, had acquired, perhaps unfairly, a bit of a 'problem-boy' tag, most notably after a bust-up with Spurs' reserve coach Ray Clemence. His arrival galvanised Guy Whittingham and the most lethal partnership in Pompey's history was born. Pre-season training was also a bit different for Knight, as, for the first time since the early 1980s, Gosney was no longer there as his sparring partner, having signed for Birmingham City when his contract ended. A quirk of the fixture list brought Gos back to Fratton in the first weekend of September, but it was no happy return as Walsh and Whittingham carved the Blues' defence apart in a 4-0 win.

However, Pompey were slow to pick up pace and a televised defeat at home to West Ham at the end of that same month had them languishing in 15th place. The game also left Knight red-faced as he and Awford left a through ball to each other, on the stroke of half time, which allowed Clive Allen to steal in and score the only goal of the game. Knight put the gaffe down to the new law which forbade goalkeepers to pick up a backpass. 'Last season I'd have stayed back and waited for Andy to knock it back to me. Now you can't do that. You have to decide to come more often than you used to and hope you're going to get the ball. That's what happened. I shouted at Awfs to leave it and didn't get it...' At least he had the consolation that a superlative second-half display kept the score respectable and even moved Neasom to give him nine out of ten in his post-match report. But for that error, he may well have got that elusive ten out of ten from Mike.

Suddenly Pompey clicked in October, and three wins and a draw sent them moving up the table, until a 3-0 thrashing at Grimsby - not helped by Knight being hit by a fruit pastille hurled from the crowd – punctured self-belief again. The 5–5 draw at Oxford, after leading 5–2 with 12 minutes to go and 5–3 as the game went into injury time, also hit morale, but thanks to Whittingham's goals, not to mention Walsh's assists, the points continued to be racked up. Knight even enjoyed a taste of 'European' football, as Pompey travelled to Bari and Ascoli in the Anglo-Italian Cup, but of more pressing concern to him was that manager Smith seemed intent on signing a true rival for his undisputed first-team spot. Since Gosney had left, Alan Gough remained the only other 'senior' keeper on the books, so news that Pompey were prepared to pay £300,000 for out-of-favour Manchester City keeper Andy Dibble had Knight on his mettle. 'Obviously I've no divine right to be in the team and I know we've got to get another goalkeeper as cover. But when there's talk of somebody with Andy's track record and a fee like that, you wonder whether the boss really fancies you or thinks it's time to bring someone else in as first choice. Sooner or later someone's got to come in, that's obvious, but I was hoping it would be a youngster making his way, not a player like Andy who's done most things and done them well,' he confessed to the *Sports Mail*, although he added he didn't feel he'd become complacent. To prove the point, not to mention make one too, he was back to his best with a close-range save to deny Notts County's Kevin Bartlett an undeserved winner, as the two sides played out a goalless draw on the Saturday before Christmas.

As the New Year dawned Knight finally got his rival. 25-year-old Brian Horne had been eased out of contention at Millwall by the arrival of Kasey Keller and arrived at Fratton on Christmas Eve, pledging to take Knight's place. The former England Under-21 international might have had an early debut as Knight picked up a hip injury that threatened his place for the FA Cup third round tie at second-division Brighton. Knight seemed relieved Horne's arrival wasn't the experienced keeper he'd dreaded: 'Sure Brian's going to be looking to get in the side, but I'm number one and I want to keep it that way. I feel I've been playing well this season. At the start, I was making a lot of silly mistakes, but those have been ironed out and I am happy with my form. I've played against Brian a couple of times. He's been around a bit and he's a good young keeper.'

In the end, Knight made the Brighton clash and the shock 1–0 defeat proved to be a blessing in disguise as the team set about making up the ground on runaway leaders Newcastle and West Ham, although not before Pompey had contrived to lose 2–0 at Upton Park in mid–January. The significance of that defeat was yet to be fully appreciated, and neither was the aborted attempt to sign former Chelsea striker David Speedie from Southampton. He eventually signed for West Ham. Not that it mattered as Pompey embarked on a run of just two defeats in 19 matches which took them to the top of the division, albeit for 24 hours, at the end of April. By this time Knight had also taken on the team captaincy, after Awford requested a break from the role, and also lost his tag as the team's 'veteran' after the signing of Blackburn utility man Chris Price. The keeper was again in form to help the team to a 2–0 win over Newcastle at Fratton in mid–February and his 477th league appearance in the next home game against Leicester – albeit spoiled by an injury–time equaliser – enabled him to ease past Joe Corrigan to 14th in the all–time goalkeeper appearance record stakes. Six straight wins in March lifted Pompey into second place, but it was apparent the team was short of cover, especially up front.

When chairman Jim Gregory baulked at paying £250,000 for Cambridge striker John Taylor, all Smith could do was recruit George Lawrence, plying his trade at Beazer Homes League Weymouth, to fill the breach. A series of late appearances as substitute, in which his speciality was to run down the clock by the corner flag, gave the former Southampton striker a talismanic quality, but his, and Pompey's luck ran out with two games to go. Pompey could have been embarrassed on the goalkeeping front after Horne picked up a calf injury, but instead it was their striking options which were confounded when Walsh got himself sent off in the 4–1 defeat at

Sunderland. Not only did the result hand the automatic promotion initiative back to the Hammers, but also a three-match ban meant Walsh was out of any play-off equation. When Speedie scored for West Ham in the last minute of the last game of the season, it extinguished any hopes Pompey might have had of overhauling them as they chased a potentially decisive third goal at home to Grimsby, amid scenes of unbearable tension. It was the play-offs and ultimately a double heartbreak, as Leicester, 12 points and three places adrift of Pompey, stole a 3-2 aggregate win in the semi-final. Some might say, rather, a combination of referee Roger Milford and his linesman, who didn't spot an apparently obvious offside, helped pinch it for them, but what was certain was it denied Knight a crack at Wembley and the club the potential riches of the by-now burgeoning Premiership.

Just before pre-season training came around again in July, Knight celebrated his 32nd birthday and confidence was high that the club could go one better the following season. However, one significant departure was the out-of-contract Whittingham, who signed for Premiership Aston Villa on the eve of the season in a deal which saw midfielder Mark Blake arriving at Fratton as a makeweight. Smith moved to sign his replacement, but Leeds' Lee Chapman was just the wrong player at the wrong time. A brace of goals in the opening fixture at Oxford was promising, but the 3-2 defeat was not. A stray elbow in his home debut saw him red-carded and by the time his suspension was purged he'd left the club, signing for West Ham. Knight was also in the wars as he picked up a rib injury in the home 1-0 win over Luton, which finally got the season up and running, in the third game. That meant he missed the trip to Grimsby – breaking a run of 97 consecutive appearances – and gave Horne the chance to shine in a 1-1 draw. 'His performance was a real bonus,' remarked Smith afterwards. 'That display suggested he can do quite a lot and it won't do Knightsie any harm.' Horne kept his place for the next game at freshly-relegated Crystal Palace, with Knight on the bench, but undid all his good work with an abject display as the home side cruised to a 5–1 win. Smith persisted, as Knight was still troubled by the knock, but another three goals conceded in a draw with newly-promoted Stoke, at Fratton the following Saturday, saw the end of his short reign as number one. His recall enabled Knight to make a nostalgic return to Millmoor, Rotherham's home ground, for a Coca-Cola Cup tie, and he kept another clean sheet, as he had on his Pompey debut 591 games previously.

Pompey were failing to match the heights of the previous campaign, although an unconvincing unbeaten run in September and October kept them in play-off contention and their Coca-Cola Cup run was gaining momentum. Knight also clocked up another personal milestone with his 500th league appearance – including 172 clean sheets – at Peterborough in October. The man who, three times previously, had tried to get away from Fratton was now setting his heart on staying for the rest of his career and beyond, as well as chasing Jimmy Dickinson's 764 league appearance record. 'I would like to see out this contract and do well enough to earn another one if I can,' he said. ' I suppose it would be nice to get close to Jimmy's record, but that's a hell of a long way away at the moment. Still, I'm only 32 and, with reasonable luck, I could have another six or seven years in the game. I'd also like to think there might be some job I could do for Pompey when I finally finish playing.' A run of four league victories as October turned to November saw Pompey established in the top six and a 'shock' 2–0 home win over Premiership Swindon set up a fourth round away tie with the winners of a replay between Peterborough and Blackpool. However, it was clear things weren't all sweetness and light behind the scenes at the club. Leading scorer Walsh was the subject of persistent rumours about an imminent transfer – neighbours Southampton being the most likely buyers – and plans for a new 25,000 stadium at Farlington had collided with planning regulations and a decision was referred to Whitehall.

A 4–1 defeat at West Brom, followed by a 1–0 home reverse against Sunderland, punctured promotion optimism, but that result was sandwiched by a 0-0 draw at Peterborough in the cup. A last-gasp, extra time Benny Kristensen goal in the replay set up a quarter-final clash with Manchester United at Old Trafford and by then the FA Cup third-round draw had pitted Pompey against Blackburn at Ewood Park. Within the space of four days in January Pompey and Knight would have to face the top two teams in the Premiership. To say they rose to the challenge was an understatement. At Rovers, Alan McLoughlin etched his name in Pompey folklore with a memorable hat-trick, the last goal of which earned an 89th minute replay. At United it was Walsh earning the plaudits with a brace of goals in a 2-2 draw which kept the Wembley dream going. Knight played his part, although Ryan Giggs' 29th minute opener ended his record of not having conceded a goal in the competition. His first-half save from Eric Cantona, when he leapt to turn aside his downward header, kept Pompey in the game. 'It was a nice save to make. I wasn't sure I was going to get to it, but I did,' he said post-match. 'In a way though, I was more pleased with the one from him towards the end when he was through on his own. I just managed to spread myself and get down and block it away which was satisfying.'

Premiership class told in the replays, as Blackburn won 3-1 at a packed Fratton seven days before United nicked a tight game through Brian McClair's first-half header. Knight was quick to point the finger. The luck in his 'lucky' tee-shirt had clearly run out. 'It's worn out anyway in any case,' he said, 'but I've grown fond of it. I first wore it for the FA Cup semi-finals against Liverpool a couple of seasons ago. Then it began to rip and I tossed it aside, but after I injured my ribs earlier this season I dug it out again and started to wear it again for a bit of protection and I've kept wearing it since. But it may have to go. We've had no luck at all recently. There was the penalty we should have had at United, the last-minute goal at Derby and then Wednesday night against Blackburn. How the referee didn't see the handball for their third goal I'll never know. It was so obvious. I know Jason (Wilcox) didn't mean to do it, but it doesn't matter, his arm knocked it in,' he moaned. After those two defeats Pompey's season nose-dived. Not even the signing of Celtic striker Gerry Creaney in a club-record £650,000 deal could lift a team whose promotion aspirations had started to crumble during a thirteen-match winless run sandwiching the cup distractions. A 3-1 win over Grimsby in February finally saw Creaney launch his Pompey career with a hat-trick and young Aaron Flahavan was on the bench as Knight's understudy for the match, recognising the enormous progress he had made since signing his first professional contract in November, along with Sammy Igoe and Deon Burton.

That win failed to stop the rot and the mood of fans was not helped when the mercurial Walsh was sold in March to Manchester City. A flurry of wins in April ensured there was no hypnotic drift towards the relegation rocks, but by now Knight was also concentrating on organising his testimonial match, fixed for the end of the season. Southampton, now managed by Alan Ball, had agreed to be the opposition and the long-serving goalkeeper was putting together an all-star Pompey side, including Mark Hateley, Guy Whittingham, Darren Anderton and, ironically now, Walsh. On the night, more than 17,000 fans turned up to pay tribute to the man who was fast becoming a Pompey legend. Even if Saints didn't quite enter into the spirit of things, ruthlessly exposing the ageing partnership of Blake and Gilbert at the back, the night was an unqualified success. Knight even got to score his one and only Pompey goal, a somewhat suspect penalty, at the Fratton End. 'He's something of a throwback to the old days,' said Burrows in his pre-match tribute. 'Players don't stay at clubs for 17 years now. When money was less of a god within the game it wasn't unusual for a player to spend his whole career at a club. Those days are now past. That's what makes Alan an exception. He deserves to be up there with Jimmy Dickinson.' Although matching that Pompey legend's record was still some way off, one record was fast coming into view. Peter Bonetti, one of his childhood heroes, played a record 600 league games in goal for Chelsea. By the time his current contract was up in 1996, Knight was on course to have passed him.

Knight shouts instructions during the 5-0 defeat at Nottingham Forest in November 1987.

Mike Walker / M&Y News Agency

Knight claims the ball during the 3-0 FA Cup win over Bradford in February 1988.

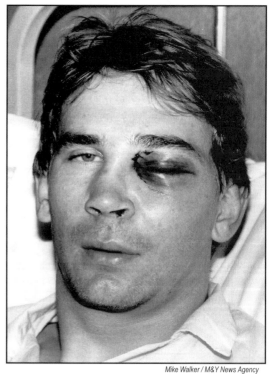

Knight recovers from his facial injuries in Queen Alexandra hospital after the Wimbledon game in April 1988

Mike Walker / M&Y News Agency

Knight keeps out an effort from John Aldridge as Pompey go down 2-0 at home to eventual champions Liverpool in February 1988.

Alan with new-born daughter Rebekah and Jade shortly before the 1992 FA Cup semi-final.

The News

Knight encourages his defenders to think about things in March 1993.

Portsmouth FC

Alan Knight collection

Knight steps up to score his one and only goal, from the penalty spot, in his testimonial match against Southampton in May 1994.

Alan Knight collection

The Pompey stars past and present who turned out for Knight's testimonial.

Alan points the way, while doing his best to look cool, in March 1994.

7 - 'There comes a time...'

When Mart Poom arrived from Estonia, the official line was that he was there to put me under pressure and Jim told us both before the season that whoever was playing the best would play. But I was in no doubt that Jim was looking to use him and, in that knowledge, I was in no mood to give up my place in the team. Jim has told me since that I played my best under him after he had brought in Mart. He was tall – at 6' 5" – and lean, with not a single ounce of fat on his body. In short, he was a super-fit guy, in fact, the fittest player I have ever known. I used to jokingly refer to him as 'a living Russian genetic experiment'. He would train, train and train – pushing weights to what I thought were fanatical lengths. Sometimes, I felt he possibly over-trained and that was why he regularly picked up injuries – such as pulls and strains – and he still does to this day. It happens with some players. Having said that, I had a lot of time for Mart and he was a very good goalkeeper, which he proved when Jim brought him back to England at Derby. Mart had some problems with the language to begin with and then eventually he had to go back to Estonia after losing his work permit. Neil Sillett and I even jokingly took him out in Portsmouth to try and find him an English wife, but, with his fitness ethic, he would have one glass of wine and then want to go home to more aerobics. Jim gave him one or two chances in the League Cup games that season but, after Terry Fenwick arrived, he preferred him to me for the first four games of the following 1995/96 season. Unfortunately, in the last of those games, at Leicester, Mart had an absolute shocker and Fen brought me straight back in for the next game.

In late September 1994, Awfs broke his leg in four places at West Brom. It was immediately obvious from where I was that he had broken it and was in real trouble. I feared it was a compound fracture and just could not bring myself to go over. It didn't look like a bad challenge from their guy and Awfs had no complaint about it. It was just one of those things which comes out of a very heavy challenge between two players occasionally. It was the worst injury I had come across and it brought back memories of that time years back, when, as a youth player, I had accidentally broken Graham Marriner's leg. It was a real worry for Awfs and his family. He had to have a rod inserted in his leg and then suffered several infections thereafter. Luckily Sills, our physio, was a good buddy of Awfs and gave him a lot of support through the long slog of the rehabilitation.

After Christmas, in the FA Cup, at home to Leicester, I got the one and only red card of my career. A new rule had come in making it an automatic dismissal for goalkeepers handling outside the penalty area, but the referee in my case showed no common sense whatsoever. The pitch was very muddy and by the time of the incident the lines were simply not visible. I had come out, dived and grabbed the ball three or four yards inside the box, but my mud-assisted momentum meant I had slithered outside the box. Twisting, I had tried hard to keep the ball inside the white line, not that I could really see it, but on the linesman's say-so, the referee penalised me for handling. Perhaps I had, by the strict letter of the law, but, with no line visible, I don't know how the linesman could possibly have made such a decision. At 19 years of age, with no previous first team experience, Aaron Flahavan went in goal as substitute and did well. We lost 1-0 with nine men, as Jon Gittens had already been sent off before my dismissal.

Pompey managers and I have never had a lot of luck against Leicester and that trend continued when Jim lost his job after that game. It had already become obvious to us that he was under pressure and that something was going to happen. The first sign of that pressure had appeared after we had been beaten in a home game a few weeks earlier. We were ordered in on a Sunday to warm down and, after running around Fratton a few times, Jim appeared, red in the face and obviously flustered. He called us all in for a meeting. He then launched into a tirade, clearly directed at Preki – a Yugoslavian winger he had bought in the close season – saying: "Some player has been talking out of turn, talking to the directors. That's really out of order to go up to the boardroom like that. What is he doing in there anyway; if he has got any problems then he should come and see me." Poor old Preki denied it vehemently, with his limited English, but obviously he had been stitched up by being asked up to the boardroom and questioned by the chairman and directors who were looking for ammunition to use against Jim.

I heard on the radio that Jim had been given a 'sabbatical' to the end of the season – that was a new way of putting it – but he turned it down nevertheless and was then sacked. He had done well in previous years but we were struggling and the Leicester cup defeat was obviously the last straw for new chairman Martin Gregory. Nobody was happy with the way it was done – everybody knows there's no easy way to sack somebody – but that was totally out of order. Typically, Jim took it on the chin and moved on. The players were very sad about it and we felt we had let Jim down. For me, Jim had brought about some of the best spells in my career and Kit, in particular, who owed a lot to Jim for giving him his chance, was really unhappy about it.

Within days Terry Fenwick had been appointed and my immediate reaction was, with both his inexperience and previous connections with QPR and the Gregory family, 'here we go; the John Gregory syndrome again'. I felt that an inexperienced, young manager, in his first job, was not what we needed at that particular time. However, none of the players had any problem or gripes with Fen. In the fans eyes, historically, he is tainted by his association with Terry Venables and, like John Gregory, is ridiculed as one of our worst managers, but

I have to say that I think that's unfair. Fen did okay by me and I found him very approachable. I respected him and he stuck by me when I was having a bad time. He would always be happy to talk with me at great length if I had a problem at any time. I well remember Fen's first training session, on a cold day, with him in a tee shirt and shorts, fresh from his playing days, trying to create a 'hard-man' image. He arranged a 12-a-side game on a small-sized pitch, with him joining in and, with everybody anxious to impress, the tackles were flying in as everybody kicked each other to bits.

Fen had some good ideas, but went over the top on the fitness side, metaphorically running us into the ground. Tactically he was sound, but I found his coaching methods very regimental, particularly on the defending side. He would make the simple things seem very complicated and we would spend hours on positioning, for instance. Theoretically, he had a good method but, given the short attention span of most players, to spend two hours out there was too much. Keith Walden came in as Fen's number two to replace Graham Paddon, who had resigned after being unhappy with the way Jim had been treated. With no disrespect to Keith, Fen might have been better off with a more experienced assistant and it was a shame things didn't work out for him.

By now, at my age and with me having been at the club for so long, I was finding that managers were becoming wary of me. They were starting to give me strong hints, usually along the lines of: "There comes a time in every player's career when..." Fen even brought in another keeper, Jimmy Glass on loan, but he had a bad game on his first start, letting in Port Vale's winner and I was promptly brought back in. John Durnin booked his place in Pompey folklore with some crucial goals in the run-in that season which probably saved us from relegation. Durns was a complex character and you had to watch for his mood swings. He was a typical Scouser and had a fiery side to him. He wore his heart on his sleeve, both on and off the field, and that passionate, committed attitude was largely why the fans took to him in a big way. He was the sort of character that fans and players liked on their side. When Adrian Whitbread arrived, they formed a 'terrible twosome' and were virtually inseparable. Durns and Whit were always happy to represent the club at many functions and people certainly appreciated that. Durns started his career at Liverpool and the joke was that he was the first at Anfield to play over 400 reserve games in the Central League. It's a tribute to his fitness that, at the age of 37, he was still playing in the league with Port Vale last season and his name keeps cropping up in the Liverpool Veterans sides on the TV. Durns was nicknamed 'Johnny Lager', which originated from his days at Oxford, but he wasn't a big drinker – certainly not compared to some of the 80s Pompey generation – and was much more of a gambler. I never knew the extent of his losses, but it was a regular thing to find Durns, Whit and Chambo in Ladbrokes in the afternoon.

Darryl Powell, for whom Jim Smith had returned to his old club to take to Derby, was the only departure during the 1995/96 pre-season. 'Cyrille' – so nicknamed by Ballie, who on his first sighting in a trial match compared him to Cyrille Regis – was only 23, and he had yet to pull up any trees at Pompey, but it was a good move for him. He didn't want to go, but once he saw the money on offer then it was foregone conclusion. Kit had been unhappy for some time in the Fen regime, in fact, since Jim left and it was no surprise when he soon moved to Manchester City. It was also a good move by Fen to show Gerry Creaney the door soon after that, with Walshie returning in exchange. Before doing the deal, Fen asked me what Walshie could do and I had told him he was an exceptional player and also made the point to him that he would win back the fans as well. I was excited about Walshie coming back and it was tragic that, just a few months later, the move was ruined by injury. The incident, against Leicester (who else?) at home, was so innocuous. There was no-one near Walshie when it happened – his leg just collapsed under him. Walshie just couldn't come back from it and it was a big blow to lose him. Again I think that if it had happened nowadays, with all the remarkable advances in treatment, it might not have been a career-ending injury. Martin Allen – the 'Mad Dog' from West Ham – came in on loan and you could see, at times, how he had acquired that nickname. He was a very strong character, even a tad eccentric, who was a non-stop practical joker with plenty of silly tricks to play. In training, for instance, he would suddenly dive into the bushes, go into hiding and start barking. I tried to keep out of his way, but there were plenty of the usual dressing room practical jokes – other players' shirts, ties and socks being cut up, unwelcome stuff being deposited in shoes and the like. He was certainly different, perhaps strange, but a 110% player, who had to struggle with one or two injuries during his playing time at Pompey.

I was never known for my penalty saves, but the Sunderland penalty-takers must have been sick of the sight of me that season. Curiously I managed to save spot-kicks against them both home and away. First Phil Gray missed at Roker Park in September and then it was Craig Russell's turn at Fratton, a few months later. You need some luck in the first place but a little homework can pay off. Sometimes I have seen the player take a penalty on the TV and I guess that they will put it in the same spot. Sometimes a team-mate knows where a player will put the ball if they have played with him at a previous club. But really it's all down to the penalty-taker. If he hits it well enough there is little a goalkeeper can do.

We were drawn to play at Southampton in the FA Cup third round in January 1996 and that game was one of the worst experiences of my career and left me severely embarrassed and upset. I've talked already about my worst feelings in football – the last-minute defeat by Saints in January 1984 and the play-off defeat by Leicester in May 1993 – but in each, although I was bitterly disappointed, I knew we had given our best. Well, in that 3-0 defeat, we totally capitulated and let everybody down. The local derbies against Saints have been few and far between in my time, but at least we had always been up for them. Fen was excited about the prospect of the derby match and seemed to grasp the enormous significance of it, but we were tactically hopeless that day. Venables was not involved at this stage and it was all down to Fen. Early on, we could have had a penalty when Walshie was brought down, but after the first ten minutes or so, Saints were in total control. It was a massive mistake to allow Matt Le Tissier free range that lunchtime and I felt that he should have been man-marked. As a result, he was left to his own devices, allowed to run riot, and proceeded to take the piss out of us throughout the game. What made it worse was that Saints were not a particularly good side at that time either. The lads went for a drink in the hotel afterwards but, for the first time ever, I went straight home. I just couldn't face anybody, I was so pig-sick.

Out of the blue in April 1996, I had my first real public recognition when I was awarded an Honorary Master of Science degree by the University of Portsmouth. It was said that it was for my work in the community and with local charities. For someone who had been so unsuccessful on the academic side at school, it was ironic I suppose, but very touching nevertheless. It was a nerve-racking ceremony, in which I had to wear a mortar board and gown of course. Some people were not too welcoming and there were some letters to the local press from parents of students complaining that their offspring had spent years working and studying for their degree, not to mention the financial sacrifice and here was I being handed one apparently on a plate. I don't know whether they thought the degree was going to open doors for me in some sort of alternative career, but what they missed completely was that the degree was of an honorary nature and merely symbolic.

The importance of meeting requests to represent the club in the community was emphasised to me by Frank Burrows in my early days at the club. He would always say: "It doesn't take two minutes to go and do these things," and I had a great role model in that respect in Peter Mellor. Peter was more outgoing than I could ever be, but he gave freely of himself and his time, so it was a good habit I picked up from him. I have always done it, even though people have sometimes said to me that I should say no more often. It doesn't matter to me whether it's helping to raise £50 for a nursery or playgroup, helping a national appeal for something like the Great Ormond Street Hospital for Children, or just something worthwhile locally, which needs support in one way or another. Don't get me wrong – an awful lot of people do a lot more than me for charity. I'm not naturally gregarious and have had to work at it. The great thing is that people are always pleased to see you, make you feel at ease, and the looks on the kids' faces usually makes it all worthwhile. Having said that, there's nothing like having a bunch of kids look up at you and exclaim "who are you?" to immediately bring you down to earth. Through my hundreds of visits in the city, I have built up a great affinity with the people of Portsmouth, the vast majority of whom have been very good to me, even when I didn't always deserve it.

During my playing days I always attended one or two functions per week in the season of one sort or another, to represent the club. In the summer it would often amount to two in one evening, with my record standing at four in one night. Sometimes it meant that I could only stay for an hour or so and occasionally people have taken some convincing that it wasn't an excuse to get away, when I said I really had to leave to get to another function. I try to help everybody, but it has meant that I have spread myself too thinly on occasions, such that I have ended up pleasing nobody. In the past, there has been some apathy amongst the players about such duties, but it has got a lot better in recent years. It's an individual's choice; some are happy to do it, others are more uncomfortable with it. The present group, under Harry, will do anything they can do to help in the community, despite the enormous demands. It was a hard day emotionally when a group of us went with some naval personnel to a neurological unit at Great Ormond Street Hospital in the early 1990s. The navy boys had raised some funds aboard ship and we took some presents to raise awareness of the hospital's appeal. None of the children knew anything about Pompey, but two things that day stuck in my mind. We were taken to see a sick young child, who had a brain disease with less than six months to live. She was surrounded by tubes and equipment and with her young mother present we felt awkward and embarrassed at intruding, by having a picture taken with her in that situation. But all the mother could think of was helping out the hospital, saying: "If you are raising money and awareness for this hospital, then it's worthwhile." Later on, while we were waiting in the corridor we sat with a huge black guy, built like Darren Moore, and whilst we were with him he was given some news about his child. He just dissolved into tears and crumpled in front of us – a quite shocking sight and bringing the reality of the hospital's role into focus. It was a quiet bunch of players who headed for home, with football and its worries put right into perspective.

After looking so comfortable that season, we hit a really bad patch towards the end and slipped into a real relegation battle. We lost 2-1 at home to Port Vale in midweek in late March, and my blunder in the first few minutes of the game cost us their first goal. On the following Saturday we went down again at home, 2-0 to West Brom, but this time you couldn't lay any of the blame at my door. Afterwards, to my amazement, Fen launched a scathing attack on me, blaming my earlier mistake against Vale for eroding the confidence amongst the younger players in our defence. I remember him saying: "The youngsters need to be able to rely on the experienced players and by failing to do his job properly, Alan's cut them down. As far as I'm concerned it's cost us two matches." It was the most ridiculous comment I had ever heard, but to me it showed the pressure he was under. To say that something which happened in the first five minutes of the previous game was still on their minds the next time they play was way over the top. After that I made a joke of it in our dressing room, saying to the lads: "Look, if I mess up today, it's not going to worry you too much for next Saturday, is it?"

Before the last and absolutely vital home game against Ipswich, we went away to Bournemouth and Fen took us all out for the night to relieve the pressure. It led to an incident involving our winger Jimmy Carter, who Fen had bought earlier in the season. Even though it was obviously unplanned, it certainly had the effect of taking our mind off the game. Jimmy was the nicest, politest guy you could ever meet and he certainly wasn't a drinker. Unfortunately, he turned from Dr Jekyll into Mr Hyde if he did have a glass or two. It didn't take that many to turn him into an out-of-character 'wild man'. That particular night, after coming out of the club, Jimmy took exception to a woman's car and proceeded to kick in the door. He was spotted on CCTV – became a 'TV star' as we put it – and before long the police were on the scene. Jimmy immediately offered to pay for the damage, which was accepted, and he wasn't charged. I had gone back to the hotel early that night, feeling unwell, and woke up the next morning to the news that Jimmy had been arrested the night before. It was so out of character and when he came to his senses and realised what he had done, Jimmy was very upset, and bitterly regretted it.

Carter was one of the great characters – a happy-go-lucky guy who was very funny and witty and great company. He would tell these outlandish stories. Allegedly his grandfather had accumulated enormous wealth in India and Jimmy was waiting on a family inheritance. We would laugh at this story and regularly pull his leg, saying: "If you're a millionaire why are you still playing football?" I gather he is now in real estate abroad and on his way to his second million. He was a gifted player, who had been at Liverpool and Arsenal, but, like many wingers, infuriating. Jimmy was like Vince Hilaire and Kevin O'Callaghan before him. He wouldn't just beat his man once, but insist on beating him four times before getting around to crossing the ball.

We lost to Ipswich, which was a bad result at the time, and it was all down to the last game at Huddersfield. We had to win and hope

Millwall dropped points at Ipswich. A tall order. The pressure in the week up to the game was immense and, unlike other times perhaps, I felt it severely. The whole season had been overshadowed by rumours about takeovers and it just seemed like one long round of survival battles on and off the field. It wore me down. I certainly didn't enjoy all the pressure and anxiety surrounding that Huddersfield game. Fen got his tactics absolutely spot-on, however. He used the 'crab system', which involved us concentrating on staying solid at the back and keeping them out for the first 10-15 minutes. The idea then, was that we would open up, go on the attack with pincer movements down the flanks and try to pinch a goal. If we were successful, then we were to retreat, close up again and stifle their efforts to get back in the game. In the event we scored after eight minutes, which put the 'crab system' out of the window somewhat and we had to 'close up' much earlier than originally planned. I must admit to being quite relieved when Andy Booth, their top scorer, went off early on, after he had collided with me. Again all sorts of scores from the other vital Ipswich/Millwall game, going on simultaneously, were being shouted across to our players and I had to keep on issuing "don't take any notice" instructions. It was a great day, but with hindsight, Huddersfield clearly had nothing to play for and we were playing for our lives. When it was all over, everybody went wild and a great feeling of relief swept over me. It was almost like getting promoted, in some ways. Jason Rees had been a bit of a peripheral figure all season, but he had a great game and a few years later he told me that he was proud of that, saying: "That was my most important contribution to the club." Jason, with some encouragement from Fitzroy Simpson and Paul Hall, also takes the 'credit' for first calling me 'The Legend', at the time when there was some fuss around my appearance record.

When Terry Venables arrived at the start of the 1996/97 season, it came as no surprise to the players, as Fen had talked about him coming to take over and anyway we had already seen him around from time to time during the previous season. Early on, he took a few basic training sessions but, as one of the goalkeepers, I had no contact with him. The players had a respect for what he had achieved in the game, but we had heard all the things which were being said about him and his business affairs. We went over to Le Havre for a friendly in pre-season, which I missed through injury, and I sat on the bench with Fen and Keith Walden. Our fans were very frustrated with the club's situation at that time and many of them decided to have a day out over to France, intent on making their feelings known. The game was played on what was the equivalent of a non-league training ground. There was a pitch invasion at half time, with a mass sit-in. As a result, the French got in a panic about the situation and abandoned the game. Fen and Keith Walden sat on the bench through all this, and took some terrible verbal abuse from our fans, mainly concerning the chairman Martin Gregory.

My injury let in Flav, and I had to sit on the sidelines until just after Christmas that season. It was a difficult, frustrating time for me, not helped by a persistent feeling that I was being encouraged to give up playing. Again I was back to drinking too much and generally wallowing in self-pity, but convinced they would need me back in the end. I had no doubt about Flav's ability, but I knew he would have a dip in form, however slight, at some time, just as most keepers do during a season. As it transpired, I felt sorry for Flav, whose form really did dip and who should have come out of the side two or three games earlier than he did. It's a sign of a good manager when he knows how to handle young players. As it was, Flav's confidence was affected, the crowd was getting on his back and it all culminated in his blunder in dealing with a backpass against Swindon on Boxing Day. I found myself back in the side for the rest of the season and just in time for the cup run through to the sixth round.

One of Venables' first moves was to bring in Matt Svensson, who had been a part-timer in Sweden whilst working as a car dealer. Sven certainly put himself about and, early on, got into a lot of trouble with his late challenges, for which he was in the habit of leaving his foot in. He was a wholehearted player, but early on his touch was raw and he had to work hard at that. He got better and better the longer he was with us and now he's playing in the Premiership with Charlton, so you have to give him a lot of credit for his progress with his game. Venables had a big influence, tactics-wise, on two games in particular that season, both in the FA Cup, at Leeds, where we had a brilliant win of course and then in the next round at home to Chelsea. At Elland Road the tactics worked perfectly, but against Chelsea they failed miserably. There could not have been more of a contrast. The win at Leeds was all down to Venables, who convinced Fen to play our twin strikers, Sven and Bradders, wide rather than down the middle and, in doing so, split their two central defenders. Leeds just couldn't come to terms with it and, on top of that, Sven and Bradders were on fire that afternoon. It was a great afternoon; away at a big club, with a full house and a huge Pompey following and to top it all, everything clicked. Their goalkeeper had a great deal more to do than I did, and even when Leeds scrambled back a couple of goals, I never felt we would lose the game.

For the quarter-final against Chelsea three weeks later, Venables' tactics were way off the mark. It was decided to stand off them, let them have the ball at the back and then try to pick it up when it came into our half of the field. The theory was that people like Frank Leboeuf couldn't pass the ball, so their attempts wouldn't reach their targets. We set out our stall wrongly and that was never better illustrated when Leboeuf picked out Mark Hughes with a 40-yard crossfield pass and he then volleyed it past me into the top corner. Even their players were very surprised at our tactics and expected us to be working hard to shut them down all over the park, particularly as one of Bradders' strengths was the pressure he put on defenders in possession. As it was, the tactics gave Zola and Company a chance to express themselves and they proceeded to murder us.

Inevitably, the question of my future came up and, after Fen had mentioned to me that a group of Chinese football officials were over here on a visit, Venables had a 'chat' with me: "China were looking to get some players in, would I be interested?" I knew that Ted Buxton, a friend of Venables and by now our chief scout, had some involvement with Chinese football, but I was never put under any pressure to go. After that one mention, Venables never came back to me. For a person like me, who throughout his career has retained a basic insecurity, when people at the club come out and say things like that it was bound to create some paranoia. But it was to become a fact of life for me, a recurring theme in the latter days of my career. As I said to the lads at the time: "I think they are trying to tell me something – not only are they trying to move me out, but they're trying to send me as far away as possible..."

*'If his response shows what
competition and hurt pride can
do then I'm delighted.'*
                    Terry Fenwick

The arrival of Estonian international Mart Poom, in a £200,000 deal from Swiss club FC Wil, was a sure sign manager Jim Smith wanted to put pressure on his long-serving goalkeeper and, with just one year left on his contract, Knight was as aware as anyone that his place was under perhaps the most serious threat yet, since he had established himself as first choice ahead of Peter Mellor thirteen years before. 'I'm sure his arrival will keep me on my toes,' he said pre-season. 'Whoever is playing the best will be picked for the team and it's up to me to get the nod,' adding that Aaron Flahavan would also be pushing for a place. Pompey had brought in Yugoslav winger Predrag Radosavjlevic – better known as Preki – but the chances of winning promotion had been substantially reduced because just two sides, and only one automatically, would go up at the end of the season as the Premiership slimmed down to 20 clubs. Of more pressing concern, ultimately, would be the fact that four sides were also destined to leave the first division from the wrong end in May 1995.

On the opening day, Pompey sealed an encouraging 2–1 home win over a Notts County side that had just missed the play-offs in the previous campaign. Knight had got the aforementioned nod, but any complacency he may have had was shattered when Smith picked Poom for the first round Coca-Cola Cup tie with Cambridge. The Estonian even kept a clean sheet, as Pompey won 2–0 and Knight had an anxious wait until the Friday to find he had regained his place for the trip to newly-promoted Reading. It was clearly a jolt to the 33-year-old's system, although his reaction at the time was diplomatic enough: 'Being dropped for Wednesday was a bit of a shock although I could understand the Gaffer's thinking. He's paid a lot of money for Mart and obviously he is looking to get that back by playing him. But I'll make it hard for him to drop me,' he added. Poom got another run out for the second leg of the cup tie, in which Pompey cruised to a 5-2 aggregate win, but it was clear Knight had seen off the pretender for the time being. Poom was reduced to a diet of reserve-team appearances, spiced up by regular international call-ups, while Knight was an ever-present as the league campaign fell away after a promising start.

Poom was also having his own highs and lows, earning the man-of-the-match award as he single-handedly defied the Croatian attack in a European Championship game in Tallinn, only to pick up a one-match ban after receiving a red card in a reserve game at Watford. By October, the goalkeeping question was further sharpened by the knowledge that, for Poom to get his work permit extended the following summer, he would have to play in 75% of Pompey's fixtures. Getting the permit in the first place had not been a problem, as Poom had been an ever-present in the Estonian fixtures since its breakaway from the Soviet Union. However, the games were already fast running out and Knight's form had made him virtually undroppable, although he acknowledged Poom's presence had improved his game: 'I know the score. All I can do is try to keep playing as well as possible, hope I'm spared injuries and avoid too many mistakes. Mart's presence has certainly sharpened me up. The competition's good for me,' he said at the end of September.

To underline the point, Knight produced one of his virtuoso performances in the second leg of the second round Coca-Cola Cup game with Premiership Everton. Pompey had stunned the Toffeemen at Goodison by winning 3-2, thanks largely to a brace of Gerry Creaney goals, but at Fratton, Everton were keen to make amends for their under-fire boss Mike Walker. They even threw in new loan signing Duncan Ferguson alongside £3 million summer recruit Daniel Amokachi, the Nigerian striker who had wowed audiences in the 1994 World Cup. Although

Everton took the lead early on through Dave Watson, Knight kept his team in the game with a string of top class saves. 'I was disappointed with myself over their goal. I went for it but couldn't get to it because there were a couple of bodies in the way,' he said post-match. 'I was pleased with the save from Amokachi when he was through and the stop from Ferguson, but I suppose it was the first one from the deflected shot which was the best. I had a bit of luck there. Normally, when you get a deflection like that there's no point going for it. This time what helped was the height it got off Jon Gittens and that gave me time to get back. Even so I was a bit surprised when I managed to scoop it off the line.' Paul Hall's last-minute goal saw Pompey through to the next round and after that performance, work permit criteria or not, Knight was going to be first choice for it.

In the end, Smith never really had to make the choice as a knee injury picked up by Poom in a reserve game was taking its time to heal, partly because of the blond giant's over-enthusiasm for returning to training, not to mention an infection in the injury, picked up when he had some minor surgery done on it on a return home. Knight was kept pretty busy shoring up a leaky defence. In November, the goals which had kept Pompey out of trouble dried up and a run of five consecutive defeats in November and December, including a 4-1 thrashing at home by Sunderland and a 4-0 defeat at Middlesbrough, had Pompey in the bottom four. Three wins against Notts County, Barnsley and Burnley over Christmas and New Year lifted the siege mentality at Fratton, which had been reinforced by the news that the controversial plan to build a new stadium at Farlington had been rejected by the Department for the Environment. When a season's-best performance dumped promotion-chasing Bolton out of the FA Cup, it seemed Smith and the team had turned the corner. It was only into another dead end. An insipid goalless draw with Bristol City, followed by a televised 3-0 drubbing at Derby, meant Smith went into the FA Cup fourth-round tie with Premiership Leicester under mounting pressure from both fans and managing director Martin Gregory, who was running affairs at the club on behalf of his ailing father Jim, who hadn't been seen at Fratton Park in almost a year. Smith's cause wasn't helped when centre back Gittens was sent off in the first half for a professional foul, then the gap-toothed, perennial scourge of Pompey, Iwan Roberts, put the Foxes one-up on the stroke of half time. When Knight slithered outside his box with ball in hand and also saw red, giving Flahavan an unexpectedly premature debut, Smith must have sensed the game was up. Gregory junior's wrapping up the sacking in terms of a 'sabbatical' until the end of the season, on the Monday, was easily seen through. Terry Fenwick, the former QPR, Spurs and England defender was the new man in charge and he had a tricky early problem, as he had to cover Knight's impending suspension.

It was all-change at Fratton, as coaches Graham Paddon and Mike Bailey were replaced by Keith Walden. Knight was also 'promoted' to become goalkeeping coach and enthusiastically threw himself into his new role, just 48 hours after having had an operation to cure a long-standing sinus problem. ' I'm looking forward to it. I've wanted to get into coaching and this is an opportunity to ease myself in,' he said at the time. With Poom close to fitness, Fenwick offered the Estonian the chance to step in for Knight when he was due to purge his suspension in the new boss's first home game against Millwall. Fenwick was stunned to hear Poom turn him down, claiming he was not fit enough, but the new boss decided to leave Flahavan out in the cold too. 'I would have expected him (Poom) to be ready to walk over broken glass to play in such a big game and I felt it was a bit too early to throw Flav in at the deep end,' commented the rookie manager. Instead, Fenwick turned to 21-year-old Jimmy Glass, whom he brought in on loan, even though the Crystal Palace reserve player had yet to make a first-team appearance. In the end, the Millwall game fell victim to the weather and Glass made his debut the following week as Pompey came from 2-0 down to draw at Sunderland. Knight was immediately back, but he gifted a couple of goals in games with Wolves and West Brom in early March, which both led to defeats. The tame Bob Taylor shot which went under his body in the latter fixture at Fratton, which Knight himself described as a 'schoolboy error', persuaded Fenwick to extend Glass's loan. With Pompey slipping back into the relegation mire, Fenwick axed Knight, claiming the veteran keeper's confidence was low, for the midweek trip to Port Vale, only to see Glass shatter the confidence his manager had shown in him with an equally banal error which gave the home side victory. All in all, March 1995 was not a happy time for any of Pompey's goalkeeping fraternity, as Poom was also disappointed to see a loan move to Premiership Leeds scuppered by the terms of his work permit. Fenwick persevered with Glass for the next home game, but then decided to cut his losses and send him back to Selhurst Park, as Poom was now back to full fitness. Knight was back between the sticks as Pompey stayed up with three wins and a draw in the final four matches of the season. As Knight finally put pen to paper on his new contract, he was also boosted by the news he had been voted the fans' player of the season.

Knight was now within 22 games of equalling Peter Bonetti's 600–game record and with three more years of contract under his belt, it seemed only a serious injury could prevent him over-taking the former Chelsea custodian's mantle. Initially, however, Knight's proud record of having started as first choice every season since 1981 was really being tested by Poom, who had been granted a further year's permit in the light of his injury problems. It was no surprise when Poom was named for the opening game of the 1995/96 season at home to Southend. There wasn't even a place for Knight on the bench as Fenwick opted to go with three outfield players. He was vindicated by a 4–2 win in which Creaney grabbed a hat-trick, but it was to prove a false dawn for Fenwick, who had been promising a promotion challenge in pre-season. A 3–0 aggregate defeat by second division Cardiff in the Coca-Cola Cup, was a stunning blow, sandwiching a (by now traditional) loss at Grimsby. Knight too was upset at his bystander role: 'After being player of the season last year and, I think, generally playing well, I'd hoped to start in the team this time and I suppose that had a lot to do with me signing that new contract. Had I thought this might happen I might have had second thoughts,' he said. Fenwick was busy reworking his squad, selling Kit Symons to Alan Ball's Manchester City for £1.8 million – and Knight almost joined him temporarily at Maine Road, as City sought to cover a goalkeeping crisis. It is perhaps fortunate for all concerned in this tale, that the move fell through. For, in Poom's fifth appearance of the season, he endured a nightmare game, as that man Iwan Roberts helped himself to a first half hat-trick. Poom was at fault for all of the goals, as Pompey trailed 4–1 to Leicester at the break, losing 4–2 in the end. Knight was back in his 'rightful' place for the next game at home to Millwall and Poom's infant Fratton career was effectively over.

Fenwick's transfer dealings were picking up pace. Midfielder Fitzroy Simpson and striker Carl Griffiths had come in the other direction as part of the Symons move, then unsettled Creaney finally got his move away. Bizarrely, it was also to Manchester City as Fenwick and Ball thrashed out a cash–plus–player deal. That player was Paul Walsh. A week later, West Ham's Martin Allen arrived on loan, with a view to a permanent £500,000 deal and the team was taking shape in its young manager's image. Knight saved a penalty to help earn a 1–1 draw at Sunderland and earned his manager's praise: 'Knightsie's performances in the last two games have been exceptional and, when he's playing like that, there's no one better in the division. It's now up to him. I left him out at the start of the season because I thought it was the right decision for the team and if his response shows what competition and hurt pride can do then I'm delighted.' Not that results were forthcoming at once for Fenwick's 'new' team. Four defeats out of five in September and October put Pompey second bottom of the table and even the point gained at Oldham had manager and goalkeeper at odds again. 'How could a man who's played hundreds of games not demand the ball in a situation like that,' moaned Fenwick after Jon McCarthy's equaliser. 'I yelled at Gitto (Gittens) to leave it but I'm afraid he didn't hear me,' retorted Knight. At the end of October, Pompey's first win since September 9, 4–2 at home to Watford, finally lifted them clear of the drop zone, while Poom was getting ready to leave Fratton. Knight had established himself as the undisputed first choice and the Estonian's work permit was due to expire on December 31, with little prospect of him playing in the requisite 75% of games to ensure its renewal, especially as he copped another three-match ban after being sent off for the reserves at Bristol Rovers. He was philosophical: 'There's nothing I can do about it. I want to stay here because I'm happy and I still believe in myself, but it's not up to me.' Fenwick was rather blunter: 'Mart had his chance at the start of the season, but the pressure got to him I'm afraid and we were punished.'

After a miserable November, Pompey perked up in December with four straight wins and the news that chairman Martin Gregory – his father's illness had finally forced him to relinquish the role – was in negotiations to sell the club to a consortium of northern businessmen led by Warren Smith. Knight also equalled Bonetti's one-club record in the 3-2 home defeat to Crystal Palace on New Year's Day, but his last-minute race into the opposition penalty area couldn't ensure a truly memorable end to the match. In the tributes, ex-boss Jim Smith was even moved to apologise for the time he called Knight a 'liability': 'That was unfair of me. He wasn't. He's a true pro and no-one plays that many games and sees off so many rivals without being an exceptional player,' he said. The record was broken in the following home game against Grimsby. Sandwiched between the matches was the wretched surrender at Southampton in the eagerly-awaited FA Cup third-round tie. In early February Whitehall, as expected, refused Poom's work permit extension. 'I'm sad to go because I know people here haven't seen the best of me. I'm a better goalkeeper than they think and I would have liked the chance to prove it to them. I'm certainly a better player than when I came – I've learned a lot here, particularly from Knight,' were his parting words. A £100,000 move to Stockport fell through, as the Department of Employment insisted he pack his bags, leaving Pompey out of pocket.

As Pompey kept their good form going, despite losing Walsh to a knee injury that would claim his career, Knight was in the headlines again as he saved a penalty in the Sunderland home game – the second time he'd stopped a kick against the Rokermen. 'I saved a penalty up at Roker Park against Phil Gray earlier this season. When the penalty was awarded I looked around to see where he was, but he was on the subs bench. Craig Russell stepped up and put the ball to his right. He made it obvious where he was going to put it and I went the right way by diving to my left. A lot of strikers put the ball straight down the middle, but you can end up looking a bit of a fool if they put them in the corners and you're rooted to the spot,' he commented.

By mid-March, Pompey were in the top half of the table and optimism was high that they could make a blind-side run for the play-offs. The Smith consortium had finally had their offer rejected by the Gregorys and chairman Martin had brought London businessman Terry Brady onto the board. His presence immediately pepped up the place, but suddenly, on the field, the team's form collapsed after a 2–0 home defeat to Wolves. The referee's final whistle, a fraction before Andy Roberts' shot for Crystal Palace hit the back of the net a week later, earned Pompey a point and Knight another clean sheet, but one win, six defeats and a draw in eight games left Pompey staring relegation in the face. The final home game of the season saw Knight presented with the fans' player-of-the-season trophy for the second consecutive season but a goal ten minutes from time, by Alex Mathie, left Pompey needing an unlikely combination of results to stay in the first division. Oldham and Reading's midweek wins saw them safe, leaving Millwall – who had topped the table in December – the only side Pompey could catch. On an afternoon of unbearable tension at Huddersfield, Pompey took an early lead through Deon Burton and never looked like losing it. The scoreboard never ticked over at Portman Road and, after an excruciating 90-second wait, after the game at the McAlpine ended, the news filtered through: Pompey were safe.

The euphoria, coupled with relief, which followed allowed Knight to make the most of the Honorary Master of Science degree awarded to him in recognition of his services to the club.

Not bad for a lad from Balham with barely a qualification to his name when he left school. It was also during pre-season training in 1996 that Knight finally acquired the nickname he sports to this day: 'The Legend'. Not that his newly-acquired status guaranteed him a place in the side. As optimism soared at Fratton Park with the news that former England manager Terry Venables – long courted by the Gregory family – was joining the club on a 'consultancy' basis, Knight found himself out in the cold at the start of a season for the second time in a row. Flahavan was in goal for the opening game, but it soon turned into a nightmare, as first Andy Awford and then Flav himself were sent off. Pompey crashed 3–1 and followed that up with a televised 2–1 home defeat by newly-relegated QPR in a ground which was a pale shadow of its former self, with just 11,000 seats bolted onto the terraces by the parsimonious Gregory. Knight got a look in, and kept a clean sheet, in the 1–0 win at Grimsby, as Flahavan served his suspension, but it was then back to the reserves and coaching duties for the veteran. As Pompey started to climb the table, after their shaky start, it seemed Knight was destined to have a long wait to get his place back. By December Pompey were in mid-table, with Venables now sharing his time between assisting Fenwick with the coaching at Fratton and managing the Australian national side. The signing of Swedish striker Mathias Svensson promised to give the side additional punch, currently provided by the fast-maturing Lee Bradbury, the Cowes-born striker whom Pompey had plucked from the army like Guy Whittingham before him.

Despite making the odd mistake, which had got the terrace critics on his back, howling for Knight's recall, Flahavan was doing more than enough to justify his place, even saving a penalty at Barnsley. Then his luck ran out – a theme which was to become sadly familiar. His gaffe against Swindon on Boxing Day when his fluffed clearance led to the winning goal, was too big to ignore and persuaded Fenwick to be 'cruel to be kind' and let Knight back in. He was vindicated as the 35-year-old rolled back the years with a couple of vintage saves in the 2–0 win at in-form Port Vale. Flahavan's misfortune was Knight's gain. Pompey suddenly found a hot streak of form, blitzing past Wolves and Reading in the FA Cup – the former their first win at Molineux since 1951 – and putting together a five-match winning run in the league to put them at the heart of the play-off race. The crowning glory though was the 3–2 win at Leeds in the FA Cup fifth round – in the same week Venables announced his intention to buy the club for a nominal £1. The win set up a quarter-final tie with Chelsea at Fratton and, before the game, Knight was appreciative of the fact he was now back in the spotlight, especially in view of the fact his contract was due to expire in the summer. 'I don't think I'm playing any better or worse than last season or the season before. Flav got in at the start of the season and did well, it's just things began to catch up with him, but I still believe he is a good keeper and will serve this club well. I want to stay here and be part of this club for the foreseeable future. I still believe I can do a good job for them and I still believe I've a few more years left in me. I like to think my form so far, since I got back in the side, supports that. I suppose in a way, it's all a bonus for me. After 1992, when we got so close, I thought that was my last chance of making it to Wembley. Now we're close again, although there's a very tricky match coming up. But after the way the season started for me it's a lovely position to be in.'

That was as lovely as it got. Mark Hughes' sumptuous strike after 25 minutes set Ruud Gullit's Premiership aristocrats on the road to a 4–1 win to shatter any illusions Pompey had of a visit to the twin towers. However, under Venables and Fenwick, Pompey had made enormous progress on the field and with the rising talent of the likes of Bradbury, Svensson and Russell Perrett, coupled with the older heads like David Hillier and Alan McLoughlin, optimism was high they could go at least one better the following season. Knight's form was rewarded with an other two-year contract but, as ever with Pompey, things were not going to turn out to be quite that straightforward.

8 - Indian summer

For the 1997/98 pre-season Fen took us to Norway, where we seemed to spend most of our time making long boat trips across fjords to where we were due to play. Terry Venables flew in one night in a flying boat to watch one of our games and we had a chat – only the second time I had spent any real time with him. Perhaps he wanted to pick my brains about tactics? Not likely, as the conversation took a similar turn to the previous one: "At your age and at this stage of your career, have you thought about playing and coaching in Australia, as I've got some contacts who could set you up." For my part I didn't dismiss the idea, but just replied: "Let me know if anything comes up." He never came back to me on the idea. It was probably down to my paranoia, but again I couldn't escape the conclusion that they were trying to move me out. When that tour was all over, it was back to crossing fjords and taking a plane to Scotland, where we stayed in Dunblane. No sooner had we arrived than Fen was back into his usual mode, caning us physically with plenty of running up and down hills. But afterwards, just as typically, he took us all out to a Glasgow nightclub and he would be one of the boys for the night, ready to sit and chat with every one of the players.

We started the season with a big influx of Australian players, after Fen and Venables had been Down Under together in the summer. It rapidly became a bit of a joke. Fen tried to make out that he had recruited them, but no-one really believed him and we knew, that with his connections out there, Venables had been a major influence in the signings. Their arrival was the beginning of the end for Fen and caused a number of problems. Immediately, there were rumours going around about the amount of money they were earning and that caused considerable resentment amongst the other players. The Aussie group found it hard to acclimatise, weren't the best mixers in the world, and formed themselves into a clique. Only two of the original Aussie bunch were good enough in my opinion – midfielders Craig Foster and Robbie Enes. Robbie looked the best of the lot to me, but he got injured early on, hated it here anyway and quickly moved back home at the end of the season. The goalkeeper, Zeljco Kalac, had been here before with Leicester, but had work permit problems. He was a big, imposing lad and his arrival was unsettling for me and really got me down. I needn't have worried, as it turned out, because he failed again to get a work permit, after a long wait. Australian striker John Aloisi was signed a few weeks later, but he was the exception in the group. He had played abroad in Italy already and was used to adapting to a foreign environment. Also, John was of a different mentality and a good mixer, who fitted in immediately.

Bradders was sold for a club record fee of over £3 million to Manchester City, followed quickly by Deon Burton for £1.5 million to Derby, where he rejoined Jim Smith. We were back to being a 'selling club' again, but left with substandard Aussie players who were picking up good wages. Like the fans, I had become bitter and disillusioned by the lack of investment in the club and the lack of interest being shown by the owner. I just didn't feel that anything was going to change. I couldn't see the club going forward and it looked to me like another season of struggle. I was having a few personal problems, was drinking far too much and was nowhere near as focused as I should have been. There were rumours that the club was about to fold and with the severe cash-flow problems, it felt like I had gone full circle back to my early days in the 1970s with the SOS appeal. All this climaxed with the non-payment of our November salaries. We had been paid late in the past and, although we had mortgages to pay or overdrafts to negotiate, it was no more than an annoyance and inconvenience for the players. We knew we would get paid, if only through the PFA. It was the office staff I felt sorry for, as they had no such guarantee of payment.

Early in the New Year, Fen was sacked. A couple of weeks later we played at Oxford and lost to a last-minute goal and, as I drove myself home, I had a call from BBC *Radio Solent* to say that Alan Ball was returning to take over as manager. My first reaction was that it was fantastic news, was just what we needed and that Ballie was sure to get the right response from the players. For some reason, my form dipped dramatically from the moment Ballie arrived. I even came up with an own goal in his very first match in charge at home to Sheffield United when, in taking a cross from my old mate Lee Sandford, I collided with a goal post and as I fell, dropped the ball into the net. It obviously caused some amusement in the city. In the following week, whilst I was dropping my girls off at school in the mornings, some of the boys, as soon as they had spotted me, would take the mickey out of me by deliberately walking into lampposts and falling over. You had to laugh, I suppose.

After all the problems with previous managers, I think the relief of Ballie's arrival meant I subconsciously relaxed and wasn't as focused as I might have been. When we lost 3-1 at Crewe, just three games after his arrival, I was at fault – slipping coming out for a cross – for the second goal and the defeat left us rooted at the bottom of the league. Crewe's Gresty Road was a bogey ground for me and Ballie got it right afterwards when he said: "I bet you love it here, you just always have a nightmare…" I wasn't making massive howlers, but my confidence was being affected. Three days later we were at home to Stockport and that game was the turning point of the season. Beforehand Ballie pulled me aside and started to say: "I think I need to make a change…", but I didn't give him time to finish the sentence. I butted in, saying: "You're right, I'm not playing well, and you should bring Flav back in." It was not a great game, but a unique experience for everybody there that night. Suddenly this wall of noise arose from the fans midway through the first half, after Steve Claridge had scored. That constant booming chanting sound just continued for the rest of the game from all corners of the ground. It was a memorable experience, even though I wasn't playing, and helped us to a vital victory.

Whilst he was caretaker for a few days after Fen's departure, Keith Walden had brought Claridge in on loan. Steve had a galvanising effect on the team and we won five out of six before he had to return to Leicester. Off the field, Steve always had a joke and plenty of banter and was a scruffy guy, even if he was dressed up in an Armani suit. Not the most elegant of players, Steve was a naturally fit bloke, who only ever seemed to need to keep it ticking over. He could run and run and had no problem with cross country of any distance. He played with his heart on his sleeve, still does, with a great will to win and a 110% attitude. How he retains that enthusiasm, after all these years, I just don't know. As a local lad, Pompey clearly has a special place in his heart and it really showed.

Flav played well during that relegation battle, which climaxed with the final-day escape through the win at Bradford. It was a nerve-racking afternoon at Valley Parade and, as a radio summariser, not having any control over events on the field was awful for me. Not taking anything away from our lads' performance on the day, but I felt the Bradford players had already booked their holidays, as they say. It was great to stay up, but when you're not playing you just don't feel part of it. It just wasn't the same for me and I didn't feel like joining in the celebrations. I just drove home and stayed in that night.

On his return, after nine years away, Ballie was more relaxed and less intense than I had been used to before and that was certainly to the benefit of his health. He was less involved on the coaching side, leaving things generally to Kevin Bond. I felt he could have taken more sessions than he did and we needed him to be more hands-on. None of this is a criticism, but there were times when his motivating skills could have been put to greater use if he had been more closely involved. It was also apparent to me, although he wouldn't admit it, that, whilst managing elsewhere, he had taken a lot of knocks that he didn't deserve and they had taken their toll on him. I felt that, generally, in this second spell at the club, his signings let him down. They simply didn't perform, and most were not strong enough, both mentally and physically, for the English game.

Flav was first choice for the new 1998/99 season, but in our second game at Plymouth in the Worthington Cup first round I had to come on as a sub to replace him after he had been injured in a collision. Not expecting to play, I had driven down to Torquay and hadn't eaten anything other than a pie on arrival at the ground. It turned out to be a rather dramatic evening, mainly through the worst refereeing display I had ever witnessed in my nearly 800 games to date. It would be an understatement to say that Plymouth were over-physical, let's just say our players were being smashed all over the pitch. Our little Greek lad Nikos Kyzeridis was carried off and I was really wound up about it all. At the final whistle I sprinted to the centre circle to confront the referee and tell him what I thought of his display. I was at pains to ensure that I didn't swear at him and even got him to confirm to me verbally that I had not done so. As it transpired he reported me to the FA, and I was found to have brought the game into disrepute and fined £500. Much was made of the fact that his report mentioned that I had sworn at him during our confrontation.

Flav's blackout during the home game against Swindon in mid-September was a worrying development for everybody, not to mention the lad himself. People immediately questioned his nerves and his ability to handle the pressure, even though we were 4-1 up at the time and cruising. In any event, he had played at Bradford in that last crucial game of the previous season, was under great pressure that day and, cool as a cucumber, had come through with flying colours. Everything was considered – was it nerves, or perhaps a viral infection, or a dietary or fluid problem, or did he just simply faint? He had all the tests in London, but no reason could be found. Our physio, Jonathan Trigg, spent hours on the internet, searching sites in an attempt to find a possible cause. Flav was prescribed some tablets, but I never found out what they were. For all I know, they may have been placebos, if the medical people thought there was some psychological reason behind the blackout. In the end, the incident was dismissed as a one-off and everybody forgot about it. However, almost a year later it happened again and then people really did start to worry.

Flav was a humorous guy, nicknamed 'Space Cadet', mainly because of the strange dreams he would have, which he would then come and tell us about. He was a very fit lad and certainly intense and highly strung about his goalkeeping. Flav enjoyed his training and we would work together every day. If we were working absolutely flat out to the point of exhaustion, we would get a bit dizzy. We would joke about the fact that at those times we would be in a state of what we called 'delusion', almost with stars in our eyes.

Ballie brought me back into the side when it was obvious that Flav's confidence had been affected, but not long afterwards he borrowed Andy Petterson from Charlton. I had nothing personally against Petts, but Ballie didn't tell me he was coming and the first I knew of his arrival was when he turned up to get on the coach to Grimsby. It was a condition of his loan that he had to play, so I was on the sidelines again and I was most unhappy. In fairness, although he continued to train with Charlton, Petts did well while he was on loan that season and it rejuvenated him. We used to joke later that it was only when he signed permanently and came down to train with us, that he didn't do so well. Inevitably players often raise their game when they go out on loan and are looking for a contract, then their form dips when they get taken on permanently as they psychologically take their foot off the pedal.

Petts certainly had a nightmare time in his three-year Pompey stay. He had a lot of injuries, particularly problems with his calves and, with the team often not playing well, it meant that even when he did play he invariably got the blame for our defeats. Later on, his cause wasn't helped when Tony Pulis arrived as manager and took an instant dislike to him and made it clear that he thought he was 'swinging the lead' when he was out. Subsequently, under other managers, he still had a bad time and became something of a forgotten man at the club.

Towards the end of February, Petts was recalled by Charlton and Ballie brought Flav back for our game at Swindon. You could say that Flav wasn't the luckiest of guys, to put it mildly. In his return match, he was caught by a totally outrageous challenge from Iffy Onoura and his face was smashed. A few teeth were broken, along with his nose, and he was severely concussed, not to mention the shoulder ligament damage. For me, it brought back vivid memories of my facial injury against Wimbledon all those years before and I was worried that Flav's cheekbone had been damaged, as mine had been. I went to hospital and sat with him for hours and he was delusional, just asking non-stop questions like "did they score?", "was it my fault?" and "how do I look?"

It was during December 1998, that chairman Martin Gregory stripped Ballie of his power to buy and sell players and brought in an agent with a view to selling as many players as possible to relieve the club's debts. Before one game the lads warmed up in tee-shirts with their 'prices' – £1.50 here, £2.50 there – marked on the front with a marker pen. We even thought of coming out holding up estate agents' 'for sale' boards, but that was perhaps going too far. The chairman was struggling financially and the situation really came home to us when we arrived at the hotel where we were due to stay for the night before our cup game at Nottingham Forest. We turned up at the hotel only to find they wouldn't let us in because they refused to take a club cheque to cover the costs of our stay. It was only when Keith Walden arrived with cash that they relented and even then all the players had to give their personal credit card details to cover any other expenses incurred. From then on, for all overnight stays, Keith had to take a briefcase stuffed with notes with him to cover any costs.

Eventually, the club went into administration and all the players could do was to be professional and try to do their job. As before, we were not being paid and initially it wasn't a real problem with the PFA   stepping in to help, but we knew they would only carry on for so long. We were hearing the rumours that Gregory was prepared to let the club go to the wall and there was a genuine worry amongst the players, shared by the fans no doubt, that the club might go out of existence. It was not for me to side with any potential buyer, but I was asked to speak in support of the 'Portsmouth United' supporters' consortium at a public meeting at the Guildhall. I wasn't into the politics of their bid and I didn't know the individuals involved, but I was happy to speak on the basis that I would support anything that might enable the club to survive. I am not the best or most eloquent of speakers and I found it very hard to go on stage in front of such an audience, but I tried to speak from the heart. The desperate situation the club found itself in did galvanise people, made everybody determined to see the club survive and had the beneficial effect of drawing the players closer to the fans.

I was out of contract at the end of that 1998/99 season. Nothing had been said to me about my future and I had a feeling that if it was down to the administrators or, in fact, any new owners, they wouldn't want to keep a 37-year-old player, who had at one time that season been the third-choice keeper. I had gone through a bad spell that season, being dropped and worn down by the continual relegation battles. I realised that perhaps the time had come for me to pack it in. The club had got to look forward and I felt Flav should be given his chance as the Number One next season. I was hoping for another playing contract, if only to play if and when I was needed and to carry on with the goalkeeper coaching work. I could sense that a big career decision was looming for me.

Suddenly my playing career seemed like it was at an end and, despite all those games and seasons I had been through, it had gone so quickly. They say you don't realise what you've got until it's gone. You always hear managers and players saying: "You are a long time not playing" and never a truer word in football has been spoken. The truth is I could have carried on playing, got myself an agent, made myself available and earned a few quid as a footballing nomad, plying my trade in the lower divisions. In some ways I regret I didn't make an effort to keep on playing. I could even still be turning out today, as Dave Beasant is. But then again, perhaps I would have made a fool of   myself and might have regretted not packing it in. Who knows?

However, the story goes that Ballie was out with Awfs and Adrian Whitbread at a golf event and in the bar afterwards the conversation got round to next season and, amongst other things, my future involvement at the club. Awfs and Whit had seen how despondent I had become during the previous season at being regularly sidelined and they suggested to Ballie that I be given a role as the goalkeeping coach. With me unaware of this conversation, Ballie pulled me in a few days later and started the familiar refrain : "There comes a time in every player's career when you have to think about..." He went on to offer me the coaching role with the goalkeepers, adding: "You've been a great servant to this club, and, whilst I am here, there's a job for life here for you. The coach's job will keep you involved and means you can stay here, rather than bang around in the lower divisions if you carry on playing." It did mean that my salary was halved but, although I really wanted to carry on playing, I didn't want to leave the club I loved. Ballie's offer solved both our problems – he didn't want to be the manager who had shown me the door and I couldn't bring myself to leave. I agreed to stay on a non-contract basis, but with the club holding my playing registration in case of emergency. At that time, few first division clubs had a full-time goalkeeping coach and it was good of the new chairman Milan Mandaric and Ballie to employ me in that job. Every Premiership club has a coach for their keepers and the role is becoming more established in the game.

If I had taken more time to think about it, even perhaps gone away to recharge my batteries before making a decision, I might have done differently. Perhaps I had allowed people to make up my mind for me, but I made the decision to go into coaching there and then and haven't lost any sleep about it since. I knew the transition would be hard and it was. In fact, I still struggle with it to this day. I can't stop myself wanting to play – I have to stop myself joining in six-a-sides.

Once I had finished playing and was not subject to the players' 48-hour curfew before a game, there was no need for me to keep ultra-fit and I found myself drinking more. I was also having personal problems with my marriage breaking up, with my drinking as one of the factors. Whilst I was playing I could always run off any effects in training and the drinking did not affect me unduly. As a player you knew when you could drink and when you couldn't and you would sort out your drinking sessions accordingly, knowing you would be in a fit enough condition to perform on match days. But now I was finding myself out more with my mates and even on the night before a game. I found the transition to non-playing difficult and, as time went on, I felt insecure in my coaching role. As I saw it at the time, my career appeared to be drifting aimlessly. I would seek solace in my drinking and there were regular binges at weekends. You can look for all the excuses in the world for it, but none will do. I am not going to blame anyone but myself for that situation, and am not looking for sympathy.

It wasn't long into that season before I was back between the posts, if only for eight minutes, when Ballie put me on as a sub at home to Torquay in a Worthington Cup. With Petts nursing an injured elbow, I was on the bench. Late on, with the tie effectively over as we led 3-0 on aggregate and the fans chanting for me to come on, Ballie sent me out so as to notch my 799th appearance and get me nearer the magical 800. There was never a dull moment with the batch of keepers working with me and plenty of problems for me to contend with in the early weeks of my new career. First Petts was in trouble with a drink-driving conviction and then he was out of action with that injured elbow, followed quickly by a pulled calf muscle. Chris Tardif

(Tards) collapsed one morning in training with what was diagnosed as nervous exhaustion, brought on by worry over his mother's cancer, which he had never spoken to us about. Tards was living on his own, with his mother back in Guernsey and we had to send him home for a couple of weeks to enable him to deal with the family crisis.

To top it all, Flav fainted in the goalmouth again, in a Worthington Cup tie against Blackburn, almost a year to the day since the first occurrence. Twelve months previously, we had thought it was a one-off and had managed to laugh it off as one of his 'delusional' spells. Now the seeds of doubt and uncertainty were really being sown in Flav's head. He just wanted to know what was happening to him. Again, physio Jonathan Trigg pursued every avenue possible to find the cause and it was suggested that a fall in Flav's blood pressure was at the root of it, with some tablets prescribed to counter the problem.

We were battered 3-0 by Blackburn in that first leg at home, and were 5-1 down on aggregate at Ewood Park in the second leg when Ballie put me on as a sub for Petts for the last seven minutes. It was my 800th appearance. Ballie had said beforehand that he might bring me on – "for the last 10 minutes" – so that I could get to the milestone figure. It was a great gesture and one that I'll never forget; he didn't have to do it and not all managers would have bothered. I had not really trained that season and we were under the cosh that night, so I was looking to be out there for as little time as possible. As I sat waiting for the call from Ballie, I even thought of slipping out to the toilet to run down some more time. When I finally went out on to the pitch, the reception from the 200 or so Pompey fans present, coupled with the ovation from the Blackburn crowd, was fantastic – it made the hairs stand up on the back of my neck. When I went over to our supporters at the end of the game there were a few faces I recognised, like John Westwood, who had travelled all that way when there was so little to play for, and to see and hear them give me their appreciation gave me a real shiver and brought me close to tears. Unfortunately Kevin Gallagher had poked one past me in injury time, which meant that I took some stick in the dressing room afterwards for my 'chocolate wrists' in letting it in.

After having lost at home to Grimsby the previous week in the league, we went to Crystal Palace and were hammered 4-0 and afterwards Ballie went mad in the dressing room. I was sitting in the corner when he turned and pointed to me, saying: "I feel sorry for this guy, he's been with this club for 20 years and he's been forced to sit through such an inept performance." Then, by now in a real temper, he turned on the players and said: "I can tell you now – some of you won't play again for this football club." I knew from previous experience that it was his way of trying to force a reaction, of throwing down the gauntlet to the players who had let him down. With some players such an outburst would strike the right chord, while others would simply not listen. Some would be destroyed by it. It all depends on the mental make-up of the player. The Pompey squad of the mid-1980s would have taken his comments as a slur and would have all pledged to turn their performance around. With that group of players, such a tactic by Ballie would have worked in his favour. After such a bollocking, they would have taken a pride in proving him wrong the following week and when they had done so they would turn and run to the bench with a clenched fist to make their point to him to his face. Modern players are not like that. Now you have to cuddle them and so many are on such good wages that they are simply not fussed as to whether they are in the side or not. Ballie lost his job in mid-December and the local press reported that there were 'not too many players disappointed' at his departure. Some of the squad had grievances about being left out but, in my experience, whenever a manager goes, there are some players who are pleased and others who are gutted. As I said before, I felt that Ballie should have been more hands-on in his second spell. He was still passionate but, like Frank Burrows when he returned, had mellowed with age.

Milan asked former Arsenal defender Bob McNab to come over from the States to have a look at things at the club and he took charge for a couple of games, with my assistance. Dave Kemp came in as coach, having achieved some success in the Premiership with Joe Kinnear at Wimbledon. He immediately introduced a more direct, high-pressure style of play, with the ball having to be played down the channels and into the corners for people to chase. It was the first major change of style at the club I had come across in my time and that was reinforced when Tony Pulis arrived as manager. Pulis made it clear on arrival that he wanted his own backroom staff installed, but retaining Kempie and me was part of the deal, although he was allowed to bring in some of his own people like Lindsay Parsons and Mike Trusson. As a result, I always felt that I was never trusted by Pulis and was continually being harassed by him. He tried my patience to the limit by, for instance, sending me up and down the country to watch games for reasons which were not apparent to me. One week I was off to Port Vale reserves of an evening, the next to Bradford City for a league game. No players were specified for me to watch, no reports were requested and Pulis never spoke to me about the games I had seen. Nevertheless, it was part of my job to watch games to look at players and to assess future opposition, but I felt that such assignments were merely tests of my resolve. Certainly, if I had refused or objected to any of them, then that would have given him ammunition to use against me.

Pulis would also interfere with the training of the goalkeepers, which irritated me. In the old-fashioned way, he liked to see them diving around continuously for up to an hour until they reached a state of collapse. What added to my aggravation, was that he insisted that I join in with that routine. I performed OK when I played in goal in games in training once or twice and this led Pulis to approach me and insist: "I think we should put you back on a playing contract." We went to see David Deacon, the managing director at the time, to pursue it contractually, but he wouldn't have it: "You can't do it, it's not possible now." Pulis then looked at me and said: "Well, that's that then," accepted what he'd been told and made it look as if it was my idea in the first place. I was left wondering whether he really wanted to do it or whether he was simply playing games with me. My feeling was that he was trying to upset me and force me out of the club.

Pulis wanted to play a rigid system and the boys worked for hour after hour on getting the right shape and getting the ball into the right channels. That approach turns players into robots and the players in our squad at that time just didn't respond well to it. I'm not knocking him for the way he wanted to play; after all it had worked for him previously at Gillingham. He would later say that it didn't work because the players at Pompey were unreceptive. The players would spend ages standing around, with every game or practice stopping and starting every 30 seconds for Pulis to make a point. It rendered the players almost brain-dead and bored the pants off them. Pulis would rely on his first impressions and therefore was quick to make decisions about certain senior players. Scott Hiley in particular, was rapidly bombed out and sent to train with the reserves. However, whatever my opinions about Pulis and his methods and style of play, you can't deny that he brought some decent players to the club – Darren Moore, Shaun Derry, and Justin Edinburgh for a start.

In early January 2000, after not having played a full game for a year, I found myself back in one-off league action at Norwich, for my 801st appearance. Flav had twisted his ankle in a practice game and it became clear that Pulis was not prepared to take a chance on Tards, due to his inexperience. When I was asked by Kempie whether I could play, I told him I was unhappy about 'leapfrogging' over Tards, who was considered to be the second-string keeper. I was concerned about what it would do for his confidence. I knew if it had been me in his position, then I would have been gutted to be overlooked. Despite my concerns it was decided that it would be best for the team at the time if I played and I had to explain it all to Tards. He knew I wasn't trying to stab him in the back, but he was pretty upset nevertheless. The chance to play again had come out of the blue and it meant that my record would show that I had played in four decades. I enjoyed it and thought I did OK, even though I let in two – one penalty and the other a close-range header. By coincidence the team played really well, the best for a while, but there was no cutting edge to our work. It gave me a taste for it again and it crossed my mind, if I got fit, maybe I could resume my playing career. The following day, I couldn't move, was as stiff as a board and mentally exhausted from the concentration. Perhaps not then...

One incident that made the headlines that season, for all the wrong reasons, arose after we had played against Southampton in a behind-closed-doors friendly one afternoon. After the game, a staff and team meal had been arranged in Southampton and afterwards some of the boys decided to go on to a local bar. I didn't go, but unfortunately, after a few drinks, Rory Allen and Flav got into a dispute with a couple there, resulting in a bit of a fracas during which the police were called. Flav was genuinely remorseful afterwards and apologised to the couple involved. However, as a result of the incident and their subsequent conviction, the two lads were each fined two weeks' wages. Steve Claridge also got into some trouble around that time after a casual, innocent remark during a radio interview following our win over Barnsley. Steve happened to mention that he had placed a bet on Pompey winning, with him scoring and suddenly he found himself being charged by the FA. It was all a bit silly; a mountain out of a molehill, if you like and Steve was guilty of nothing more than being unaware of the rules. Besides, if he had wanted to beat the system, then he could have got one of his family to place the bet for him.

Pulis continued to pile the pressure on me, clearly hoping I would quit the club. By now Jennifer and I had separated and I was beginning to feel that I ought to look elsewhere for a job, when I was approached by the then Brighton manager Micky Adams to have a trial down there. Their goalkeeper Mark Kuipers was injured and Micky had a problem with cover. So I agreed to play for them in a behind-closed-doors friendly against Crystal Palace, but unfortunately the goal in our 1-0 defeat was down to me dropping the ball in making a save. Afterwards Micky said that he was worried that I had not played enough games and nothing came of it. However, any lingering thoughts I had about a playing comeback at Pompey disappeared with the arrival of Russell Hoult from Derby, who I knew was a very good keeper.

As a player I didn't enjoy the close seasons – they seemed to go on for ever. I would soon get bored and want to get back playing again. We regularly used to go to Florida as a young family. Now, I favour Mexico as a holiday destination and, after seven years of rushing around Disneyland with the girls, I am happy, at my age, to be lazy and sit by the pool in the shade. But in the summer of 2000 I wouldn't have been in my usual rush to get back to pre-season training if I had known what Pulis had in mind for us. That gave us our first taste of his pre-season schedule and it was an absolute beast. He took us initially to the New Forest and started us off on a round of circuits and weights, but the real pain for me came with the running. A six-mile run on the first day with plenty of hills along the way, was followed by eight miles and then finally a 12-mile half-marathon on the Saturday. Despite my non-playing status, I was made to do them all and that last one killed me. I couldn't run when I was a player, let alone as a coach. I am not saying that it was unsuitable for the players, but I had not done anything like that for so many years, since those days up at HMS Mercury and it was a massive culture shock.

There was major unrest in the dressing room as the season got under way, and the players were clearly unhappy. Pulis had lost the players' respect and confidence and then in October 2000 came the news that he had stepped down. I don't like to see anybody lose their job, but in this case you could say that I wasn't too upset to see him go. The departure of Pulis wasn't too much of a shock, but nobody could have foreseen who the chairman would go for as his replacement. Life had never been dull at Pompey and soon it was to become even more interesting.

*'I don't think he knows any
different than Pompey. He was
always prepared to put his
body on the line for the club.'*
Neil Sillett

To describe pre-season training at Pompey in the summer of 1997 as 'interesting' barely does justice to the word. Knight's continued presence was at least a constant factor as Fenwick and Venables set about a radical re-working of the squad. Lee Bradbury was sold to Manchester City for £3.5 million, while Deon Burton was also off to Derby for a third of that amount. The Australian influx – John Aloisi, Craig Foster, Robbie Enes and the hapless Hamilton Thorp – in retrospect smashed the team spirit the previous season's heroics had engendered. To Venables, apparently owner and now chairman of the club, they represented a good deal. In footballing terms it was a disaster. Despite his new one-year contract, Knight was no longer secure as first choice and had been challenged to earn another deal. Venables was keen to recruit another Aussie, 6' 7" international goalkeeper Zeljco Kalac, who had cost Leicester £750,000 three years previously, but was now playing in Sydney. 'I've got every confidence in my ability and I want to play in the Premiership like every player and I believe I am good enough. But time is on my side, I'm only 24 and I believe I can get there with Portsmouth,' he said. Now 36, time was the one thing not on Knight's side, but bureaucratic red tape rode to his rescue as the Kalac move got mired in another work-permit wrangle.

So Knight started as first choice on the opening day of the season for the first time in three years, as Pompey pinched what was ultimately to prove a vital point at Manchester City thanks to Paul Hall's late goal. Any thoughts that the luck was with him though evaporated soon after as a calf strain picked up meant Aaron Flahavan found himself back in goal for the Coca-Cola Cup tie with Peterborough. Of the Aussies, only Aloisi had found his feet and, as summer gave way to autumn, Pompey were in freefall. Six straight defeats put them second from bottom of the table by mid-October. After the 3-2 defeat at home to West Brom, Knight – now fully recovered from his injury – returned for the home game with Bradford. A point was a step in the right direction, as was the one which followed at Huddersfield, but home defeats to Swindon and Sunderland offset points gleaned on the road at Middlesbrough and a first win in 11 league matches at Bury. By the time Pompey lost 2-1 at Birmingham on November 29, they were bottom. On the same day, Venables was enduring the agony of his Australian national side giving away two late goals to gift their World Cup final place to Iran.

Matters came to a head when Venables and Martin Gregory had an angry exchange over his supposed controlling stake in the club and it was announced in early December he was no longer chairman. That the players wages weren't paid in November and safety chiefs were threatening to close down the new £2.5 million Fratton End stand, only added to the sense of chaos. Things were temporarily patched up, but it was only delaying the inevitable. Three home wins in December kept Pompey in touch with safety although, as the New Year dawned, Pompey were still rock bottom. Fenwick toyed with dropping Knight for the FA Cup third-round tie at home to Aston Villa, but in the end stuck by experience. Foster finally showed his international class to put Pompey two-up, but two late goals denied Pompey a famous scalp. By the time the replay came around, Fenwick and Venables were Pompey history. A 3-0 home defeat to relegation rivals Manchester City on January 10 was the last straw. Fans vented their discontent and Fenwick and Venables were forced to take both barrels. On the Monday Venables picked up a 'six-figure sum' and cleared his desk, if indeed he had a desk, at Fratton Park. Fenwick followed on the Tuesday. Caretaker Keith Walden presided over three more defeats, despite signing Portsmouth-born Steve Claridge on loan for his last game and Pompey – six points adrift of safety – were looking all but doomed.

Enter Alan Ball. Reportedly on the back of a proposed takeover of the club by rock singer Brian Howe and his American backer Vincent Wolanin, the former World Cup winner and the man who guided Pompey to the old first division in 1987, was drafted out of semi-retirement since his bitter split from Manchester City. His effect, while not immediate, was ultimately remarkable. Unfortunately, it took the dropping of Knight – Ballie's biggest backer when he arrived – before things began to change for the better. Ball's first home game against Sheffield United saw Knight uncharacteristically spill a run-of-the mill looking cross into the back of his own net to deny him a winning start. Two games later, he was badly at fault with the second Crewe goal, on the way to a 3-1 defeat which left Pompey still rooted to the foot of the table and seven points adrift of 21st place. It looked a hopeless task, but Ball rang the changes and Flahavan was back in goal for the Tuesday night game with Stockport at Fratton Park. Inspired by a the noisy and persistent backing of the 8,000 or so loyal souls still minded to turn out and support an increasingly lost cause, Pompey clung to Claridge's first-half goal and the Great Escape was born.

Within a fortnight, three more wins had been picked up and Pompey were out of the bottom three. Knight was a frustrated spectator, but he appreciated the change the manager had wrought and he also detected a change in Ball himself. 'He seems a lot more mellow and isn't jumping about in the dug out so much these days,' he said. With his trademark flat cap, Ball seemed to be guiding Pompey to safety, only for form to collapse again in March and April. An Andy Thomson goal in the last minute at least rescued a point in Pompey's centenary match against Birmingham on April 4, but another three defeats in the next four matches left the club on the brink of second-division football for the second time in three years. A 3-0 home win over Huddersfield rekindled hopes however, and when the news filtered through that Manchester City could only draw with QPR, Pompey's destiny was back in their own hands. For the second time in two years an army of Pompey fans descended on West Yorkshire – Bradford's Valley Parade the venue this time – and saw their favourites pull it off with a 3-1 win, John Durnin scoring two of the goals. Flahavan also played his part, making a couple of vital saves as City finally roused themselves out of end–of–term mode in the second half. That the win sent Stoke and Manchester City down – two clubs that had fired him in the past – was not lost on Ball.

Having been offered the manager's job on a permanent basis, Ball set about drawing up his retained list and Knight was on it, but it was clear his role was increasingly moving towards coaching. Despite picking up a calf strain in pre–season, Flahavan was fit enough to start in possession of the green shirt, but was immediately courting controversy as he and Thomson blamed each other for the own goal which sparked a Watford comeback on the opening day of the season. The newly–promoted side sneaked all three points to puncture the optimism surrounding Fratton Park. The news that Claridge had finally signed permanently after an on–off transfer saga lifted the atmosphere, but Flav's luck was about to take a further turn for the worse. A heavy challenge in the first half by Plymouth's Sean McCarthy left him nursing a rib injury which forced him off to be replaced by Knight before half time. He hadn't recovered by the Saturday and Knight lined up at Tranmere, only to be left cursing as he let Micky Mellon's soft shot skip over his dive, to cancel out Aloisi's opener.

Flahavan was back and in fine form to help keep Ipswich at bay in a 0-0 draw, but he was in the wars as he picked up a head injury during the 3-3 draw at Huddersfield and had to play with stitches in the wound as Pompey secured their first league win of the season on Bank Holiday Monday, against QPR. Ball pointed the finger at his young goalkeeper for the two goals which condemned Pompey to defeat at Bury and Flahavan himself was big enough to accept the blame, but that was but nothing compared to the events during the next match at home to Swindon. With Pompey 4–1 up and cruising with 15 minutes to go, an innocuous ball into the box turned into a goal for George Ndah, as Flahavan lay prone in his penalty area, having apparently fainted. He saw out the game with physio Jonathan Trigg watching anxiously behind the goal and a subsequent barrage of tests could find nothing wrong, although medical advice decreed he should not play in the next match and Knight was back for the Coca-Cola Cup game with Premiership Wimbledon. Pompey's players even devised a fainting routine to celebrate Aloisi's opening goal in a 2–1 win. Flahavan was given the all-clear, returned for the Port Vale match and kept a clean sheet, but his confidence was clearly affected. A clutch of late goals had denied Pompey vital points and, when Flahavan was at fault for another such goal, which earned Bristol City a draw, Knight got his chance to return to the side. And he was at his best, making a couple of excellent saves in the 1–0 home win over Wolves, a performance which rekindled his enthusiasm: 'You don't realise how much you miss playing until you're watching from the stands,' he said post-match. 'I enjoy my coaching but I love playing. I don't know how long it will be for, but I want to stay in the side for as long as possible.' Ball recognised his goalkeeper's contribution, but was less than encouraging about his future prospects. 'I put the old man in and he responded with a fantastic performance when needed, but let's not get carried away. He didn't actually have much to do.' Knight kept his place, but Pompey continued to leak goals.

A 4–1 defeat at Crystal Palace in early November was bad enough, but the fact the London side were now managed by Messrs Venables and Fenwick made it harder still to bear. Knight looked decidedly ill at ease in the following home game with Norwich on the Tuesday night as Pompey slumped to a fourth consecutive defeat, so Ball acted. Charlton goalkeeper Andy Petterson was signed in time to play at Grimsby on the Saturday and looked the part as he helped ten-man Pompey to a point. It was perhaps the signal that Knight's long and distinguished, if perhaps unfulfilled, playing career was all but over. As ever in football, things didn't quite turn out the way you might expect.

Pompey were a club in crisis. After the death of Jim Gregory in late September, his son Martin's enthusiasm for allowing Portsmouth Football Club to drain the family fortune was decidedly on the wane. At the end of November matters came to a head when the club went cap in hand to the PFA for a loan to pay the salaries of players, while an unpaid £500,000 bill for work on the Fratton End came due after a protracted court case. Gregory's response was to stage a fire sale. Stripping Ball of the power to buy and sell players, agent Athole Still was appointed to get what he could for the players. The only one to leave was leading scorer Aloisi in a cut-price £650,000 – and it may not have even been that much – move to Premiership Coventry. At least by the time Robbie Pethick, Matt Robinson and Sammy Igoe left the club in January, it was, however reluctant, the decision of the boss that they should go for the greater good.

Knight got another run out – Charlton didn't want Petterson cup-tied – and turned in a faultless display as Pompey dumped Premiership Nottingham Forest out of the third round of the FA Cup, thanks to Claridge's goal. Knight was also in his familiar place for the fourth-round tie against Leeds at home which saw the Yorkshire side thump five goals past Pompey with only Luke Nightingale's reply. In early February, Pompey went into administration and Petterson was forced to return to the Valley as his maximum three-month loan period was up and the club were in no position to buy him. It was touch and go at times, as the accountants charged with finding a buyer for the club – or in the worst-case scenario winding it up – went about their work. Knight gave his support to the Portsmouth United group, which was drawing up contingency plans to form a community club, should the need arise.

With Petterson gone, Knight may well have thought he could be in with a chance of returning to the side, but instead Ball opted to recall Flahavan for his first game since

October as Pompey travelled to Swindon. It was no doubt a disappointment for Knight, but as he was already contemplating semi-retirement from playing in the summer, Ball's decision made sense. Once again fate was to intervene and give the old man one last crack at regular first team football. Flahavan and Iffy Onuora were involved in an horrific collision on the half hour, requiring a five-minute stoppage as the club doctor raced onto the field. Flav was stretchered off, his teeth and face smashed, while substitute Russell Perrett was forced into goal. By half time Pompey were 3-1 down and their recent run of form in adversity looked set to end. A second goal by Claridge and a superb long-range effort from Jeff Péron preserved an unlikely, and ultimately crucial, point.

Knight's tenuous playing position was underlined by director Terry Brady's plea to the administrator to allow the club to pay £100,000 to sign Petterson. 'Alan Knight is more than capable but we have to look at our options,' commented Brady, who pointed out the club would have just Knight and teenager Chris Tardif until the end of the season. 'Flav came round in the casualty department and was in a pretty poor way. He looked like he'd done a few rounds with Mike Tyson,' added Brady, who accompanied the keeper to hospital. 'When he came round he couldn't remember what had happened and kept asking what the score was.' Predictably, the administrator wouldn't countenance paying Petterson's wages, so Knight was back for the home game with Port Vale. Afterwards, he reflected on what it was like to still be playing at 37. 'I ache like hell after a game. I can't do what the young lads do – I wouldn't be able to move. I had a little sprint into the corner in the second half. It was a rush of blood. The thing I couldn't believe was I got to the ball first,' he commented. Pompey won 4-0, in part thanks to on-loan striker Guy Whittingham's hat-trick – 'It's nice to have someone around almost as old as me,' quipped Knight – but once he returned to Sheffield Wednesday in March, Pompey's problems began to mount.

Not that Knight was to blame, despite a rash of letters in the local press claiming he was past it. Certainly, Sunderland boss

Peter Reid made Knight man of the match as he single-handedly kept the score respectable in a 2-0 defeat during the keeper's first appearance at the Stadium of Light and he was in form a week later with a match-winning save from Marcelo, as Pompey clung to a lead against Sheffield United, given to them by a rare Andy Awford goal. Knight's Indian summer suddenly put on hold his plans to retire: 'I haven't spoken with the manager yet and I don't suppose he really knows what's happening at the moment, but there obviously comes a time when it needs sorting out. It all depends on the manager's view. I would   imagine he would be looking to play a younger keeper next year and will be looking to Flav. But I think there is possibly a good case for me to carry on the goalkeeper coach side of things and play if I was needed. I'm pleased with the way I'm playing at the moment, although I don't like to talk about form too much, in case it goes pear-shaped.' On the field things did start to go wrong, however, as Ball's emasculated squad began to succumb to injuries and inevitable suspensions. A seven-match winless run took them to the fringes of the relegation zone until April 24, when Stockport were seen off 3-1, to all but assure safety barring an arithmetical Armageddon. It had been a long and difficult season, but ended on a high, as news that Serbo-American businessman Milan Mandaric had been successful in his bid to buy the club. A new era was dawning.

And Knight was part of that future. He got his wish of a playing contract, with Ball proclaiming there was a job for Knight at Fratton Park all the while he was there. However, it was clear his chances of extending a career, which now counted 798 league and cup games, were going to be slim. Petterson had been signed on a free transfer and Flahavan was back from a summer playing in Scandinavia and raring to go. Knight was clearly third in the pecking order. In the end, he was quickly able to make it 799, as an elbow injury to Petterson allowed him to take a place on the bench in the Worthington Cup tie with Torquay. With eight minutes to go and Pompey cruising in the next round, leading 3-0 on aggregate, Ball gave the fans chanting 'Bring on the Legend!' their wish. A standing ovation greeted his entrance and he was even able to pull off a fine save before shaking hands at the end with another long-standing keeper legend Neville Southall, who was between the posts for the Gulls. Knight also had the honour of receiving the most votes in a summer *News* poll to name the Pompey 'team of the century'. The chance to give Knight his 800th match came in the next round of the cup, as Pompey trailed 5-1 on aggregate in the second leg of their tie with Blackburn. That Knight was on the bench again was in part down to the seemingly jinxed Flahavan, who had fainted in his goalmouth for the second time in less than 12 months in the first leg. As a result Knight came on for the last seven minutes, to another standing ovation as Ewood Park rose to acclaim his achievement, although there was time for Kevin Gallagher to stick a goal past him in the final minute. Former physio Neil Sillett, by now at Derby, summed up the moment: 'Knightsie has given tremendous loyalty to the club and that makes him one of a dying breed in the game. I heard the story about him wanting to have his ashes scattered on Fratton Park when he dies, and that doesn't surprise me at all. I don't think he knows any different than Pompey. He was always prepared to put his body on the line for the club, diving in among the boots to make a save. He has a massive heart and all the character going. When I was with Pompey I had to treat him for all kinds of injuries because he dived in where it hurt to stop the ball at all costs.'

For Knight though, that seemed to be it, although he refused to close the door on another game: 'You can never say never. If the call comes again, I would be there to play again if needed, but now I would love to bring another keeper through who could play 800 games for the club.' His protégé was clearly Flahavan and the 23-year-old got his chance as Ball dropped Petterson after a miserable run of results left Pompey in familiar territory near the foot of the table. Petterson's career had taken a nosedive after he had been arrested for drink-driving in August and a series of niggling injuries to the Australian meant Knight was on stand-by for the first team once more.

By now, Ball was once again part of Pompey's history. Results had been poor, despite ten signings, and Mandaric displayed the ruthlessness which was to become his trademark by firing the likeable Lancastrian. In temporary charge was Mandaric's colleague and former Arsenal defender Bob McNab, assisted by new coach and former Fratton favourite Dave Kemp. And McNab was forced to turn to Knight once more as Flahavan picked up a knock in training. With Petterson suffering from a calf strain too, it was a toss up between the experience of Knight and the untried potential of Tardif for the trip to Norwich on New Year's Day. 'It was a surprise to be called up to be honest,' said Knight afterwards. 'I didn't travel up there with the team and had to drive up there when the call came. I thoroughly enjoyed myself, although it was shame there was no fairytale,' he added as Pompey slumped to a 2-1 defeat.

And that truly was it: 801 and out. The final curtain on a professional playing career that spanned four decades; it was January 1, 2000 after all. Under new manager Tony Pulis, who was appointed later that month to dig Pompey out of the relegation mire once more, his role was now going to be exclusively that of coaching the club's goalkeepers. In Flahavan Pompey had a talent, with the right nurturing, more than equipped to match the Legend's exploits, but fate would intervene to cut down that young man's career in the cruellest of fashions. Knight was about to enter a phase in his life which was to be touched by honour, tragedy and triumph. Perhaps more importantly however, it was a period which would be marked by his on-going struggle with an attachment to the drink culture which has been as much part of his life since he arrived in Portsmouth as a 16-year-old in July 1977 as the football club itself.

The last word is his.

Dermot Gallagher shows Knight his one and only red card in the FA Cup fourth round tie with Leicester City in January 1995. Darryl Powell can't believe it either.

Alan with Jade (left) and Rebekah in 1994

Sir Alan, Knight of Fratton Park, prepares to slay the Saints in the FA Cup third round in January 1996. Except Pompey lost 3-0...

Mike Walker / M&Y News Agency

A safe pair of hands.

Portsmouth FC

The old picture ideas are the best ones. Alan marks his record-breaking 601st league appearance for Pompey.

Knight dives to deny Steve Claridge, playing for Birmingham in October 1995.

Knight dives to keep out Keith Curle's penalty against Wolves in December 1997.

Master and pupil: Knight in his pre-match warm-up routine with Aaron Flahavan in 2001.

Portsmouth FC

Knight and Flav work out on the training field.

The News

Alan proudly shows off his MBE to Jade and Rebekah (left).

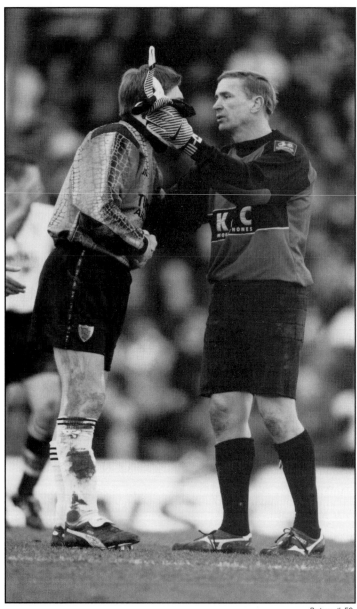

Mutual respect. Alan commiserates with Port Vale's Portsmouth-born goalkeeper Paul Musselwhite after his side had been thrashed 4-0 by Pompey in February 1999.

9 - Honour, tragedy, triumph

It was a massive shock to me when I heard that Steve Claridge had been given the manager's job, with Guy Whittingham as his assistant. There had been no previous whispers and it seemed like a strange decision to me initially. If it had come off, then it would have been fantastic, but from the start I felt that it would be difficult for him and so it proved. Steve never really got it confirmed whether or not he had the job on a caretaker or permanent basis, but as it transpired the job came too soon for someone so inexperienced in management. With no disrespect to Guy, Steve needed an older head alongside him and, with hindsight, it might have helped his cause if an experienced man, a Jim Smith-type say, had been brought in to assist him. As it was, Steve was trying to perform both on and off the pitch. I certainly think he could have made a go of it with someone alongside him who knew the ropes. As a player it's all laid on – largely all you have to do is turn up at a certain time at a certain place, whether for training or to play. You don't get to know how the club is run and all that goes on behind the scenes with such things as travel arrangements, training facilities and routines, players' contracts, discipline and so on. I know that I have learnt more about all that in the two or three years since I moved on to the management/coaching side, than I did in the previous 20 years as a player.

I felt it would be difficult for Steve and Guy to make the transition initially and, in particular, to impose the necessary discipline. For the lads, one day the two of them were their team-mates, the next they were their manager and coach. I had seen the problems both John Gregory and Fen had experienced in dealing with former team-mates. They've previously seen the manager misbehave as one of the lads and now, suddenly, he's telling them not to do it. Steve had, for instance, always been notorious for being late for training and now, here he was laying down the law on it. But Steve had a good crack and his appointment did create harmony in the dressing room again. Unfortunately, after a good spell initially, we picked up some injuries and suddenly the results were hard to come by. Scott Hiley was immediately reinstated and he did fantastically well for Steve. I was pleased to be much more involved in things, with Steve regularly asking for my opinions. On matchdays, however, with Steve out there playing, it was difficult to get messages relayed back and forth. Guy would sit up in the director's box to get a good view and I would be down below him at pitchside. I became a go-between, trying to interpret and then relay messages between Guy, up above me, and Steve, out on the pitch. It made getting decisions on things, like substitutions and tactics, difficult, with the need to get Steve's agreement first. During this time, I felt that Steve showed his inexperience by continuing to pop up on most TV and radio football shows as a commentator or pundit, or at least that was the public perception. By appearing that way to the fans, they began to wonder why Steve wasn't wholly working for the club. He was watching games at the same time, of course, but the fans didn't see it that way and I thought it was a mistake on Steve's part, particularly as it was his first managerial job.

After his injury problems, Awfs had retired and Steve looked after him by appointing him as his chief scout. That gave me the chance to engage in some serious banter with Awfs – amongst other things calling him 'the youngest and best-paid scout in the history of the game'. It was also during Steve's time in charge that Russell Hoult came to leave the club. Russell had looked shaky for a couple of weeks and then he gifted Barnsley a winner at Oakwell, with a real ricket when he was robbed on the by-line, whilst he was trying to shepherd the ball out for a goal kick. When Steve asked me if Flav was ready to come in, I said he wouldn't let us down and so Russell was dropped. When Flav kept his place for the next home game, Russell had a sulk, wouldn't sit on the bench and remained in the dressing room for the entire game. He subsequently made it clear in the local paper that he wanted to leave and Steve felt that it might be in everybody's interests, if that was the way he felt. Russell went to West Brom, and has since done really well, getting promotion and playing in the Premiership, and at one time being on the verge of an England call-up.

I first heard of Steve's dismissal on the radio and that same evening I was at Fratton Park for a Sportsmen's Dinner and found Steve up in the offices clearing out his desk. He was devastated, very emotional and tearful when I spoke to him. I felt really sorry for him. To his credit, he's put it behind him now. Coming back into the dressing room as players made Steve and Guy's positions completely untenable. Things became even more difficult when new manager Graham Rix arrived and it made for an uncomfortable situation for all parties concerned. There had been rumours about Rixie coming and we knew he was in the frame for the job. He came with a good reputation and I had heard positive things about his time at Chelsea, where it was said he ran the show when Ruud Gullit was manager. It looked like an inspired appointment and even more so when it soon became clear that Rixie was very much a 'players' manager'. He created a very professional impression with his new training sessions, wanted his team to play football and it soon became apparent that his aim was to build a young, successful side over a three or four-year period. His assistant Jim Duffy, a more relaxed person, came with great credentials. He is one of the very few coaches in the country to hold the same UEFA licence as Gerard Houllier and Arsène Wenger. From the start, it was apparent that Rixie was a deep thinker, who always seemed to have an element of insecurity in his personality. Early on, Rixie did speak to me about my length of service and added: "With the greatest respect, I could see that as a lack of ambition." In reply I said: "I see it as loyalty and it's my ambition to see this club play at the highest level – that's what I've always been working towards."

It was in late March 2001 that I paid a visit to Buckingham Palace to be presented with the MBE by Her Majesty, The Queen. I heard subsequently that there had been a campaign amongst some fans on the internet to nominate me and that some letters of support had been passed to the FA and the Prime Minister. A gesture like that from the supporters meant a great deal to me. When, out of the blue, I had received an official-looking envelope at the club some months earlier, with an OHMS logo on it, I imagined it was just another tax bill. But when, on opening it, I saw a 10 Downing Street heading and then read the letter, my immediate reaction was that it was some sort of wind-up. After I had checked it out with Paul Weld, the club secretary – he seemed to think it was genuine – I immediately began ringing and texting family and friends, despite the request in the letter not to inform any-one. I'm not a strong royalist, but I must admit to having a sneaking wish to be given the honour by the Queen rather than Prince Charles.

A friend was kind enough to be my chauffeur for the day and he drove me and my two daughters, Jade and Rebekah, to the hotel which the club had paid for us to stay in and then on to Buckingham Palace for the morning ceremony. I had hardly slept the night before and on the day my emotions were all over the place. I was eventually ushered into a room where, along with all the others waiting for their investiture, we were given a briefing on the etiquette for the ceremony. There, I met Everton chairman Bill Kenwright and a couple of Royal Navy guys who came over to talk to me about football, which was a great tension reliever. I waited in a picture gallery for my name to be called among groups of ten. It felt like I was waiting for half my life in my top hat and tails as they went through Knighthoods, Dames and OBEs before, suddenly, it was my turn to go through the side door, walk along the red carpet, stop and turn to face the Queen. She was on a podium slightly above me and when I reached her she asked me if I was still playing football. I told her I was a coach now and she asked me if I taught kids.

I told her I did and she said: "Children do love football, don't they." The Queen pinned on my MBE and shook my hand, which was my cue to take three steps backwards – you are not allowed to turn your back on Her Majesty – and turn and move away. It had been one of the biggest days of my life and had taken about four hours, but it had all gone so quickly and in a way it was quite a surreal experience. When it was all over however, and the nerves had all gone, it felt brilliant. I had loads of cards, letters and messages congratulating me. Awfs was immediately teasing me about it, saying that when Alan Ball got his MBE it stood for 'Member of the Best Eleven', after the World Cup winning team of 1966, so mine must stand for 'More Beer Everyday'.

The subsequent battle against relegation that season, especially going to the last game, was a real eye-opener for Rixie. The penultimate home game against Crystal Palace was a very low point and so embarrassing for everybody. It's difficult for me to say whether it's the worst performance I have ever seen from a Pompey side, but the timing and manner of that 4-2 defeat was horrendous. Not for a very long time had I heard the Pompey fans dish out such abuse to their team and it was probably the worst I had ever known from them. It was another high-pressure last day of the season, when we beat Barnsley at home to stay up. They didn't put up much of a fight and there was a great party afterwards. The number of such occasions was becoming embarrassing and I seem to remember the parties to celebrate avoiding relegation as usually being better than those celebrating promotion. It's ironic that there has always been such happiness over what amounted to under-achievement.

During pre-season 2001/02, Flav had another scare before a friendly match at Newport, in the Isle of Wight, when he suffered a slight blackout. It was whilst I was warming up him and Tards that Flav stayed down on the ground after diving to make a save. He came to, saying, in our usual joking fashion: "I'm feeling delusional again!" But we realised something was amiss and a decision was made to play Tards in the match instead. After this latest occurrence, Flav began to seriously worry about his career and he did even talk about retiring and opening up a bar abroad. Everyone was always confident about sorting out the problem, but it bugged Flav that nobody really knew what was wrong with him. While the squad were away in the West Country it was decided to refer Flav to the Brompton Hospital for investigations where he underwent a minor operation. I took him up to the hospital on the Friday, drove to Yeovil for the Saturday game and then collected him on Sunday to take him home to Southampton. We were assured that the operation was 'a perfect job' and it was confirmed later that it was not a contributory factor in his subsequent accident. Flav was hoping to play against Leicester in a friendly at Fratton Park the following Saturday, but the necessary incision in his groin for the operation was still sore and he watched the game from the stand.

Before that Leicester game Rixie told me he was worried about starting the season with Flav, on the basis that he had not played enough games in pre-season. He then said he had spoken to Dave Beasant (Bes) about coming down to help us out in goal. I wasn't overly happy about it, my immediate reaction being: "He's older than me." After the game, in which Tards had done well, I went looking for Flav in the players' bar, but he had left the ground. I telephoned him to tell him of Rixie's concern over his lack of match practice and to explain the Beasant situation, but added that nothing had finally been decided. He didn't seem to be particularly worried about the news and appeared to be in good spirits. I asked him what he was doing that night and he said he was meeting his girl friend for a meal. It was about 6.30 pm on that fateful Saturday evening when I made the call and it was the last time I spoke to him. It was between 8 and 9 am on the Sunday morning that I had a call from Ceri Hughes. He asked if I had heard the news about Flav's death in a car accident the previous night. I was stunned, just numb. We had been very close, having been together every working day for nearly ten years. I had always felt an affinity with Flav; we were very similar in so many ways and I could see much of myself in him. I felt guilty that maybe I had set him a bad example with my drink-driving and I felt that I could have been partly responsible. That sense of guilt stayed with me for a long time afterwards.

There was an enormous outpouring of grief in the city and beyond and Flav's death affected a number of the players at the club, not to mention several ex-Pompey players who had known him. Tards is a sensitive lad who was close to Flav and it upset him greatly. With the considerable media interest, I found it difficult to grieve privately. Even when I placed flowers it was a media event, accompanied by photographers, as if it was some sort of exhibition on my part. It was as if I wasn't hurting any more than anyone else and could handle it like everybody else. I tried to steer clear of any cameras for fear of having my picture taken or having to talk about it all yet again. In addition, I was always conscious that if I was seen in the media too often, then I could be accused of exploiting the situation for my own publicity. The hardest bit for me was seeing Flav in the funeral parlour, but throughout it all, including the minute silences at two games, the lads pulled together and rallied around me. The funeral was very difficult for me – it seemed to go on forever – and indeed for everybody who knew Flav. I became very emotional looking at his picture in church, whilst waiting for the service to start. Afterwards, with Flav's brother Darryl, I was able to go to the graveside before the burial and have some precious private moments, almost for the first time.

Flav had great natural ability as a keeper, but he needed to stay injury free and to play 30-odd games to get the confidence and the experience he needed to progress. He had all the attributes of a great keeper, but with his blackouts, his severe facial injury and several other injury setbacks, he never got the chance to prove himself over a sustained spell. He had great determination and, to his credit, despite the continuous worry of his blackouts, it was only after the latest occurrence that he began to think about giving up the game. With the success the club has had in getting to the Premiership, it would have been so nice to have had him around and involved. It was great to hear our fans at Bradford at the last game of last season, in the midst of celebrating the championship, thinking of Flav by singing his name. That will be something I will always remember from that great day.

After the drink-driving element had emerged at the inquest, I was very disappointed with the reaction of some people to this and was angry to hear comments like: "He got everything he deserved". I had to work hard to restrain myself from responding to such remarks. His death was such a waste of a life and it still hurts me to have to talk about it all. Flav's death taught me some lessons, which unfortunately turned out to be only temporary. I felt the need to make changes in my lifestyle particularly in regard to my drinking, but I must say, with no great pride, that I soon slipped back into my old ways.

With all his experience, Bes brought some new ideas with him and freshened up our keeper sessions, but you can't begin to coach a guy two years older than yourself. It was a case of Bes telling me what he wanted to do and me adding a few bits of my own to the sessions. Training overall was difficult that season, with constant problems with the pitches at the HMS Collingwood ground being unfit. Peter Crouch was a great signing for the club by Rixie and repaid his £1 million fee with his goals. For his height, he was a lot better on the ground than he looked and Crouchie profited from the service from Robert Prosinecki, who could pick him out from up to 50 yards. People forget that Crouchie is still only a young lad, who was playing last season in a struggling side at Villa. When Harry Redknapp sold him in March 2002, people were unhappy about the club selling its top scorer, but, with hindsight, it looks now like a really good deal.

Prosinecki was a fantastic player, with unbelievable ability and skill. Ten years earlier in his career he must have been wonderful to watch and, on his day that season, no-one could get near him. The transition to the first division was hard for Prossie and the pressure to perform his miracles each and every week started to tell on him. Also, lads like Gary O'Neil and Neil Barrett had to work very hard to cover for him and do his running. Similarly, that began to tell on them. On top of that Prossie was a problem for me, pinching all my fags.

No sooner had the season started than we had to suffer the humiliation of going out of the Worthington Cup at home to second division Colchester. It was a shocking performance. With ten minutes left I could stand no more, got off the bench and headed for the dressing room. I was just too embarrassed to watch any more. That defeat marked the end of Darren Moore's Pompey career, with Rixie feeling that he wasn't mobile enough and the club sensing that they could get good money for him. For myself, I had been keeping fit playing in the Havant Sunday League for Sewards, along with Andy Awford, Kevin McCormack, our kit manager, and Mick Jenkins, the Havant and Waterlooville manager. It started as a bit of fun to get me out on a Sunday morning and then got serious with us eventually finishing as runners-up. Despite having passed my 40th birthday, I also had a couple of run-outs in goal for Pompey reserves when Tards and young Craig Bradshaw were injured.

There had been talk of Japanese keeper Yoshikatsu Kawaguchi moving to Fratton Park and I first met up with him when he came over for acclimatisation. He trained with me for a couple of days, along with the youth team and I took him for his medical, on his last day, which coincidentally was the fateful September 11. A national hero in Japan, there was considerable media interest from the foreign paparazzi, who chased us in motor cycles and cars to the examination. Yoshi's recruitment was seen as a commercially-viable venture and, after he joined the club, the interest from home and abroad was unrelenting. The ever-present Japanese journalists, always polite and courteous, would continually want to know where Yoshi was, how he was, when and where he would be training or playing and so on. It was a regular thing to see photographers in the trees around the training ground trying to take pictures of him in action.

From the start, Yoshi was a truly dedicated professional, with a lot of character and such great dignity. He was someone who was a pleasure to work with and wanted to train all the time. He always had a smile on his face, no matter what, and he was universally popular amongst the lads.

The supporters have come to respect him a great deal, as do Harry Redknapp and Jim Smith, the current management team. Unfortunately though, at the outset, the enormous hype and expectation around his arrival made it doubly difficult for him to settle in what was a completely different culture. He initially spent a lot of time on his own, but happily has acquired a few friends now and he spent Christmas with Alex, my new partner and I.

When he finally got into the side at Sheffield Wednesday, in November 2001, he conceded a goal in 26 seconds and that seemed to set the tone for his Pompey first-team experiences. Unfortunately, keepers live or die with what's in front of them defensively and he had come into a struggling side that was poor at the back. Then, he was clearly at fault with two of the goals in our defeat at Grimsby and somewhat unfairly he was bearing the brunt of the defeats in our poor run. The media were adamant that Pompey's slump had coincided with his arrival and it was summed up for me when I overheard the press boys taking the mickey and questioning whether he could even catch the ball. Then came the *coup de grace* , with the disastrous 4-1 FA Cup defeat by Leyton Orient at Fratton, for which Yoshi carried the can and lost his place. Bes came back in. Kawaguchi had conceded 25 goals in his 12 appearances, but as subsequent results confirmed, the problems ran deeper than Pompey's keeper.

Bes had been bitterly disappointed to lose his place at Hillsborough, but typically accepted it graciously and was one of the first to wish Yoshi all the best. It's rare to find keepers bearing a grudge towards each other, mainly because they know that there is only one place up for grabs. As a keeper, it's a strange experience watching someone else in goal in your place – for their sake and that of the team you don't want to see them concede a goal or get injured, but equally you're hoping that they will give the manager some cause to prefer you back in goal. The lads used to pull my leg that, as his coach, Yoshi's situation was all down to me. He had come to England to learn to be a better goalkeeper, but that I had destroyed Japan's national hero. To Yoshi's credit, with a different mentality to many of our players, he accepted his demotion to the reserves with good grace and retained his pride and dignity, which is a Japanese trait. Being out of the side probably cost him his chance to play in the World Cup finals in his home country, but he was determined, come what may, to work to make the grade with Pompey and see it through. He has improved since he arrived and it has benefited him to work with the other keepers every day. But he needs to play games regularly, if not at Pompey then somewhere else, even it means going back to Japan. I desperately don't want his career to be ruined.

Late in February that season we went to West Brom, were very poor and ended up battered 5-0. Like many of the fans, chairman Milan Mandaric was embarrassed and frustrated by the club's lack of progress and results and you could hardly blame him. He decided to withhold the players' wages in return; it was his way of showing his disgust at the lack of heart in the performance. Rixie's position, in the face of such performances and our position close to the relegation zone, became even more precarious. He had always seemed to be under pressure, but he never lost the players' respect, unlike other managers I had known. They knew what he was trying to do. He was a manager who was close to his players, but I never felt that the players ever took advantage of him. He would have been harder with them if he had needed to be. I liked Rixie, who had plenty of good ideas, but my feeling was that he was on a hiding to nothing at Pompey and that it was a case of 'wrong time, wrong place' for him as manager. Losing Mark Burchill, who was his big signing and looked capable of scoring a lot of goals, was desperately unlucky. But looking back, he must have regretted his publicly-stated aim of 'mid-table mediocrity' as the limit of his ambition for the season. That immediately seemed to conflict with the chairman who, having invested so much money in the club, was looking for a quicker fix than that, with the play-offs as his target. Maybe Rixie was too honest for his own good and was not adept at the political side of things. His level of insecurity seemed even more marked (and perhaps understandable) as the season progressed. When his assistant Jim Duffy left, in the wake of the Orient defeat, it got to the stage where he clearly felt that everybody was out to get him. He seemed to visibly age about 20 years in the year or so he was at the club. For his last few weeks it was a case of not if, but when he would be sacked.

In the spring of 2002 Mick Jenkins, who was a mate of mine, asked me to help them out Havant and Waterlooville when they had a keeper crisis, so I travelled with them to play at Folkestone one evening. It turned out to be a real eye-opener for me. I discovered that most of the Havant lads had been up since 6 am, had gone to work in the morning and then caught the coach at 2 pm. I knew they would have to go to work again the next morning after arriving back in the early hours from Folkestone. The floodlights were dim – I couldn't see a thing – the pitch was very wet and then I had to suffer a woeful referee. I confess that I verbally abused him after a series of bizarre decisions and I was cautioned. As he walked away after taking my name, I called out to him "and don't forget the MBE", which the lads thought was hilarious. The referee just looked bewildered. I had other games against Stafford Rangers and Tamworth, but had to come off at half-time in the latter game with a pulled hamstring, bringing an end to my non-league exploits.

It looked as though the chairman might not make the change until the end of the season, but Rixie was sacked with five games left. Director of Football Harry Redknapp had stayed in the background up until then and had never forced himself on Rixie and had never got involved on the playing side unless he was asked. Initially, when he took the manager's job, no-one was sure how much really wanted it. He rapidly decided that many of the players were not what he wanted, but it wasn't clear at that stage how he was going to achieve the big changes he had in mind.

In the close season – summer 2002 – I found myself, for the first time ever, actually confronting my drinking problem. It came through the Tony Adams book *Addicted*, which my partner Alex had bought for me at the airport before we departed on holiday, with the words "I think you should read this". I found great similarities between what Tony had gone through and my own current situation. My drinking was affecting me mentally and putting immense pressure on my relationship with Alex, as it had done with Jennifer previously. I was not an alcoholic in that I didn't need a drink as soon as I got up in the morning or even every day. But through my lifestyle as a player I had become a 'binge drinker' or 'power drinker', who would get smashed through consuming large quantities over a short period, usually socially, at a weekend and then no more for the rest of the week. Instead of going out in company and settling for a couple of pints, I would have to go up to ten pints and beyond to get the buzz I craved.

The Adams book spurred me into making an attempt to give up drinking and, without any real effort or difficulty, I managed just that for the first six months of the 2002/03 season. Football is an environment where alcohol is always to be found and in those months I made an effort not to stay around for too long in such situations. From that experience I could sympathise with Paul Merson when he had to work hard to keep himself away from the champagne in those promotion celebrations. It was easy enough for me to give up, but it wasn't with the idea that I wouldn't ever drink again. I never ever thought that I would be able to refrain forever. Inevitably, I got some stick from my mates and it got boring, but most people were very supportive, congratulated me and reassured me that I was doing the right thing. Adams talked in his book about getting into poetry and learning to play the piano instead, but I couldn't see myself going in those directions.

Through the subsequent pre-season Harry played the market superbly, with wheeling and dealing which was out of this world. He took full advantage of the state of the game, with the transfer market being depressed, and virtually built a new team. The squad got together for a pre-season 'camp' in Devon to play a few games and to get to know each other, just as we had done the previous season. With Rixie one could detect an animosity brewing between the manager and the chairman. This time there was a completely different atmosphere of togetherness, boosted by Jim Smith's return and the realisation that Harry had brought in some more-than-decent players. With the wholesale changes – seven players made their debut on the opening day of the new season, with a completely new back three – I really thought it would take a while for the team to gel. We were quietly confident of perhaps grabbing a play-off spot, but little did we know we were in for a season beyond anyone's wildest dreams. We went off like an express train, which never came off the rails.

At this time, Harry was always talking about that one final piece in the jigsaw and he was, of course, working hard to bring Paul Merson in. Merse's signing was pivotal and with his record and sheer presence, he commanded great respect in the dressing room. Merse was that extra little bit of star quality Harry wanted. Right from the word go he was carving teams open and they just didn't know how to cope with him. We would give him the ball and he would look to open things up, at the same time making it all look so simple. The players around him, like Nigel Quashie, were saying "I can do that", and soon his presence was encouraging them to try things they hadn't previously had the confidence to attempt. He got everyone playing and, under his influence, the team raised its game to new levels. Merse is a quiet bloke, a deep thinker who is very knowledgeable on the game, but nevertheless likes a laugh and a joke in the dressing room. Occasionally, we would find ourselves talking about drinking in his presence, but he would joke about it and the embarrassment we felt would soon pass.

Harry has the respect of all the players which is important. He's never one to shout or scream – he has Jim for that, although even he has mellowed. Harry's man management is top class. He is great in the dressing room – a real cool customer with no tantrums or cups being thrown. Harry's a nice bloke, who nevertheless doesn't suffer fools gladly. His knowledge of players, not to mention his dozens of contacts, is phenomenal, extending all over Europe and he regularly comes up with the names of players that none of us have heard of. Harry and Jim's coming-together seemed a strange one to me at first. I wondered if, given that they were both big names in the game, they would find themselves clashing. But Jim seemed to be quite happy to be Harry's number two, a role he had already filled earlier, under Roland Nilsson at Coventry. Not that they didn't disagree at times – they did have the odd 'healthy discussion' – but it was never in front of the players. I wondered whether there might be 'too many cooks' at training with Harry, Jim and Kevin Bond around, but they worked it out between them, split the sessions and it was never the problem I knew it had been at some clubs. Not that the calibre of players Harry brought in needed too much coaching – it was only ever a question of keeping them fit and getting them ready to play. With the results we were having all that was needed was to keep it ticking over, there was no need to tinker with anything.

We got off to a great start with a win over Forest and a goal from Vincent Péricard. For the first two weeks of pre-season, Vincent looked like he had never kicked a ball before in his life. Everyone was tearing their hair out over him, but he was, after all, only 19 years of age and having to adjust to a different country and culture. Then, to confound us all, he was unbelievable in that first game and never looked back. That good start included a decent draw at Sheffield United and the confidence was growing. It was the result and the character we showed at Crystal Palace that first made everyone realise that we could do really well. Coming in two-down, Harry and Jim launched into the lads at half time and the second-half comeback was the catalyst for the whole season. That result built enormous belief that we could win any game and from then on we never really looked back. I was a radio summariser that afternoon and it struck me forcibly that this team could really win something – but even then I never imagined how much we would go on and achieve. Winning became a habit, just as losing had so often in the past, which was hard to break. This was a group of players who knew no fear, who had no preconceptions of what had gone on before and who went on to break all the 'we never win there' hoodoos. As the season rolled on, it seemed to fuel itself and things got better and better, such that my natural wariness was overtaken by an unusual optimism. When quizzed publicly about our prospects I would jokingly say "well you know what Pompey are like", but deep down I didn't feel like that this time. I knew that this was a different kettle of fish to anything which had gone on before. We were all guarded about our chances publicly – there was no one to be found who was shouting and screaming from the rooftops – but there was a great belief amongst the squad. People talked about us having a wobble through December, but we were still picking up draws against some decent sides and stayed top of the league. If we had suffered six defeats, I could understand it, but nevertheless the press tried to talk it up, whilst recalling the Wolves scenario from the previous season. It only served to increase our determination to prove them wrong. We knew that everyone has some sort of stutter on the way and we knew we would come through it. Jim had a graph upon which he charted our path to promotion, with various targets along the way and he would show it to us as proof that we were still well on course.

Harry had it in mind to bring in some extra faces when necessary, and knew that he needed to freshen it up as we went into the New Year. He had been after Tim Sherwood since pre-season and his signing showed that we could now attract Premiership players with an international background. Tim added more steel in midfield and, with teams beginning to work out Merse's role, his knowhow and experience helped us get back on track. Fresh faces in the form of Tim, Yakubu Ayegbeni and Steve Stone lifted everybody at the right time. The system Harry employed worked a treat, with the whole thing based on attacking at pace, although initially I worried that it might leave us exposed with just three at the back. He had got in the right players for it, particularly at wing back where Matthew Taylor was a sensation – I couldn't believe the engine on the boy – it made me tired just watching him. Kevin Harper also did a great job out on the right.

Harps deserves a lot of credit for responding to the challenge. With his great pace you always knew he could beat defenders but, with his increased confidence, it was noticeable how his delivery became much improved. He had some stick from the crowd early on, but by the end of the season he had turned them around. Rarely have I seen a player achieve that. Once a player gets stick from the fans it's usually the beginning of the end for him. Harps, like Linvoy Primus and Matthew Taylor, also deserves credit for playing on through injuries. We didn't have the biggest squad in the world and they responded in the right way when Harry asked them to stay in for as long as possible. Harry had every faith in Shaka Hislop in goal, who is a laid-back, lovely guy, and nothing rattled him. His concentration was good and it needed to be, in a season when he went for long periods in games with nothing to do. He made the odd mistake, once or twice punching the ball outside the area, but nothing major. It's easy to play well if you are kept busy in a struggling side, as I well know. Goalkeeping requires a different mentality to other positions, with confidence and feeling good about yourself as vital components. I heard that a small minority amongst our fans felt that he didn't command his area enough, but some people will always find something to complain about in their keeper.

Shaka was an experienced keeper and not in any need of much coaching. He liked certain routines and I was there to help him if he had any problems, to keep him ticking over and make sure that he didn't aggravate any previous injury problems. There was a running joke on the bench during games concerning Shaka. If he made a great save I would say: "We've worked on that all week, you know," but if he made a mistake then they would all turn and stare at me and I would be made to feel as if it was all my fault. I call them 'my keepers' and I get a lot of pride from their performances and equally, I feel for them if they make a mistake. Yoshi wanted to train morning, noon and night and I had to work on getting him to relax. I was pleased for him when he got on for the second half at Bradford, after patiently waiting all season for a chance. It was only fair that Shaka be allowed to start so that he could retain his 'ever present' tag, but after a long discussion beforehand we decided to put Yoshi on, whatever the situation was in the game at the time. It was the least he deserved.

Linvoy Primus wasn't one of the original pieces in Harry's jigsaw, but literally forced himself into the boss's plans with his approach to the situation he found himself in. We had one or two injuries in defence at the start of the season and when Linvoy came in he shocked everyone with his great performances. He deservedly went on to sweep the board at the end-of-season awards. With Gianluca Festa, Arjan De Zeeuw and Hayden Foxe fit, Harry found that four into three at the back wouldn't go, but he managed to juggle it around successfully even if Linvoy had to play on the right. Whether it helped Linvoy to play with better players or not, there's no doubt he raised his game to new levels. De Zeeuw, Foxe and Festa, were all experienced, strong defenders who could read the game well. They had great confidence in each other, which is a major plus at the back, and each had the ability to get the ball down and play. Above all, for the first time in a long time at Pompey, they knew that if we went behind, we could come back and score the goals we needed. Svetoslav Todorov had a slow start after arriving at Fratton in the previous season and could look lazy, but we saw a great change in him, like others, once he had gained strength and confidence from the players around him. His close control and unbelievable feet, coupled with his masterly finishing, were a joy to watch at times.

Our performance at Burnley in October was memorable – I had never seen football like it from a Pompey side. It was men against boys and we didn't get the goals we deserved. Two weeks earlier, at Rotherham, it had been a completely different situation which had shown the two sides to our game. It was a tough, horrible game, in which we had dominated the first half with our class, but had to show real steel in the second half. Shaka's great save in the last 30 seconds brought us the points that day. Our display at Manchester United in the cup also told us a lot. For the first 20 minutes we froze – the one and only time all season – and showed United too much respect. In the second half we were the better side and, if Nigel Quashie had scored with the great chance he had, we might have caused an upset. There were plenty of positives to take from Old Trafford and it stood the team in good stead for the rest of the season. It was while we were staying up in Manchester, for a few days before the game, that I started drinking again. On the Thursday night the players had their meal together in the hotel at 7 pm, but the staff meal was delayed an hour, while Jim and Harry met up with Sir Alex Ferguson for a chat in the hotel lounge. It was during that meal that for some unbeknown reason I had a couple of glasses of wine and then some more, as the evening wore on. Within weeks, I was a back in the old routine again, on the same treadmill, but this time it was to take on a new dimension.

With the finishing line agonisingly in sight, our defeat at home to Sheffield Wednesday brought everyone down to earth with a bump, just when we thought we had promotion sewn up. But curiously, winning it a few days later against Burnley made it even more special. It was great to do it at home and, for me, when we did our lap of honour afterwards, it brought back memories of going round the pitch after losing in the play-offs to Leicester ten years earlier. This time there was no crying on the terraces, just thousands of smiling faces. Winning the title at home brought out all those flags, making it a very special, unique sight, turning Fratton Park into a continental stadium. Becky, my daughter, and Harvey, Alex's son, came on to the pitch at the end, were at the back of the stage for the presentations and joined in the lap of honour – something they will never forget. Then, at Bradford, we played some of the best football of the season to lay on a final treat for our fans. I have built up a great admiration for our supporters over the years. For so long they have been short-changed and let down in so many ways, but they have stuck by us through thick and thin and it was great for them to get what they richly deserved. The players were thrilled for the chairman Milan Mandaric. When he came to the club originally, it was at the lowest point I had ever known. I have seen him, at times, at a very low ebb, and as anyone might, he has made mistakes which he has admitted. It has probably cost him much more than he anticipated, but he has stuck by his promises to the supporters and hasn't been too far off his target in taking the club to the Premiership.

The promotion celebrations were another excuse for me to binge drink, but now it makes me feel very depressed and guilty afterwards. To add to that, I never used to get hangovers, but now I suffer afterwards – perhaps it's something to do with my age – and that increases the pain. It's now a vicious circle and I don't know what comes first, the depression or the drink. My bouts of both have put my relationship with Alex under great strain, but she has stuck by me for three years now, when not many others would have and I will always be grateful for that. It's been difficult for her, but she is always there for me and has a lot to put up with. All the people close to me have to suffer my mood swings and personality changes. It makes me hard to live with – I know I couldn't stand living with myself. After a binge I go through the whole gamut of negative emotions, mainly remorse and regret. When I wake up sober on a Monday morning, after a long weekend wasted spent drinking, I am tortured by such thoughts as: 'Why did I do it?', 'What might I have said?', 'I can't believe I have done it again', 'I can't remember any of it' and 'I have let everyone down again'. The subsequent guilt of what I have put those close to me through is overwhelming, but then I find myself doing it all over again.

I was interested to hear Merse saying that suicide crosses his mind as he grapples with his problems and there have been times, at my lowest points, when that has really crossed my mind. I have not yet sought any help, other than once to have a chat with the club doctor. He referred me for counselling, which I did not pursue, on the basis that I thought I could cope with it and my feeling, prejudice perhaps, at that time that counselling was for wimps anyway. It was nice to talk it through with Andy Rimmer our club chaplain recently, but I am not in any way religious and he could only deal with it on a purely spiritual level. Once Adams and Merson had come out and admitted their problem, it opened the floodgates, so to speak, and soon the depth of the   problem in the game became apparent. Some players will admit to it, others won't. I know there are very many out there who have had   similar experiences to mine. I am uncomfortable talking about it, but then I have always kept things to myself and maybe that is part of the problem. I know it frustrates the people close to me that I don't let them know what I am really feeling. I put my drink problem firmly down to my early days at the club and the drinking culture into which I became embedded. Most players survived such an upbringing, but I am unfortunately one of the few who have had residual problems – perhaps it's something to do with my character or personality. I have cut back on my regular drinking through the week, but it's the 'benders' which are now the problem. These three or four-day sessions, every couple of months or so, are usually triggered by my finding myself in situations or mind frames that I can't deal with, which I have allowed to build up and during which I can't express my feelings or let anybody get close enough to help me. I kid myself into thinking that I am facing up to it, that I can control it, but I know I am not really. It wouldn't surprise me if it got to the stage where I found myself being forced to stop drinking and to seek help. I don't know if I will have the courage to do it myself, or whether I will eventually need someone to come and drag me there.

As the team headed relentlessly to the Premiership, I would have dearly loved to have been out there in goal, but it was still a real pleasure to sit and watch some of the best football I've ever seen. I've been able to savour our success and have taken it in a lot more than I did as a player. After a period when I began to wonder whether my future lay in such a coaching role, the promotion season has revitalised me. Like everyone, I felt very proud, not only as a member of staff, but as a fan and I am looking forward to going to new and redeveloped Premier League grounds. It has been disappointing to hear people making us favourites for relegation, but that will harden our determination to stay up. It is hard to get out of the first division and the last thing we want is to go straight down again. Hopefully, with the present management and our magnificent chairman, it won't come to that and we can establish ourselves and perhaps even think of Europe.

Things are a lot different from the days when we got promoted to the first division in 1987. Then, our first game at the top level was away to Oxford and we found ourselves going down to the cramped, tiny Manor Ground. The camaraderie amongst the squad was our main strength, with the booze culture as an integral part of all that. That culture was half preached to you – that it was important to go out together and bond. We would regularly drink together, party together, but also work hard together. That bonding worked out on the pitch. We were all mates in it together and you wanted to die for each other on the pitch. It's different today. That social culture doesn't exist now and with the introduction of foreign players to the English game, the culture in clubs has changed dramatically. To add to that, there are differences in terms of dieting and fitness, with the players being more athletic today than we ever were. Nowadays the lads don't socialise with each other so much – and that's the way it has to be. But in their own way, they have a terrific team spirit, with some close friendships and a real mutual respect.

Inevitably, people will try to compare the side which won the first division championship last season to the 1987 promotion team. In the same way, our team was compared to the first division championship side of the 1940s and 1950s. It's all relative really. If Jimmy Dickinson or Duggie Reid played today, then I'm sure they would have adapted and been successful. I see and hear what certain players up and down the country are earning nowadays and I've never been jealous exactly, but I do resent it a little. I don't blame the players at all. Clubs have been willing to pay that sort of money and in some cases have been spending money they didn't have. Often the players were not worth it, but it is the players who have been calling the tune. Now, football is paying the price for such over-indulgence and the clubs are trying to regain control. I suspect that the unbelievable sums which are still being earned will soon be a thing of the past. I missed out on all those big pay-days, but it's all relative. I talk to Len Phillips, an England international from our 1950s championship team and he reminds me that he used to have to catch a bus to the ground on a Saturday to play.

I still miss playing, like all ex-pros, but after pulling on the gloves again in Steve Claridge's benefit match at the end of the season, I knew I was past it. The reflexes had gone and I found I couldn't pick up the ball in flight – you only maintain the eye-hand co-ordination through daily training. Not only that, I know that my body couldn't take the daily training and, of course, you get more tired as you get older. I have said in the past that I am not interested in management, but I think now that I would like to give it a go at some time in the future. I think it would depend on the circumstances, where it was, who I had around me to help out and whether I had complete trust in my employer. My ultimate ambition is to manage Pompey, but I would need to learn the ropes and serve the necessary apprenticeship at the right level. I won't know whether I am the right type until I try it, but I have seen from close quarters that it is a 24-hour, seven-days-a-week job for Harry and it's just as hard for Mick Jenkins at Havant and Waterlooville. Both have their mobile phone never far away from their ear and are in constant demand. This summer I am continuing to take my UEFA coaching badges, to include my goalkeeping badge, so that should stand me in good stead, given that they are likely to become compulsory.

For the moment I count myself as extremely lucky to have spent over 25 years at a fantastic football club, to have played as many games as I have, and to have played in front of the best supporters in the country. I have been lucky beyond measure. I wouldn't change a thing in my career, except perhaps to have won more trophies, but that would be greedy, given the wonderful life I have enjoyed in football. Portsmouth Football Club has been my life since the age of 13. It is in my blood now. I don't know anything else but football and my life revolves around it. This is me, the way I am, and I don't think that will ever change.

Index

WE ARE
WHAT WE
LISTEN
TO
The Impact of **music** on individual and social **health**

PATRICIA **CAICEDO**
M.D., PH.D.

mundoarts

Music and Health Collection N.1
We are what we listen to: the impact of music on individual and social health

ISBN 978-1-7339035-4-7
Paperback
October, 2021
MA00012

First edition in Spanish:
Somos lo que escuchamos: impacto de la música en la salud individual y social. Barcelona, Septiembre, 2021

English translation
Neha Iyer

Cover Design
Stephanni Vega
Patricia Caicedo

Interior Design
Patricia Caicedo

Mundo Arts Publications
Patricia Caicedo

www.mundoarts.com

E-mail: **info@mundoarts.com**
Phone US: +1-678-608-3588
Phone Spain: +34-696-144-766

Barcelona - New York

WE ARE
WHAT WE
LISTEN
TO
The Impact of **music**
on individual and
social **health**

PATRICIA **CAICEDO**
M.D., PH.D.

*To my parents Jorge and Patricia
and my brother Juan Pablo.*

INDEX

FOREWORD

By Tess Knigthton, Ph.D.

What is the soundtrack of your life? Which music gives you goosebumps? How can a song, like Proust's proverbial *madelaine* dipped in lime-blossom tea, effortlessly and involuntarily, bring back a hundred memories? Have you thought about which music attracts you and why? Do you lose yourself in music or listen to it with a conscious desire to understand it? Or both, depending on circumstances, on the moment in time? How is it that music seems to be able to express our deepest emotions without need for words? Can we ever really know how music works its magic? These are just some of the questions posed by the singer and musicologist Patricia Caicedo in her new book *We are what we listen to*.

Music holds meaning for us, she argues, for each of us as an individual, and for all of us collectively, as a community of the world. That meaning may be influenced – even conditioned – by social and cultural context, but we all participate in 'musicking', the term coined by Christopher Small to indicate that each musical act is experienced by all those present, whether as performer or ear-witness. Music is quintessentially inclusive, even when it may appear to be exclusive, a music with which we are not familiar, a music that can make us feel uneasy even as it draws us to it, a music associated with a particular social group that we do not immediately identify as ours. Music can transcend all barriers, if we allow it to do so. And in this – and many other respects – music is wonderful in its effects – its impact – on our daily life, filling us with wonder at its power, its creative energy, its unswerving companionship from before we are born until after we die, as – often unwittingly – we write our musical autobiography in the course of our lived experience.

Caicedo's book is itself a wonderful introduction to thinking about how music is an integral part of our lives, because, as she describes, it is good for us. During my childhood in England, there was a country saying 'An apple a day keeps the doctor away', and some parents, including my own, would take this quite literally – at least during the apple season. Caicedo, as a trained medical doctor who was known in the hospital where she worked as 'the singing doctor', would say – or, rather sing – 'A song a day keeps the doctor away', and it is an enlightening combination of medical knowledge and musical experience that she brings to this brief survey of, essentially, how music *works*. It is a book that you will want to devour in one sitting (we are what we eat!), but it is filled with ideas that you will want to savour, and with ideas that may take a little while to digest. Music, she argues, is a biological, chemical and psychological process: our physiological, rational and emotional responses are inextricably bound together, even though science is able to detect and chart these responses with increasing accuracy and an unprecedented rapidity with each technological advance. The discovery that our biological cells actually emit sound – they sing! –, that a rich chemical cocktail is mixed inside us when we 'musick', and that the parts of our brain that light up in response to both environmental and organised sound connect to memory and enhance a sense of interconnectedness within ourselves and with others, certainly gives pause for thought.

Caicedo, as doctor and performer, explains these complex processes with clinical clarity and draws on her own experience to elucidate what they mean in practice: how we can listen to our body – our pulse, our rate of breathing, our sense of physical equilibrium – through listening to music; and how we can take stock of our mental well-being by allowing ourselves to enter into the flow of the music and engage with the now of life, emerging able to face the future, to look back at the past without being in thrall to it, and to make the most of the present. Should we, then, regard music as a panacea for all ills? Studies show that 'musicking' can alleviate pain, can reduce sickness from radiotherapy, can prolong life or at least mitigate the aging process, can release emotional tension and restore mental equilibrium, though probably not to the same extent in all people, nor in all situations. A lively debate followed the piping of Classical music in certain stations of the Paris *métro* with the idea of reducing crime. The move appeared to be remarkably effective, until it became apparent that the crimewave itself just moved to other stations where Bach and Beethoven were not to be heard. Did the experiment prove that Classical music had a salutary effect on the criminal mind, or were the criminals deterred simply by their sense of musical taste?

The positive impact of music has been charted by writers from ancient times to the present day, and Caicedo cites many authorities from the past three thousand years and more, from western and eastern traditions. Observation on how music can assuage the sadness and grief felt at the death of a loved one, often leading to a sense of catharsis by which loss is gradually transformed into memory and acceptance, or how it can arouse a sense of exhilaration among a crowd that results in a wave of emotion contagion, as at a spectacular event, whether in coliseum or football stadium, is not new, but reappears in different modes of expression over the centuries. Caicedo's writing is refreshingly free of jargon; it is aware of present-day sensibilities, but wokeness is, thankfully, absent. The book is thoughtful and will make you think; it is affirmative, but grounded in real experience rather than the chimera of fantasy. The reader is drawn into a shared soundscape that is constantly in a state of flux and reflux and in which music is both constant and ever-changing.

Caicedo is surely right to conclude that the role of music in our lives has become even more important in the time of a pandemic, even when live performance has been for almost two years confined to Zoom and podcasts. The ban on singing in choirs has been particularly destructive in terms of sociability and the sheer joy of participating in music-making in the company of others. This is something that many of us have experienced and still miss in a masked, distanced and confined world. But what I didn't know, before reading this wonderful book, is that singing in groups strengthens the presence of oxytocin in the body, a hormone that is released naturally at childbirth to stimulate bonding between mother and child. We may all have sensed that music is a catalyst that can bring elements together and transform them, but it now appears that our sixth sense can be confirmed by a bodily chemical reaction.

This need not take the mystery out of music-making. The fifteenth-century philosopher – and medical doctor – Marsilio Ficino (one of the many authors cited by Caicedo) wonderfully evoked this mystery – or magic, as Caicedo calls it – by describing music as the 'decoration of silence': an increasingly poignant metaphor in an age of unprecedented sound contamination. Ficino, and other thinkers of the time, saw the role of the performer as someone with the ability to channel higher creative activity: performance was considered, essentially, to be a ritual that could create the conditions for contemplative awareness. For them, as for Caicedo, the energy generated by music can be gathered and sustained through the performer, who serves as conduit during the unfolding of the musical performance in an infinite exchange of ebb and flow with the listener. It is this intangible dialogue that can lead to that frisson of understanding, of recognition of all that is beauty, all that is positive, all that is health-giving – and which gives us the goosebumps.

Tess Knighton, ICREA Research Professor
Universitat Autònoma de Barcelona

PRELUDE

I'm sure you can think of pieces of music which have defined the most important moments of your life, songs which have been there for you in difficult times, which have helped you express your emotions in a way like no other. Perhaps you have felt an uncontrollable energy after attending a huge concert, an inner peace while listening to a symphony or the desire to cry while listening to a love song.

The fact is that all of us, no matter the time or our culture, have experienced the power of sound, vibration and music.

In the Kybalion,[1] a compilation of texts from Ancient Egypt, published in 1908, we find the seven principles that rule the universe, one of which states: *Nothing is immobile, everything moves, everything vibrates.*[2] This supposedly simple affirmation has been validated right from quantum physics, resulting in string theory which explains how the universe and all its objects function in terms of vibrations of thin supersymmetric strings that move in ten dimensions space-time and one temporary dimension.

The universe is a symphony of objects in constant vibration, life itself is vibration, sound. For example, as proven recently by Pelling, Gralla and Gimzewski,[3] the cells in our body sing, and their song varies depending on health and sickness.

According to my parents, my relationship with music began in my mother's womb, when, very ahead of their time, they played music hoping that it would have a positive effect on my brain development. At five years old, I began my studies in the conservatory, immersing myself in the universe of sounds and finding my most loyal partner in music, my refuge in difficult times and my therapeutic, cathartic tool.

Just like for you, in my own life, music has played different roles, all of which have been of vast importance. When I was eleven years old, when I began to sing, music helped me with social integration, something which was very difficult for me considering I was a profoundly shy child. Singing became my way of expressing emotions, and helped me fit into a group in school, something which I would never have been able to do without it. During my adolescence, it became key to the construction of my identity, a symbol of rebellion, a vehicle of values and ideologies. If I take a look back at my life, music has been present in the most important moments of my life, the celebrations, the sorrows, the loves or the heartbreaks.

Medicine entered my life when I was sixteen, and I began a degree in the Colombian School of Medicine. I remember that the first thing I did when I arrived at the faculty was look for the college choir. Once again, music became the key which opened all doors. Throughout my years at university, I took part in the choir, where I met some of my best friends. When I began clinical practice, in every hospital I was in, I performed concerts for patients and doctors, raising funds for the many hospital services, even becoming known as "the doctor who sings".

I've always known, intuitively so, that music had a healing effect, that patients who listened to it felt better, that even for a few moments, their pain was eased, that they felt happier and more relaxed, which was a feeling also shared by the doctors in the hospital environment, a very demanding environment from a physical and psychological viewpoint.

However, it was only a few years later that I could myself confirm the therapeutic power of music, when the study of singing and the discipline associated with it, which consists of breathing, posture, body consciousness and sound, cured me of an eating disorder that I sustained for many years. It was through music that I became healthy, and learned to listen to myself, even realising that my mental and physical health depended on musical practice, which was the moment I decided to dedicate myself professionally to music and do a complete 180 degree turn in my life.

Although in that moment it felt like I had abandoned medicine, when I began my role as a singing teacher, I realised that every lesson was like a therapeutic session, a medical session where we worked on psychological conflicts and physical pains, and we relearnt how to sense and express using the body and emotions, all through the medium of sound.

I was able to confirm that the journey to health and wellbeing is made up of the conscious composition of a harmonious piece of music, unique to each person and each object in this universe. This piece must also be rhythmic because the universe, as highlighted by the Ancient Egyptians, is also rhythm.

Everything in the universe has its own sound and its own rhythm, the heart and even Covid-19, which, while I'm currently writing this book, is devastating the planet. While I am writing these lines, I am listening to the decoded melody by professor Markus Buehler from MIT, who, along with his team, assigned each aminoacid, the building blocks of protein, a unique note, which then an algorithm turned into musical notes. According to Buehler, listening to the melody offers a more intuitive form of understanding protein: "I would need many different images, a lot of different magnifications to see what the ear can capture with just a few seconds of music."[4]

Perhaps in the future, this auditory comprehension will be key to understanding many pathologies, which until this day have been difficult to understand and treat. Through sound and music, we can more quickly and directly reach the core of the things which surround us, and understand this universe, in which everything from the most microscopic to the most gigantic of objects vibrates.

This makes sense considering it is through sound that we experience life for the first time. As we are born, we interact with the sounds of the environment, creating emotional ties through the voices, songs, and whispers.

I'm sure that now you are thinking about your own relationship with music, about the role that it has played in your life and your relationships, in the construction of your identity, in your health, or you may even be remembering shared musical experiences that have stayed with you.

Music, apart from being an individual experience of the senses, is also a communal experience with a strong symbolic meaning, a space to represent the values that define our identity. Part of its beauty is that it transcends the sphere of the individual to unite us in a shared experience.

There are so many ways that we could discuss the impact of music at a physical, psychological and social level that I have decided to write this book to try shed light on the important role of music and sound in the human experience, the age-old relationship between music, medicine and health, and the ways in which we perceive and process music at a cerebral level.

This journey into this topic is a reflection of my interdisciplinary training in music, medicine and musicology and for this reason, I'll be looking at historical, social, scientific and musical aspects.

In light of recent neuroscientific research, I aim to explain the cognitive processes of music, to understand how the brain of musicians works and the many benefits of musical practice at a cognitive level, such as protecting the brain and delaying the process of aging.

We will discover the ancient relationship between rhythm, movement and health, the mysterious brain mechanisms that link music, pleasure and emotion, and the many ways in which music improves our quality of life, leads to wellness, happiness and provides us a sense of purpose and meaning in life.

The perception of sound and music, one of the most intimate and personal human experiences, as deep as thought itself, has been key to the evolution of our species and it could also be key to creating an individual who is more conscious of themselves and their surrounding, an individual with a global ecological conscience.

The road to physical, mental and emotional health is sure to be filled with sounds and music. I invite you on this journey so you can start to understand the many ways in which music can change your life for the better.

Chapter 1

MUSIC AND MEDICINE
THE HISTORY OF A RELATIONSHIP

Taking shelter in the maternal womb, we begin life floating in a space similar to the sea, in constant movement and vibration. We are accompanied by the rhythmic beat of our mother's heart and the many sounds made by her organs. Upon arriving into the world, a cry is our first mark of independence, an affirmation of *I am*. Gestation and birth are sonorous experiences just like they were for the first hominids hundreds of thousands of years ago. From then on, sound and music have been a central part of human experiences, tools of communication and of healing and above all, spaces of symbolic representation in which our individual and collective identities are built and dealt with.

Because of its ephemeral nature, in that it only exists during the performance, and due to its intangible character, throughout history, music has been associated with magic, spirituality, sublime experiences of the being which transcend the ordinary and transport us to other times, to other states of emotion and consciousness.

Different disciplines, like anthropology, philosophy and archeology have confirmed that music could have preceded the existence of the paleolithic man. Its uses have been as varied as culture itself; right from the origins of humanity, it has been linked to ritual, being a vehicle of ideologies and a social marker.

In his text, *The expression of emotions in animals and man,*[5] published in 1872, Charles Darwin developed the hypothesis that music was necessary for sexual selection, having existed before language itself. Seemingly our Neanderthal ancestors communicated through gestures and vocalizations where they made variations in tone or pace[6].

It is precisely the ability to differentiate the variations of rhythm, tone, timbre and volume in language which allows us to distinguish emotions and the context of a conversation, even in languages that we don't know. It seems that we recognize a primary, very ancient form of communication, based on the musical aspects of communication. According to Daniel Levitin, "humans discovered communication through language, and then, at some point, they rediscovered music."[7]

How did this first human communicate and express himself? What ancestral mysteries were uncovered by this primitive voice?

It was precisely the voice, that first form of contact and uniting bond, a cry which expressed pain, sorrow and joy, which discovered the sounds of the depths of the human soul.

For the current-day man, the voice is the umbilical cord which connects him to the past, the manifestation of life right from the first cry, the affirmation of his presence in the world. The voice, a sound emitted from the body, an inseparable part of it, through orality becomes a space of representation. From the oral sphere, we learn to call out and experience being heard; whatever makes noise gives meaning to the ability to hear.

It is precisely the fact that sound is a part of the body, not just through voice, but also through the multiple sounds made by the organs, in a sort of symphony, perfectly balanced and with the same purpose, which makes it impossible to separate the concepts of music-sound and medicine-health.

The French surgeon René Leriche (1879-1955) defined health as "life in the silence of organs", suggesting that when we have good health, we are not aware of the existence of our body. When our body is silent, we don't need to give it a second thought. Personally, I believe that health and illness both express themselves through sound. The variations of harmony, frequency and rhythm of these sounds are what differentiates health from illness.

In 2002, professors James Gimzewski and Andrew Pelling from the University of California inaugurated the campus of *sonocytology*,[8] upon having discovered through nanotechnology that cells emit frequencies of sound as they vibrate between themselves; cells sing.[9] This surprising discovery is evidence that life consists of vibration and rhythm and that sound is an integral part of the body and of human experience. It also explains the ancient relationship between music and medicine, two disciplines which at the beginning were related to the supernatural, the spiritual and the magical.

There is numerous evidence about the use of music and sound in magic and religious rituals in which shamans, who were the main interlocutors between gods and men, experts of botany, interpreters of dreams, doctors and mystics, used music to cure and to reach altered states of consciousness. The paleolithic figure of the "masked dancer", also known as "the tiny wizard with a musical bow", found in the caves of *Les Trois Frères*, shows an individual in an upright position, wearing the skin and head of a bison, celebrating a type of dance ritual, accompanied by an object which could be interpreted as a wind instrument or a small musical bow similar to those that are used by some tribes in Africa in the present day[10.]

Right from the corners of Siberia to deep in the Amazon, having been a part of the North American and Asian tribes, the shaman has had prominent roles within the community, as a spiritual and social guide, as well as a healer, or medicine-man as it's called in some indigenous tribes.[11] The role of the shaman, undertaken in many cultures by women who were deemed fit to reach out to other realities, was always linked to music and dance, key elements to reach these altered states of consciousness.

Practically all systems of thinking and spiritual traditions have used some type of musical expression to adore, invoke or ask a favor from its deities. Likewise, numerous scientific, religious and philosophical theories, both old and new, credit the structure and existence of the universe to sound.

In Western culture, we usually refer to the *New Testament*, to the moment when Saint John says: "In the beginning, there was the Word, and the Word was with God, and the Word was God", however, much earlier, around 2000 BC, in old Babylon, in the *Code of Hammurabi,* the Assyrians wrote about the therapeutic use of music in one of the most important documents in history, in which the medical practice is regulated in great detail.[12]

Later on, between the 5th century BC and the 4th century BC, the Ancient Greeks gave great importance to music, considering it an integral part of medicine. Plato stated in *The Republic*, "music is extraordinary because rhythm and harmony make their way to the most intimate part of the soul, and they bestow it with strength and grace". Also, Aristotle studied the effects of music, focusing on its cathartic properties. According to him, music helps "overcome feelings like pity, fear or enthusiasm" and mystic music helps "cure and purify the soul".[13] Both philosophers believed in the healing power of music.

For Pythagoreans, music and mathematics were closely tied. Music, made up of intervals which represent numerical relations, had the same moral attributes as numbers. Their daily routine included playing music in the morning to prepare themselves for their day and night, helping them clear their minds and fall asleep.[14] Pythagoreans also maintained that audible music on the Earth reflected the *Music of the Spheres*.[15]

In his book, *Life of Pythagoras*, Porphyry says:

He himself held morning conferences at his residence, composing his soul with the music of the lute, and singing certain old paeans of Thales. He also sang verses of Homer and Hesiod, which seemed to soothe the mind. He danced certain dances which he conceived conferred on the body agility and health. Walks he took not promiscuously, but only in company of one or two companions, in temples or sacred groves, selecting the quietest and pleasantest places. His friends he loved exceedingly, being the first to declare that the goods of friends are common, and that a friend was another self. While they were in good health he always conversed with them; if they were sick, he nursed them; if they were afflicted in mind, he solaced them, some by incantations and magic charms, others by music. He had prepared songs for the diseases of the body, by the singing of which he cured the sick. He also had some that caused oblivion of sorrow, mitigation of anger and destruction of lust.[16]

Between the 9th and 11th centuries, the Golden Age of Arabic medicine, the famous doctor Ibn Sina (980-1037), author of the *Canon of Medicine*, a book translated into Latin and for centuries considered the reference point for Western doctors, makes special reference to the use of music as therapy. During the Caliphate of Cordoba, mentally ill patients were prescribed a daily dose of listening to beautiful voices and songs[17], and Sufis stated that all of the proceedings of the universe, whether visible or invisible, are musical - we are music. Our bodies vibrate reflecting the symphony of the universe.[18]

While medicine and arts flourished in the Arabic world, in Europe during the Middle Ages, music was an anonymous and collective art, in the same way illness was as well. Together, people suffered the terror, pain and death brought on by successive epidemics, with unknown causes.

When the *Black Death* surfaced, one of the most traumatic events in European history, music and medicine began to have a unexpected association: hoards of men, women and children travelled all over cities and fields dancing frenetically. When the illness began to appear in a city, it wasn't the doctor, but rather the musician to whom they went, believing that only dance would make it disappear. Flagellants, groups of singers, sang songs called *Geisslerlieder*,[19] begging for divine intervention and repenting their sins, and music became like a direct path to God, a tool for healing.

As testament to the relationship between music and medicine during this period came the famous *Decameron*, written not long after bubonic plague which ravaged Florence in 1398. In this, Bocaccio uses ten songs which he wrote in confinement to piece together a story. With the clear purpose of healing, every song is sung in a group as a method of protection against the imminent plague.

So much power was given to music as a healing power that by law, those who wished to be doctors had to appreciate and study music as it was considered essential for maintaining the wellbeing of patients. It was believed that curing the psyche through music also healed the body, and there were even specific melodies recommended for different illnesses. For example, the cure for gout was to listen alternately between the sound of the flute and the harp, but of course, these remedies were only within the reach of a few privileged members of society.

Medical and musical theory are associated with the Hippocrates' four humors - blood, phlegm, yellow bile and black bile - and with the four elements of the cosmos - air, water, land and fire -, stating that both good and bad health depended on the perfect balance between these elements. The pleasure caused by music was clinically prescribed as a remedy for rage, sorrow and fear.

In Italy, Marsilio Ficino (1433-99), physician, musician, astrologer and priest, and one of the most prolific translators of Plato in modern history, wrote in *De vita*[20] (book of life) that music embodies perfection and harmony and induces the feeling of tranquility in its listeners and performers. Ficino also translated the *Song of Orpheus* into Latin, revealing the power of music about nature.[21] According to him, if music is performed with regularity, the spirit adopts the characteristics of the music being listened to. He equated music to the soul, to the intangible, and to the celestial. Like many Renaissance thinkers, he believed illness to be the result of an imbalance of the four humors, in direct relation to nature, so much so that when he treated a patient, he linked their unique nature to the music of the planets.

"Music is influenced by divine power in such a way that when certain tones are chosen, they reflect the model of the skies and the seven planets. The planets have their own voices and sounds. The sounds of Saturn are slow, profound, jagged and querulous; Mars' are fast, sharp, fierce and threatening; Jupiter has profound and intense, yet always sweet and cheerful harmonies; the music of Venus is voluptuous with a with both wildness and softness, while Apollo's is marked by its grace, reverence and simplicity, and Mercury's by its vigour and joy".

The Venetian Gioseffo Zarlino (1517-1590), one of the great theorists of Renaissance music, wrote *Istitutioni harmoniche,* a monumental work in which the views of this period of time about the relationship between music and medicine were represented.[22] In his first book, titled *From praise to music*, he states that "absolutely nothing can be found in places where music is not of the greatest interest".

According to Zarlino, knowledge of music was essential to be a doctor:

> If the doctor does not understand music, how will he understand the pulse of his patients in the way Herophilus recommended, based on musical proportions?[23]

From 1550 onwards and until the beginning of the 17th century, a lot of effort was put towards elucidating the relationship between music and emotions. It was in *The doctrine of emotions*[24] where the first attempts to link empirical reason with music were expressed, linking science and music to explain the various emotional states like rage, desire, amazement, love, vigor, joy - feelings which, according the theorists at the time, were the opposite of sadness, gentleness and sweetness. This doctrine had a huge influence on Baroque music, as seen in the great works by J.S. Bach or Handel.[25] It is worth noting that during the 17th century, healing arts were represented by Apollo, god of music and medicine.

Important figures at the time brought this topic to the center of their discourse. In 1618, a young René Descartes (1596-1650) published the *Compendium musicae*, in which he explains the pleasure of music using mathematics, which he called the geometry of the senses. In this, he states that music brings pleasure and awakens emotions, giving the sensory organs a predominant role.[26] In 1649, in *Les Passions de l'âme*, he described the six passions in terms of their effects on the mind and their relationship with the movement and spirits of the blood.

In 1650, the German Jesuit, mathematician and philosopher Athanasius Kircher (1601-1680) wrote *Musurgia Universalis*, a piece of work which influenced such important composers as Handel and Bach.[27] In this, he explores the existence of different musical styles and states that the emotional and physiological characteristics of an individual determine their musical preferences in such a way that you can treat a person with different types of music to induce different emotional and physiological states. According to Kircher, the body and soul adopt the spirit of the music.[28]

Up until the 17th century, studies about the relationship between music and health were confined to the intellectual elites of society and although music was used as therapy for many illnesses, it was not known how it worked. The physiological effects of music on health remained a mystery[29] and moreover, music was a phenomenon that occurred in private spaces, to which only a select few had access, and only on special occasions.[30]

It was in the 18th century, accompanied by the Age of the Enlightenment, when texts about music and health became increasingly scientific and focused on understanding the physiological effects of music, including its changes on blood pressure, breathing and digestion.[31] As an example, we can look at the works of *Richard Browne, Medicina musica: or, A mechanical essay on the effects of singing, musick, and dancing, on human bodies* (1727).[32] and those of Richard Brocklesby, *Reflections on Antient [sic] and Modern Musick, with application to the cure of disease* (1749).[33]

Browne begins his book by saying:

"Singing is the enemy of melancholic thoughts, which we are constantly trying to suppress, and therefore singing is a pleasing promoter of mirth and joy. Singing brings serenity of mind, as well as being beneficial for digestion, due to the use of abdominal muscles and the diaphragm. Singing causes muscular elasticity and awakens the mind and body."

Later on, in the 19th century, the German physicist and physician, Hermann von Helmholtz kickstarted the field of acoustic physiology. Considered one of the precursors of experimental psychology, Helmholtz invented the Helmholtz resonator, a piece of apparatus to analyze the combination of tones made by complex natural sounds. His research about the emotional effects of harmonies on the psyche boosted the application of music in a clinical environment and opened the doors to numerous studies in the fields of perception and musicology.

Also in the 19th century, the first use of music therapy in an institutional environment took place on Roosevelt Island (previously named Blackwell Island) in New York, as well as the first systematic experiment of music therapy, in which music was used to alter sleep states during psychotherapy.[34]

In the field of surgery, Dr Evan O'Neill Kane was the first to use music in a surgical environment, and in 1914, he published a report about the use of the phonograph in the operating theatre.[35] The following year, Dr W.P. Burdick published a more detailed description of the experiment in the American Annual of Anaesthesia and Analgesia: "I discovered that patients that listened to music were better able to tolerate the anesthesia and they had a reduced level of anxiety before suffering the "horrors of surgery".[36]

Four decades later, the effect of auditory analgesia was shown while observing a reduced need for painkillers in patients who were undergoing painful dental procedures when exposed to both strong auditory stimulus as well as music in the background. Previous research suggested that being exposed to music reduces haemodynamic variability, postoperative pain, the amount of sedative or painkiller needed and the time of recovery post-operation.[37] It also lowers the levels of dehydroepiandrosterone, epinephrine, interleukin-6 and various other substances associated with stress, and it significantly increases the plasma concentration of the growth hormone, with its subsequent positive impact on immunity.

In the 20th and 21st centuries, new areas of study arose which combined music and medicine, gradually revealing the effects of music, the way in which we process it in the brain and its relationship with our health. We have slowly responded to the questions asked centuries ago and we understand the complex mechanisms that take place in perception of music, not just from a biological point of view but also a cultural one, because although we perceive music through our body, we cannot separate it from its cultural environment. Music is loaded with symbolic content, which reflects the social and cultural values of the context in which it was created.

Although music has an important social role and unquestionable healing powers in all cultures around the world, some people wrongly believe that the only music with therapeutic effects is Western classical music; we remember the famous *Mozart Effect*, which made millions of people believe that listening to the music of Mozart, and only this, made their children more intelligent. This could not be further from the truth. This was so widely believed because of Enlightenment rationalism, which placed Europe at the centre of history and seeped its way into the whole of academia and science, and caused only music coming from Western Europe to be considered legitimate, and therefore the majority of research about the effects of music on health were carried out using this particular type of music.

The truth of the matter is that listening to the music of Mozart positively impacts our health, but luckily it isn't the only music to have this effect. The effect that music has on us is linked to the culture in which we have grown up and the experiences and associations we have with it. The numerous and diverse pieces of music around the world have positive effects on health, on both a physical and emotional level.

Another wonderful aspect of music is that as well as being an individual experience to help us perceive, it is also a collective experience, a way for us to communicate, to fit into a group, to relate to one another. This is why all of us, regardless of the context in which we are born, can identify songs that have marked different periods of our life, that make up, so to speak, our soundtrack, the different moments of our existence. Music therefore has become a social marker and it is linked to emotions, memory and, above all, our identity.

Let's ask ourselves: Why do some songs make us cry, others reawaken our patriotic pride and others transport us to the past? Why do we want to sing some, but we skip others? Why do the same songs change their role and meaning over time, as if they have their own life and write their own story?

Tell me what you listen to and I will brand you with the relevant label. The music that we listen to identifies us and associates us with a set of values, with a class, a place, a generation, a mood, a desire or an aspiration. It speaks about our history, making it the foundation of memory.

It is incredible that a thing so abstract as music is such an integral part of human experience. Its ubiquity and intangibleness means we rarely stop to reflect about its importance, its key role in our lives, and how critical it is for our physical and emotional balance.

In the next few chapters, we will get to know the ways in which the brain processes music, its many therapeutic uses in the 21st century and the ways we can consciously incorporate it in our everyday life, in order to achieve a healthy and balanced life.

Chapter 2

MUSIC AND COGNITION

We have all experienced the excitement of listening to a song that reminds us of a special moment in our lives, a certain period, a love, a separation. We know intuitively that when we listen to music our brain is taking part in a much more complex process than just listening to and processing a sound.

Numerous cultural traditions around the world recognize that sound isn't just auditory perception. For example, the Tuvan people, throat singers from the south of Siberia,[38] paint landscapes through sound and vocal gestures, and the Yoreme community in Mexico paint sonic drawings to transform their spatial perception through specific musical progressions.[40]

From a neurological standpoint, many studies have shown evidence that sound affects the frontotemporal parietal regions of the brain, which causes a multimodal processing of sound.[41] This means that when we hear a sound, our brain activates a number of processes all at once, which connect various regions of the brain. These connections make it possible, for example, for Alzheimers' patients, who have lost the ability to recognise even their closest relatives, to recognise or perform complex melodies.[42] They also make it possible for a song to make us dance or for us to decipher complex poetic metaphors in the lyrics.

In fact, our perception of the world depends on our ability to establish multimodal cross-connections within our senses.[43]

To understand these processes, many researchers have studied synesthesia, a condition which allows some people to perceive sensory stimuli using two or more senses at once. Coming from the Greek words "syn", which means "with", and "aisthesis", which means sense, synesthesia occurs in approximately 1 out of every 200 people in the United States,[44] with these people possessing a neurobiological hyperconnectivity that allows them to involuntarily perceive simultaneous stimuli, e.g. see the colors of sounds or listen to tastes etc.[45]

A famous example of a synesthetic person throughout history is the Russian composer, Alexander Scriabin (1872-1915), who could see the colours of music and suggested the creation of an *Omni-art*, a synthesis of music, philosophy and religion with an aesthetic language that unified music, image, sound, drama, poetry and dance. With this, he aimed to bring the human mind towards a higher and more complex reality, towards ecstasy. His interest in the relationship between sound and colour led him to compose *Le poème de l'extase* and *Prométhée, Le poème du feu, op.60*, works which mixed both these elements. He was so convinced that the experience of colour would intensify the auditory experience that he declared that the audience would absorb his *Prométhée* more completely if they bathed in the colour which corresponded to the music.[46]

Although only a small percentage of the global population is synesthetic, in 1929, with his famous experiment *Kiki, Boulba*, Köhler showed that 90% of participants related the word *Kiki* to an angular shape and the word *Boulba* to a rounded shape.[47]

Perhaps you yourself relate sharp sounds to the cold or to sour tastes, or deep sounds to dark, warm and rounded colours. Everyone has different associations with music, colour, textures and tastes, which shows that a significant amount of the general population exhibits synesthetic tendencies and therefore, multimodal perception exists, although it is not present in such an extreme form, as it is in those with synesthesia. This hypothesis is used to study the different levels of connectivity in the brain upon hearing a sound and therefore it argues in favour of the relationship between music, movement and emotion.[48]

How do we hear?

Understanding how we hear is the first step in understanding the perception of sound. A sound is essentially the impression made in the ear by a mix of vibrations that are spread by an elastic medium, such as air or water. The sound is spread from one particle to the next. When the sound reaches the ear, for example a word or a song, it is initially captured by our auditory system in a basic or elemental form. The human ear can capture sounds between 20 Hz - 20 kHz. It is most sensitive between 2 kHz and 5 kHz. It has been noted that the upper limit decreases with age.

The auditory system is marvellous because it is capable of detecting even the most minute variations in pressure. The ear is divided into the outer, middle and inner ear. Soundwaves travel from the outer ear, through the ear canal, making the eardrum vibrate. In turn, this makes the three ossicles in the middle ear, known as the hammer, anvil and stirrup, move. These vibrations travel through the oval window to the fluid in the cochlea of the inner ear, stimulating thousands of little cilia cells. These vibrations turn into electric impulses which the brain perceives as sound. If any one of these components loses its ability to move, whether this be the result of an infection, a scar or a pathology, it will have a negative effect on the auditory capacity. Despite being a very sensitive organ, luckily the ear has mechanisms to protect itself against very intenses sound, or sounds with a very high frequency.

The perception of sound, however, is much more complex that the mere transmission of waves though an auditory apparatus - this is just the beginning of a complex process.

Upon listening to music, numerous regions in the brain are activated, in what we call multimodal perception, in other words, a multitude of processes, areas and networks are activated, which means we are not just limited to listening to the sound. The perception of sound is linked to emotion, memory, images. Studying the perception of sound and of music implies studying the mechanisms of cerebral cognition.

What is cognition and how is it studied?

Cognition is a human characteristic without which we could not survive. It has been defined in many ways, from the processes of general thinking and the intellectual capacity that includes memory, attention and learning, right until the acquisition of knowledge of surroundings and sensory systems. It also includes the processing and acquisition of languages.

Although there is an overlap of the regions of the brain which are involved in carrying out the different cognitive functions, there is also a certain specificity depending on which cognitive abilities we are referring to.

The part of the brain which is usually associated with complex cognitive processes such as episodic memory, reasoning and spatial abilities[49] is the prefrontal cortex.[50]

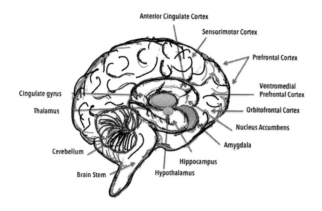

Meanwhile, the control of attention can be attributed to the convolution of the anterior cingulate cortex inside the frontal lobe,[51] although, as it is also necessary to carry out other cognitive functions in an effective manner, it is located in multiple regions of the brain.[52] Attention can be defined in many ways, as it implies a system of functions which includes the ability to focus on a task and at the same time, filter out the unnecessary stimuli for the task at hand. It simultaneously involves different regions of the brain,[53] as it links various cognitive and perceptive processes and motor actions.[54,55]

Memory can be linked to the prefrontal and temporal regions of the brain, in particular to the hippocampus.[56] These processes are carried out by the limbic system, which is also responsible for the processes of learning alongside the thalamus and the cerebellum, and memory, a structure associated with the learning of complex movements necessary for playing musical instruments.[57]

The cognitive processes which involve attention, memory and learning are only possible due to the stimuli acquired by the senses, through our system of perception, that includes touch, taste, sight and sound, in fact so much so that often cognition is defined as the learning that we develop thanks to information obtained from our surroundings through the senses.

Until relatively recently, studies about cognition were dominated by two paradigms, the cognitivist and the adaptationist. These models aim to explain how exactly the brain works, how mental operations are carried out, and what evolutionary mechanisms have contributed to the development of these cerebral abilities. These ways of understanding and studying the brain have influenced the way in which we study the perception and cognition of music.

We have to go back to the 1940s to find the beginnings of the cognitive science we now understand. In the boom of the cybernetic movement, researchers of the brain introduced the idea that mental processes resembled the functioning of computers.[58] The influence of this model on the study of cognition promoted a disembodied view of cognition and of musical experience. Under this paradigm, cognition of music was studied just as an analysis of symbols, concepts, representations, ignoring the role of emotions and corporal perception.

In contrast, the cognitivist conception of the mind promotes a view that the mind is organised into modules which gradually adapt to the extent that they evolve.[59] As a result, the complexity of human thinking is analysed in terms of evolution of modules of cognition that adapt through natural selection in order to aid the survival of the individual.[60]

Numerous authors have questioned the cognitivist-adaptionist model, believing that it does not take epigenetic or environmental factors into account, in other words, it partially ignores the influence of surroundings and by doing so, it creates a division between mind, body and environment. [61]

In recent times, a paradigm has been developed which understands cognition as a permanent process of exchange and conversation between the body and the surroundings, in which multimodal perception, sensory-motor activity, emotions and metabolic processes are in constant and continuous movement.[62,63]

Studying the perception and processing of music is of great interest to neuroscientists as it requires the simultaneous activation of multiple parts of the brain. For example, when we learn to play a musical instrument, we are simultaneously carrying out multiple motor and sensory actions, which are very demanding at a cognitive level.[64,65]

Let's imagine a piano or guitar student, who presses the keys or the strings and at the same time is reading the score. In this action which seems so simple, the brain perceives through seeing the notes on the score and translates them into movements. The brain simultaneously captures the sounds produced and corrects the movements.

The act of playing an instrument requires extremely specific functions that are spread around numerous regions of the brain. The more complex the music, the more attention it requires. The musical experience also includes even more elements like rhythm, tempo and tuning. However, when we talk about cognition of music, we're not only referring to processes which happen when you perform an instrument, as even listening to music, without playing it, also stimulates various zones of the brain and requires complex processes. Our relationship with music could be both active and passive.

Without a doubt, the musical experience is much more than the mere acquisition and processing of auditory stimuli. We perceive music and we give it meaning according to the social, cultural and historical context in which we live. The meaning of music for us depends on our context, but at the same time, music gives meaning to this context. In other words, music should not be thought of as something external, separate from us. To exist, it has to be an integral part of our psychological, historical and social environment. This inspired Small to argue that music should not be used as a noun, but rather as a verb, and he proposed the term musicking.

> "Musicking is participating, in whatever capacity, in a musical performance, whether you are performing, listening. learning or practising, providing material for the performance (what we call composing) or dancing. Sometimes, we can even extend its meaning to include the person who checks tickets at the door

or the people who move pianos and drum kits, or those who set up instruments or do soundchecks or clean up after everyone has left. All of these people are also contributing to the nature of this event which is a musical performance".[66]

Looking at it this way, music does not rely on objects external to us, music is not defined as the instruments or objects that make it, it is not defined as the people that play it. In reality, music is an action, something that we do, something we participate in, whether that be through listening, performing, dancing, practicing, etc.[67] *Musicking* is an action which is carried out, lived, experienced by the body - a body which is in a permanent relationship and conversation with its surroundings.

This view of music takes us away from the cognitivist model which reduces music to a concept, symbol or mental process and brings us closer to a model that needs the body; music is lived through the body, it is embodied. By doing so, it is placed into the social, historical and cultural environment. In other words, when we *musick*, we do it from a social, historical place, from a gender, an age, a culture, a level of education. We can only musick from a body in constant conversation with its surroundings, in constant change and biological adaptation. The body becomes a space for cultural expression, shaped by our environment and culture.

Perhaps it would surprise you to know that in many cultures, the concept of music doesn't exist, at least not in the way we know it to be in the West, a purely sonorous experience. In many places, what we call music is an integral and inseparable part of cultural practices that include dance, performing arts and even paintings. For example, the Patua people in East Bengal in India, a nomad caste of painters of scrolls, sing through the scenes that they paint, that is to say, painting and music are inseparable. In many other cultures, music and dance are the same thing, which makes sense as they both involve movement. When the movement of the body produces sound, it produces music and when this movement is expressed purely as a form, it is dance.

If you think about it, when we are making music, we are always moving, not just to produce sound, for example when we move our fingers to play an instrument, but rather we also carry the rhythm in our bodies, we dance. Can you imagine a salsa, bossanova, opera or rock singer performing without moving? Or a jazz performer playing their instrument stood frozen like a statue? It is impossible to imagine this because music implicitly implies movement.

It is then easy to understand that the perception of music is much more complex than the processing of a sound in a concrete area of the brain; far from it, the sound is the initial stimulus that births a number of processes in multiple areas of the brain. Upon receiving the musical stimulus, many types of connections begin, which impact spheres such as emotion, motor functions, memory, affection and an endless number of metabolic reactions that take place in the body.

The study of music confirms that there is no such thing as division of body and mind, nor does thinking exist as an abstract thing, a mere processing of symbols at a neuronal level. Cognition begins in the body, a body which cannot be separated from the environment which provides it stimuli.

According to this view, cognitive processes are not limited only to the brain, but rather pass through the body without limiting it. Everything in my surrounding environment which I touch, see, listen to, the objects and devices I use all form part of my cognition, a cognition extended and embedded in the environment.

This ecological view of cognition is what we call 4E cognition. It is called *4E* because it refers to the four concepts which begin with the letter E: *Embodied, Extended,*[69] *Enacted* and *Embedded.*[70]

The evolution of the study of cognition of music, which in a relatively short time has transformed from the cognitivist-adaptavist model to a multimodal 4E cross-model, reflects the trend of Western society in the 21st century to question the compartmentalization of knowledge, to accept the need of transdisciplinarity and to recognise that we are inseparable from the environment that surrounds us.

Now that we understand how we perceive and process sounds, we will discover how the marvelous brains of musicians work.

Chapter 3

THE MARVELOUS BRAIN OF MUSICIANS

The brain is a marvelous and often mysterious organ. We still have a lot to discover about how it works, about the thousands of processes that are constantly happening even during the most simple of tasks.

In complex activities, like playing an instrument or singing, our brain activates multiple zones and functions at the same time. It simultaneously activates cortical mechanisms related to the execution of highly specific cognitive and motor functions and multiple sensory systems. To put it simply, playing music is actually the brain carrying out a high-performance task.

In fact, many studies which compare the cognitive skills of musicians with those of non-musicians of the same age show that the former performs functions significantly better and responds more quickly in all cognitive skills tests, showing that musical training is a protective factor against neuro-cognitive aging. While playing an instrument, we are exercising our perception, attention, memory and learning processes.[71]

Knowing these benefits should inspire us to include music in our daily activities, especially if we think about how we live in a society where life expectancy is increasing day by day, meaning it is likely we will live for quite a long time, hopefully with full access to our cognitive skills. This awareness is very important if we consider that one in every nine people over the age of 65 and one in three over the age of 85 have cognitive limitations.[72] These figures tend to multiply when we take into account that between 2019 and 2100, the percentage of people over 80 years in the European Union is expected to multiply by 2.5%, a jump from 5.8% to 14.6%. In the US, it is predicted that by 2060, the population of elders is expected to increase by 105.2%.

How do we get to such an age while still maintaining our cognitive skills? What can we do so that the natural decline in our cognitive abilities is slow and we reach old age while still in possession of our mental faculties?

There are many factors which determine cognitive aging, including level of education, physical activity and diet.[73] In other words, once again we can see that our daily habits are the most important factor to maintain our mental and physical health. For example, a lot of evidence has shown that habits, such as reading or playing an instrument reduce the risk of developing dementia.[74] What these protective activities have in common is that all of them present a cognitive challenge - they are activities which require the simultaneous coordination of various functions.

What could be a bigger challenge than playing an instrument and singing at the same time? Or learning different pieces which require the development of increasingly complex technical skills? When we play an instrument a number of sensory systems (sound, sight, touch) need to be coordinated with our motor activity,[75] and this coordination also requires us to keep constantly changing the focus of attention. The development of these skills is the reason why professional musicians get higher marks in all cognitive tests compared to non-musicians.[76] It has also been shown that musicians in professional orchestras, who require a higher level of cognitive complexity in their activities, develop dementia less frequently than the general population.[77] Without a doubt, musical practice is a protective factor for the brain.

But are there differences between the brain of a musician and that of a non-musician?

There is a lot of evidence that musical experience shapes the brain structurally[78]and physiologically.[79] From a structural viewpoint, in other words, the makeup of the brain and its different regions, we know that the anterior part of the corpus callosum of musicians is larger than that of non-musicians. This is also the case with the central sulcus in both hemispheres of the brain, which is deeper for musicians, and with the parts of the brain associated with the primary auditory cortex, Broca's area and the inferior frontal gyrus.[80] The cerebellum of musicians is also larger. Some studies have shown that people who play instruments have more grey material in the primary and somatosensory motor, premotor, frontal parietal and inferior frontal gyrus areas.[81]

However, the most remarkable differences between the brain of musicians and non-musicians are not structural, rather those related to perception and processing of sounds and their different features. Musicians process multisensory musical stimuli more quickly[82] and develop greater skills like auditory memory, attention and the ability to distinguish keys.[83]

Comparing the results of musicians and non-musicians in variations of rhythm and key shows that the former are quicker than the latter, which isn't surprising due to musical training. What is surprising, however, is that non-musicians detect differences more easily with the left ear, while musicians don't show any preference, which is also called lateralization.

This difference could boil down to the fact that musical training stimulates inter-hemispheric communication[84] which results in a level of cortical reorganisation more pronounced in those who begin to study music at a young age, as the brain is more malleable in the first few years of development.[85] This means that for musicians, the two hemispheres of the brain share functions and communicate with each other more fluidly.

Just a few years of musical training during infancy (a minimum of two years according to some studies) can have an impact on the neuronal codification in adulthood, even years after not studying.[86] These positive effects can extend to the sphere of memory, attention and cognitive skills in general. The good news is that even if we haven't received musical training during our childhood, simply growing up in an environment full of auditory stimuli leads to cerebral plasticity.[87] Even better news is knowing that this cerebral plasticity will remain throughout our whole life, in other words, at whatever age, we can reap in the benefits of music.

Musical practice doesn't just strengthen useful skills for the performance of music, like for example being able to identify the sound of an instrument in an ensemble, but rather it also leads to a more precise and efficient processing of sound, important for other types of communication.[88] This ability to extract meaning from complex sonic landscapes is an important factor in the transferring of skills to non-musical domains, such as the learning of languages. For example, musicians are more able to pick up languages or identify errors in second languages.[89]

Whether it be distinguishing a sound, or recognizing a voice in a noisy place, the brain of a musician is able to discern an auditory signal and extract it from a complex sonic landscape more easily than the brain of a non-musician.

Although I have not explicitly mentioned it, what we are talking about when highlighting the plasticity of the brain is our habits and the impact that they have on our health or sickness. When we consider that only two years of musical training during childhood can heighten cognitive abilities, we are recognising the importance of maintaining habits that stimulate our brain, and our body in all its aspects, in other words, placing myself in an environment rich in cognitive stimuli, whether they are sonic, visual, interpersonal, etc, is imperative for my cognitive health. Throughout life, we continuously redesign our neural routes. By being exposed to sonic stimuli, our auditory system dynamically modulates the processing of signals which have been accumulated through time, developing a sensory experience. In other words, all my auditory experiences fuse together so that my brain learns cognitive and sensory processes through experience, and my responses to stimuli slowly form. Sounds which we have picked up on in the past help shape our automatic response to new sounds in the present.

Through this experience, we learn to select the auditory stimuli most relevant to us. With time, this accumulated experience births a *"neuronal signature"* of experience, which is different for each person[90] This neuronal signature causes, for example, a musician's brain to respond and adjust to the specific timbre of the instrument they play. In other words, the brain responds better to this familiar timbre than to the sound of another instrument. The wider the stimuli we receive, the wider too becomes our spectrum of pleasure, in other words, we learn to enjoy new sounds.

The existence of this "neuronal signature" explains why, for example, the style of musical performance also affects the processing of sound. This can be clearly seen in jazz musicians who show a greater sensitivity to subtle acoustic variations in their cerebral responses if you compare them with musicians from other genres, as they are used to improvisation and are hyper aware of changes in the music to which they have to adapt in a matter of seconds.[91]

During a musical performance, there are also multiple physiological changes, such as hormones and neurotransmitters being released, which are chemical substances that send, receive, amplify or modulate messages in the brain and in the whole body.[92] This chemical *cocktail* is responsible, among other things, for the phenomenon commonly known as "performance adrenaline", the anxiety we feel before going on stage that sometimes becomes the dreaded stage fright.

You don't have to be a musician to have experienced this anxiety, for example think of when you might have had to do a presentation in public or go out on stage. This anxiety we feel just before going on stage, that mix of desire to finally get out on stage and share the work we have dedicated so much time to, the fear of thinking that it won't turn out as we hope and the apprehension of how the public will react sometimes paralyses us. Your heart starts beating fast, your breathing gets shaky, your hands become sweaty and cold, your senses are heightened and you become more sensitive.

For some people, this anxiety paralyzes them, turning into that infamous stage fright, while others overcome it and rush out on stage to perform their music.

All of these feelings are due to the release of many substances including endorphins, neurotransmitters known as natural opiates, as they produce a similar effect to morphine. These endorphins reduce breathing rate and produce a vasodilating effect which lowers blood pressure, and are produced normally in situations of stress, helping to control pain, body temperature, sexual activity, memory, hunger and thirst. Its most notable effects are the slowing of breathing rate and decrease in blood pressure, due to its vasodilating effect.[93]

During a singer's performance, for example, they are essential to regulate breathing, the foundation for the production of sound.

During a performance, there is also a release of serotonin, a neurotransmitter which has a large effect on behavior, mood, memory and attention.[94] For the performer, it is especially important as it helps to recognize the emotional states in the facial expressions of those who are surrounding them, and it improves attention and memory, and leads to the best possible performance.[95]

Another part of this neurotransmitter *cocktail*, which heightens our senses during musical performance is dopamine, which is involved in both thinking as well as regulation of motor functions and mood. Dopamine is released in situations of environmental change, and it helps us adapt and it prepares us physically and emotionally for what is to come. Dopamine is linked to the prediction of rewarding events, which is speculated to be the origin of aesthetic criticism.[96]

However, the neurotransmitter which is more often linked to musical performance is adrenaline, a substance which incidentally acts like a hormone and like a neurotransmitter on multiple levels. Adrenaline is released in stressful "fight or flight" situations. Primordial mechanisms are activated, the same mechanisms which were activated in the first hominids in their fight for survival against the elements, and these mechanisms directly tie us to our remote ancestors. In these situations, the body increases its heart rate and undergoes vasoconstriction in order to send blood to the skeletal muscles to prepare us to defend ourselves from danger. Our energy and strength are increased and our breathing rate, blood pressure and blood sugar level elevates. Adrenaline prepares us for battle, but its effects can be devastating during a musical performance, especially during a singing performance, where we need a regulated breathing rate, and so to speak, we need to take it down an octave to be in complete awareness and control.

An important part of musical training, especially for singers, whose instrument is our own body, is learning to observe ourselves and be aware of our body in order to balance the chemical storm inside us during a public performance. This is why singers study relaxation, breathing and body awareness techniques, so that we can be fully conscious and in control during our performance. The goal of these exercises is to reach our full potential, to give 110% when we're out on stage.

Although musicians, like elite athletes, use these exercises to achieve their peak performance, learning these techniques has a positive impact on their general health. Musical practice and performance present a number of unique challenges for the nervous system that cause the brain of musicians to be different to that of non-musicians, and cause them to develop cognitive skills which protect them from the degeneration associated with aging.

These findings should be enough to encourage us to play an instrument or sing, not just for the positive changes to the brain but also because it has been proved that musical practice makes us happier, and improves our quality of life.

Music helps us socialize, connect to one another, express ourselves, share with the world who we are or what we want to be. When we sing, play an instrument, attend a concert or dance, we express ourselves in the most authentic way, we introduce ourselves to others as who we truly are, with no filter. We free our bodies and vibrate together with others and with the universe, expressing the purest essence of who we are and by doing this, we merge with a group, forming part of something bigger, a community.

Chapter 4

PLEASURE, EMOTION AND MUSIC

I remember when I was ten years old, when I started to sing, often people who listened to me would tell me that they got goosebumps, and at the time I didn't understand exactly what they meant by that, although I felt as though it was something positive since they said it like praise. With time, I myself began to feel different sensations while listening to music which I liked a lot; the pit in my stomach, the knot in my throat, goosebumps and even the desire to cry.

Later on, I learnt that more than 50% of the population experience these types of physiological and emotional reactions while they listen to music or live through similar intense aesthetic experiences. Music has the power to alter our physical and emotional state, which is perhaps why music is all around us these days, it accompanies us in all the circumstances and moments of our life. In fact, many studies have shown that one of the most important reasons to listen to music throughout the day is to experience and regulate emotional states.[97] Some of these experiences can be so intense that they can trigger long-term effects on the person's wellbeing.[98]

The emotions caused by music are intimately linked to memory, they trigger our past experiences and they make it easier to access autobiographical memory. This explains why we link certain songs to certain moments in our lives that are important or packed full of emotions. Loss, pain, love, heartbreak are all associated with songs, which become the soundtrack of a certain period of our lives, referential moments in our existence, like sound chapters of our autobiographies.

The ability to identify emotions in music appears at an early age during development. As early as some time between the second and fourth month of life, we are able to relate pleasant feelings with consonant sounds and unpleasant feelings with dissonant sounds.[99] Around the third and fourth year, we gain the ability to identify happy music and around the sixth, we recognise a wide range of emotions in music, including sadness, fear and anger.[100]

Initially, we form connections with basic musical emotions, such as associating fast-paced music with joy and slow-paced music with sadness. As time goes on, we gradually refine our ability, being able to link different emotional states with more complex characteristics of music; for example, we associate sadness with music in a minor key and happiness with music in a major key.

This raises a number of questions: what do we mean when we talk about emotion? What goes on inside our body when we listen to music? How are music, pleasure and emotion connected?

Defining emotions is complicated. From the dawn of time, man has tried to explain them from different viewpoints, such as philosophy, psychology, and more recently neuroscience. According to the first philosophers, emotions were a category of feelings, separate from other proprioceptive or sensory sensations. From the 19th century, with the rise of experimental psychology, a number of theories emerged making it difficult to reach a consensus about what an emotion is made up of.[101]

Some emotions seem automatic, consistent and universal[102], and others seem to be determined by the sociocultural context in which they are triggered.[103] To make things even more difficult, many scientists discuss whether emotional experiences are a result of autonomous physiological changes[104] or whether they are triggered by environmental changes,[105] - it seems like the age old question of whether the chicken or the egg came first. The distinction between basic and complex emotions[106] gets lost in these discussions, making it even more elusive to define.

One of the most widespread theories, initially hypothesised by Darwin,[106] proposes that there are basic, uncompromising emotions, which come as a result of evolution[108] and respond to adaptative, universal, biologically determined processes.[109] A prime example of this is fear, a behavioural motivator in response to a threat, that seems to have a common psycho-physiological response[110] and seemingly is processed mainly in a part of the brain called the amygdala.[111] However, the amygdala is related to many other processes, including the recognition of emotions in the music,[112] which confirms that there aren't localized regions of the brain for specific emotions.

One of the main criticisms of this theory is that there is no consensus about what the basic emotions[113] are and how many of them exist. Some researchers have stated that the only basic emotions are pleasure and fear, however the most widely accepted definition includes basic emotions such as joy, wrath, fear, sadness, disgust, embarrassment, surprise, scorn, interest, blame, acceptance and anticipation.[114]

In contrast, the theory of assessing emotions focuses on how we judge, evaluate and understand stimuli, in other words, more than the stimuli itself which triggers the emotion,[115] it is important how we assess it, and this depends on cultural and environmental factors. This explains how a single stimulus can cause different emotional reactions in different people.[116]

Finally we come to the constructionist approach to emotion, which focuses on the effects of stimuli on the cultural, social and biological surroundings. In other words, according to this paradigm, emotional response and it's varying intensity are the result of the interaction between the stimulus, the culture, the society and somatic markers, similar to the 4E model of cognition mentioned earlier. In this context, emotions and social interactions make up an unbreakable system, in other words, emotions are expressed socially and historically and are recognised, simulated and controlled in different ways, in accordance with the social, historical, class and gender context.

Therefore, when we try to understand the emotional effects of music, we must keep in mind its cognitive, social, therapeutic and aesthetic effects on the listener.

In 1871, Darwin stated: "Music awakens various emotions within us, but not the most awful ones like horror, fear, anger etc. It awakens the gentler emotions, like tenderness and love, that quickly turn into devotion."[117] These statements of Darwin have recently been confirmed by researchers that found that although music is able to produce a wide range of emotions, it usually stimulates positive emotional states, like happiness-euphoria and nostalgia-longing.[118] Emotions like wrath, irritation, boredom-indifference or anxiety-fear are found more often in daily emotions rather than when we listen to music. Zentner, Grandjean and Scherer also showed that music usually triggers positive reactions like relaxation and joy than negative ones like aggression, anxiety, depression and wrath.[119]

Darwin also stated that emotions generated by music fulfil an evolutionary role, that, along with songs, dances or rites of a community, foster social ties, leading to survival. An example of this are the sounds that a baby and its carer exchange. The musical properties of this first communication have been shown to be essential for the survival of the infant.

Recent authors have suggested that there are two types of emotions, the utilitarian ones, linked to the interest and wellbeing of an individual, and musical aesthetics. According to researchers, the terms used by subjects to describe emotions that they feel while listening to music correspond with the nine musical aesthetic emotions: amazement, transcendence, tenderness, nostalgia, peace, power, joy, tension and sadness.[120]

A controversial point that arises from this analysis is whether music evokes emotions in listeners or whether they just recognize the emotion expressed by the musical piece. In the first instance, musical stimulus triggers a series of psychological, physiological or motor reactions, like for example, the feeling of calmness, relaxation or happiness, or the tendency of our bodies to follow the rhythm. A different situation from this would be when we recognize that a piece is sad or happy, but this doesn't trigger emotional responses, in other words, my relationship with the music is purely cognitive. I recognize that the music is happy but I don't feel happy or I listen to sad music but feel happy, that is to say, the perceived emotions do not coincide with the emotions felt.

In general, scientific literature suggests that the amygdala and numerous regions of the temporal lobe are the areas involved in the perception of emotion in music. The ability to perceive music and the ability to perceive emotions in music have been clinically differentiated, having observed that patients with damage to their temporal lobes are impeded from recognizing emotions in music despite being perfectly able to perceive it.[121]

We also know that environmental and social factors determine our emotional response to music; it is not the same to listen to a sad song after a breakup or at a funeral of a loved one than listening to it as background music while I do other things or as Muzak in a lift.

Certain songs which are played in battlefields, in political or religious demonstrations, or in football stadiums have the effect of energizing, uniting and exciting a group of people who share ideals and ideologies. This proves that emotions triggered by music are also linked to non-musical factors. The same song can trigger different physiological and emotional responses in different contexts.[122]

A way to evaluate the emotional response to music is through analyzing psycho-physiological responses to it. The most common responses include changes in blood pressure, pulse, skin conductance and changes in muscle tension. It has also been shown that upon listening to clips of musical pieces which express sadness, fear, anxiety, the level of physiological excitement of the body changes. Sad music alters, above all, heart rate, blood pressure, skin conductance and body temperature of listeners. Music which expresses fear causes, above all, changes the beats per minute of the pulse. Finally, happy music causes changes in breathing.

Within these observed changes, we can also find the so-called "goosebumps" or "the chills", which I mentioned at the start. This feeling, described as pleasurable, consists of a type of electricity that begins in the neck and is felt the whole way down the spine, is usually associated with making your hair stand on end.

Defining pleasure is also complicated. We surely all agree that pleasure is subjective, relative, and that what is pleasurable for you is revolting for others. Human beings are as simple or as complex as our pleasures.

Several authors differentiate between the so-called fundamental pleasures, the necessary ones for survival of the species, like sex, food, belonging to a group and those of "high priority", more conscious pleasures, such as financial earnings, social acceptance, religious beliefs, musical and aesthetic pleasure. Although these pleasures are not necessary for survival, they activate the same parts of the brain as fundamental pleasures.[123]

Despite the brain having many networks and circuits related to the reward system, it seems as though pleasure mechanisms are much more specific, and in other words, rarer. Some of these structures that play a role in pleasure are tethered to the back of the brain, for example in the striatum or in the brain stem and some are found in the cerebral cortex,

It also seems that there are very small regions in the subcortex structures, called "*hedonic hotspots*" by researchers, which are separated but also connected like an archipelago and are involved in pleasure responses.[124]

Barridge and Kringelbach described the cycle of pleasure, which starts with an initial desire, an anticipation that, at a cerebral level, triggers the release of dopamine. When we obtain and enjoy the object of desire, for example experiencing an orgasm or winning a bet, other neurotransmitters called opiates are activated. After having escaped the initial tension, we enter into a phase of learning and relaxation. These phases of pleasure combine conscious and unconscious elements, in other words, we can consciously identify some of these states, but there are factors which do not enter our consciousness and operate at a much deeper level.

The same pleasure cycle also happens with the musical experience. Neuroimage studies of subjects that experience goosebumps when listening to music show activation of the bilateral amygdala, the left hippocampus, the ventromedial prefrontal cortex, and various other regions related to pleasure and euphoria.[125] Also the ventral striatum is activated, a region associated with the processing of gratification, hedonistic impact, learning and motivation.[126]

Neuroimaging scans such as PET and fMRI show evidence that listening to music which we like activates the same regions of the brain as those activated when we experience euphoria, when we receive erotic stimuli or when we eat chocolate. For this reason, many refer to the sensation of "goosebumps" caused by music as a musical orgasm.

Like always, there are people who experience musical pleasure more intensely. These differences are determined by a number of factors, including personality type and also genetic factors. This is what happens to those with congenital musical anhedonia[127] who don't experience any pleasure while listening to music. This condition affects 5.5% of the population,[128] though it can also be a result of neurological damage.

There is no doubt that music connects with emotion and produces pleasure, just think of how many times you have listened to a song, or performed in a concert, and felt a rush of emotions, or when you have felt energized at a fast-paced rhythm. As performers, we know that through music, we can express certain emotions that can't be communicated through words. The minute we begin our performance, it's as though time stops. When a musician has moved past the stage of technical learning, they experience transcendent moments in which they connect intimately with music, they become one with sound. In these moments, they reach an almost mystical state of absolute connection with the present, they truly live in the now and they freely express the musical message.

For singers, this moment represents the meeting point between music and poetry. Music and poetry merge with singing in a profoundly cathartic and transcendent way that links the modern-day singer with the ancestral figure of the shaman, the man/woman/medicine responsible for curing the community, for representing it, for floating between the real world and the world of ideas, of dreams.

During shamanic possession, the shaman, similar to the modern musician, experiences all the beings, all the lives and becomes one with the universe. As a singer, when I sing, I live a thousand lives, I experience every emotion, situation and event that although is not part of my reality, is close to me, as they are human experiences.

I always say that thanks to singing, I have been able to live as a man and a woman, a king and a beggar, an old person and a young person. I have been in love, abandoned, hopeful, alone, hurt and all-powerful.

While performing in full awareness of the poetry of the songs, I can express emotions which can only be accessed through the union of music and poetry. These moments of complete connection with the music, of mindfulness, that give us performers pleasure and happiness coincide with the moments that Csikszentmihalyi describes as *flow*. In these moments, every thought, intention, emotion and feeling is focused on the same goal.

When the flow experience takes place, we feel more connected, we reach a higher level of complexity, a complexity which is the result of two supposedly opposing movements: the differentiation which causes us to be authentic, unique, to separate ourselves from others, and the integration that brings us closer to others, that unites us, that joins us. The dialectic between these two supposedly contradictory forces produces a more complex and rich individual.

Whether it be performing or listening, music is a source of aesthetic pleasure. The great Russian composer, Igor Stravinsky described it like this:

> There is no better way to define the sensation produced by music than saying that it is the same feeling as the contemplation of the interaction of architectural forms. Goethe understood it perfectly when he called architecture petrified music.

Chapter 5

MUSIC, HAPPINESS AND THE MEANING OF LIFE

From the dawn of time the search for happiness has been one of the deepest desires of humanity. A number of philosophies have equated a good life with a happy life. Many disciplines study this phenomenon, including psychology, philosophy, sociology and economics. It seems like everyone wants to be happy.

For some people, happiness seems to be a question of resources, of GDP. However, many studies have concluded that some of the most happy societies are not necessarily the richest. This idea challenges the values of the capitalist society where, in the last few decades, happiness has become a million dollar industry which leeches off our need to buy happiness.

Every year, millions of self-help courses and books which suggest recipes and methods to achieve it are sold.

Mihaly Csikszentmihalyi, renowned researcher of happiness defined it as the ability to reach a state of flow:

> A state in which people are so involved in an activity that nothing else seems to matter; the experience is so enjoyable that people will continue to do it even at great cost, for the sheer sake of doing it.[129]

In his studies, he notes that all flow experiences share seven characteristics: they bring those who experience them a sense of competence in the activity, they combine action and concentration, they have clear objectives, they require complete and focused attention on the activity, they provide a sense of being in control, even if the situation itself isn't fully under control, they imply a loss of self-consciousness and of interpersonal connection and while experiencing them, all sense of time is lost.

There are two conditions which are always present in flow experiences. Firstly, participants feel that the activities seem like a challenge to their abilities and it provides them the opportunity to improve, to further develop their skills, and then, they should be able to evaluate their accomplishments so that they can define clear goals for the future. In these flow experiences, people develop their skills and continuously face more complex challenges, which keeps them motivated. Therefore these activities last for a long time, increasing the feeling of wellness.

Being a subjective state associated with the level of satisfaction that we have in different aspects of life, happiness is often confused with wellness, a concept which combines both the subjective aspects of happiness with objective aspects related to the quality of life. Wellness, a concept coined in the first decades of the 20th century, is defined as the optimum state of an individual, community or society as a whole. It is expressed in different ways in different cultural contexts, in fact, each society creates their own idea of wellness.

Bill Hettler, director of the National Wellness Institute in the United States[130] defined it as an active process through which people become conscious and choose options which bring them towards a fulfilled existence.[131] Hettler defined the six main dimensions of wellness, namely physical, social, emotional, intellectual, spiritual and occupational wellness.[132] Wellness is about achieving the balance of these six dimensions.

This holistic vision of the human being and his environment closely resembles a concept in medicine called homeostasis. At a biological level, homeostasis represents the optimum state in which organisms maintain a constant equilibrium and the physiological conditions to maintain life.

Personal homeostasis is therefore achieving this bio-psycho-social balance, which involves physical and psychological health and the ability to integrate and form an active part of a community. Illness occurs when there is a lack of balance in one of these dimensions. It makes sense that we link the concept of wellness to health, as wellness is a necessary condition to achieve health.

So what role does music play in happiness, wellness and consequently, in health? Recent studies carried out on professional musicians to evaluate their level of wellness at a mature and old age have shown that music is a key factor for maintaining their health and physical, cognitive and social skills during old age.[133]

Musical practice apart from providing intellectual and cognitive stimulation, also provides the feeling of belonging to a group and it facilitates the adaptation to changes associated with aging. Studies have shown that musicians stay healthy until very old, much older than the non-musical population, because playing an instrument requires them to maintain a healthy lifestyle, including their diet, posture, breathing, and it keeps them connected to their environment.

There is also a direct relationship between musical practice and happiness, as musicians constantly challenge themselves to learn new repertoires which leads them to this aforementioned flow. The feeling of happiness stems from the process of learning, achieving your goals, developing a sense of self-fulfillment, and feeling like you are achieving your potential. These findings are especially relevant in a society in which life expectancy has increased enormously in the last few years and hopefully will increase even further in years to come.

From a brain health point of view, many studies link listening and performing music to the increase of neurotransmitters which lead to relaxation, stimulate emotions such as enthusiasm, strengthen the immune system and facilitate social integration. The main neurotransmitters associated with these changes are dopamine, cortisol, serotonin and oxytocin.[134]

Although it was initially believed that oxytocin was only released during physical contact, such as the trust that develops between parents and children due to close contact, it has now been shown that group activities related to music, like singing in a choir, cause an increase in its levels, which explains how singing in a group can strengthen bonds of trust and cooperation between performers.[135]

Nuclear Magnetic Resonance (NMR) has also shown that upon receiving a musical stimulus, the cerebral arteries are oxygenated, triggering the release of neurotransmitters in many parts of the brain. Music is a catalyst in brain activity that promotes wellness, happiness and therefore a better quality of life.

One of the aspects that determine wellness is feeling like we have a purpose in life, an end goal, something that gives meaning and makes it worthwhile to be alive. This purpose or reason to live in Japanese is known as *Ikigai*, a concept that overlaps in many aspects with Csikszentmihalyi's definition of happiness, which relates the ability to experience states of flow with self-fulfillment and the feeling of being able to develop our skills to their maximum potential.

Music is marvelous because through it we can reach this state of flow in a collective or individual way. Our participation in this phenomenon of music gives rise to many ideas and actions, we respond to sensory impulses, we interpret and convey emotions.

Body, emotions and music fuse together, sound is embodied in the individual. While merging with sound, we become one with it and upon doing so, we experience one of the characteristics of flow; the merging of action and awareness.[136] This convergence of knowing and doing is especially meaningful in music, making it one of the activities that most easily produces this greatly desired state of happiness.

This statement itself should encourage *musicking*; it should encourage us to listen to more music throughout our lives, to study music from childhood, and to include it as an essential part of education.

Music acts as a tool for social integration, as a shared language that helps us to overcome our differences, to find similarities in our diversity, to build a consensus.

When we *musick*, we pour in every last drop of who we are, and our past, present and future, our memory, our perception of the now and our desire to share, to build all fuse together; everything merges when we musick.

To *musick* means to share an aesthetic experience in which I express my uniqueness and I give it generously to others. I hand it over so that they can experience it in their own way, so they can decode it and feel its presence in their body and their culture, in the values that define them, in their being. When I make music, I hand myself over, and by doing so, I leave a space for another to enter, for exchange, for growth, for transformation, for compassion.

This way of making music, of sharing the phenomenon of sound, is sadly far from the teachings of conservatories and institutions of professional musical education, where often intuition and playing by ear have been wiped out and the real use of music has been forgotten, in favour of a exceedingly rationalistic and technical learning.

Obviously a musician must learn technical skills which are developed through practice and through learning certain methodologies, but it is just as important to learn about the development of intuition, how to share music and incorporate it into all aspects of life, and also giving the same value to all musical traditions around the world.

In order to achieve a more healthy and happy, a more fair and compassionate society, music should be the base of the emotional, aesthetic and intellectual education for all the children of the world, as sagely demonstrated by the existence of the *Five Music Rights*, promulgated by the International Music Council.[137]

Chapter 6

RHYTHM, MOVEMENT AND HEALTH

"Everything flows, out and in; everything has its tides; all things rise and fall; the pendulum-swing manifests in everything; the measure of the swing to the right is the measure of the swing to the left; rhythm compensates."

The Kybalion[138]

The universe is constantly expanding and moving in response to a rhythm and to a periodicity. Right from the smallest of subatomic particles to the biggest of stars, the universe is vibrating in a rhythmic movement. In the same way, our body is in constant movement, cells don't stop performing their biochemical processes, they regenerate. Every new interaction with the environment causes changes within our brain and body. We are constantly changing right from birth to death.

Emilie Conrad Da'Oud stated that what we call a body is not material, but rather movement.[139] The body is a rhythmic orchestration of many forms of movement and sound, in which many different rhythms overlap; the rhythm of the heart, of breathing, of the digestive tract, the actions and reactions of the nervous system and even the cells and the auditory cortex that have their own inherent rhythm, independent of external stimuli.[140, 141]

When we are healthy, the rhythms of the body flow naturally. Physical or emotional illness are brought about by a change in the rhythm, they occur when we are off rhythm. Just like in a game of mirrors, we constantly reflect our internal, emotional, corporal movements in our social interactions and the environment around us. In the same way, the rhythms of our surrounding environment have a positive or negative impact on the rhythms of the body.

In Ancient Greece, philosophers like Plato proposed a difference between the knowledge gained through the body and that gained through reason, the latter which he linked to the soul, and which he placed more value to.

Following this Platonic tradition, Christianity condemned the knowledge gained through the body, associating it with sin and sexuality, placing the body on the opposite end of the spectrum to the desired virtues. Centuries later, Carthesian philosophers, with their famous *"I think, therefore I am"* further legitimised this way of thinking, giving rise to the philosophical dualism that influenced all the sciences and paradigms of thought, assigning greater value to the mind and to the rational than to the experiences acquired by the senses. This paradigm of thought, that remains even to this day a big part of academics, is completely the opposite of current neuroscientific evidence; just like we learnt in the chapter about music and cognition, the body is also a cognitive apparatus, through which we perceive the world and shape thought. There is no separation between body and mind, they are dependent on each other. Intelligence is first an intelligence of the body, an intelligence which develops by doing.

This means the experience we gain through our bodily interactions shapes our brains, creating new neural connections, a continuous process which happens throughout life thanks to our brain plasticity. Body, mind and environment make up an inseparable trinity. Health and illness are the result of the interaction between these three inseparable elements, we are bio-psycho-social beings.

Despite the evidence, and probably due to the fact that we've been living through centuries of this Carthesian paradigm, educational institutions, in all areas of knowledge - medicine, music, philosophy to name a few - keep perpetuating compartmentalized models of teaching which separate mind and body, assigning greater value to rational knowledge and separating science from the arts and humanities. As a result, medical training is mainly of a biological nature and arts, in particular, music is taught in a way that separates mind and body, turning musical performance into a purely rational, and therefore incomplete exercise.

Luckily, throughout history, in many cultures, forms of knowledge have recognized the importance of maintaining the balance between physical and emotional rhythms and the rhythms of our surrounding environment.

The first relationship we think of between rhythm and health is that which is usually found in shamanic ceremonies in which percussion instruments are played with a regularity and rhythms that induce altered states of consciousness, causing many diseases to be cured.

Now we know that the acoustic stimulation of drums affects the electrical activity of the brain and leads to synchronization or rhythmic entrainment. Entrainment is a physical phenomenon which causes the rhythms from different systems to synchronize. It was discovered in the 17th century by Christiaan Huygens, inventor of the pendulum of clocks, who observed in his workshop that the pendulums that were close to one another tended to synchronize.

There are different types of rhythmic entrainment: intra-individual entrainment, which happens when two or more systems within the individual themselves synchronizes, inter-individual which happens when two or more individuals synchronize, or inter-grupal, which happens when the activities of two or more groups synchronize.

We can observe this phenomenon, for example, when an

energetic rhythm wakes up the autonomic nervous system, producing an increase in breathing, heart rate, cortisol, adrenaline and many other hormones, or when a musical stimulus affects heart rate, in other words, increases or decreases the number of times the heart beats per minute.

It is worth noting that Plato himself, in the *Timaeus*, one of his last works in which he describes numerous diseases, recommends to never move the soul without the body and the body without the soul, because it is the equilibrium of these two that keeps you in good health.

In the 11th century, the famous Arabic doctor Ibn Butlan recommended in the *Taqwim al-Sihha* - a text which had a great impact on Europe during the Middle Ages, known by its Latin translation *Tacuini or Theatrum sanitatis* - to make music and dance (*sonare et bailare*) as a way to maintain good health. The book, which lays the foundation for preventive medicine, outlines a set of recommendations to maintain good health which is the result of the balance of the so-called "six unnatural things" (*sex res non naturals*): (1) air, (2) food, (3) sleep, (4) movement and rest, (5) secretions and excretions, (6) emotions.

This codex, which in many ways remains current, is not just the source of information for doctors, but is also an exceptional iconographic source for the study of life during the Middle Ages. The remaining copies have been brightened with beautiful illustrations, which, in the section dedicated to *sonare et ballare*, show people dancing to the sound of music played by wind instruments. According to Ibn Butlan, the benefits of singing and dancing are received in equal parts by the performers and the audience.[142]

During the Middle Ages, there were records of a number of episodes which we would now call collective hysteria, when large groups of people started to dance frantically until the point of exhaustion.[143] Experts say these episodes, which some called Saint Vitus's dance, were a result of an epidemic of *Sydenham's chorea*, an infectious disease that produces involuntary muscle movements.

Throughout history, a good number of treated patients have described the benefits of movement and rhythm on their health, including the six books *De arte gimnastica* by Girolamo Mercuriale (1530-1606), published in 1569, the treaty *Sanitate tuenda* by Pierre Gontier, published in 1668 and the treaty by the French Michel Bicaise, published in 1669. According to Bicaise:"

> Music and sound make the mind dance by causing a harmonic motion, rhythm, swing. The swing of the body moves the mind.[144]

More than just discussing the benefits of movement, the treaties recommended specific dances for different diseases, depending on the age, gender, social class, profession and morphology of each patient. Different types of music were linked with the promotion of different virtues, for example, the Dorian mode, with its major key of today, was linked to virtues such as modesty, sobriety and prudence, while other modes and their related dances were linked to unbridled passions, which should be avoided.

In his book *Anatomy of melancholy*, published in 1621, Robert Burton links music, movement and emotion. In it, he recommends dance, hunting, walking and horse riding as a treatment for depression, which was then called melancholy and he explains how certain melodies and dance foster infatuation, which he calls the melancholy of love.

In the 19th century, the composer and teacher Emile Jacques-Dalcroze (1865-1950), the creator of the famous *eurhythmics* method stated that the rhythms of the body and of our surrounding environment, such as walking, running or the heartbeat, lead to the development of our intelligence right from infancy. According to Dalcroze, musical rhythm develops which we feel and we correlate our internal and external rhythms, in other ways, the rhythms of our own body and those of our surroundings.

Although Dalcroze's theories are relatively recent, the relationship between rhythm, movement and health dates back to more than 30,000 years ago, when shamanic ceremonies, considered the oldest systems of organised healing, were practised everywhere. In them, the shamans would play repetitive rhythms on the drums with regularity, which according to some studies was three taps a second, just the right number to evoke altered states of consciousness and trances in participants that would lead to healing.

The ancient practices of healing are linked to modern therapies such as the so-called *Neurodrumming*, a therapy which involves the use of drums and mantra chants following predetermined rhythms which have been shown to improve the cognitive and emotional capacities of participants, reducing levels of anxiety, stress and depression.

For people with autism and schizophrenia, there has been a lot of success when using a therapy known as *Rhythmic Entrainment Intervention* (REI), a treatment which consists of making a patient listen to the sound of drums to stimulate the central nervous system. This rhythm therapy has a positive effect at a cognitive level, an effect which is amplified when this activity takes place in a community setting.

Because of its benefits at a cognitive level, these types of therapy are considered mental or brain training, which most people traditionally associate with exercises to improve memory or maths problems, but in reality, this term can cover many areas, including participation in social activities which are essential for cognitive health.

Mental training is necessary and positive at every age as we know that neurogenesis, that is, the regeneration of brain cells, happens throughout your whole life.[145,146] Our brains are plastic, they regenerate constantly and they can be shaped and stimulated at any age.[147]

It has been shown that simple activities such as dancing, or participating in a group drum activity,[148] can lead to longevity and the development of a healthy aging process as they require the activation of numerous cortical circuits and of complex cognitive processes. Attention, perception, mobility and many brain areas get exercised simultaneously. Although it seems easy to us, perceiving rhythm is both one of the most fundamental and one of the most complex experiences of our bodies.

What is rhythm?

Generally when we talk about a rhythmic song, we mean that the music induces a sense of temporary regularity, it is organized according to a pattern which gives it a regularity. However, there is a difference between the regularity of music, the rhythm of music and the rhythm that we perceive, in other words, when we talk about rhythm, we're talking about two phenomena, one external, the object sound with its regularity, and one internal, the subject which perceives the regularity of the sound.

The way in which we perceive rhythm is also influenced by the culture in which we are brought up. Many studies demonstrate that the perception of rhythm is different in Western and Eastern culture which confirms that biology and surroundings interact to shape our sense of rhythm.

Through dance, which is beautifully defined by some researchers as a type of organized energy that gives form to feeling,[150] the values of a society are represented. Dance becomes a space for resolving conflict and representing values that deeply express who we are as individuals and as a society.

In a study based on the analysis of Bolivian songs in Quechua, Stobart and Cross,[151] showed that when we listen to music, we perceive the beat in different ways depending on the culture in which we grow up. The authors attribute these differences to the rhythm of the Quechua languages, in other words, the "music" of the language we spoke, its prosody, determines how we perceive rhythm.

It has also been shown that the ability to perceive complex rhythms is increased when we have more exposure to different languages and types of music,[152] in other words, this skill can be developed if we stimulate our brain by exposing it to music and languages from different cultures.

Although all humans are born with the same skills to perceive simple and complex rhythms, they are then shaped by their culture. Already at nine months old, infants are able to distinguish different rhythms and show a preference for the rhythms of their own culture. When they reach twelve months, cultural preferences similar to those of adults arise, that is to say, a brief exposure to music develops our ability to perceive certain rhythms.[153]

Body movement and pleasure are related - it just takes us remembering moments in which we have danced to the rhythm of music for the body to start moving almost automatically, in sync with the music. Some studies have shown that we find music which is somewhat complex, but not too complex, pleasurable. To produce this pleasure, music should surprise us in some way, that is to say, it should have a structure that in any moment could suddenly change, whether it be removing a note or changing the rhythmic structure.[154]

Of course, what some find complex could be very simple for others, and therefore the pleasure that music produces depends fully on the person listening to it, on their cultural context. However, we could say that a certain level of syncope, that is, a certain level of irregularity and surprise in music makes it more pleasurable and more likely to make us move.

Although there is still a lot to discover about the brain mechanisms which produce pleasure and the ways in which rhythm and music affect us, we can state that pleasurable and playful activities like dancing and singing can greatly improve our quality of life. It has been shown that dancing or playing percussion instruments reduces anxiety, stress, as well as levels of testosterone and it regulates the hormone system.

Knowing the impact that our corporal experiences and habits have on our health grants us an incredible power, but also a great responsibility; we can shape our brain with our actions, slow down the aging process and live until an old age while maintaining good health. Let's dance!

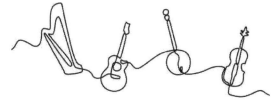

Chapter 7

MUSIC IN PAIN AND DEATH

Pain is a shared human experience, something which we have all experienced. Whether it's physical or emotional, pain is our body's way of warning us about an imbalance, something which is hurting us that we must pay attention to. According to the International Association for the Study of Pain (IASP), pain is a displeasurable subjective emotional or sensory experience related to tissue damage. By recognizing it is subjective, we accept that it cannot be generalized or compared between individuals, and we also understand that it is an experience which combines many physical, social, cultural and psychological elements. Pain is a complex and multidimensional phenomenon which should be dealt with in a transdisciplinary way.[155]

Our experience of pain is determined by factors as diverse as the memories we have of trips to the hospital, our anticipation before a specific procedure or our psychological state at the exact moment we're undergoing it.

Even more complex than physical pain, emotional pain can also not be measured, evaluated or compared, and the only thing we can say for certain is that we all suffer from it at some point during our lives and in these moments, music is there for us, it soothes us. It expresses what we cannot put into words, and it acts like a cathartic tool.

I'm sure you have lived through moments where music has calmed you or helped you express emotions which you wouldn't be able to express in any other way. Sometimes you might have used it to calm down in moments of stress or to encourage you when you may be suffering from pain, loss or separation.

Many of us use music as something cathartic. I remember when a friend of mine was upset and he listened to the same sad song for hours and days, it seemed like he needed to listen to music that vibrated at the same frequency of the pain he felt, and according to him, it soothed him. Music allowed him to represent what he felt and what he could not express in any other way through sound.

The opposite also happens when we are overwhelmed with happiness and we get lost in the rhythmic music turned up to the highest volume to express through the vibrations and sound the ecstasy that we feel, that feeling that goes beyond the realm of explanation, of word. Sometimes only music can express the depth of the emotions that we harbor.

In hospitals, music began to be used to treat pain after World War I in the hospitals of veterans when groups of volunteer musicians performed for soldiers who had lost limbs, were recovering from serious injuries, and also for many who had lost friends and lived through intense emotional experiences. The results of this encounter between music and pain were so grand that the field of music therapy arose and nowadays has become a profession for thousands of people. From then on, many studies have shown that music reduces stress, anxiety, depression and the pain of physical and emotional scars.

Music began to be "prescribed" for specific purposes in so-called musical interventions, where music therapists expose patients to different types of music in controlled environments once or several times a day. The "dosage" of music depends on the ailment and can be administered in one and several sessions.

To select the appropriate music, the therapists strike up a relationship with the patient to discover their tastes and associations that they have with different types of music.

Although the general belief is that the music that has a greater effect of calming pain or anxiety is Western classical music, that could not be further from the truth. This false belief has developed as the majority of studies about the use of music in clinical environments have been carried out in Western countries, where this type of music is associated culturally and socially with certain codes and sociocultural environments. Surely if we did studies in countries outside of this Western axis, we would find that every culture responds to different types of music. In other words, the use and effects of music must be culturally, socially and historically contextualized.

This requires a personalized approach for each patient, where the patient is seen in their entirety, as a bio-psycho-social being, and the patients themselves are studied, not their illness and from that point, their sound treatment can be designed. In other words, if we had to design a musical handbook, we would be faced with the challenge of creating one for each and every cultural and social environment.

Contrary to what we might think, music therapy treatments aren't just limited to listening to music. They include any type of musical activity like performing, composing, learning an instrument and singing. Music is created and experienced through the body and through it, physical and emotional pain is relieved and motor and cognitive skills are developed. The benefits of music go far beyond the relief of pain and are supported by an infinity of studies.[156,157,158]

From a physiological point of view, the relationship between pain and music is backed by *Gate Control Theory*, one of the most accepted theories about pain, developed by Melzack and Wall, who recognized the emotional and cognitive components of pain. This theory postulated that pain signals travel through the thin nerve fibers, while tactile sensations like vibration, touch or pressure travel through wide fibers. When we receive a pain stimulus, the nerve sensors send both signals to the spinal cord, which acts as a gateway to decide which of the signals should be let in, the tactile or the pain one. The most interesting and relevant thing for our relationship between music and pain is that the wide fibers, apart from processing tactile stimuli, also process auditory and visual stimuli.[159]

Gate Control Theory explains why sometimes we massage a painful area and it soothes us, in other words, the tactile stimulus of the massage competes with the pain stimulus and in essence, it gains entry to the spinal cord. Thus, what we feel is the touch of the massage, not pain.[160]

If we consider the fact that music is a multimodal experience which doesn't just impact the ear but also tactile perception through vibration, visual perception through the associations that it evokes and the emotional and cognitive spheres, we all have the elements that allow us to explain, at least empirically, the effect of music to control pain.

A more recent theory about pain, also developed by Melzack, called *Neuromatrix Theory*,[161] proposes the involvement of the limbic system and cerebral cortex in pain mechanisms, giving the phenomenon of pain an even wider and multidimensional aspect which further reinforces the relationship between music and the control of pain.

Numerous studies have shown that the involvement of music reduces the intensity and anguish related to pain, and it also reduces heat rate, blood pressure, breathing rate and the need for both opioid and non-opioid painkillers. In other words, music has a proven effect on the treatment of pain.[162]

For cancer patients, who frequently suffer from intense physical and emotional pain, numerous studies have shown that the active listening of music reduces the anxiety associated with pain and death,[163,164] reduces the severity of symptoms like nausea and vomiting associated with chemotherapy,[165] and it soothes anxiety and pain during radiotherapy.[166] Music also increases motivation, the feeling of wellness and the ability to exercise for patients with a bone marrow transplant,[167] as well as reducing pain for patients with severe burns[168] and the post-operatory pain for heart patients.[169]

Although the benefits of music at a physical level are highly important, perhaps it's psycho-social effect is even more important, in other words, its effect on emotional health and on our ability to fit in socially, to accept those changes that will inevitably befall us at some point in our lives; after all, life is just a constant adaptation to new environments, people, challenge, physical and social transformations.

One of the changes that each and every single one of us will have to face at some point in our lives is illness. When it impedes our lives, it transforms it, causing changes and losses that lead us to mourning. Illness launches a whole lot of bio-psycho-social processes which have an impact on all aspects of our daily life, affecting our habits and relationships. Illness also makes us confront our own mortality, the fact that our days have a date of expiry, and that we are not here forever. Death represents the most fundamental crisis of being.

In these moments of loss and confrontation, throughout history, music has played a very important role. In some of the first ever tombs which can be dated back to the Neolithic period, remains of harps and other musical instruments have been found, which apparently seem to be buried to accompany the deceased in their journey to the other world.[170] Similar figures have been found in the 5 BC tombs of Ancient Egypt and China. In the Egyptian tombs, musicians are playing percussion instruments, probably to keep away the bad spirits, a still-present tradition in Egypt.

Etruscan Iconography shows dancers and musicians playing the aulos, a wind instrument similar to a flute, in funeral ceremonies. This custom was maintained until Roman times when it was a requirement to have two guilds of musicians participating in all festivals, public games and funeral processions,

In the old Mesopotamia and in the near East, communal funeral songs were sung. In China, famous poetry called *"lamentations for the south"* was sung, and in Ancient Greece, funeral songs were accompanied by the three-stringed lyre. But it is perhaps in Greek mythology where we find one of the main figures in Western culture who showed the relation between music and death: Orpheus, the Sirens and the Muses.[171] Although the representations of these figures have been dated to the Helenistic era, the myth of *Orpheus* probably had its origins way back in 6 BC.

Orpheus, the one who tamed wild beasts with music, the one who could move trees and rocks and change the course of rivers just with the sound of his lyre, who dodged all the dangers of the underworld with his music in order to save his beloved Eurydice from the clutches of death.

The Sirens, birds with a human head, used music to seduce travelers in order to bring them to an island where they would meet their death, and the Muses appear in the works of Homer as musicians at Achilles' funeral, acting as guardians of the order of the cosmos and choir members during the parties of the gods. Musicians and music are there to help us pass to the other world, to protect and guide us in our journey into the unknown.

But apart from assisting the departed in their journey, music also helps to preserve the memory of the community, to have hope and move on with our lives.

In Iran, while the women cry for the deceased, the men sing and dance. In rural areas of China, el *xisang* (happy funeral) is celebrated for those who lived a long life and the *xiongsang* (unhappy funeral)[172] for those who had a short life. The atmosphere of these two types of funerals is made up of musical and aural events, including representation of folkloric music for friends and family of the dead. In the Colombian

Pacific, communities of African descent sing songs called *Alabaos*, which are lively celebrations in which the whole community participates. Similarly, within the black community in New Orleans, jazz funerals are celebrated, a tradition that can be dated right back to the history of the city. In these celebrations, groups of musicians form a parade in honour of death. These rituals help the mourning process and the mental health of those closest to the deceased.[173]

In the Christian tradition, we are familiar with many musical works composed since the 16th century to accompany the Office of the Dead and to declare the existence of eternal life, an act of faith and hope for believers.

The first *Requiem* recorded was composed by Johannes Ockeghem (1461), followed by numerous works including Brumel's Requiem (1483), Jean Richafort's Requiem for six voices, Antoine de Févin's (15th century), Tomás Luis de Victoria's (1603), just to name a few from that period. More recent and well known requiems have been composed by Mozart (1791), Cherubini (1816) Brahms (1865–68), Verdi (1874), Saint-Saëns (1878), Berlioz (1837), Faure (1887), Durufle (1947), Britten (1961) Ligetti (1963), Stravinsky (1966), Penderecki (1980–2005), Lloyd Webber (1985), Rutter (1985), Jenkins (2005), and an infinite number of compositions of Western musicians intended for the Office of the Dead.

What all of these funeral rites of the past have in common is that they aim to restore the balance of the community, which was lost due to the death of one of its members. The words of the songs, the music, the speeches and the lamentations are there to remind and preserve the memory of the deceased. Through songs and lamentations, the community is able to restore the memory, experience catharsis of pain, connect this earthly life with life beyond and preserve collective memory.

Although these rituals are directed at the dead, in reality they serve as spaces to reaffirm life, spaces of resilience where passions and emotions are exuberantly expressed through word, music and dance, with the body acting as a vehicle.

Death is without doubt one of the most important social and vital events, the only certainty that we have in our constantly changing and flowing existence. Sadly, despite its importance, in our current society we tend to deny it and glorify all representations of youth and beauty. For many people, being faced with death causes conflict and most of the time it is denied and we prefer not to talk about it, to sidestep, to believe that its something which happens to others and when it happens, it's a tragedy. Unfortunately death isn't seen as what it essentially is, a natural occurrence, a process which we will all inevitably go through and therefore, something we should be prepared for.

Music can also help prepare us for our own death and for the death of our close ones. In one study, patients who had terminal illnesses or those who had sought assisted suicide, as well as their close ones, were asked to create a playlist to listen to during death or during their last hours or days of life. Some people chose music which made them relaxed or happy, others chose songs that had a special meaning in some moment of their life, songs which reflected their values or experiences. For example, some patients made playlists which included music from their childhood, adolescence and youth, a sort of musical autobiography which ended with songs that they would like to be played during their funeral. Music helped them to build a narrative that linked their past, present and future.[174]

Projects, like the one done by *Chalice of Repose,*[175] are based on music accompanying patients with terminal illnesses and their families through musical intervention in the final days of their life and during their death. These interventions include passive and attentive listening of music and composition of songs, a very powerful exercise as by combining text and music, we reach levels of expression which you normally would not be able to access, we can express the depths of our pain, our fear, our vulnerability, our hope.

In this context, music serves as a narrator and a tool by which we release our memories and emotions, and it's as though music is an extension of our being, a part of who we are that it is expressed outside of our body and it makes us, and those who join our listening experience, vibrate. Music allows us to directly access emotions and create a narrative, an autobiography in which you make amends between your expectation of who you wanted to be and who you are in reality, in other words, we can look back on our lives and build a bridge between the real us and the idealized version of us, which helps us accept who we really are, including accepting our mortality and viewing it as a natural process.

Composing songs, even if we are not musicians, is a very powerful exercise and within everyone's reach. Why don't we compose songs for the person that we were, who we are now and who we would like to be? Why don't we write for those who we leave behind, songs to say goodbye to our loved ones, to express our gratitude or love for them or to give them hope? Why don't we start to think about the songs that would play at our funeral?

These exercises that seem superfluous are in reality very powerful confrontations with our own mortality, transformative exercises which help us to reflect about who we truly are and about the mark we want to leave on the world, about our values and about the impact that our actions have on society and the environment.

The beautiful thing about music is that it is within the reach of everybody; you don't need special musical training to create a song or enjoy a melody and reap in its positive effects on our mental and physical health.

Chapter 8

VOICE, SONG AND THE SOUNDS OF THE BODY

Do you remember the tunes that your parents sang to you when you were a child to calm you down, make you happy or to guide you? Or perhaps your first school songs come to mind, those songs that you happily shared with your family and that led to family evenings together?

In our childhood, we sing and dance freely, we shout, we cry melodiously and our cries are heard far away as our breathing and vocal emission mechanisms have not yet been "tamed". We still haven't internalized the rules that determine what is correct or the valued judgment that limits us as adults when we sing and when we constantly evaluate whether we're singing well or badly or if we're making a fool of ourselves.

Singing is something inherent in human beings, in fact, when an adult begins to learn singing, the first steps are to remember and relearn the freedom and relaxation with which we made sound during our childhood. We start by learning to breathe in a completely relaxed state, conscious of our body, of our posture, relaxing our jaw muscles, our tongue, our neck, our rib cage. The process of learning to sing becomes a journey in self-awareness which has a physical component that connects us to our body, makes us conscious of it, makes us introspect, look into ourselves, be in touch with ourselves. The body is the instrument of the singer.

But perhaps the most important component when learning to sing is the emotional component. Our voice becomes the metaphor for our being, for the space of representation where part of our being is projected in the most pure and authentic manner.

Some people find it hard to listen to their own voices, they get nervous or embarrassed listening to a voice recording of themselves and they don't like what they hear. Learning to sing therefore becomes a journey of accepting ourselves, and recognising who we are, without facades or exaggerations. We are simply who we are and that is enough. We don't need to be anything else to be loved, accepted, or valued.

The process of getting used to and accepting my own voice is a process in which I get used to and accept myself. Throughout this process, I have come to love who I am. But this journey doesn't end here, as the process of learning to sing teaches us that each person's voice is unique, a digital footprint that differentiates us from others and one which is in continuous construction and development.

The study of the technical side of singing also teaches us that although we begin the journey with a *tessitura* or a vocal extension, our voice can develop to its full potential, a potential that we didn't even know we possessed. Our voice, like the rest of our body and brain, changes throughout life, mirroring the experiences and physical and emotional stages that we go through during our life cycle.

The process of taking both our real and metaphorical voice to its highest level of expression is a process of self-awareness and acceptance where we are aware of our bodies and we learn to coordinate relaxation, breathing and sound emission mechanisms in an environment of complete awareness and freedom.

Perhaps many of you are now thinking that your voice isn't beautiful, that you're not able to sing. Luckily, although we would all love to have a beautiful singing voice in line with the aesthetic ideals of our society, the act of singing transcends these ideals, and therefore we all can and must sing.

Singing is essentially communicating, giving the world a part of me, expressing my beliefs, my ideals, my dreams. The singer, while reflecting the reality around them, transcends this reality, transforming themselves. When singing, they can reach other planes of reality, forms of perception and subtle expression. In this almost magical act, they connect with that ancestral shaman and priest, and become the bridge that connects the ordinary world with the symbolic world, the ethereal, abstract and transcendent world.

Throughout history, singing has been used to heal, soothe pain, express happiness, give strength to those who are sent off to war, energize those who work long, dull hours, comfort those who are suffering, provide company to those who feel alone.

They say that Isabel of Farnesio, the second wife of the Spanish king, Felipe the 5th, invited the Napolitan castrato Carlo Broschi, the famous Farinelli to court, in order to pull the king out of his depression, as songs were the only way to rescue him from isolation and apathy. This anecdote that may seem funny can be backed up by science. Listening to happy music or music that has an emotional connection to us has proven effects on our wellbeing and mood.

A recent study by the *British Academy of Sound Therapy,*[176] using the *Oxford Happiness Questionnaire*[177], concluded that after listening to music, 32.07% of people were more prone to happiness, 64.97% felt happier, 89.31% more energetic, 64.97% laughed more, 86.31% felt more satisfied with their lives, 84.67% felt like they had a positive effect on others, 82.4% felt more in control of their lives and 80.06% said that feeling happier helped them make decisions more easily. Singing and listening to others sing has positive effects on physical and mental health.

The key part of a song is voice, that digital footprint that differentiates us from others, and it's important both when it makes noise and when it doesn't. Voice is essentially produced through vibrations of the vocal cords due to air.

As well as being a cathartic tool, songs help to convey the values of a person or of a community, as a badge of personal and social identity. This is why we identify with songs from a generation, political party or artist themselves, because songs transcend the musical aspect to become a gate to a culture, to the values and aspirations of people and nations, they are an essential part of our heritage, for both us as individuals and for our species.

Music and song in particular date back to the dawn of our species. Although proponents of musical proto-language tend to place its beginnings in evolutionary scenarios prior to 400,000 years ago, recent studies have shown that from an evolutive standpoint, the ability to produce complex vocalizations appears 400,000 years ago, as both Homo Sapiens and Neanderthals, and by extension, their last common ancestor, have the same anatomical adaptations when it comes to speech, while previous species were likely different. According to these findings, we can assume that speech and language are at least 400,000 years old and probably developed together in a process where cognitive and anatomical adaptations coevolved in a gradual manner. There is also a process of coevolution between vocalizations, gestures and communication skills; and between culture and biology, all linked by self-organization.[178]

Music and song are related to biological and adaptive processes in different species. Just like the human language, the sounds made by animals carry a lot of meaning, they express information about territories, reproduction, social groups, alliances, predation, dangers and resources. For example, the songs of birds have communicative, adaptive and reproductive purposes[179] they're used to woo their partner, to define territory and to stand out in a group. Chimpanzees adjust their sounds depending on the social group they're in and the male species of the South African clawed frog (Xenopus laevis) produces a song as part of their reproductive rites.[180] Their song is possibly due to complex adaptive processes where there are an infinity of hormones and neuromodulator substances at work. Their larynx has androgen receptors which allow it to grow eight times more than that female of the species so that they can sing.

When it comes to humans, the first social interactions are of a musical nature. When the mother sings and whispers sweet melodies to the newborn child, hormones, such as oxytocin and vasopressin[181] sre released which are essential for the development of the social brain which fosters attachment, trust and affection between mother and child. The newborn's attraction to the familiar sound of the voice and song of their mother has an impact on their central psychological responses, like for example, the secretion of cortisol.[182]

Visual and auditory perception develop in parallel, complement each other and are just as important as each other for our development. As Sterne says:

> Hearing is spherical, vision is directional; hearing immerses its subject, vision offers a perspective; sound comes to us, but vision travels to its object; hearing is concerned with interiors, vision is concerned with surfaces; hearing involves physical contact with the outside world, vision requires distance from it; hearing places you inside an event, seeing gives you perspective on an event; hearing is a primarily temporal sense, vision is a primarily spatial sense.[183]

Although we have evidence that through hearing we can get to know and understand reality in a more complete way and sometimes in a faster way than through sight, our society favours the sense of sight.

It is paradoxical given that gestures, languages and sound, all essential skills for social integration and belonging to a community, seem to have arisen through adaptation, almost at the same time, to help us survive.

This situation has mainly arisen due to the fact that in Westen culture, for centuries, especially since the Enlightenment, great narratives were constructed through the written word. From then on, humanities and sciences have distanced themselves away from tradition and folklore, legitimizing themselves through the written word, while oral tradition is associated with premodern, remote, backwards societies, and this caused the audible sphere to be demoted to second place. Sciences began to use the eye of the scientist as a reference point. And from then on we have lived in a vision-centric society.

Before the 19th century, sound was studied exclusively as language or music, idealizing music and linking it to God and to the harmony of the universe. When the concept of frequency was popularized in the 19th century, a concept previously developed by those such as Decartes or Bernoulli, sounds began to be studied as a form of vibration, giving rise to the physics, acoustics, otology and physiology that would later be developed from the 19th century onwards. In a way, the sphere of hearing was legitimized once it began to enter the scientific rationalist discussion.

In medicine, just like in philosophy, vision is studied over hearing. According to Sterne, this was partly due to the difficulty to access the miniscule structures of the ear and the difficulty to study them in human bodies, something only normalized from the mid-19th century onwards when doctors finally were allowed to carry out the dissection of cadavers and were able to observe these structures.[184]

Medical semiology, one of the most valuable bodies of knowledge within medical practice, which gives doctors the tools to observe in order to diagnose complex pathologies, was mainly developed based on visual observation. Thanks to the study of semiology, doctors diagnose by observing posture, way of walking, colour of the skin, breathing rate, eyes, movement and an endless number of physical and psychological characteristics. Although semiology also deals with sound phenomena, such as heart rate, breathing rate or timber of the voice, the majority of our evaluation is visual.

However, it was a tool for listening which became one of the key elements for the professionalization of medicine. From the incorporation of the stethoscope onwards, medicine went from being purely theoretical to being perceptual. Examining the patient using sound equipment, listening and interpreting the sounds of the body became a necessity for doctors.

Although Hippocrates had already written about the important of immediate auscultation, which consisted of putting the ear directly on the body of the patient, and in 1761, in his *Inventum novum*,[185] Leopold Auenbrugger advocated for the use of percussion, which required interpretation of the sounds produced by the percussion in specific areas of the body, before the invention of the stethoscope and audio examining (through the means of an instrument), the doctor exclusively depended on visual observation and the patient's narration to draw up the diagnosis. The voice of the patient, their narration and visual observation were the most important pillars of information for the diagnosis.

From the incorporation of the stethoscope onwards, and the development of the ability to link certain sounds in the body, picked up by the stethoscope, to illnesses, the internal sounds of the body became the most important source of information for diagnosis and voice began to be important for its timbral qualities, in other words, being analyzed based on the type of sound it produces.

In 1816, when Rene Laennec wrote that he could hear the sounds of a patient's heart better while listening through a rolled up cylinder of paper over the chest, his innovation didn't exactly lead to the invention of the tube itself, but rather to the ability to link the sounds of the body, the internal organs, to possible illnesses. From this moment on, a series of observations began which culminated in the publication of his *Treaty on mediate auscultation,*[186] a founding work in which, for the first time, auscultated sound was linked to disease of the lung, heart and thoracic cavity.

Listening became essential for doctors and the stethoscope allowed them to listen to what they could not see. Sounds became signals which indicated good health or illness, and doctors thought it necessary to refine the sense of hearing, to develop auditory skills for scientific purposes, and the sphere of hearing was made rational.

The sounds of the body have also had a long relationship with music and the arts. The heartbeat, the rhythmic sounds that have been a metaphor for love throughout history, the emotions and life, were described for the first time by the Greek doctor Praxagoras of Kis (340 BC) and later by Erasistrus (304-250 BC). However, it was Herophilos (335-280 BC) who deduced that the pulse was a result of the contraction and dilation of the arteries, being the first person to reference its musical qualities.

His theories, which bestowed the pulse with a musical

metric, had a considerable impact on musical creation during the Middle Ages and the Renaissance, when people such as Boethius (480-524 AD) distinguished between three types of music: *musica mundana,* which comes from the celestial spheres, *musica humana*, caused by the pulse, breathing and heartbeat and *musica instrumentis,* the only type of music that humans can hear.[187]

From then on, the heart became a common theme in art, being associated with love, kindness and other Christian values. From the 20th century onwards, thanks to digital technology, the heartbeat was used to create interactive artistic works which connected body, emotion, creativity and music. A recent example is the *Heart Chamber Orchestra*, an audiovisual spectacle made up of 12 classical musicians and the artistic duo *Terminalbeach.* Linking the heartbeats to a composition and visualization software in real time, musicians can interpret sheet music made by their own hearts.[188] The creation of this orchestra is an example of the so-called biometric art, which is based on the sounds and shapes of the body to make art, a true fusion of knowledge which reflects the interdisciplinarity which we are returning to in the 21st century. Biometric analysis allows us to create music based on data taken from the body, but it also opens the door to make medical diagnosis easier.

Taking advantage of the sensitivity we have as humans to distinguish variations in sound, biochemists at Michigan State University invented the analysis of musical urine,[189] a type of research that allows, for example, doctors with a visual disability to analyse the results, just like those who are performing a surgery and who don't have their hands or eyes free. Musical analysis allows a high specificity because humans are more sensitive to variations in tone than to numerical variations. This caused the geneticist Susumo Ohno to turn DNA sequences into their musical equivalents, allowing him to discover genetic patterns that would have been difficult to find any other way.[190,191]

The body is literally a symphony, a set of sounds that we can now listen to thanks to experiments which turn our electric signals and muscle movements into music by using a simple electronic instrument called the *Biomuse*.[192]

Digiti Sonus, an artistic system that turns digital footprints into sound also shows that our bodies are music. The system uses algorithms so the audience can explore their sonic identities through unique sounds generated by the patterns of their fingerprint. The most interesting thing about this is that the participants can alter the sounds, experimenting with their sound identities.[193] According to Yoon Chung Han: "given the system's ability to locate the sound in the 3D space, it is likely that the sonification of fingerprints can be used as an effective method to represent complex biometric data".[194]

Yoon Chung Han and Byeong-jun Han have also experimented with turning the many patterns and qualities of the skin into sound, in what they call sonification of the skin. The artists split up the body into its different parts: head, neck, arms, legs, chest and pelvis. In order to sonify the numerous qualities of the skin, they used an algorithm to take an average of the pixels of color specific to each part of the body and then they assigned this average color to a default range of frequency. Like this, someone could explore the skin from their whole body and examine the different sonic representations.

These experiments open the doors to a myriad of possibilities for the future and allow us to explore our bodies in different ways than we have ever done before. Soon we'll be able to listen to the sound of our skin, eyes, hands, hair and I'm sure we will also be able to distinguish between the sounds of health and sickness. This technology could also lead to endless therapeutic possibilities. If organs can sound different in health and in sickness, why not consider changing the sonic frequencies of the sick organs so that they sound like healthy ones?

If, as shown by Pelling, Gralla and Gimzewski,[195] cells can sing, who says that we can't make cells vibrate at the frequency of health? The possibilities are endless!

Sounds themselves, of both the individual and the environment, define who we are and they place us in the socio-historical context. We can create music from the sounds of the body and also from the sounds of our surrounding environment. The act of listening to ourselves and to the surroundings is in itself therapeutic, it connects us to our environment, it anchors us in the here and now. By listening, we open ourselves up to the world, we direct our attention to one another, and we begin a relationship with the exterior. As Gadamer says, "anyone who listens is fundamentally open. Without such openness there is no genuine human bond. Belonging together always means being able to listen to one another".[196]

Chapter 9

MUSIC AND CREATIVITY

One of the first things we think about when we hear the words music and creativity is the composer. They have the ability to create music which represents and unravels the values, desires and fears of a society in a specific moment of history, and they turn their emotions and experiences into sounds that are chock-full of meaning.

How are they able to create works which entire generations can identify with? Are they geniuses, gifted with exceptional talent? Special people?.

In Ancient Greece, it was believed that those who took part in activities or produced output that we would now consider creative were possessed by a spirit or inspired by the muses.[197]

During the Middle Ages, creativity was considered a gift of God, coming from divine inspiration.[198] In the Romantic period, creativity was attributed to super gifted humans, people who were special in some way.

Research started in the 20th century revealed that creativity is within the reach of everyone, and that the great creative achievements in the fields of arts, sciences or sports weren't solely due to talent or genius; they were mainly a result of perseverance, studying and years worth of practice. Nobody has put it better than Pablo Picasso when he said "Inspiration exists, but it has to find you working."

Defined as an individual's ability to produce something new, original, suitable and valuable for a specific task, creativity is often associated with individuals[199] in other words, we tend to believe that innovation comes exclusively from the brain of a creative individual. However, creativity, like cognition, is also a sociocultural phenomenon, given that the output of the creative process is used by, appreciated, rejected or incorporated into the society in which it is created. This means that creativity isn't just limited to an individual, but rather it's a process which extends to the environment in which the individual develops their ideas.

Although there are personality traits that are more frequently associated with creative subjects, like, for example, extroversion, willingness to take risks[200] or seek out new experiences,[201] creativity also depends on factors such as habits, motivation and the conditions of our surrounding environment. This means that we can develop it, and we can cultivate habits and create environments which stimulate it.

Although we might think that creativity is a solely human characteristic, it can be found extensively in the animal kingdom.[202] Hinde and Fischer described how in order to survive, a species of bird in the UK learned to make holes in the aluminium caps of the bottles of milk left at the door, a practice that started in one area and became the norm in most of the country.[203]

According to Wallas,[204] during creative processes, there are conscious and unconscious factors involved that develop at different stages. In order to create, we have to go through a phase of preparation and acquisition of knowledge that continues the incubation of the idea. Then we arrive at that awaited moment of enlightenment, when innovation takes place. In the final stage, the idea is tested and validated.

The unconscious plays a very important role in creativity. Many composers and creators from all fields have told us how their ideas appeared, how they sprung out from nowhere, as if someone was controlling it. I personally get surprised sometimes when I'm composing songs, as ideas come to me so quickly, in an almost magical, mysterious way.

When I compose, I usually put music to poems by famous authors and I've always found it strange how sometimes when I'm reading the poetry, suddenly I come across one poem that inspires music in my head. It's as though the music is jumping out of the page. And this phenomenon only happens with some poems, not all.

In 1997, when Karlheinz Stockhausen was asked what is intuition, he answered:

> Intuition transforms every normal action into something special that one doesn't know oneself. So I am a craftsman, I can start working with sounds, with apparatuses and find all sorts of new combinations. But when I want to create something that amazes me and moves me, I need intuition. …something happens every now and then which is amazing and which is also for me unknown. Intuition comes, according to my own experience, from a higher world.[205]

The composer Pierre Boulez said that the fundamental components of creativity are imagination and intelligence: "creative processes can't exist without imagination, but they also can't exist without training the skills to create".

When the composer Lucas Foss was asked the definition of an idea, he answered: "an idea occurs when there is chaos and suddenly you see relationships, when you find meaning where you looked before and there seemed to only be disorder".[206]

What Foss was referring to was *divergent thinking*, a type of thinking that comes up with creative ideas through exploration of many possible solutions. It is a type of thinking that, in contrast to logical thinking which looks for the one correct answer based on previous knowledge, usually happens spontaneously, fluidly, which allows many ideas to emerge in a short amount of time, connecting things in an unexpected way.

This explains why when he had a difficult problem to solve, Einstein would shut himself in and play the violin, an instrument he played since he was six years old. The physicist even stated that his famous theory of relativity came to him through intuition and that its discovery was a result of musical perception.[207]

The famous Italian composer, Edgar Varese, stated that his inspiration came from maths and astronomy because they stimulated his imagination and gave him the impression of movement and rhythm. Son of an engineer, from a young age, Varese studied in a school which specialized in maths and science. Here he discovered Leonardo da Vinci and became interested in the study of sound.

> "When I was around 20, I found a definition of music that changed my life. Józef Maria Hoene-Wroński, Polish physicist, musicologist and philosopher from the first half of the 19th century, defined music as "the corporealization of the intelligence that is in sounds". It was this definition that first made me think of music as something spatial, as bodies of sound moving in space, a conception that I gradually made my own.".[208]

From a physics point of view, music, and by extension all sounds, are viewed as energy that vibrates through a medium and is transferred to our body and senses.[209] The vibration activates our auditory system, touch[210] and the vestibular system in the inner ear. From the moment in which we perceive sound, we assign it an aesthetic value, we situate it culturally and we classify it as music or noise, as beautiful or ugly.

The history of music is intimately linked to physics. It has been said that when Einstein got to know of the quantum theory proposed by Max Planck, who won the Nobel Prize for physics in 1918 and was also a gifted pianist and cellist, he stated that it was "the highest form of musicality in the sphere of thinking".

We could cite hundreds of examples of scientists-cum-musicians and musicians-cum-scientists who provided us with massive contributions throughout history, all thanks to an education which allowed them to develop divergent thinking.

According to Root-Bernstein, this is an example of *correlative talents*, that is to say, skills or abilities in different fields that can be merged together to produce surprising and innovative results.[211]

Creative thinking is transdisciplinary by nature and can be transferred from one field to another. The skills associated with music, like the training and recognition of patterns, synesthetic skills, imagination, aesthetic sensitivity, rhythm, the ability to interpret and express emotions and the understanding of music itself, all united by the discipline required in the field, have been important components of the correlative talents of famous scientists.[212]

The doctor Hector Berlioz (1803-1969) found worldwide fame as one of most innovative composers of the 19th century.

Aleksandr Borodin (1833-1987), respected medic, chemist and founder of the St Petersburg Women's Medical School, was also one of the greatest Russian composers throughout history, a member of the *Group of Five*.[213] Virginia Apgar, a doctor from the USA who was a reputed anesthesiologist, obstetrician and creator of the Apgar Score, a test carried out on all newborn babies to evaluate their neurological health, played the violin from a young age and learned how to build instruments. Camille Saint-Saëns (1835-1921), apart from being a composer, was also an avid astronomer. Edward Elgar (1857-1934), isn't just famous as a composer, but was also a chemist with many registered patents. The Anglo-German astronomer William Hershel (1738-1822), who discovered the planet Uranus, had a noteworthy career as a composer and helped his sister Caroline Hershel (1850-1948) to first establish herself as a singer and later as an astronomer. Caroline discovered a number of comets and was a pioneer in many ways, as she was the first woman to receive a salary as a scientist and the first woman to be accepted as a member of the Royal Astronomical Society. The famous guitarist and composer Brian May, part of the band Queen, is a doctor of astrophysics with numerous publications in the field.

The cardiologist and composer Richard Bing has said that his discoveries were a result of the transdisciplinary education he received. Nobel Prize winners, like the neuroanatomist-cum-visual artist Santiago Ramón y Cajal, and the immunologist-cum-novelist Charles Richet, have stated that the big advances that have taken place in science aren't due to monothematic specialists, but rather to people with a wide range of interests and hobbies.[214]

There is a need to develop hobbies, to promote the study of music and arts, not just as a secondary subject, but as the main one, recognizing that it is essential for cognitive and creative development. This statement can be verified by numerous studies carried out on thousands of students gifted in the field of science and maths which showed that the most important factors predicting their professional success weren't what we would expect, i.e. their IQ or academic results. The determining factors were whether they took part in cognitively challenging activities in their free time or not.[215]

With so much evidence, I once again would like to invite you, dear reader, to fill your life with music, to brighten all the aspects of your daily life with sounds, to learn an instrument and to sing. We can develop skills and environments that stimulate creative and innovative thinking, and live a fuller and healthier life. Pay attention to the sounds in your surroundings, walk around with your ears open, listen to the birds chirping, to the trees swaying in the wind, to your neighbors singing, to the music you come across during your daily strolls. Take note of your surroundings, prepare your senses for creativity. When you're having a mental block or you feel tired, stop for a minute, listen to music, take a deep breath, dance. If you are a musician, improvise, leave aside the sheet music for a second and explore the sounds of your instrument.

Cognition and creative processes interact with the surroundings, they become embodied, meaning that the environment in which you live and the habits that you develop manifest themselves in your ways of thinking and in your creative being.

Chapter 10

GLOBAL HEALTH, PANDEMIC AND THE EXAMPLE OF ORCHESTRAS

There is no better example of working in a team or managing diversity than how an orchestra, choir, theatre or musical group works. These represent the perfect metaphor for how society should function. Every instrument, every member of the choir has a unique voice, a digital print, a stamp of their identity, however, despite differences in the forms and sounds of the instruments, each of them join to play a piece, each one bringing to the table what makes them unique, listening to others, following a rhythm and a shared melody, all united by a common goal. What each person does affects the global result.

Defining health is a very complex matter, and sometimes we fall into the trap of thinking we are healthy if we don't feel any pain, if we aren't taking medication or if we don't visit the doctor. We usually fall into the trap of thinking health is an individual concept, something which happens to me, disconnected from our surroundings. This individualist view of health is a reflection of the values of a society in which we are all competing with one another, where there is the survival of the fittest; as long as I am well, who cares about the rest.

This manner of thinking can be seen at every level, from governments that watch over their borders and implement protectionist policies which only benefit themselves, without caring about the disastrous consequences it has on other parts of the world, the methods of production that seriously harm the environment, the selling of weapons and drugs that wipe out millions of humans, high and low level corruption, our daily consumption habits, our diets, the way we dress, how we travel. It is difficult to find an area of human existence that isn't tainted by this capitalist individualism. Our health and our own body, being the first territory we have access to and control over, are no exception.

In order to understand health and sickness, we must have a holistic view of things, which links the individual and their physical and emotional aspects to their surrounding ecosystem and their cultural and social environment. In other words, health and wellbeing can only be achieved when there is a bio-psycho-social equilibrium which acknowledges the individual and their surrounding environment as inseparable, dependent on one another.

One of the most recent pieces of evidence of this individualist - I'd go so far as to say egotistical - concept of health has been the reaction to the COVID-19 pandemic, which we are living through at the time of writing this book. Thanks to the incredible advances in sciences and communication, during this pandemic - the most recent version of a long series of similar ones that humans have lived through since records have been kept - the mechanisms of transmission and the measures of containment of the virus were quickly identified, with this information very quickly reaching most of the world population. We recognized that measures as simple as using a mask or washing hands were critical to contain the spreading of the virus.

One of the greatest learnings during the pandemic has been that our actions have repercussions on the life and health of the people around us. Our habits directly impact the health of our neighbors, our friends, the people in our country, in the world, on the planet. The lesson to be taken out of all this is that this situation isn't just limited to the transmission of a virus, it extends to all areas of life.

Although the conclusion seems obvious, during the pandemic we are seeing that despite the evidence, millions of people around the world are not following these preventative measures. Interviews with people who don't wear a mask or break the rules show that they believe they are simply exercising their right to freedom, and that they're doing nothing wrong because ultimately it's their own life they are risking: "if I get sick, it's my problem, not anyone else's". This way of analyzing the situation reflects an individualist concept of sickness that places me at the centre, a me which is isolated and disconnected from my environment.

In contrast, the individual that sees themselves as part of a community knows that their actions and habits will impact those around them, their environment, their community, their country, their planet, and they are aware of this social impact on both a local scale and a global one.

How can we internalize correctly from childhood this social conscience when we live in a world that promotes individualism? Music and art are once again the answer.

There are many examples where participation in artistic activities has been successfully used to mobilize communities, include and empower marginalized groups, educate people about issues related to health or to raise awareness about healthy practices. As tools of representation of the values of the community, arts are critical for the education and health of individuals and the community at a global scale.

From a public health point of view, the pandemic has also led governments to a long overdue paradigm shift, which transcends the interests of the local community, and cares about making sure every town in the world is equipped to deal with it and has access to healthcare. The need for herd immunity to be able to force this pandemic out has made rich countries recognize the need to help poorer ones, not as an act of generosity or charity but rather as a crucial step for their own public health. It means nothing to be a rich country with the whole population vaccinated if one part of the world isn't, as the virus still would not have gone away.

We've moved away from the paradigm of "public health", in which policies are made focusing on topics affecting the health of local communities of cities and countries, onto the paradigm of "global health", based on issues that transcend national borders, and directly or indirectly affect the health of communities.

Achieving a global health paradigm that aims to secure an equal and fair access to healthcare, requires a high level of cooperation between governments. Due to its complexity, this global health paradigm crucially requires a transdisciplinary approach that goes beyond the sciences of health.

By recognizing that health and sickness are also cultural concepts, a global approach views the humanities and arts as indispensable tools. There will no longer be arrogant public health interventions in which a member of the health system goes to a community to teach or impose measures which are completely out of context or incoherent with the people and their territories. We are working towards an ecological approach, which recognizes the relationship between the individual, their social context and their surrounding environment.

In this context, music, apart from its positive effects on personal and collective health, serve as a resource for individuals and their communities to build habits, express civil unrest, mend relationships within the community, bring together different generations and in general, promote physical and emotional health. If we look at it this way, music is an essential part of the ecosystem of health, fundamental for the development of the individual and community at a local and global level.

Understanding this should be enough to incorporate music and arts into the lives of every person, as well as into government policy. This understanding should suffice for budgets given to arts and humanities to be just as important as those given to the sciences. It should be enough for the government to start campaigns to encourage the participation of boys in arts and humanities, in contrast to the current climate which pushes women into STEM. We should celebrate the fact that girls show interest in the arts rather than discourage them. Understanding that music is vital for health should be enough for access to musical education and expression to be seen as a right, as promulgated by the International Music Council in their *Five Music Rights*.

EXERCISE
BOOK

I hope that after having read this book and understood the importance of music for your physical, emotional and social health, you're ready to take action and incorporate it into your life, and consciously use it as a tool to improve your health and make you feel happier.

Therefore, in this section, I invite you to complete some exercises based on some of the studies I based my research on. Come reflect about the role of music in your life, create playlists with your favourite songs or with music you associate with different moods. These exercises will help you understand yourself better, discover who you once were and who you will become, prepare you for your death and the death of your loved ones. I'm sure you'll also have fun doing these exercises, so let's get going!

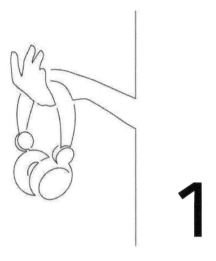

1

THE
SOUNDTRACK
OF YOUR LIFE

Autobiographical exercise

In this section, I invite you to reflect on the music that has accompanied you throughout your life. Right from your childhood to the present day, let's make a note of the music that is linked to your history, your dreams and your beliefs. At the end of the section, I also invite you to create a Spotify playlist with your favourite music and share it on social media with the hashtag *#wearewhatwelistento*

A. Write down the most important songs from your childhood.

_____

_____

_____

_____

_____

_____

_____

_____

B. Write down the music of your adolescence, the songs or soundtracks that marked this stage of your life.

.

_____

_____

_____

_____

_____

_____

_____

_____

C. Write down the songs that have accompanied you in your sad moments.

.

_____

_____

_____

_____

_____

_____

D. Write down the songs that have accompanied you in the happy moments of your life, or the music that makes you feel happy.

.

_____

_____

_____

_____

_____

_____

_____

E. Write down the songs that make you feel most relaxed, that help bring you to inner peace with yourself.

.

_____

_____

_____

_____

_____

_____

_____

F. Write down the songs that you will pass on to your children and grandchildren or to the young people you love.

_____

_____

_____

_____

_____

_____

_____

G. Write down the music that you'd like in your funeral

_____

_____

_____

_____

_____

_____

H. Write down the ten songs that have accompanied you in the most important moments of your life and explain why each one is important. Create a playlist on Spotify or Youtube with your favourite versions of each.

1._____

_____

_____

2._____

_____

_____

3._____

_____

_____

4._____

_____

_____

5._____

_____

_____

6._____

_____

_____

7._____

_____

_____

8._____

_____

_____

9._____

_____

_____

10._____

_____

_____

Remember, share your playlists on social
media with the hashtag
#wearewhatwelistento

2

CREATION EXERCISE
Your essence in music

The creation or composition of songs is within the reach of everyone. You don't have to be a professional musician to write a text which reflects who you are, your beliefs, aspirations, dreams, sadness, losses and desires. This creation exercise is an invitation to reflect upon the beliefs and qualities that define you, and is also an opportunity to ponder over who you want to become, the habits you want to develop, the bonds you want to strengthen.

This autobiographical exercise is very powerful, and through it, we can come to terms with who we are, forgive ourselves and even prepare ourselves for our death and that of our loved ones.

CREATE SONGS THAT EXPRESS YOUR ESSENCE

A. Write a song which expresses your beliefs and your outlook on life.

._____

_____

_____

_____

_____

_____

_____

_____

_____

_____

_____

_____

_____

_____

_____

_____

_____

B. Write a song in which you describe the person you want to become.

_____

_____

_____

_____

_____

_____

_____

_____

_____

_____

_____

_____

_____

_____

_____

_____

_____

_____

_____

3

SOUNDSCAPES

The sounds of your everyday life

We are immersed in a sea of sounds. Although usually we ignore them, we encounter the voices of others, the sounds of cars, the birds, the wind, the cries of street vendors, the metro, sirens, the conversations of people on the street, our home appliances, the noises of animals on a regular basis. Our surrounding environment makes noise, and even when we think we're in silence, in the background, there is a gentle gust of wind, a chirping of crickets, a rustling of leaves on a tree, a swishing of waves in the sea. The sounds of our surrounding environment affect our mood, usually in ways we are not even aware of, but that are ever-present. This exercise aims to make you aware of this reality and to help you foster healthy soundscapes. It also aims to make you aware that the sounds of a place are its fingerprints, its hallmark, not just every person, but every place in the world and every moment in history has its own sound.

A. Your everyday sounds

_____

_____

_____

_____

_____

_____

_____

_____

_____

_____

B. The sounds of your city

_____

_____

_____

_____

_____

_____

_____

C. The sounds of your favourite natural landscape

_____

_____

_____

_____

_____

_____

_____

_____

Remember, share your music and experiences on social media with the hashtag #wearewhatwelistento and follow Patricia Caicedo on Spotify where you will find hundreds of playlists.

Follow her on Instagram as well at @patriciacaicedobcn

BIBLIOGRAPHY

1. Three initiates, (2009). *The Kybalion: A Study of the Hermetic Philosophy of Ancient Egypt*. Mineola,New York: Dover Publications Inc.

2.Requena Rodríguez, A. (2008). "Nada está inmovil; todo se mueve; todo vibra". Academia de Ciencias de la Región de Murcia, Internet [https://www.um.es/acc/nada-esta-inmovil-todo-se-mueve-todo-vibra/]. Consultado 5 de mayo, 2020.

3. Pelling AE, Sehati S, Gralla EB, Valentine JS, Gimzewski JK. (2004). "Local nanomechanical motion of the cell wall of Saccharomyces cerevisiae", *Science*. 2004 Aug 20;305 (5687):1147-50.

4.Reuters (2020). "Coronavirus, the musical" en Medscape. Internet [https://www.medscape.com/viewarticle/929061]. Consultado 3 de mayo, 2020.

5. Darwin, C. (1872). *The expression of the emotions in man and animals*. London: John Murray.

6. Steven Mithen (2005). *The Singing Neanderthals: The Origins of Music, Language, Mind, and Body*. Cambridge: Harvard University Press.

7.Levitin, D. (2008). *The World in Six Songs: How the Musical Brain Created Human Nature*. New York: Dutton/Penguin and Toronto: Viking/Penguin.

8.Roosth, Sophia. (2009) "Screaming Yeast: Sonocytology, Cytoplasmic Milieus, and Cellular Subjectivities." *Critical Inquiry*, vol. 35, no. 2: 332–350. JSTOR, www.jstor.org/stable/10.1086/596646.

9. Pelling AE, Sehati S, Gralla EB, Valentine JS, Gimzewski JK. (2004). "Local nanomechanical motion of the cell wall of Saccharomyces cerevisiae", *Science*. 2004 Aug 20;305 (5687):1147-50.

10. Begouëm, M. y Breul, H. (1934). "De quelques figures hybrides (mi-humaines et mianimales) de la caverne des Trois-Frères (Ariège)." *Revue Anthropologique,* vol. XLIV, n° 4-6, p. 115-119.

11.Vitebski, P. (1996). *The Shaman: Voyages of the Soul. Trance, Ecstasy and Healing from Siberia.* Macmillan and Duncan Baird Publishers.

12. Sibbing Plantholt, I. (2017). "The image of divine healers: Healing goddesses and the legitimization of the Asû in the Mesopotamian Medical Marketplace". Ph.D. Diss. University of Pennsylvania.

13. Aristotle. *Politics in The Complete Works of Aristotle*: *The Revised Oxford Translation*, ed. Jonathan Barnes, 2 vols. Princeton, NJ: Princeton University Press, 1983, Book VIII, 1338b 1, 2122.

14.West, M. (2000). "Music Therapy in Antiquity," in *Music as Medicine: The History of Music Therapy Since Antiquity*, ed. Peregrine Horden. Burlington, VT: Ashgate Publishing Limited, 56.

15. Portnoy, J. (1954). *The Philosopher and Music: A Historical Outline*. New York: The Humanities Press: 8.

16. Porfirio (1987). *Vida de Pitágoras ; Argonáuticas órficas ; Himnos órficos*. Introducción y traducción Miguel Periago Lorente. Gredos. Madrid. 1987.

17. Istambouli, M.N. (1981). 'The history of Arabic Medicine based on the work of Ibn Abi Usaybeiah 1203 - 270". Ph.D. Diss. Loughborough University of Technology.

18. Khan, Hazrat. I. (1996). *The Mysticism of Sound and Music. The Sufi Teaching of Azrat Inayat Khan*. Boston: Shambhala Dragon Editions, 9.

19. Salmen, W. (1980) "Geisslerlieder", in *The New Grove Dictionary of Music and Musicians*, ed. Stanley Sadie. 20 vol. London: Macmillan Publishers Ltd.

20. Ficino, M. (1980). *The Book of Life*, trans. Charles Boer. Dallas: Spring Publications, Inc.,1980.

21. Voss, A. (2002). "Marsilio Ficino, the Second Orpheus," en *Music as Medicine: The History of Music Therapy Since Antiquity*, ed. Peregrine Horden. Burlington, VT: Ashgate Publishing Limited, 155.

22. Zarlino, G. (1998). "Istitutioni harmoniche", en *Source Readings in Music History*, ed. Oliver Strunk. New York: W.W. Norton Company, 294.

23. IBID, 296.

24. Hall, S.K. (2017) "The Doctrine of Affections: Where Art Meets Reason," *Musical Offerings*: Vol. 8 : No. 2 , Article 2.

25. Fink, H.J. (1953). "The Doctrine of Affections and Handel: The Background, Theory, and Practice of the Doctrine of Affections With a Comprehensive Analysis of the Oratorios of G.F.Handel". PhD diss., Western Reserve University: 116.

26. Bertrand, A. "Descartes's Compendium of Music," *Journal of the History of Ideas* 26, No. 1 (Jan-March 1965): 128-129.

27. Gouk, P. (2004), "Raising Sprits and Restoring Souls: Early Modern Medical Explanations for Music's Effects," in *Hearing Cultures: Essays on Sound, Listening and Modernity,* ed. Veit Erlmann. New York: Berg Publishers, 92.

28.Monk, E. S. (2010). A Case for Music as Therapy: "Healing and Purgation," and the Expressiveness of Music from Antiquity through the Eighteenth Century. Bachelor of Arts Diss. Presbyterian College.

29.Agrawal,S. R. (2005) "'Tune thy Temper to these Sounds': Music and Medicine in the English Ayre". PhD diss., Northwestern University, 30.

30. Gouk, P. (2002). "Sister Disciplines? Music and Medicine in Historical Perspective." In *musical Healing in Cultural Contexts*. Burlington, VT: Ashgate Publishing Limited.

31. Alvin, J. (1966). *Music Therapy*. New York: Basic Books Inc.

32. Browne, R. (1728). *Medicina Musica: A mechanical essay on singing, musick and dancing containing their uses and abuses; and demonstrating, by clear evident reasons, the alterations they produce in a human body*. London: J. Pemberton, 1727: 2.

33.Brocklesby, R. (1749). *Reflections on ancient and modern music, with the application to the cure of diseases. To which is subjoined, an essay to solve the questions, wherein consisted the difference of antient musick, from that of modern times*. London: M. Cooper, 1.

34. https://www.musictherapy.org/about/history/

35. O'Neill Kane, E. (1914). "Phonograph in operating-room", J*ournal of the American Medical Association*, vol.62, no.23, p. 1829.

36. Burdick, W. P. (1915). "The use of music during anesthesia and analgesia". in F. H. McMechan (Ed.), *The American year-book of anesthesia & analgesia*. New York: Surgery Publishing Company: 164- 167.

37.Bernardi L, Porta C, Sleight P. (2006). "Cardiovascular, cerebrovascular, and respiratory changes induced by different types of music in musicians and non-musicians: the importance of silence." In *Heart* 92: 445- 452

38. Levin, T. and Edgerton, M. E. (1999). "The Throat Singers of Tuva", *Scientific American*, September, 80-87.

39. Levin, T. (2019). *Where Rivers and Mountains Sing: Sound, Music, and Nomadism in Tuva and Beyond.* Indiana University Press.

40. Simonett, H. 2014. "Envisioned, Ensounded, Enacted: Sacred Ecology and Indigenous Musical Experience in Yoreme Ceremonies of Northwest Mexico." *Ethnomusicology* 58 (1): 110–132.

41. Schlaug, G. (2008). *Music, Musicians, and Brain Plasticity.* Oxford Handbooks. Online. Web.

42. Leeds, J. (2010). *The power of sound: How to be healthy and productive using music and sound.* Rochester, VT: Healing Arts Press.

43. Rieger, A. (2016). "Crossmodal cognition". Doctoral Diss. Dartmouth College.

44. Sagiv, N., & Frith, C. D. (2013). *Synesthesia and Consciousness.* Oxford Handbooks Online.

45. Cytowic, Richard E. (2002). *Synesthesia: A Union of the Senses.* Cambridge, MA: A Bradford Book.

46. Triarhou, L. C. (2016). "Neuromusicology or Musiconeurology? "Omni-art" in Alexander Scriabin as a Fount of Ideas". *Frontiers in Pshycology.* Vol.7, Article 364, March 2016.

47. Köhler, W. (1929). *Gestalt Psychology.* New York: Liveright.

48. Sievers, B. & Polansky, L. & Casey, M. & Wheatley, T. (2012). "Music and movement share a dynamic structure that supports universal expressions of emotion". *Proceedings of the National Academy of Sciences of the United States of America.* 110. 10.1073/pnas.1209023110.

49. Verhaeghen, P. (2011). "Aging and Executive Control: Reports of a Demise Greatly Exaggerated." *Curr Dir Psychol Sci*, 20(3), 174-180. doi:10.1177/0963721411408772

50. Bengtson, V. L., Gans, D., Putney, N. M., & Silverstein, M. (2009). *Handbook of Theories on Aging* Vol.2

51. Parasuraman, A., Zeithaml, V. A., & Berry, L. L. (1998). "Alternative scales for measuring service quality: a comparative assessment based on psychometric and diagnostic criteria." *Handbuch Dienstleistungsmanagement.* Springer:449-482.

52. Gazzaley, A., & Nobre, A. C. (2012). "Top-down modulation: bridging selective attention and working memory". *Trends Cogn Sci*, 16(2): 129-135. doi:10.1016/j.tics.2011.11.014

53. Attention processes involve almost all brain structures, including the striated cortex, the prestriate cortex, the medial temporal cortex, the inferior parietal cortex, the frontal eye fields, the prefrontal cortex, the cingulate gyrus, the nucleus pulvinaris, the nucleus lateral geniculate, the substantia nigra, and the superior colliculus..

54. Leclercq, M., & Zimmermann, P. (2004). *Applied neuropsychology of attention: theory, diagnosis and rehabilitation.* Psychology Press.

55. Gazzaley, A., & Nobre, A. C. (2012). "Top-down modulation: bridging selective attention and working memory". *Trends Cogn Sci*, 16(2): 129-135. doi:10.1016/j.tics.2011.11.014

56. Bengtson, M., Martin, R., Sawrie, S., Gilliam, F., Faught, E., Morawetz, R., & Kuzniecky, R. (2000). "Gender, Memory, and Hippocampal Volumes: Relationships in Temporal Lobe Epilepsy". *Epilepsy Behav,* 1(2): 112-119. doi:10.1006/ebeh.2000.0051

57. Yinger, O. S., & Cevasco, A. (2014). "Understanding neuroscience within the field of medical music therapy" en *Medical Music Therapy: Building a comprehensive program.* Silver Spring, MD: American Music Therapy Association.

58. Gardner, H. (1985). *The Mind's New Science: A History of the Cognitive Revolution*. New York: Basic Books.

59. Fodor, J. (1983). *The Modularity of Mind*. MIT Press.

60. Pinker, S. (2009). *How the Mind Works*. New York: Norton.

61. van der Schyff, Dylan. (2013). "Music, Meaning and the Embodied Mind: Towards an Enactive Approach to Music Cognition". MA Diss. University of Sheffield.

62. Changizi, M. (2011). *Harnessed: How language and Music Mimicked Nature and Transformed Ape Into Man*. Dallas: BenBella.

63. Tomasello, M. (1999). *The Cultural Origins of Human Cognition*. Cambridge, MA: Harvard UP.

64. Kempler, D. (2005). *Neurocognitive disorders in aging*: Sage.

65. Pascual-Leone, A., & Hamilton, R. (2001). "The metamodal organization of the brain". *Progress in brain research*, 134: 427-445.

66. Small, C. (1999). *Musicking: The Meaning of Performing and Listening*. Middletown, CT: Wesleyan UP.

67. Blacking, J. (1976). *How Musical is Man?*. London: Faber.

68. Korom, Frank J. (2006). *Village of Painters: Narrative Scrolls from West Bengal*. Santa Fe: Museum of New Mexico Press.

69. Andy Clark & David Chalmers. (2008). "The extended mind" en *Analysis*, 58(1), 7-19.

70. James Gibson. (1966). *The Senses Considered as Perceptual Systems*. Boston: Houghton-Miffflin.

71. Campbell, M. R. (1991). "Musical learning and the development of psychological processes in perception and cognition". *Bulletin of the Council for Research in Music Education*: 35-48.

72. Ortman, J. M., Velkoff, V. A., & Hogan, H. (2014). "An aging nation: the older population in the United States". United States Census Bureau, Economics and Statistics Administration, US Department of Commerce.

73. Kramer, A. F., Humphrey, D. G., Larish, J. F., Logan, G. D., & Strayer, D. L. (1994). "Aging and inhibition: beyond a unitary view of inhibitory processing in attention". *Psychol Aging,* 9(4), 491-512.

74. Hall, C. B., Lipton, R. B., Sliwinski, M., Katz, M. J., Derby, C. A., & Verghese, J. (2009). "Cognitive activities delay onset of memory decline in persons who develop dementia". *Neurology,* 73(5), 356-361. doi:10.1212/WNL.0b013e3181b04ae3.

75. Rodrigues, A. C., Loureiro, M. A., & Caramelli, P. (2013). "Long-term musical training may improve different forms of visual attention ability". *Brain Cogn,* 82(3), 229-235. doi:10.1016/j.bandc.2013.04.009

76. Lehmann, A. C., & Davidson, J. W. (2002). "Taking an acquired skills perspective on music performance." T*he new handbook of research on music teaching and learning,* 2, 542- 560.

78. Grant, M. D., & Brody, J. A. (2004). "Musical experience and dementia. Hypothesis". *Aging Clin Exp Res,* 16(5), 403-405.

78.Gaser, C. and G. Schlaug (2003). "Brain structures differ between musicians and nonmusicians." J. *Neurosci.* 23(27): 9240-9245.

79. Schlaug, G. (2001). "The brain of musicians. A model for functional and structural adaptation." Ann. N. Y. *Acad. Sci.* 930: 281-299.

80. Wan, C. Y., & Schlaug, G. (2010). "Music making as a tool for promoting brain plasticity across the life span". *Neuroscientist,* 16(5), 566-577. doi:10.1177/1073858410377805

81.Gaser, C., & Schlaug, G. (2003). "Brain structures differ between musicians and nonmusicians", *JNeurosci,* 23(27), 9240-9245.

82. Schulz, M., Ross, B., & Pantev, C. (2003). "Evidence for training-induced crossmodal reorganization of cortical functions in trumpet players". *Neuroreport,* 14(1), 157-161. doi:10.1097/01.wnr.0000053061.10406.c7

83. Kraus, N., & Chandrasekaran, B. (2010). "Music training for the development of auditory skills". *Nat Rev Neurosci,* 11(8), 599-605. doi:10.1038/nrn2882.

84. Bever T.& Chiarello, R. (2009) "Cerebral dominance in musicians and nonmusicians". *The Journal of Neuropsychiatry and Clinical Neurosciences.* Winter; 21 (1) :94-7.

85. Habibi, A.(2011). "Cortical activity during music perception; comparing musicians and non-musicians". Ph.D. Diss. University of California Irvine.

86. Skoe, E. and N. Kraus (2010). "Auditory brain stem response to complex sounds: a tutorial." *Ear Hear.* 31(3): 302-324.

87. Percaccio CR, Pruette AL, Mistry ST, Chen YH, Kilgard MP. (2007) "Sensory experience determines enrichment-induced plasticity in rat auditory cortex". *Brain Res.* 2007 Oct 12;1174:76-91. doi: 10.1016/j.brainres.2007.07.062. Epub 2007 Aug 9. PMID: 17854780.

88. Kraus, N. and B. Chandrasekaran (2010). "Music training for the development of auditory skills." *Nature Reviews Neuroscience* 11(8): 599-605.

89 Keverne, E. B. (2004). Understanding well-being in the evolutionary context of brain development. *Proceedings of the Royal Society of London,* 359: 1349–1358.

90. Krizman, J., J. Slater, E. Skoe, V. Marian and N. Kraus (2015). "Neural processing of speech in children is influenced by extent of bilingual experience." *Neurosci. Lett.* 585: 48-53.

91. Vuust, P., E. Brattico, M. Seppänen, R. Näätänen and M. Tervaniemi (2012). "Practiced musical style shapes auditory skills." *Ann. N. Y. Acad. Sci.* 1252(1): 139-146.

92. "Neurotransmitter," in *The Columbia Encyclopedia,* New York: Columbia University Press, 2013, consultada December 17, 2014, http://literati.credoreference.com.

93. Anthony L. Vaccarino and Abba J. Kastin, "Endogenous Opiates: 2000," *Peptides 22* (2001): 2257.

94. Berger,M. Gray, J.A. and Roth, B. (2009). "The Expanded Biology of Serotonin," *Annual Review of Medicine* 60 : 356.

95. Nakajima, S. et al. (2013) "The Potential Role of Dopamine D3 Receptor Neurotransmission in Cognition," *European Neuropsychopharmacology* 23, no. 8 : 800-1.

96. Falk, D. (1983). "Cerebral cortices of east African early hominids". *Science*, 221: 1072–1074.

97. Saarikallio, S., and Erkkilä, J. (2007). "The role of music in adolescents' mood regulation". *Psychology of Music*, 35(1), 88-109. Doi: 10.1177/0305735607068889.

98. Schäfer, T., Smukalla, M., and Oelker, S-A. (2014). "How music changes our lives: A qualitative study of the long-term effects of intense emotional experiences". *Psychology of Music*, 42(4), 525-544. Doi: 10.1177/0305735613482024.

99. Trainor, L. J., Tsang, C. D., & Cheung, V. H. W. (2002). "Preference for Sensory Consonance in 2- and 4-month-old Infants". *Music Perception*, 20: 187-194.

100.Cummingham, J., Sterling, R. (1988). "Developmental Change in the Understanding of Affective Meaning in Music". *Motivation and Emotion*, 12: 399-413.

101. Izard, C. (1977). *Human emotions*. New York, NY: Plenum Press.

102. Ekman, P. (1999). "Basic emotions". In T. Dalgleish and M. Power (Eds.), *Handbook of cognition and emotion*. New York, NY: John Wiley and Sons Ltd.:45-60.

103.Barrett, L. (2006a). "Are emotions natural kinds?". *Perspectives on Psychological Science,* 1(1), 28-58. Doi: 10.1111/j.1745-6916.2006.00003.x.

104. Russell, J. (2003). "Core affect and the psychological construction of emotion". *Psychological Review*, 110(1), 145-172. Doi: 10.1037/0033-295X.110.1.145.

105. Scherer, K., Schorr, A., and Johnstone, T. (2001). *Appraisal processes in emotion: Theory, methods, research.* New York, NY: Oxford University Press.

106. Ekman, P., and Cortado, D. (2011). "What is meant by calling emotions basic?". *Emotion Review*, 3(4), 364-370. Doi: 10.1177/1754073911410740.

107. Darwin, C. (1872). *The expression of emotions in man and animals.* London, UK: John Murray.

108. Izard, C. (2007). "Basic emotions, natural kinds, emotion schemas, and a new paradigm". *Perspectives on Psychological Science*, 2(3), 260-280. Doi:10.1111/j.1745-6916.2007.00044.x.

109. Ekman, P., and Cortado, D. (2011). "What is meant by calling emotions basic?". *Emotion Review*, 3(4), 364-370. Doi: 10.1177/1754073911410740.

110. Kreibig, S. (2010). "Autonomic nervous system activity in emotion: A review". *Biological Psychology*, 84(3), 394-421. Doi: 10.1016/j.biopsycho.2010.03.010.

111. LeDoux, J. (2003). "The emotional brain, fear, and the amygdala". Cellular and *Molecular Neurobiology,* 23(4-5), 727-738. Doi: doi.org/10.1023/A:1025048802629.

112. Peretz, G., N I., Johnsen, E., and Adolphs, R. (2007). "Amygdala damage impairs emotion recognition from music". *Neuropsychologica,* 45(2), 236-244. Doi:10.1016/j.neuropsychologia.2006.07.012.

113. Bannister, S. Craig (2020). "A Framework of Distinct Musical Chills: Theoretical, Causal, and Conceptual Evidence", Durham theses, Durham University. Available at Durham E-Theses Online: http://etheses.dur.ac. uk/13582 /

114. Tomkins, S. (1984). "Affect theory". In K. Scherer and P. Ekman (Eds.), *Approaches to emotion*. Hillsdale, NJ: Erlbaum:163-195.

115. Scherer, K., and Coutinho, E. (2013). "How music creates emotion: A multifactorial process approach". In T. Cochrane, B. Fantini, and K. Scherer (Eds.), *The emotional power of music: Multidisciplinary perspectives on musical arousal, expression, and social control*. New York, NY: Oxford University Press:121-145.

116. Gross, J., and Barrett, L. F. (2011). "Emotion generation and emotion regulation: One or two depends on your point of view". *Emotion Review*, 3(1), 8-16. Doi:10.1177/1754073910380974.

117. Darwin, C. (1902). *The Descent of Man and Selection in Relation to Sex, part II*. New York: P.F. Collier & Son.

118. Juslin, P., Vastfjall, D. 2008. "Emotional Responses to Music: The Need to Consider Underlying Mechanism". *Behavioral Brain Sciences*, 31: 559-621.

119. Zentner, M. Grandjean, D., K. Scherer. (2008). "Emotions Evoked by the Sound of Music: Characterization, Classification, and Measurement". *Emotion*, 8(4): 494-521.

120. IBID.

121. Papp, G., Kovac, S., Frese, A., & Evers, S. (2014). "The impact of temporal lobe epilepsy on musical ability". *Seizure*, 23, 533–536.

122. Sloboda, J. (1991). "Music Structure and Emotional Response: Some Empirical Findings". *Psychology of Music*, 19: 110-120.

123. Kringelbach, M. L., & Berridge, K. C. (Eds.). (2010). *The pleasures of the brain*. New York:Oxford University Press.

124. Kringelbach, M. L., & Berridge, K. C. (2010). "The Neuroscience of Happiness and Pleasure". *Social Research: An International Quarterly*, Volume 77, Number 2, Summer.

659-678.

125. Becker, S., Bräscher, A-K., Bannister, S., Bensafi, M., Calma-Birling, D., Chan, R., Wang, Y. (2019). "The role of hedonics in the human affectome". *Neuroscience and Biobehavioural Reviews*, 102, 221-241. Doi: 10.1016/j.neubiorev.2019.05.003.

126. Liu, X., Hairston, J., Schrier, M., and Fan, J. (2011). "Common and distinct networks underlying reward valence and processing stages: A meta-analysis of functional neuroimaging studies". Neuroscience and Biobehavioural Reviews, 35(5), 1219-1236. Doi: 10.1016/j.neubiorev.2010.12.012.

127. La anhedonia, proveniente del griego hedoné que significa placer, es la incapacidad para experimentar placer.

128. Mas-Herrero, E., Zatorre, R. J., Rodriguez-Fornells, A., & Marco-Pallarés, J. (2014). "Dissociation between Musical and Monetary Reward Responses in Specific Musical Anhedonia." *Current Biology*, 24, 1–6.

129. Csikszentmihalyi, M. (1990). *Flow: The Psychology of Optimal Experience; Steps Toward Enhancing the Quality of Life*. New York: HarperPerennial.

130. NIMH (2016). Mission. Obtenido en: https://www.nih.gov/about-nih/what-we-do/nihalmanac/national-institute-mental-health-nimh.

131. Ch. Wickramarathne, J. Chun Phuoc, J. Tham. (2020). "The impact of wellness dimensions on the academic performance of undergraduates of Government universities in Sri Lanka". European Journal of Public Health Studies. Scientific Figure on ResearchGate. https://www.researchgate.net/figure/Six-dimensions-of-wellness-model-Source-Hettler-1977_fig1_342769817 [consultado 23 Aug, 2020]

132. Hettler, B. (1977). *Six Dimension Model*. Stevens Point, WI: National Wellness Institute.

133. Hutchison, B. (2016). "The Role of Music Among Healthy

Older Performance Musicians". North Dakota State University. Doctoral Diss.

134. Chanda, M. L., & Levitin, D. J. (2013). "The neurochemistry of music". *Trends in Cognitive Sciences*, 17(4), 179-193. DOI 10.1016/j.tics.2013.02.007.

135. Keeler Jason, Roth Edward, Neuser Brittany, Spitsbergen John, Waters Daniel, Vianney John-Mary. (2015)."The neurochemistry and social flow of singing: bonding and oxytocin". *Frontiers in Human Neuroscience*, V. 9 , 518. Online: https://www.frontiersin.org/article/10.3389/fnhum.2015.00518

136. Lori A. Custodero. (2012). "The Call to Create: Flow Experience in Music Learning and Teaching", David Hargreaves, Dorothy Miell and Raymond MacDonald (eds.), *Musical Imaginations: Multidisciplinary Perspectives on Creativity, Performance and Perception*. Oxford: Oxford University Press, 369-84.

137.The five musical rights include the right of all children and adults to express themselves freely through music, the right to learn musical languages and skills, the right to interact with music through direct participation, appreciation, creation, and access to information. The right of all musicians to develop their careers and to disseminate their artistic work through all available media and the right to obtain recognition and fair compensation for their work. https://www.imc-cim.org/about-imc-separator/five-music-rights.html

138. Three initiates, (2009). *The Kybalion: A Study of the Hermetic Philosophy of Ancient Egypt*. Mineola,New York: Dover Publications Inc.

139. Conrad-Da'oud, E. (2012). *Life on Land: The Story of Continuum, the World-Renowned Self-Discovery and Movement Method*. North Atlantic Books, Berkeley.

140. Schroeder, D. Poeppel and E. Zion Golumbic (2017). "Neural Entrainment to the Beat: The "Missing-Pulse" Phenomenon" en *Journal of Neuroscience* 28 June, 2017, 37 (26) 6331-6341;

DOI: https://doi.org/10.1523/JNEUROSCI.2500-16.2017

141. I. Tal, Large,E. W., Rabinovitch, E., Wei, Y., Schroeder, Ch. E., Poeppel, D. and Zion Golumbic, E. (2017). "Neural Entrainment to the Beat: The "Missing-Pulse" Phenomenon" en *Journal of Neuroscience* 28 June, 2017, 37 (26) 6331-6341; DOI: https://doi.org/10.1523/JNEUROSCI.2500-16.2017.

142. Arcangeli A. (2000). "Dance and Health: The Renaissance Physicians". Dance Research: *The Journal of the Society for Dance Research*, Vol. 18, No. 1. Published by: Edinburgh University Press. Edimburgh. 3-30.

143. Paul Krack, "Relicts of Dancing Mania: The Dancing Procession of Echternach," *Neurology* 53, no. 9 (1999): 2169-72.

144. Bicais, M. (1669). "La manire de regler la sante par ce qui nous environne, par ce que nous recevons, et par les exercices, ou par la gymnastique moderne" (Aix: chez Charles David, 1669), pp. 280-8.

145. Shaffer, J. (2012). "Neuroplasticity and positive psychology in clinical practice: A review for combined benefits psychology." *PSYCH*, 3(12A), 1110-1115. doi: 10.4236/psych.2012.312A164.

146. Eriksson, P. S., Perfilieva, E., Björk-Eriksson, T., Alborn, A. M., Nordborg, C., Peterson, D. A., & Gage, F. H. (1998). "Neurogenesis in the adult human hippocampus". *Nature medicine*, 4(11), 1313-1317.

147. Kempermann, G., Gast, D., & Gage, F. H. (2002). "Neuroplasticity in old age: Sustained fivefold induction of hippocampal neurogenesis by long term environmental enrichment". *Annals of Neurology*, 52(2), 135-143.

148. Lynn-Seraphine, P. (2016). "Neurodrumming: Towards an integral mental fitness training for healthy aging". Diss. Master Psychology, California State University, Irvine.

149. Geiser, E. Zähle, T., Jacke, L. & Meyer, M. (2008). "The neural correlate of speech rhythm as evidenced by metrical speech processing." *Journal of Cognitive Neuroscience,* 20(3), 541-552. doi:10.1162/jocn.2008.20029.

150. Dale, J.A., Hyatt, J., Hollerman, J. (2007). "The Neuroscience of Dance and the Dance of Neuroscience: Defining a Path of Inquiry". *The Journal of Aesthetic Education,* Volume 41, Number 3, Fall 2007. 89-110.

151. Stobart, H. & Cross, I. (2000). "The Andean anacrusis? Rhythmic structure and perception in Easter songs of northern Potosi, Bolivia." *British Journal of Ethnomusicology, 9(2), 63-94.*

152. Kalender, B. Trehub, S.E., & Schellenberg, E.G. (2012). "Cross-cultural differences in meter perception". *Psychological Research,* 77(2), 196-203. Doi:10.1007/s00426-012-0427-y

153. Hannon, E.E., & Trehub, S.E. (2005b). "Tuning in to musical rhythms: infants learn more readily than adults." *Proceedings of the National Academy of Sciences of the United States of America,* 102 (35), 12639-12643. Doi:10.1073/pnas.0504254102

154. Witek MAG, Clarke EF, Wallentin M, Kringelbach ML, Vuust P (2014) "Syncopation, Body-Movement and Pleasure" in *Groove Music.* PLoS ONE 9(4): e94446. doi:10.1371/journal.pone.0094446

155. Davies, J., & McVicar, A. (2000). "Issues in effective pain control". 1: Assessment and education. *International Journal of Palliative Nursing,* 6(2), 58-65.

156. Allen, J. (2013a). "Pain management with adults". In J. Allen (Ed.), *Guidelines for music therapy practice in adult medical care* (pp. 35-61). University Park, IL: Barcelona Publishers.

157. Dileo, C. (1999). *Music therapy and medicine: Theoretical and clinical applications.* Silver Spring, MD: American Music Therapy Association.

158. Bradt, J., Dileo, C., & Potvin, N. (2013). "Music for stress and anxiety reduction in coronary heart disease patients." *The Cochrane Database of Systematic Reviews,* 12, CD006577

159. Gatchel, R. J., Peng, Y. B., Peters, M. L., Fuchs, P. N., & Turk, D. C. (2007). "The biopsychosocial approach to chronic pain: Scientific advances and future directions". *Psychological Bulletin,* 133(4), 581-624.

160. Melzack, R. (2010). Pain theories. In I. B. Weiner, & W. E. Craighead (Eds.), The corsini encyclopedia of psychology (4th ed.,). Hoboken, NJ: John Wiley & Sons, Inc. doi:10.1002/9780470479216.corpsy0630

161. Melzack, R. (1999). "From the gate to the neuromatrix". *Pain,* Suppl 6, S121-S126. doi:10.1016/S0304-3959(99)00145-1

162. Bardia, A., Barton, D. L., Prokop, L. J., Bauer, B. A., & Moynihan, T. J. (2006). "Efficacy of complementary and alternative medicine therapies in relieving cancer pain: A systematic review". *Journal of Clinical Oncology,* 24(34), 5457-5464.

163. Gallagher, L. M., Lagman, R., Walsh, D., Davis, M. P., & LeGrand, S. B. (2006). "The clinical effects of music therapy in palliative medicine". *Supportive Care in Cancer,* 14, 859- 866.

164. Hilliard, R. (2003). "The effects of music therapy on the quality and length of life of people diagnosed with terminal cancer." *Journal of Music Therapy,* 40, 113-137.

165. Ferrer, A. J. (2007). "The effect of live music on decreasing anxiety in patients undergoing chemotherapy treatment". *Journal of Music Therapy,* 44, 242-255.

166. Clark, M., Isaacks-Downton, G., Wells, N., Redlin-Frazier, S., Eck, C., Hepworth, J. T., & Chakravarthy, B. (2006). "Use of preferred music to reduce emotional distress and symptom activity during radiation therapy." *Journal of Music Therapy,* 43, 247-265.

167. Sahler, O. J. Z., Hunter, B. C., Liesveld, J. L. (2003). "The

effect of using music therapy with relaxation imagery in the management of patients undergoing bone marrow transplantation: A pilot feasibility study." *Alternative Therapies in Health and Medicine,* 9(6), 70-74.

168. Edward, J (1998). "Music Therapy for children with severe burn injury." *Music Therapy Perspectives,* 16: 21-26.

169. Zimmerman, I., Nieveen, J., Barnason, S. & Schamaderer, M. (1996)."The effects of music intervention is postoperative pain and sleep in coronary artery bypass graft (CRGB) patients". *Scholarly Inquiry for Nursing Practice: An International Journal,* 10. 153-170.

170. Galpin, W. (1937) *The Music of the Sumerians: And their Immediate Successors, the Babylonians and Assyrians.* Cambridge University Press.

171. Meyer-Baer, K. (2015). *Music of the Spheres and the Dance of Death.* Princeton University Press. 224-241.

172. Qi Kun (2014). "Sonic expressions of cosmological awareness: a comparative study of funeral rituals among Han Chinese living in the Yangzi River Valley". Yearbook for Traditional Music Vol. 46. Cambridge University Press :159-169.

173. Coclanis, A., Coclanis P. (2005). "Jazz Funeral: A Living Tradition". *Southern Cultures,* Volume 11, Number 2. The University of North Carolina Press. 86-92.

174. Austin, D. (2009). *The Theory and Practice of Vocal Psychotherapy: Songs of the self.* London: Jessica Kingsley Publishers.

175. https://chaliceofrepose.org/

176. Cooper, L. "Your Healing Voice - The benefits of singing for health and wellbeing" en https://www.britishacademyofsoundtherapy.com/wp-content/uploads/2020/07/Your-Healing-Voice-Article-sing-for-health-research-3.pdf

177. The Oxford Happiness Questionnaire http://www.blake-group.com/sites/default/files/ assessments/ Oxford_Happiness_Questionnaire.pdf

178. Bart de Boer (2017). "Evolution of speech and evolution of language". Published online: 3 August 2016, Psychonomic Society, Inc. 2016 Psychon Bull Rev (2017) 24:158–162 DOI 10.3758/s13423-016-1130-6.

179. Darwin, C. (1872/1998). The Expression of the Emotions in Man and Animals. Oxford: Oxford University Press.

180. Kelley, D. B. (2004). "Vocal communication in frogs". Current Opinion in *Neurobiology*, 14: 751–757.

181. Insel, T. R. (2010). "The challenge of translation in social neuroscience: A review of oxytocin, vasopressin, and affiliative behavior". *Neuron*, 65: 768–779.

182. Kanwal, J. S., and Ehret, G. (2006). *Behavior and Neurodynamics for Auditory Communication.* Cambridge: Cambridge University Press.

183. Sterne, J. (2003). *The Audible Past: Cultural Origins of Sound Reproduction*. Durham: Duke University Press.15.

184. IBID, 54.

185. Auenbrugger, L. (1936). "On the Percussion of the Chest" Translated by John Forbes. *Bulletin of the History of Medicine* 4. Cit. Sterne, J. (2003).

186. Laennec, R.T.H.A. (1830) *Treatise on the Diseases of the Chest and on Mediate Auscultation.* 3 ed. Translated by John Forbes. New York: Samuel Wood; Collins and Hannay. Cit. Sterne, J. (2003).

187. Arozqueta, C. (2018). "Heartbeats and the Arts: A Historical Connection". *Leonardo* 51 (1): 33–39. doi: https://doi.org/10.1162/LEON_a_01152

188. http://musicwithmachines.org/hco/

189. Sweeley, C.C., Holland, J.F, Towson, D.S., Chamberlin, B.A. (1987) "Interactive and Multi-Sensory Analysis of Complex Mixtures by an Automated Gas Chromatography System," Journal of Chromatography 399: 173–181.

190. Ohno, S. y Ohno, M. (1986) "The All Pervasive Principle of Repetitious Recurrence Governs Not Only Coding Sequence Construction but Also Human Endeavor in Musical Composition," *Immunogenetics* 24: 71–78.

191. Ohno, S. (1993) "A Song in Praise of Peptide Palindromes," *Leukemia* 7 Supp. 2 S157–S159.

192. Morey, L.W. (1989) "Musings on Biomuse," Science News 135: 307.

193. Han, Y.C., & Han, B. (2014). Skin Pattern Sonification as a New Timbral Expression. Leonardo Music Journal 24(1), 41-43. https://www.muse.jhu.edu/article/561861.

194. IBID.

195. Pelling AE, Sehati S, Gralla EB, Valentine JS, Gimzewski JK. (2004). "Local nanomechanical motion of the cell wall of Saccharomyces cerevisiae", Science. 2004 Aug 20;305 (5687):1147-50.

196. Gadamer, Hans-Georg. (1989). *Truth and Method.* 2nd ed. Translated by W. Glen-Doepel, translation revised by Joel Weinsheimer and Donald G. Marshall. London: Continuum. First published 1960 as Wahrheit und Methode: Grundzüge einer philosophischen Hermeneutik (Tübingen: Mohr). 2nd ed. of translation first published 1989 (London: Sheed and Ward): 355.

197. Dacey, J. (1999). *Concepts of creativity: A history.* In M. A. Runco & S.R. Pritzer (Eds), Encyclopedia of creativity, Vol.1 A–H. San Diego, CA: Academic Press.

198. Albert, R. S., & Runco, M. A. (1999). "The history of creativity research". In R. S. Sternberg (Ed.), *Handbook of human creativity.* New York, NY: Cambridge University Press: 16–31

199. Vartanian, O., et al. *Neuroscience of Creativity*. The MIT Press, 2013. Project MUSE. muse.jhu.edu/book/46971.

200. Roe BE, Tilley MR, Gu HH, Beversdorf DQ, Sadee W, Haab TC, et al. (2009) "Financial and Psychological Risk Attitudes Associated with Two Single Nucleotide Polymorphisms in the Nicotine Receptor (CHRNA4) Gene". PLoS ONE 4(8): e6704. https://doi.org/10.1371/journal.pone.0006704.

201. Zuckerman , M. (1994). *Behavioral expressions and bio-social expressions of sensation seeking* . Cambridge : Cambridge University Press.

202. Miller, G. F. (2001). "Aesthetic Fitness: How Sexual Selection Shaped Artistic Virtuosity as a Fitness Indicator and Aesthetic Preferences as Mate Choice Criteria". *Bulletin of Psychology and the Arts*, 2, 20-25.

203. Hinde, R. A. & Fisher, J. (1951). Further observations on the opening of milk bottles by birds. *British Birds*,44, 393-396.

204. Wallas, G. (1926). *Art of thought*. New York, NY: Harcourt Brace.

205. http://www.furious.com/perfect/stockhauseninterview.html

206. Lapidaki, E. (2007). "Learning from Masters of Music Creativity: Shaping Compositional Experiences in Music Education." *Philosophy of Music Education Review*, 15(2): 93-117. Revisado May 20, 2021 en http://www.jstor.org/stable/40327276.

207. P.A. Schilpp, ed., (1959). *Albert Einstein: Philosopher-Scientist*. New York: Harpers,Vol. : 2:45.

208. http://www.personal.psu.edu/faculty/m/e/meb26/INART55/varese.html

209. Eidsheim N. S. (2015). *Sensing sound. singing & listening as vibrational practice*. Durham, London: Duke University Press: 16.

210. Huang J., Gamble D., Sarnlertsophon K., Wang X., Hsiao S. (2012). *Feeling music: integration of auditory and tactile inputs in musical meter perception*. PLoS One 7:e48496.

211.Root-Bernstein, R.S. (2001). "Music, Creativity and Scientific Thinking". *Leonardo* 34(1), 63-68. https://www.muse.jhu.edu/article/19631.

212. IBID.

213.The Group pof Five was a grup of prominent nationalistic Russian composers formed by Mili Balákirev (el líder), César Cuí, Modest Músorgski, Nikolái Rimski-Kórsakov y Aleksandr Borodín.

214. Root-Bernstein, R.S. (2001). "Music, Creativity and Scientific Thinking." *Leonardo* 34(1): 63-68. https://www.muse.jhu.edu/article/19631.

215. Milgram, R., Dunn, R. y Price, G.E. eds., "Teaching and Counseling Gifted and Talented Adolescents: An International Learning Style Perspective". New York: Praeger.

ABOUT THE AUTHOR

Patricia Caicedo is a soprano, musicologist and physician whose scholarship and performances center Latin American and Iberian art song. She has released eleven albums and published numerous scholarly editions of scores and books, including *The Latin American Art Song: Sounds of the Imagined Nations*, the go-to history on its subject.

She is also an avid performer of these works, having performed at important halls in Europe and the Americas in addition to founding and directing the *Barcelona Festival of Song*, which focuses on the performance and study of Latin American and Iberian art songs in Spanish, Catalan, and Portuguese.

She is the host of the podcast, *Latin American and Iberian Art Song*, in which she interviews composers and leading experts from across the world.

Patricia holds a Ph.D. in musicology from the Universidad Complutense de Madrid and a Medical Doctor's degree from the Escuela Colombiana de Medicina. She is an Executive Board Member of the International Music Council a UNESCO partner organization.

PATRICIACAICEDO.COM

Follow **Patricia Caicedo on social media,** communicate with her, listen to her music and podcast, invite her to speak at your institution, ask her questions or simply share your ideas about the book

 @patriciacaicedobcn

Instagram

 https://spoti.fi/2XQwHHS

Spotify

 @PatriciaCaicedo

Twitter

 youtube.com/singerpat

 /FansPatriciaCaicedo

Facebook

 /in/patriciacaicedo

Linkedin

www.mundoarts.com